Social and Solidarity-based Economy and Territory

From Embeddedness to Co-construction

P.I.E. Peter Lang

Bruxelles · Bern · Berlin · New York · Oxford · Wien

CIRIEC
Xabier Itçaina & Nadine Richez-Battesti

Social and Solidarity-based Economy and Territory

From Embeddedness to Co-construction

Social Economy & Public Economy
Vol. 7

CIRIEC activities, publications and researches are realized with the support of the Belgian Federal Government – Scientific Policy and with the support of the Government of the Belgian French Speaking Community – Scientific Research.

The book was subject to a double blind refereeing process.

Éditions scientifiques internationales
Brussels, 2018
1 avenue Maurice, B-1050 Brussels, Belgique
www.peterlang.com; brussels@peterlang.com

Printed in Germany

ISSN 2030-3408
ISBN 978-2-8076-0812-2
ePDF 978-2-8076-0813-9
ePub 978-2-8076-0814-6
Mobi 978-2-8076-0815-3
DOI 10.3726/b14135
D/2018/5678/38

CIP available from the British Library and from the Library of Congress, USA.

Bibliographic information published by die Deutsche Nationalbibliothek Die Deutsche Nationalbibliothek lists this publication in the Deutsche Nationalbibliografie; detailed bibliographic data is available on the Internet at ‹ http://dnb.d-nb.de ›.

Table of Contents

Part II
Towards new heterogeneous forms of territorial cooperations?

Acknowledgements

The present volume is the result of the CIRIEC International Working Group on Social and Solidarity-based economy and Territory. The editors want to thank the authors for their patience in what has turned to be a long but fruitful process of publication. The book could not have been produced without the support of the Social Economy & Public Economy CIRIEC Series at Peter Lang. Our thanks go to Christine Dussart, research assistant at the International scientific commission Social and Cooperative Economy at CIRIEC International, to Barbara Sak, managing director CIRIEC International and CIRIEC Belgium, to Philippe Bance, President of the CIRIEC International Scientific Council, to Bernard Thiry, General Director of CIRIEC International, and to Benoît Lévesque, professor emeritus at UQAM and former president of the CIRIEC International Scientific Council. Finally, our special thanks go to Armelle Jézéquel (Centre Émile Durkheim) who prepared the final manuscript of this book. In addition, Xabier Itçaina thanks the *Région Aquitaine* for its support through the research programs *Vers une gouvernance transfrontalière en réseau ? Expériences transfrontalières du tiers secteur en France et au Royaume-Uni* (Sciences Po Bordeaux, Centre Émile Durkheim-Région Aquitaine, 2010-2014) and *ESSAQUI : Institutionnalisations en miroir de l'économie sociale et solidaire en Aquitaine* (Sciences Po Bordeaux, Centre Émile Durkheim-Région Aquitaine, 2015-2019).

Introduction

Changing Social Economies in Changing Territories

Nadine RICHEZ-BATTESTI

Aix-Marseille University, LEST-CNRS UMR 7317

This book is the result of an International Ciriec Working Group on social and solidarity economy and territory. It is the fruit of an interdisciplinary dialogue among researchers from nine countries and two continents, Europe and America. If contexts widely vary from one country to another, the different contributions underline the capacity of social and solidarity-based economy (SSE) to elaborate original inputs to social, economic and sustainable development. Generally focused on original case studies, at a geographical or organizational level, papers illustrate different strategies of SSE in their territories: answer to socio economic or political changes, renewal and increased heterogeneity of territorial cooperations? More specifically, they show the diversity of links between SSE and territory at a meso-economic scale and different articulations with politics and policies. Most of the time, their embeddedness depends on the intensity of their networks and their capacity to renew it along the time.

We first present the general framework elaborated for this book before introducing the two parts and their components.

1. A neo-institutionalist framework

1.1. Territory as a social construction

The relation to the territory is a central element of the social and solidarity-based economy (SSE) to the point of being presented by the actors from the field as one of its constitutive values. The forms of anchorage and territorial dynamics of the SSE are diverse, subject to institutional arrangements and deserve careful analysis.

At the meso-theoretical level, the SSE can be analyzed from a dialogue between the various institutionalist, proximist and territorialist approaches. These approaches share a critical stance towards those asserting the uniqueness of a rational agent, axiologically neutral and aspatial, for which the territory is reduced to an external spatial variable with low explanatory value.

In contrast, we consider the territory as a social construction, or "a gathering of players in a given spatial context that seeks to bring out, then attempt to resolve under environmental constraint, a shared societal or production problem" (Pecqueur, Itçaina, 2012). Territory builds up through the activities of its players in a spatial context which dimensions are not only geographical but also organizational and institutional. In the best case, the territory becomes a player itself who can rely on a governance form that gives him the possibility to speak with one voice. From this angle, the SSE, given its origins and characteristics, is not only part of the territory but also contributes to its building, in particular at the governance and social aim levels, overpassing the sole economic logic.

Territorial governance, in that sense, takes on a transversal meaning, both socio-economic and political, as referring to a mechanism "of coordination of players, but also of appropriation of resources and construction of the territoriality" (Leloup, Moyart, Pecqueur, 2005) in which the public policy-makers are nodal but not monopolistic. The whole challenge then consists of enrolling the territorial actors, including the SSE organizations, in this process, in order to "encourage their adhesion, participation and involvement in an idea of collective construction of systems of public action" (*Ibid.*: 329).

1.2. "New" status for the SSE and the renewal of sectors as territorial constructions

From then on, and from a methodological viewpoint, the interactions between the SSE with all its diversity (associations, cooperatives, mutual societies, foundations and social enterprises) and the territory should be reviewed regarding corporate governance as well as territorial governance. Indeed, is governance revealing to be strategic given the objectives that are put forward, especially as these objectives cannot be reached by one category of players alone? Are dominant governance forms characterized by more horizontality and cooperation by opposition to verticality and constraint?

More widely, the territorial reference is situated at the confluence of entrepreneurial models, public policies and socio-territorial mobilizations. In particular, the emergence and consolidation, in many countries, of multi-stakeholder statutes for the organizations of the SSE bringing together private, SSE and public players in the name of the territorialized general interest provides a solid base for comparison. If the Italian social cooperatives, for instance, are the classic example of multi-stakeholder organizations, similar institutional innovations have also emerged elsewhere. For Southern Europe alone, the SCIC in France, the social initiative cooperatives in Spain, the social cooperatives and the community cooperatives in Italy are significant examples of these institutional arrangements with strong territorial anchorage.

It is then relevant to address SSE and specifically these new organizational forms by combining a socio-economic approach (socio economic level) and a twofold political approach (public policies and social movements; political level).

– At the socio-economic level, this book is an opportunity to better understand the contribution of the SSE to territorial regulation in the sense of the "mode of interaction and coordination of activities, employment and incomes and capital flows that allow a guarantee of the regularity of the production system" (Demoustier, Richez-Battesti, 2010: 8). Is territory only one single element of contextualization, one resource among others or is it a real strategic actor in social and economic initiatives?

How did the organizational innovations proper to the SSE contribute over the past 30 years to transform the relation of the "civil economy" (Bruni, Zamagni, 2009) with its territory? How did the organizational innovations contributed to internalize the territory within the SSE organizations? Are we witnessing strategic changes within organizations, given the development of a more territorialized and open governance in the territory? How does the link with the territory find expression and affirm itself within the organization: is it embodied only in its governance bodies? Or does it draw support from the new internal coordination mechanisms (strategic committees and other scientific committees…)? What are the effects of the local context on these organizations? Finally, how could the risks of localism and enclosure be avoided?

From another perspective, how do we address the emergence, the development and the first effects of these new territorial networks of the SSE, most often carried by the players of the SSE themselves: we refer here to the territorial clusters of economic cooperation that are developing in France or, again, to the SSE clusters. What links do these experiences maintain with the remaining actors of local development? What does the situation look like in distinct national contexts?

Beyond that aspect, at the meso-economic scale, how should we address the renewal and diversification of the short production chains, often initiated by the SSE organizations, whether they concern agriculture, trade, energy production, or the taking into account of waste management? How do we assess the effects on a territory in terms of modes of cooperation, price-setting behavior, strategies for coproduction and their forms of incorporation in the territories? Can we define sectorial ideal-type or national models?

Finally, this work is mainly interested by emerging forms of SSE that mobilize multiple stakeholders without neglecting more institutionalized forms, represented for instance by cooperative groups. Because the organizational and statutory innovations are also likely to affect indirectly the more traditional forms of the SSE, such as the cooperative banks or agricultural cooperatives, generally of large size, do these organizations reinvent their relation to the territory and if so, according to which rules and procedures?

– At a political level, the relation with politics and policy must then be analyzed from two angles.

The first one, centered on public policies, refers to the contribution of the SSE to territorial governance, here understood as a "framework of institutional rules and procedures for decision-making on the mode of territorial development through public debate, public action and, more precisely, the production of public policies" (Demoustier, Richez-Battesti, 2010). The participative imperative was able to bring different actors together in a joint approach to territorial governance and the institutionalization of the SSE (Bassi, 2010; Ségas, 2007; Jérôme, 2010). However, the assumption of perfect congruence between the SSE and horizontal territorial governance, in particular *via* the new statutes and cooperation mechanisms, needs to be challenged (Itçaina, Pecqueur, 2012). How do we approach the relation between social capital, social economy and local development policies (Kay, 2005; Evans, Syrett,

2007)? What are the territorial processes for publicization of support for the SSE, including their contentious dimensions? Are their different processes of institutionalization of the SSE as a policy sector? How should we characterize the resulting process of standardization? Finally, what is the impact of the scale of sectorial policies (Jullien, Smith, 2008) on the dynamics of the SSE?

The second political dimension refers to the links between the SSE and social movements, considered here from their territorial dimension. Social movements research manifests a new interest in cooperative and SSE organizations as organizational supports for movements in search of alternative ways of action, in order to compensate for a lack of access to policy-making (Soule, 2012; Schneiberg *et al.,* 2008). By way of an example Arthur *et al.* have also seen in the mobilizations around the takeover as a cooperative of the Tower Colliery mine in Wales the expression of a contentious social space (Arthur *et al.,* 2004). Through the ethnographic analysis of the Hotel Bauen, set up as a workers' cooperative in Buenos Aires, Faulk (2008) points out how cooperativism, as a social movement (distinguishing between formal cooperativism, affective cooperativism or *compañerismo* and community participation) creates space for the emergence of new conceptions of work and citizenship, alternative conceptions to the dominant neoliberal model. In Southern Italy, social cooperatives have managed to become one of the organizational instruments of mobilizations of the civil society fighting organized crime (Buccolo, 2013). In the Basque Country and in Quebec, the complex historic articulation between cooperativism and territorial identity mobilizations, under various banners, has also been emphasized. More recently, we could observe whether the anti-austerity mobilizations, particularly in Southern Europe, have completed their protest by local innovations in the matter of the social and solidarity-based economy. This opens up a field of discussion, still largely unexplored, on the role of social movements in the production, implementation and acceptance of organizational innovations of the SSE.

Since SSE develops very differently from one territory to another and since territories are also contrasted (in terms of public policies and social movements) we consider that relations between the territory and the SSE take a large diversity of configurations constituted by social innovations. This explains the choice of cases which components rest upon a large diversity of organizational and institutional forms and trajectories.

2. A book in two parts and twelve chapters

Once the general frame of the book is presented, two thematics structure the work.

The first part of the book, *SSE and territory an answer to the socio-economic and political changes?*, tries to analyze the effects of socioeconomic and political changes on the link between SSE and territory. Is it a context encouraging, maybe by default, local innovations on SSE, with the development of new experiments, e.g. short food supply chains, new modalities of job and social and economic value creation, responsible finance, or management of common goods as water, etc.? Are there new ways to articulate global and local dimensions through experiences based on proximity and control of the whole economic circuit? To which extent are these initiatives related to social movements (notably anti-austerity ones) but also to local policy makers?

The second part, *Towards new heterogeneous forms of territorial cooperation?* presents the restructuring of local cooperation strategies between heterogeneous actors at the territorial level. What role do civil society and public actors play in these processes, which might result in territorially contrasted forms of institutionalization of SSE as a policy-sector? If responses to social needs are dominant in several articles, this second part is more centered on the dynamics of public actors.

2.1. Part 1: SSE and territory: an answer to the socio-economic and political changes?

In the first chapter, Marie J. Bouchard and Tassadit Zerdani start by presenting a theoretical approach of territories and underline the role of networks of SSE "as spaces of interaction and co-construction". More precisely, they analyze the institutionalization of reticular spaces with a neo institutionalist perspective focused on institutional work. Their case study concerns the emergence of a local network of solidarity and responsible finance in Quebec. Authors show that the institutionalization of this project contributes to build an institutional field (solidarity and responsible finance) centered on finance, distinct from its contribution to local development, in a meso and macro dynamic.

In a second chapter, Nadine Richez-Battesti and Béatrice Chauvin show how territorial anchorage improves performance. They start from the observation that links between cooperative banks and territories are more frequently postulated than demonstrated. After stressing the difficulty to comprehend the notion of territory, they show the double nature of these links in terms of governance and of economic results as well. They essentially base their reflection on a case study coming from the experiment of an itinerant banker conducted recently at the NEF (New fraternal economy), a small French banking cooperative, first linked with Crédit Coopératif, in the BPCE Group. They underline both the capacity to innovate and to structure commercial activity and the weight of normative isomorphism in the recent evolution of NEF.

Chapter three focuses on the recent increase in cross-border experiences by the SSE actors in the Basque borderscape. Xabier Itçaina and Marc Errotabehere paid attention to changing relations between SSE actors on both sides of the French-Spanish border. This chapter is based on the qualitative analysis of 26 cross-border projects located within the social economy (or social and solidarity-based economy: SSE), with different themes (Basque language and culture, agro-ecology, fishing, media, women's entrepreneurship, social integration and social services). Authors show that the involvement of Basque SSE actors in cross-borders cooperation has been a proving ground for the transformation of social governance and the structuring of alternative economic spaces. They underline the ability of civil society to embrace the new policy instruments in the 1990s and to contribute to the governance. But after 2008, the process of hybridization of the governance began with a growing part for private business. The building cross-border governance networks is faced with four types of asymmetries: institutional, political, organizational and finally market asymmetry. These issues are further complicated by the risk that unintegrated and functional cooperation might be motivated purely by access to EU-based or bilateral funding opportunities.

For the fourth chapter, Andrea Bassi and Sarah Fabbri are working on short food supply chains, a global phenomenon in industrialized countries, and especially on the Farmers markets phenomenon in Italy. Their case study concerns the city of Cesena (a medium size town in the North East area of Italy), the most important agri-food center of the Region. After a theoretical approach of these markets, their main contributions are about the characterization of clients of these local markets and the proposal of a conceptual framework of social value added to evaluate the social impact of the Farmer's Market.

The fifth chapter is about Romania in a specific context. Cristina Barna and Ancuţa Vameşu pointed out the role of social and solidarity economy and social enterprises, for a sustainable territorial development and their contribution to the reduction of territorial inequalities. Their case study exemplifies the process of reconfiguration of social economy. It concerns inter relations between social enterprises, local production and use of social capital in the Horezu territory, a rural and mountainous region. They foster the role of cooperatives and social enterprises on re-thinking the production and trade chains putting into attention the capacity of social and solidarity economy to join economic and social dimensions. The originality of their analysis is to focus on dairy and forest production as commons.

Chapter six is about SSE trends in Venezuela. Benito Díaz, Angel Higuerey, Mario Fagiolo, Leonardo Argüello and Fernando Aponte analyze the role of SSE and public policies in the local management of water industry in two regions of Venezuela. They first show the increasing role of SSE, even if there is a debate about its boundaries, in the local public policy level. Authors highlight that this growing role is not taken into account at the national planning level. Then they analyze two cases studies: the Nucleus for endogenous development (NUDE) in Trujillo State and the Technical water roundtables, a community organization working with organized community support and helping the people to meet their common needs. Their role could be to go over the sole water management in order to deal with other problems encountered by territorial public authorities.

2.2. Part 2: Towards new heterogeneous forms of territorial cooperation?

In their contribution, Nathalie Vallet, Simon De Nys-Ketels and Michelle Bylemans put their attention on urban territories in Belgium and specially about conceptualization and design of the concept of inclusive economic participation for labor and consumption. A lot of Flemish urban municipal governments are therefore confronted with the following challenge: how can socially deprived urban citizens participate economically as a provider of labor and as a consumer in a more solid i.e. sustainable and structural way? What kind of alternative policy solutions does exist there, and which of these solutions are focused on the remediation of the poorly coordinated and spatially dispersed initiatives? Authors emphasize "Inclusive Economic Participation (IEP) site" as a particular territorial network that accommodates partners who try to resolve under the environmental constraints of an urban setting, the objective of an inclusive economic participation. This IEP site works as a spatially concentrated *hub* cities that accommodates public, (social) profit, non-profit and for-profit organizations that jointly strive for a (more) solid economic participation of socially deprived citizens, both as a consumer and as a provider of labor. Consequently, IEP sites may associate providers of public services (e.g. employment, social housing and child care support), SSE organizations (e.g. sheltered workshops, social restaurants and production co-operatives) and for-profit organizations (e.g. eco-design stores, recycling pop-up shops, repair cafés,[1] training experts and co-working facilitators).

Chapter eight from Susan Bernardino, Deolinda Meira and J. Freitas Santos from Portugal, show how the recent development of SSE and social enterprises contribute to solve old problems such as the lack of social cohesion, economic wellbeing or housing. They choose to present social innovation in the Portuguese context and their link with local development in a context of economic crisis. The Portuguese social stock exchange (PSSE) is a social initiative that aims to reproduce, with some adaptations, the environment of a conventional stock exchange. The main objective is to mobilize resources for promising new social ventures. Social investors are donors who choose to finance projects with social goals. One case study is extracted from this system: the Bee interpretation and biodiversity centre. The second case study concerns the Production cooperative of the Porto masons' workers. These two initiatives share common factors as their capacity to be sustainable in the long term and to contribute to local development by involving private and public actors in participatory processes. The two case studies demonstrate that the innovation and creativity of social entrepreneurs could facilitate the transformation of a social problem into an opportunity to create social and economic value in a lasting way.

Chapter nine concerns the possible transformation into cooperatives of the social services in the province of Gipuzkoa, in the Spanish Basque Country. Enekoitz Etxezarreta Etxarri, Eusebio Lasa Altuna, Anjel Mari Errasti Amozarrain and Juan Carlos Perez de Mendiguren show the main results obtained from the Delphi study, which was made of politicians and technicians from the Department of social policy in the County Council of Gipuzkoa, concerning the possibility of gradually

---

1 See: <http://repaircafe.org/>, consulted on 1 November 2017.

transforming into cooperatives the provision of social services in this province. Even if there is a tradition of collaboration with the third sector, they show that the spread of the cooperative form in the social sector is not a primary public objective.

Chapter ten is about professional inclusion of disabled people in South Brazil. Maurizio Serva and Júlia Graeff analyze social and solidarity-based economy organizations that work on labor training for visually impaired people and people with intellectual disabilities. That action has got the characteristics of sustainable territorial development particularly to their social aspect and possibility of including a portion of the population that is outside labor market. It happens not only for the lack of training access but also because it requires special management and organizational environments prepared for their insertion. Such actions may start from public policies or public-private partnerships, without going into ideological aspects, but aware the public sector performance, in these aspects, has been somewhat failure, in Brazil. They support their analyses with two case studies in the field of social and solidarity-based economy organizations that work with people with visual impairments and mental disabilities, respectively. They underline the fact that the economic aspects of their practices are so embedded in the non-economic dimension that social sustainability stands out and guarantees the continuity of the organizations. The core of these processes is the ability to establish partnerships with other social economy organizations in the territory, with governmental organizations, companies and the community. All these relationships are based on the legitimacy and credibility built by the two organizations from their commitment to the causes they fight for concerning the context of visually impaired people and those with intellectual disabilities.

Chapter eleven concerns territorial clusters of economic cooperation (TCEC) that recently appeared in France. These new dynamic questions both the social and solidarity economy and the territorial development. Danièle Demoustier analyses this measure as the territorial cooperation "process" and as the territorial development of "new actors". Taking into account the most TCEC experiences in France, she builds a first typology of TCEC to distinguish priorities surrounding member's consolidation, business or population services diversification, a sector construction or consolidation, the response in terms of functionality. In this sense, she underlines the role of TCEC to generate social and technological innovations and more generally to promote sustainable development.

She also promotes the role of TCEC to sustain and develop social and solidarity economy. But she emphasizes the difficult equilibrium between economization and socialization of territorial development.

Chapter twelve from Alexandrine Lapoutte, Martine Vézina and Marie-Claire Malo concerns the territorial legitimacy of large SSE's through the analysis of a speech by the president of a cooperative group. While the local rooting of small social and solidarity-based economy enterprises is taken for granted and large globalized enterprises do not have to justify a lack of local rooting, this is not the case for large social and solidarity-based economy enterprises. Though the latter belong to the field of social and solidarity-based economy due in part to their territorial identity, their identity as large enterprises propels them toward a more globalized territory, often leading to question their legitimacy as social and solidarity-based economy enterprises. Their purpose is to explain how large social and solidarity-based economy (SSE) enterprises legitimize their relation to their territories. To explore this question, the authors analyze a speech by the president of a cooperative group in the banking sector. The results reveal a strong will to account for the relationships that the large SE enterprise maintains with its territory of origin. The speech analyzed proposes also a vision of the broader territory as meeting local stakeholders' expectations. Stakeholders are proposed a win-win deal, a common project and an expansion consistent with the original mutual model. This discourse conciliates development with cooperative identity.

To conclude, facing persistence of the crisis and increasing inequalities, SSE promotes new ways of intervention through a diversity of models. Their common point is the link with territory considered as a resource. Divergences come mainly from the place of policy-makers in the different local networks and the role of SSE in the governance framework at local level. The connection between SSE and social movements remains less taken in account and is still a dimension to be discussed further.

References

Arthur L., Keenoy T., Smith R., Scott Cato M. and Anthony P., 2004, "Cooperative production – a contentious space?", paper for the *22nd Annual International Labour Process Conference*, Amsterdam, 5-7 April.

Bassi A., 2010, "La mosaïque coopérative. Stratégies de réseau de la coopération sociale à Ravenne", *in* X. Itçaina (dir.), *La politique du lien : les nouvelles dynamiques territoriales de l'économie sociale et solidaire*, Rennes, PUR, p. 109-27.

Bruni L., Zamagni S. (eds.), 2009, *Dizionario di economia civile*, Roma, Città Nuova.

Buccolo E., 2013, "L'Économie Sociale et Solidaire et la création d'espaces d'action publique territoriale : le cas des coopératives sociales gérant des biens confisqués à la Mafia", communication ST 9, *12e congrès AFSP*, Paris, 9-11 juillet 2013.

Demoustier D., Richez-Battesti N., 2010, "Les organisations de l'économie sociale et solidaire : gouvernance, régulation et territoire", *Géographie, économie, société*, 12 (1): 5-14.

Demoustier D., 2010, "Économie sociale et solidaire et régulation territoriale. Étude sur quatre zones d'emploi en Rhône-Alpes", *Géographie, économie, société*, 12 (1): 89-109.

Evans M., Syrett S., 2007, "Generating social capital? The social economy and local economic development", *European Urban and Regional Studies*, 14 (1): 55-74.

Faulk K.A., 2008, "If they touch one of us, they touch all of us: cooperativism as a counterlogic to neoliberal capitalism", *Anthropological Quarterly*, 81 (3): 579-614.

Jérôme V., 2010, "L'économie sociale et solidaire : une subversion institutionnelle et politique ?", *in* X. Itçaina (dir.), *La politique du lien : les nouvelles dynamiques territoriales de l'économie sociale et solidaire*, Rennes, PUR, p. 149-64.

Jullien B., Smith A. (eds.), 2008, *Industries and Globalization: The Political Causality of Difference*, Houndmills, Palgrave.

Kay A., 2006, "Social capital, the social economy and community development", *Community Development Journal*, 41 (2): 160-73.

Leloup F., Moyart L., Pecqueur B., 2005, "La gouvernance territoriale comme nouveau mode de coordination territoriale ?", *Géographie, économie, société*, 7 (4): 321-32.

Pecqueur B., Itçaina X., 2012, "Économie sociale et solidaire et territoires : un couple allant de soi ?", *RECMA – Revue internationale de l'économie sociale*, 325: 48-64.

Schneiberg M., King M., Smith T., 2008, "Social movements and organizational form: cooperative alternatives to corporations in the American insurance, dairy, and grain industries", *American Sociological Review*, 73: 635-67.

Ségas S., 2007, "Le détour de l'action publique : enthousiasme et déception des acteurs de l'économie sociale face aux politiques de développement territorial", *in* X. Itçaina, J. Palard, S. Ségas (dir.), *Régimes territoriaux et développement économique*, Rennes, PUR, p. 247-60.

Soule S.A., 2012, "Social movements and markets, industries and firms", *Organization Studies*, 33 (12): 1715-33.

Part I

SSE and Territory: An Answer to the Socio-economic and Political Changes?

Chapter 1

Financing the Social and Solidarity Economy in Québec

At the Crossroads of Territorial Development and Solidarity-Based Investment

Marie J. Bouchard & Tassadit Zerdani

Université du Québec à Montréal

Introduction[1]

In the social and solidarity economy (SSE), the notion of territory has several meanings, among them: social territory, reticular territory, physical territory, administrative territory and action territory (Bouchard *et al.,* 2005). However, overall territory is understood as the place where the differentiated and complementary actions and logics of social actors involved in SSE projects meet, intersect and complement each other. As such, territory is a space that allows for concerted action between development actors (entrepreneurs, funders, support actors, municipalities, etc.) and from there the promotion of economic development at the local level. In that process, these actions give shape to formal and informal spaces of relationships between the development actors with a view to strengthening and confirming a distinctive practice in the field of economic and social development, namely that of the SSE. These spaces promote and formalize inter-organizational relationships and socio-territorial mobilization, establishing links between local actions – and interactions – as well as global development strategies at

[1] We would like thanks the reviewers for their comments on a previous version of this article as well as Cathleen Pohler for the translation into English.

different territorial levels. Let us recall that local development actions and collective projects are what initially gave rise to SSE initiatives. In turn, each of these initiatives contributed to shaping territories within various types of proximities (geographical, organizational and institutional) (Richez-Battesti, Gianfaldoni, 2008). In this study, we examine networks of the SSE as spaces of interaction and co-construction, from the angle of the logics (Lounsbury, 2007; Thornton, Ocasio, 2008) that characterize their governance, in particular during their transition from the informal to the formal mode. We thus analyze the institutionalization of reticular spaces which are composed of actors with different identities and objectives, yet which also have a common objective serving the public interest, namely that of the development of their territories.

To explore this question, we conducted an in-depth longitudinal study of one case: the *Réseau de la finance solidaire et responsable au Québec* (Québec Responsible and Solidarity-based Finance Network), hereinafter the "FSRQ Network." This network is a good example of the reticular spaces of the SSE, in the sense that it combines a sectoral and a territorial dimension and fosters interaction between local, regional and national actors as well as between actors involved in the funding, support and the promotion of the social economy. The founding members of the Network are active either in solidarity-based financing, where they support the SSE, or in development capital, where they focus on sustainable development and the maintenance and creation of quality jobs both within and outside of the social economy. All seek to fund local and regional development in Québec. These funders complement each other to ensure the financing and development of these projects at all stages and funding levels and across all regions of Québec. The FSRQ Network brings together financial actors but also has members who are active in supporting territorial development (support actors). The Network thus combines two unique and complementary logics of economic development: the logic of solidarity financing and that of territorial development. These two approaches, finance and development, although different in many ways, are nonetheless compatible, if not consubstantial, with each other. The case study shows that between its emergence and institutionalization – in other words, on its way from an informal network to a more formal organization – the Network favored the logic of financing over that of local development.

To examine the institutionalization of the FSRQ Network as a reticular space, we resorted to two concepts proposed by what

Ben Slimane and Leca refer to as neo-institutionalism revisited (2010): the concept of institutional logics (Friedland, Alford, 1991) and that of institutional work (Lawrence, Suddaby, 2006). The mobilization of this conceptual framework helps explain how actors working with logics that are different but nevertheless compatible and complementary collaborate to collectively build and institutionalize their network. Note that we have not addressed the tensions that arise invariably as part of this process (Théret, 2003). The Network is composed of actors who, although sharing goals that are of public interest, each have their own goals and interests, in addition to being of very different types and sizes. This inevitably leads to certain tensions or rivalries. Without undermining the importance of these tensions, we focused on what unites these actors and the way in which their shared identity evolves, namely from a sector to an institutional field specifically dedicated to finance.

This paper presents the emergence and formalization of the FSRQ Network, and the issue raised by the relationship between the domains of finance and support. It also identifies and describes the practices that these actors have collectively developed to conclude the Network's institutionalization process. Finally, the paper shows that the formalization of the Network induces another logic, that of building an institutional field (the field of solidary-based and responsible finance – FSR field), which is distinct from local development. However, another logic also emerges that reconfigures these actors and their respective logics – of finance on the one hand and support on the other – within a partnership-based context.

The content of this article is structured in five sections. The first section presents research that analyses the relationship between the SSE and territorial development, and clarifies the key concepts mobilized and the issue raised by this study. The second section explains the methodology (qualitative and longitudinal case study, spanning a period of ten years from 2000 to 2010). The third section presents the main actors of solidarity-based and responsible financing in Québec (FSR actors). The fourth section features the FSRQ Network by describing three phases of its development, and the fifth section discusses the results as well as the institutional practices that led to the creation of specific institutions in the Network and the emergence of a new institutional logic that is more sectoral, namely that of developing a new institutional field. The conclusion presents and illustrates the main contributions of this study to research on SSE networks and territories.

1. Literature review and issue at hand

This section is intended to clarify the problem targeted by the study and to justify its importance for the field by analyzing the link between the SSE and territorial development. It presents a non-exhaustive account of the research analyzing this link, clarifies key concepts used in this study and explains its conceptual framework.

1.1. Social economy, territorial action and networks

A territory is not just a physical or geographic location. Pecqueur and Itçaina (2012: 48) define it as "a tug-of-war between actors of a given spatial context that aims to identify, and then solve, under ambient stress, a societal problem or shared asset."[2] Here, the territory is a resource pool, generator of systems of territorial actors and generator of collective actions (Bouchard *et al.*, 2005).

In the SSE, defining territory also involves considering notions of proximity and the local. The latter is a space that serves as the basis for systems of actors and their initiatives, and that evolves with them. It is a breeding ground for many initiatives which usually come from different stakeholders but whose aims converge and generate, according to Enjolras (2010), a horizontal type of local or territorial governance system. This system of governance is defined by Coissard and Pecqueur (2007) as:

> [...] a complex phenomenon that involves both stability (compromise and negotiation) and instability (divergence and conflict) in which heterogeneous actors must mobilize around a common goal. In countries where the state has traditionally been centralized, the system of governance implies that public institutions no longer have the monopoly of territorial organization and, on the contrary, that decision-making involves the participation of actors pursuing different interests.[3] (quoted in Demoustier, Richez-Battesti, 2010: 8).

The sense of belonging to a local territory is an important factor in people's willingness to engage in initiatives or collective projects aimed at solving a shared problem (Arocena, 1986). Territorial collective action results from the synergy between a diverse set of actors working together and acting collectively. Local development is defined more as

2 Our translation.

3 Our translation.

a synergy of various activities (market and non-market) than the mere juxtaposition of productive initiatives (Artis *et al.,* 2009: 18). Note that the strength or weakness of a community depends on "organizational density"[4] (Klein, Fontan, 2004) or on mobilizable socio-territorial capital (Fontan *et al.,* 2003) that enables the sharing of resources and information (Klein, Carrière, 1999). The local community is thus a pool of resources and a base for restructuring social ties at once (Klein, Fontan, 2004; Lévesque, 2002).

Organizations from the Social and solidarity economy organizations (SSEOs) are known for their commitment to communities (Demoustier, Richez-Battesti, 2010), which is also what distinguishes them from conventional organizations (Pecqueur, Itçaina, 2012). For this reason, the SSE is a key partner in building and implementing local development policies aimed at overcoming sector- and community-based barriers to endogenous development (Artis *et al.,* 2009: 21). SSEOs are both actors of territorial governance and agents of territorial regulation. Given this role that is both sociopolitical and socioeconomic, they are an important actor in the structuring of new institutional territorial compromises (Demoustier, Richez-Battesti, 2010: 8). The SSE thus emerges as a set of actors that finds strength through solidarity (Vienney, 1994).

To fully play these roles, SSEOs have developed an ability to connect with each other and with other development actors. The groups they form are either of a sectoral or cross-sectoral nature, at different territorial scales (Lévesque, 2016). Networks take shape at many levels; some are homogeneous, such as the sectoral federations of cooperatives, and others are heterogeneous. In the latter case, some are of the multi-sector type, such as the Conseil québécois de la coopération et de la mutualité, which groups cooperatives of different sectors as well as mutual insurance societies, or intersectoral, such as the Chantier de l'économie sociale, which brings together SSEOs as well as representatives of other social groups, such as the women's movement and trade unions. SSEOs also group locally, mainly in order to optimize synergies between them and other actors of the territory. They thus form intersectoral heterogeneous networks, such as consultative tables at the neighborhood level. These include actors from the SSE, local social and health care institutions, elected officials and other stakeholders and play the role of custodian of the territory's assets and also see to their development.

4 Our translation.

The networks, as a mode of organization and governance of relations between the SSEOs, have multiplied, due to a context marked by the increasingly pronounced participation of the SSE sector in the socio-economic development of territories (Trouvé *et al.*, 2010), the withdrawal of the state in the provision of certain social services, and the emergence of a new model of governance that is more local or territorial. This new context prompted SSEOs to network with each other and assign representatives in order to better assert themselves as true stakeholders *vis-à-vis* the state and other partners involved in the development of geographic and sectoral territories. In Québec, this has allowed SSE actors to participate in the co-construction of public policies, at the central level, and in the co-production of their implementation at the regional or local level (Vaillancourt, 2013).

Local development policies are based on a transversal structuring logic that requires concerted action that is oriented toward the territory (Artis *et al.*, 2009). These policies also encourage collective action that inspires and engenders the formation of a web of networks that can also be seen as so-called reticular territories. "The reticular territory is brought about by the networking of actors. Regardless of the type of network, cooperation, consultation and coordination between actors creates networks. This set of networks becomes a territory within which the actors act and where places are interrelated"[5] (Bouchard *et al.*, 2005: 8). The composition of the reticular territory may likewise be either homogeneous or heterogeneous, varying depending on the functionality or the objectives targeted by the network. Moreover, the scale of the territory may be micro (within an organization), local (district, town), regional, national or international. In Québec, organizations with the rather broad mandate to support local or regional development – as opposed to those focused on a particular cause or sector of activity, such as housing or workers' cooperatives – often have an intersectoral pluralistic governance composed of representatives of SSEOs, trade unions and business and civil society.

According to Monnet (2010), in a context where reticular territories proliferate (Balligand, Maquart, 1990), networks can no longer be juxtaposed, or opposed, to territories (Painter, 2009: 57 in Monnet, 2010: 7); instead, networks emerge as a "tool, among others, for the production of multiple territories [...]" (Dupuy, Offner, 2005: 45

5 Our translation.

in Monnet, 2010). These networks, as network spaces, thus have the capacity to produce or define territories (Monnet, 2010).

Networks are presented as forms of governance in many SSE sectors, such as, in France, that of the services for the elderly (Trouvé *et al.*, 2010). They are defined as "an organizational model connecting actors and resources to allow for an improved engagement with the public in the framework of a given sector and territory"[6] (Demoustier, Richez-Battesti, 2010: 11). Through their networks, SSEOs can reconcile not only individual interests with collective interests but can also contribute to public interest objectives (Enjolras, 2010; Bernier, Bouchard, Lévesque, 2003). These networks are generally considered to be collaborative networks (Mandel, Keast, 2007):

> In these types of networks, the participants are no longer just independent actors trying to coordinate activities but rather are interdependent organizations or groups looking to make changes in existing institutions and systems and to build a new whole. Accountability in a collaborative network is based on the actions of this new whole rather than the individual organizations. [...] Each of these participants is considered an equal partner, and power is shared among all of them. (Mandell, Keast, 2007: 577).

In addition to defining and clarifying certain concepts, the studies presented in this sub-section show that collective projects, such as those focusing on local development, are at the very root of the emergence of SSEO networks. These networks, as network spaces, contribute to shaping territories in a context influenced by multiple factors (geographic, organizational and institutional) (Richez-Battesti, Gianfaldoni, 2008). Moreover, to ensure their role in governance and territorial regulation (Demoustier, Richez-Battesti, 2010), SSEOs form and operate in networks and thus produce geographical and sectoral territories. With reference to these studies, the following sub-section clarifies the main issue of this article and its analytical framework.

1.2. Issue and conceptual framework

The above-mentioned literature shows that research done in this field covers the following topics: the dynamics of the relationships between the territory and SSEOs, and the "natural" (taken for granted) links between these two entities (Demoustier, Richez-Battesti, 2010; Monnet,

---

6 Our translation.

2010; Pecqueur, Itçaina, 2012); the role which SSEOs play in local development (Richez-Battesti, Gianfaldoni, 2008; Artis *et al.*, 2009; Vaillancourt, 2013); and their involvement as actors of governance and territorial regulation (Demoustier, Richez-Battesti, 2010; Enjolras, 2010; Klein, Fontan, 2004; Lévesque, 2002). These studies also show that, to fulfill their role of territorial development actors, SSEOs operate in networks and form network spaces (Bouchard *et al.*, 2005; Trouvé *et al.*, 2010). These network spaces are described, although it is not explained why or how these networks become institutionalized (formalized).

We posit that to contribute in a sustainable way to the development of a territorial heritage, and more specifically to local development, the institutionalization or formalization of SSEOs networks is important. These organizations represent the collective interests and manifest social aspirations. Fueled by social movements and other efforts seeking social change, they also offer innovative strategies for resisting the breakdown and transformation of lifestyles (Lévesque *et al.*, 2014; Demoustier, Richez-Battesti, 2010). Moreover, these organizations "demonstrate their ability to express new social needs, to experiment with new solutions (explaining their being referred to as "laboratories") and to influence – through their presence or clout – the workings of some sectors of activity, employment relations or financial flows"[7] (Demoustier, Richez-Battesti, 2010: 8). To increase their legitimacy, these actions with multiple objectives (economic, social and even political) must be performed by groups of actors (networks) that have a formal status. This article examines the issue of the institutionalization of SSEO networks. We view these networks as structures or network spaces (Musso, 2003) where several action logics intersect.

The conceptual tools usually used to study interorganizational networks (IONs) are insufficient for examining the roles of the actors, including the ways in which they contribute to moving their network from an informal to a formal stage. By mobilizing two concepts brought forth by the so-called neo-institutionalism revisited (Ben Slimane, Leca, 2010) – that of institutional work (Lawrence, Suddaby, 2006) and that of institutional logics (Battilana, Dorado, 2010; Friedland, Alford, 1991) – we identify and describe the institutional practices which SSE actors mobilize to formalize their networks above and beyond the differences between the various logics they embody.

---

7 Our translation.

Institutional work is defined by Lawrence and Suddaby (2006: 215) as the "purposive action of individuals and organizations aimed at creating, maintaining and disrupting institutions." Its analysis is focused on the activity of institutional creation, maintenance or disruption and not on providing a static description of results (Lawrence, Suddaby, Leca, 2009: 10). The work is not led by a single actor but by many, namely in a collaborative effort; it allows to understand the institutional process of organizational transformation. The concept of institutional logic developed by Friedland and Alford (1991) is defined as "a central logic that constitutes a principle of organization and legitimacy"[8] (Leca, 2006: 75). Institutional logics are assumptions, beliefs and rules with which the actors organize and give meaning to their institutional reality (Friedland, Alford, 1991; Thornton, Ocasio, 2008). A number of these are conflicting or complementary, whereby inconsistencies, tensions and contradictions constitute a leeway for the organizational actors (Friedland, Alford, 1991), who develop capacities for action by manifestly exploiting these tensions and contradictions. This diversity of logics gives these actors the opportunity to learn from other models in order to envision new rules (Seo, Creed, 2002) and to generate institutional changes.

2. Methodology

This section presents the methodology of our study and describes our field of research as well as the strategies chosen to analyze the collected data.

2.1. Research paradigm

Our research approach is based on a constructivist paradigm; it covers a little-studied issue and thus is of an exploratory nature. The interorganizational network (ION) being complex, we opted for the case method, as it allows for a longitudinal and in-depth study (Langley, 1999) of the institutional practices that may influence the dynamics and institutionalization of that network. The choice of the FSRQ Network was motivated by the importance of the financial sector and the strategic position of this network as a pillar of territorial and sectoral development, particularly in the SSE. In addition, the FSRQ Network constitutes a

---

8 Our translation.

collaborative type of network (Mandell, Keast, 2007) founded by a core of heterogeneous financial actors from different sectors (trade unions, private SSE, public and community) following many years of informal interaction between them. Each of these financial actors certainly have their particular logic, yet the latter differ overall from those of the support actors with whom they collaborate at the local level. Despite their differences, all of these actors intervene in a complementary fashion to finance development projects at the territorial and sectoral levels. Our selected case of the FSRQ Network seems to be fertile ground for analyzing the issue primarily addressed in this article: *Why and how do SSEO networks become institutionalized in order to achieve their mission of territorial and sectoral development?*

2.2. Data collection tools and analysis strategy

Our study is based on data from three sources: interviews, non-participant observation and document analysis. Various public documents and internal documents produced by the FSRQ Network and its members were consulted. We also had access to all the email exchanges between the members of the Network through their mailing list. To triangulate the data (Langley, 1999), 25 semi-structured interviews were conducted with people directly involved in the Network. The interviews were recorded and fully transcribed to ensure a faithful reproduction of the content of the exchange.

Our focus on a single ION from a longitudinal perspective also required our involvement in the field. We conducted the non-participant observation during 12 meetings held by members of FSRQ Network and at other events (e.g. inaugural assembly of the Network and subsequent informational meeting to present itself and recruit members).

To analyze the data, we started, as recommended by Langley (1999), with the selection of relevant data to draw a portrait of the evolution of the FSRQ Network and to identify key events and practices developed during this phase. These data were used to establish the baseline, identify three phases of development, and identify the issue raised by the relationship between its two types of members, being the financial actors and the support actors. The data was then analyzed by structuring them around the main institutional practices proposed in the analysis grid developed by Lawrence and Suddaby (2006). This allowed us to identify the modes of action and objectives of all members and the dominant institutional practices in each of the three development stages of the FSRQ Network. To this end, we analyzed and coded, using the NVivo software, the interviews (verbatim) as well as the notes we took from our observations and from our readings of the documents.

3. Territories of action of solidarity-based and responsible financing in Québec

This section presents the specificities of action of FSR actors and explains their mode of intervention in sectors and territories.

3.1. Specificities of the interventions of FSR actors

The sector of solidarity-based and responsible financing (FSR sector) has an important social and economic role, particularly with regard to the SSE and territorial development (local and regional). In addition to supporting the creation and development of SSEOs, the FSR pursues socio-economic objectives, such as the creation and maintenance of jobs, local and regional development, cooperation and sustainable development. The sector is composed of financial actors but also of support actors (e.g. Centres locaux de développement [CLD], Coopératives de développement régional, Corporations de développement économique communautaire [CDÉC], Groupes de ressources techniques, Sociétés d'aide au développement des collectivités [SADC]). The financial actors contribute funds in the form of loans or loan guarantees for the pre-start-up, start-up, expansion or consolidation of SSE projects, while the support actors offer grants and guidance to firms (technical assistance, business plan development, market analysis, etc.). For example, support actors help enterprises obtain financing from financial actors by assisting with the development of the business plan and by offering an initial monetary contribution; essentially, they serve as a bridge leading to the financing of social economy projects. Financial actors, for their part, collaborate in determining and providing the financing package required by these projects while simultaneously distributing financial risk among several financial institutions. In that process, analysts and portfolio managers refer projects to each other and consult about their assessment. Note that a main criterion for financing SSE projects (Tessier, 2005) is their territorial rootedness, as manifested through the mobilization of local resources (financial, material, human), contribution to job creation and inclusive governance structure. For the financial actors, this criterion also translates into financial risk mitigation, since the community is mobilized to back up the project in the case of failure.

In principle, each of the financial actors offers different investment products, even if these sometimes overlap. Some of them offer solidarity-based financing intended only for financing SSEOs and local economic community development. Other actors offer development capital; these actors are comprised mainly of the two labor-sponsored investment funds (Fondaction CSN and Fonds de solidarité FTQ) as well as Capital régional et coopératif Desjardins (CRCD), who provide funding to all businesses that meet certain environmental and social conditions (Bourque *et al.,* 2009). Note that although differences exist between the logics embodied by these financial actors (trade union, community and cooperative), the latter work in tandem to achieve their shared mission of serving the public interest, which is to participate in the economic and social development of Québec and its regions. Some of them (the "principal actors") have even collaborated to create a formal network, the FSRQ Network.

As shown in the table below, the FSR actors (financial actors and support actors) each have different action and reticular territories. Some of them (Fiducie du Chantier de l'économie sociale [Fiducie du Chantier], Réseau d'investissement social du Québec [RISQ], Caisse d'économie solidaire Desjardins [CÉCOSOL]) have mandates that are limited to certain sectors (financial services, investment in SSE); nevertheless, they belong to reticular territories that are close to yet distinct from each other (SSE, cooperation or trade union networks). Others (Fondaction, Fonds de solidarité FTQ, CRCD, Investissement Québec [IQ], Filaction, support actors) have mandates that concern a territorial aspect, their interventions being aimed at various territorial scales. Here as well, the reticular territory varies between the networks of the SSE actors, the trade unions, the cooperative world and that of the public actors. To pursue either of two types of mandates, these actors have gradually developed common practices, followed by an informal network, which then evolved to the stage of the formal network, namely the FSRQ Network which we present in section 5.

Table 1: Action territories and reticular territories of the FSR in Québec

FSR actors	*Action territories*	*Network territories*
Actors of the FSR sector who became members of the formal network		
Caisse d'économie solidaire	Sectoral and territorial: Finances primarily SSEOs and their groupings, but also unions and socially responsible businesses. Offers responsible savings products and solidarity-based financing in Québec	Union (CSN) *Caisses Desjardins* *Chantier de l'économie sociale* *Réseau* FSRQ (founding member)
Fiducie du Chantier de l'économie Sociale	Sectoral and territorial: Finances exclusively SSEs. Solidarity-based financing offer (patient capital) in all regions of Québec	*Chantier de l'économie sociale* Unions (FTQ, CSN) *Réseau* FSRQ (founding member)
Filaction	Territorial and sectoral: Funding for SMEs and micro-enterprises and for funds from the SSE, women's entrepreneurship, cultural communities and the tourism sector. Offers financing products in all regions of Québec	CSN union network through Fondaction, its founder *Réseau* FSRQ (founding member)
Fondaction CSN	Territorial (macro or national): Funding of Québec socio-economic development by providing growth capital to companies in all regions (all sectors)	Union (CSN) Research networks (CIRIEC Canada; ARUC-ÉS) International development network *Chantier de l'économie sociale* *Réseau* capital *Réseau* FSRQ (founding member)
Fonds de solidarité FTQ	Territorial (macro or national): Funds Québec socio-economic development by providing growth capital to companies in all regions (all sectors). Intervention at the regional level: *Fonds régionaux de solidarité* FTQ; and local: *Fonds locaux de solidarité* FTQ	Union (FTQ) *Fonds régionaux de solidarité* FTQ *Fonds locaux de solidarité* FTQ *Chantier de l'économie sociale* Capital *Réseau* FSRQ (founding member)
Réseau d'investissement social du Québec (RISQ)	Sectoral and territorial: Finances exclusively SSEOs. Offers social financing (quasi-equity) in all regions of Québec	*Chantier de l'économie sociale* Private investors *Réseau* FSRQ (founding member)

FSR actors	*Action territories*	*Network territories*
Réseau québécois du crédit communautaire	Territorial (local): The members of this network intervene to finance micro-enterprises at the local level and also fund communities with specificities	Community *Réseau* FSRQ (founding member)
Actors of the FSR sector who did not become members of the formal network		
Capital régional et coopératif Desjardins	Territorial (resource regions) and sector (cooperatives): Financing of corporations and cooperatives in remote resource regions in Québec	*Conseil québécois de la coopération et de la mutualité* *Caisses Desjardins* *Réseau* FSRQ (potential member of the category of member investors)
Investissement Québec	Territorial (macro or national): Financing of development capital for SSE projects in all regions of Québec through its cooperatives and other social economy enterprises Branch	Public sector *Réseau* FSRQ (potential member of the class of member investors)
Support actors (CLD, CDÉC, SADC)	Territorial (local): Support and sometimes grants for SMEs and SSEOs at the local level. These actors collaborate with other local stakeholders to implement development projects in a given territory	Public (CLD mandate) Community (CDEC, SADC) (potential members of the category of partner members)

Source: the authors

3.2. *Joint financing package for successful territorial interventions*

The actors of the FSR sector use performance criteria and methods for supporting enterprises that are different from those of traditional financial institutions. In addition, these actors have developed a specialized niche type of intervention with SSEOs and other enterprises that pursues social and environmental goals in addition to economic objectives. The organizations they support have common values as well as local and regional roots. However, they present higher risks than traditional enterprises due mainly to their extra-financial (social and environmental) objectives and their collective ownership structure, in the case of SSEOs.

The financing of their investment projects is often made possible thanks to the participation of many actors in the financing package, which significantly reduces the relative risks of each.

Sectoral linkages and organizational proximity between the FSR actors have favored the development of partnership relations between them. Each financial actor provides a financial product that is coordinated and *a priori* complementary to the products offered by the other actors. To build a joint financing package, some actors have even created exchange forums to facilitate the flow of investment projects, ideas and tools to support collective entrepreneurship. They also share sector analyses, investment reports and internal reports on the businesses to finance. This complementary approach to funding takes place in collaboration with the support actors. The latter orient the investment project files to the different financial actors, sometimes contribute to down payments with loans or grants, and ensure the follow-up of projects. The analysis of these files is done in accordance with the *Guide d'analyse des entreprises d'économie sociale* (Guide for the analysis of social economy enterprises), designed and written by certain financial actors with the help of the support actors. In fact, the history of the FSRQ Network begins with the design of this Guide as a common standard.

In sum, the projects emerge at the level of communities and territories; they materialize with the support and follow-up of the territorial support actors who ensure their start-up by providing technical assistance, loans and grants, and by orienting them towards financial actors who guarantee or supplement their funding. Thus, these two categories of actors jointly participate in the launch and development of projects that have positive impacts on territorial development and form a network (reticular territory) that has evolved over time, as outlined in the next section.

4. The FSRQ Network: emergence and institutionalization

In 2009, a group of financial actors founded, pursuing institutional objectives, a formal network – the FSRQ Network. The mission of this network is to promote solidarity-based financing and development capital for the public and for its stakeholders, and to improve the expertise of professionals working in responsible financing.[9] The Network also represents social values: diversity, fairness, respect, democracy and transparency. The formal FSRQ Network did not emerge out of the blue; rather, it is the result of many years of collaboration between the two main groups of financial actors (those from solidarity-based financing and those from development capital) as well as between these and the support actors. Our analysis identifies three phases of its evolution.

4.1. Phase 1: Decentralized action

Looking back on their many years of collaboration in the financing of development projects at the sectoral and territorial levels, the financial actors identified their weaknesses in analyzing the funding files submitted, among others, by SSEOs. The consensus was that the analyses had not been based on standardized methods and that some financial analysts tended to lack familiarity with the specific reality of these organizations. The identification of this common problem, deemed complex by all FSR actors, led some of them in the early 2000s to call for the creation of a collective standard (a guide) that would help them to perform standardized, comprehensive and fair analyses of social economy enterprises.

This guide – the *Guide d'analyse des entreprises d'économie sociale* – was then produced with the participation of many actors, including: CÉCOSOL, Fondaction, Filaction, Fonds de financement coopératif, RISQ, IQ, the Direction des coopératives du ministère du Développement économique, de l'Innovation et de l'Exportation, as well as MCE Conseils[10] and L'Agence Pythagore.[11] The Guide proposes an approach and tools allowing financial analysts and support actors to recognize the specific characteristics of SSEOs; to identify the key risk as well as success factors of such enterprises; and to evaluate their missions, activities and ownership structures in a more appropriate and representative way. The Guide contains a multitude of grids, tools and recommendations which analysts and managers of SSEOs now regularly use to make wise and informed choices. It is used by almost all FSR actors and has

---

9 <http://capfinance.ca/pdf/presentationCapFinance.pdf>, consulted on 25 September 2015.

10 See: <http://www.mceconseils.com/index.html>, consulted on 25 September 2015.

11 See: <http://economiesocialequebec.ca/?module=directory&uid=2686&division=16&subject=73>, consulted on 25 September 2015.

become a standard working and reference tool. With its publication and dissemination in Québec, elsewhere in Canada and around the world, the Guide has become an official reference document; in other words, it has become "institutionalized." Interestingly, one of the main dimensions analyzed to assess the risk of a project is its "community rootedness," measured by the quantity and strength of the relationships between an SSEO and the actors of its local environment.

In sum, in the life cycle of the FSRQ Network, this initial stage characterized by the mobilization of certain financial actors around the production of the Guide can be considered as a process initiated on a voluntary basis by actors belonging to the core of the network. The Guide indicates a change in behavior with regard to the assessment of territorial and sectoral development projects, especially those of SSEOs. It was also the driving motor of the more structural changes that subsequently took place within the FSRQ Network and the FSR sector.

4.2. Phase 2: Expansion, standardization and partnership-based research

This phase began when the actors of the initial informal core group, following their positive and conclusive collaboration around the production of the Guide, formed links to university researchers. Building on the work of certain researchers of PROFONDS, created by Benoît Lévesque (UQAM) and Margie Mendell (Concordia University), and at the request of certain financial actors, a partnership-based activity site (Chantier d'activité partenariale-CAP) was created in 2003 within the Alliance de recherche universités-communautés en économie sociale (ARUC-ÉS),[12] namely CAP Finance responsable.[13]

Initially this CAP was composed of, in addition to researchers, a limited number of financial actors (RISQ, CÉCOSOL, Fondaction,

[12] In English: Community-University Research Alliance in Social Economy (CURA-SE). Since this study was performed in a French-speaking environment, this paper will retain the French acronym of the alliance.

[13] CAP Finance was a structure within ARUC-EC that was funded by a grant from the Social Sciences and Humanities Council of Canada (SSHRC). It also received financial support from the Université du Québec à Montréal, the Fonds de développement académique du réseau (FODAR) of the Université du Québec and its trade union partners: Confédération des syndicats nationaux (CSN), Fondaction de la CSN; Fédération des travailleurs et travailleuses du Québec (FTQ)-Fonds de solidarité FTQ.

Filaction, RQCC, IQ and CRCD). Eventually, other financial actors became involved, such as the Fonds de solidarité FTQ, in 2006, and Fiducie du Chantier, in 2007. The Chantier d'économie sociale and certain support actors (e.g. CLD) were also members of this CAP but later withdrew.

CAP Finance conducts research on several topics with the goal of assisting the financing and support actors in their interventions at the territorial level. Initially, CAP-funded work focused on the development of secondary markets and ethical investment. During this phase, the collaboration between the actors of the FSR sector and researchers was a success, since it resulted in the realization of many research projects[14] and led to the organization of several conferences and scientific symposia. Thereafter, from 2005 to 2006, the work of this CAP focused on the analysis of structural and institutional issues (e.g., public policy development and analysis of links between territorial development and solidarity-based financing). Among the outputs is a document that was discussed in the workshop *Investir solidairement* (Solidarity-based investing; our translation) organized in 2006 as part of a conference commemorating the 10th anniversary of the *Chantier de l'économie sociale*. The workshop participants agreed on a set of guidelines of action proposed by the CAP Finance partners, including that of establishing a formal network of solidarity-based and responsible funders in Québec.

Immediately after the conference, the financial actors (who were then members of CAP Finance of ARUC-ÉS) along with researchers mobilized to set up this formal network. In 2007, they launched discussions relating to the statutes of the network and jointly prepared its articles of incorporation and bylaws. The details of this phase of institutionalization of the FSRQ Network are presented in the following section.

4.3. Phase 3: Consolidation and specialization – toward the co-construction of an institutional field (FSR field)

Beginning in 2007, the financial actors who were members of CAP Finance of ARUC-ÉS mobilized, with the help of researchers, to form an association of professionals working in solidarity-based and responsible

[14] See the projects of CAP Finance at: <http://www.aruc-es.uqam.ca/Portals/0/docs/pdf/RapFinalARUC2009Web.pdf>, consulted on 25 September 2015.

financing. The latter was aimed at strengthening their joint action and resulted in the formalization of their network. Indeed, the formal FSRQ Network was officially launched in December 2009 under the name of CAP Finance, le Réseau de la finance solidaire et responsable.[15] Its founding members are Fondaction CSN, Filaction, CÉCOSOL, RQCC, Fonds de solidarité FTQ, RISQ and Fiducie du Chantier. These financial actors sought to equip their network with a legal structure to meet the challenges and issues of their sector; find new members, new areas of activities and research topics; and integrate all actors from the sector who pursue financing as their core activity.

Just after the announcement of the formalization of the FSRQ Network, its founding members met and formed an interim board of directors consisting of nine members (seven founding members and two researchers who had successively co-directed CAP Finance of ARUC-ÉS). One of the researchers, who was a former director and founder of ARUC-ÉS, chaired the board and was given the mandate to draft the strategic plan of the Network and to ensure its transition into a formal network. The strategic planning process consisted of: determining the positioning of the FSRQ Network; clarifying its objectives, values and mission; defining its activities; establishing governance structures; identifying potential members; and preparing its financing plan. One of the most important topics discussed at the meetings of this interim board was that of membership to this formal network. The goal was to clearly identify and target its potential members and find a way to integrate the support actors (CLD, SADC, CDÉC and others) without losing the specificity of a financial network. In the end, the four categories of members of the FSRQ Network were determined to be: founding members, investor members, partner members and associate members, whereby support actors have the status of partner members.

The above account shows that the institutionalization of the FSRQ Network somewhat changed the attitudes of its founding actors and the partnership practices (establishment of a strategic and institutional type of partnership). The goal of this institutionalization was to gain more legitimacy; protect the survival of their sector, and by extension the participants' survival; take positions on government policies; and deal with external threats. The founding members ultimately sought to

---

15 <http://capfinance.ca/page_accueuil.php>, consulted on 25 September 2015.

co-construct their institutional field (FSR field) such that it would be different from the traditional financial field.

5. Co-construction of the FSR field: the intersection of logics of development and financial democratization

The first sub-section explains how the joint actions of members of the FSRQ Network and the compatibility of their respective logics (financing and support) in the action on the field (local, regional or national)[16] and in the sectors (financial, labor, SSE) gave rise to the first two institutional pillars of their new field (FSR field): that of the cognitive and normative dimensions of their joint action. The second sub-section shows how the implementation of the political pillar of this field, which called for the formalization and institutionalization of the FSRQ Network, induced two processes, or phenomena. One was the distinction between the two logics it had internalized, and the other was the emergence of another logic that, unique to this field, views financing and regional development from a solidary-based and responsible perspective.

5.1. Compatibility of the logics of the members of the FSRQ Network and design of the normative and cognitive dimensions of the FSR field

The content presented in sections 3 and 4 shows that prior to its formalization, the FSRQ Network internalized two logics that were different yet nevertheless compatible (finance and development). In addition to the actors dedicated to financing SSEOs and other businesses focused on job creation and sustainable development, the FSRQ Network integrated a set of support actors (local, regional and sectoral structures) who had been created, either from the initiative of these financial actors or from a public policy, to manage collective and social entrepreneurship projects and to guide enterprises with regard to the financing of these projects. Due to the particularities of these projects, support presents an important factor in ensuring the longevity of the funded enterprises and, as a corollary, the financial efficiency of the financial actors (Bouchard *et al.*, 2017). Thus, although they are different, the financial actors and support actors form the same institutional field, namely that of territorial

16 In Québec, the term "national" refers rather to the provincial level.

and sectoral development dedicated to the deployment of projects having a public interest. By engaging in this field, these actors mutually reinforce each other to promote this development path in Québec. However, the interactions between the actors and the characteristics of their intervention embody a new institutional logic that contributes to qualifying the FSR sector as an institutional field (FSR field). The institutional pillars (normative, cognitive and political) of this new field were designed, as shown in section 4, collectively by the members of the FSRQ Network and evolved at different points in its life cycle.

First, to improve interventions in the field of territorial development, a core of financial actors belonging to the FSRQ Network collaborated informally to develop a common standard, the *Guide d'analyse des entreprises d'économie sociale*. The development of this Guide required the establishment of practices of negotiation, mobilization and activation, and legitimation. The Guide was co-written by the financial actors but was assisted by support actors and other SSE actors. No fewer than 15 organizations were part of the editorial board, including a ministry, a sectoral workforce committee, and academics (Tessier, 2005). The adoption of the Guide by several local development bodies confirms the "organizational proximity" (Colletis *et al.*, 2005) between the actors of the field of territorial development. We point out that with the development of the Guide, the financial actors aimed to create, in a collaborative process, the tools required to advance their practice as well as a new dynamic of cooperation with each other, the support actors and other institutional stakeholders. The Guide, as a common standard, thus represents the first institutional pillar of the new FSR field which the financial actors sought to create.

Secondly, after the publication of the Guide, the partners continued to work together and, in concert with researchers, formed CAP Finance within the ARUC-ÉS partnership research infrastructure of the social economy. Their goal was to together produce studies and analyze all the issues of their sector. Participation in this CAP by new financial actors (CRCD and Fonds de solidarité FTQ) and local and regional development bodies and their Québec associations broadened the FSRQ Network. Working together, these actors with different but compatible logics were able to develop a common discourse and new concepts (e.g. concept of development capital). This dynamic of research and conceptualization allowed for a rapprochement between the logics of the different actors and for the development of the cognitive dimensions that form the second pillar of the institutional FSR field. The institutional practices developed by these actors to develop this pillar are: co-construction of knowledge, development of a common discourse and mediation.

In sum, we see that the initial joint actions of the actors of the FSRQ Network and the compatibility of their respective logics (finance and development) in action on the field (local, regional or national) and in the sectors (financial, labor, SSE) led to the formation of the first two institutional pillars (Scott, 1995) of their new field (FSR field), namely the cognitive and normative dimensions. The *Guide d'analyse des entreprises d'économie sociale*, designed by the financial actors as a common standard, was then adopted by several local development organizations, confirming an organizational proximity between the actors of the field.

5.2. Formalization of the FSRQ Network and construction of the political pillar of the FSR field

The desire among certain financial actors to have an institutional field that would be different from the traditional finance field or from territorial development was fulfilled with the establishment of their formal association. The FSRQ Network thus became institutionalized, and this process resulted in the establishment of its formal governance structures (board of directors, assembly of members and working committee), the development of practices and activities to publicize and raise its profile (website, press releases, information meeting), and the regulation of power between its members. These practices required by the formalization of the FSRQ Network thus engendered the political pillar of the new institutional field (FSR field). We remind that this formal network was founded by certain financial actors considered to be the "founding members." However, other financial actors may obtain the status of "investor members," a membership category reserved for actors involved in funding as their core business activity. The FSRQ Network also sees itself as a network of financial institutions; the development and support actors can join the Network, but only as partner members. We point out that not all financial actors involved in the informal phase belong to the core of the founding members; for example, the CRDC and IQ do not, to this day, belong to the FSRQ Network.

Our analysis shows that the political pillar required by the formalization and institutionalization of the FSRQ Network induces a distinction between the two logics that it previously internalized (finance and development) as well as the emergence of a new logic that is more sectoral than territorial. This is because the Network aims, at the macro level, to build a particular institutional field, that of solidarity-based and responsible financing, which differs from that of territorial development. This new institutional field reconfigures financing and regional development in a solidarity-based and responsible perspective that allows for an improved handling of territorial development and finance issues. The diagram below illustrates how the territorial logic of the FSR actors, which is based on organizational proximity, produces, through the process of the institutionalization of their network, a sectoral logic that is based on greater institutional proximity.

Figure 1: Evolution of institutional logics in the FSRQ Network

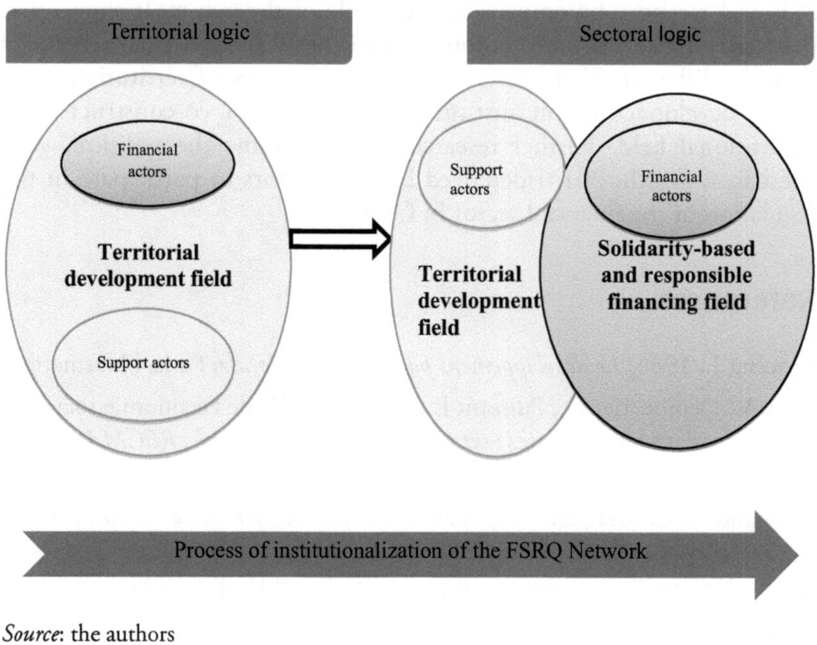

Source: the authors

Conclusion

The analysis presented in this chapter brought forth two main findings: the collective projects that emerged and developed locally with the help of the support actors were at the origin of the emergence of the

FSRQ Network; and the latter, as a reticular space, contributes to shape territories in the context of geographical, organizational and institutional proximities (Richez-Battesti, Gianfaldoni, 2008). The analysis also shows that organizational collaboration based on the compatibility of the logics of the FSR actors (financial logic and development logic) allowed for an institutional collaboration that manifests in the construction of a new institutional field (FSR field). These results demonstrate that the collaboration of financial and support actors in the field of territorial development (mesoscale) generates a new "territory" at the macro level, that of an institutional field. More specialized and sectoral, this territory is the result of institutional practices (normative, cognitive and political) that were collectively developed by these actors. Overall, this article contributes to the body of literature that examines the link between the SSE and territory by emphasizing the role of the actors. It shows that the actors in the SSE have action territories as well as reticular territories that are different. To intervene in these two types of territories, these actors develop common institutional practices to co-construct their institutional field. Further research could examine the political work (Besharov, Smith, 2014) deployed by these actors to participate in the regulation of the financial sector in Québec.

References

Arocena J., 1986, *Le développement par l'initiative locale*, Paris, l'Harmattan.

Artis A., Demoustier D., Puissant E., 2009, "Le rôle de l'économie sociale et solidaire dans les territoires : six études de cas comparées", *RECMA – Revue internationale de l'économie sociale*, 314: 18-31.

Balligand J.-P., Maquart D., 1990, *La fin du territoire jacobin*, Paris, A. Michel.

Battilana J., Dorado S., 2010, "Building Sustainable Hybrid Organizations the Case of Commercial Microfinance Organizations", *Academy of Management Journal*, 53 (6): 1419-40.

Ben Slimane K.B., Leca B., 2010, "Le travail institutionnel : origines théoriques, défis et perspectives", *Management & Avenir*, 7 (37): 53-69.

Bernier L., Bouchard M.J., Lévesque B., 2003, "Attending to the General Interest: New Mechanisms for Mediating Between Individual, Collective and General Interest", *Annals of Public and Cooperative Economics*, 74 (3): 321-47.

Besharov M.L., Smith W. K., 2014, "Multiple Institutional Logics in Organizations: Explaining their Varied Nature and Implications", *Academy of Management Review*, 39 (3): 364-81. <http://dx.doi.org/10.5465/amr.2011.0431>, consulted on 16 August 2015.

Bouchard M.J., Carrière J., Klein J.-L., Marceau S.G., Michaud V., Saucier C., 2005, "Les repères territoriaux de l'économie sociale et solidaire", *Cahier de la Chaire de recherche du Canada en économie sociale*, No. R-2005-05.

Bouchard M.J., Léonard M., Rousselière D., Tello-Rozas S., 2017, "Impacting Social Economy through Solidarity Financing. The Case of a Solidarity Finance Institution", *6th EMES Research Conference on Social Enterprise*, Louvain-la-Neuve, 3-6 July 2017, <https://emes.net/content/uploads/Bouchard-Leonard-Rousseliere-Tello-Rozas-ECSP-6EMES-04.pdf>, consulted on 17 December 2017.

Bourque G.L., Mendell M., Rouzier R., 2009, *La finance responsable au Québec : portrait, enjeux et défis d'une finance au service d'un développement durable et solidaire*, Montréal, Éd. Vie Économique.

Coissard S., Pecqueur B., 2007, "Les dynamiques territoriales : débats et enjeux des différentes approches disciplinaires", *XVIIIth colloquium of ASRDLF*, Grenoble/Chambéry, 11-13 July.

Colletis G., Gianfaldoni P., Richez-Battesti N., 2005, "Économie sociale et solidaire, territoire et proximité", *RECMA – Revue internationale de l'économie sociale*, 296: 8-25.

Demoustier D., Richez-Battesti N., 2010, "Introduction. Les organisations de l'Économie sociale et solidaire : gouvernance, régulation et territoire", *Géographie, économie, société*, 12: 5-14.

Dupuy G., Offner J.M., 2005, "Réseau : bilans et perspectives", *Flux*, 62: 38-46, *in* Monnet J., 2010, "Le territoire réticulaire", *Anthropos, (Nuevos territorios e innovación digital)*, 22.

Enjolras B., 2010, "Gouvernance verticale, gouvernance horizontale et économie sociale et solidaire : le cas des services à la personne", *Géographie, économie, société*, 12: 15-30.

Fontan J.-M., Klein J.-L., Lévesque B. (eds.), 2003, *Reconversion économique et développement territorial*, Québec, Presses de l'Université du Québec.

Friedland R., Alford R., 1991, "Bringing Society Back in: Symbols, Practices and Institutional Contradictions", in W. Powell, P. DiMaggio (eds.), *The New Institutionalism in Organizational Analysis*, University of Chicago Press, p. 232-63.

Itçaina X., Palard J., Segas S., 2007, *Régimes territoriaux et développement économique*, Rennes, PUR.

Itçaina X., 2011, "Les dynamiques territoriales de l'économie sociale et solidaire : pistes de recherche en sociologie politique", *in* A. Ndiaye (dir.), *Économie sociale et solidaire : animation et dynamiques des territoires*, Paris, l'Harmattan, p. 61-81.

Klein J.-L., Carrière J., 1999, "Les réseaux territorialisés d'information face à la communication-monde : une expérimentation québécoise", *Canadian Geographer/Le géographe canadien*, 43 (2): 161-70.

Klein J.-L., Tremblay D.G., Fontan J.-M., 2003, "Systèmes productifs locaux et réseaux productifs dans la reconversion économique : le cas de Montréal", *Géographie, économie, société*, 5 (1): 59-75.

Klein J.-L., Fontan J.-M., 2004, "Innovation sociale et territoire", *Géographie, économie, société*, 6 (2): 113-4.

Langley A., 1999, "Strategies for Theorizing from Process Data", *The Academy of Management Review*, 24 (4): 691-710.

Lawrence T.B., Suddaby R., 2006, "Institutions and Institutional Work", *in* S.R. Clegg, C. Hardy, T.B. Lawrence, W.R. Nord (eds.), *Handbook of Organization Studies*, 2nd ed., London, Sage, p. 215-54.

Lawrence T.B., Suddaby R., Leca B., 2009, "Institutional Work: Actors and Agency in Institutional Studies of Organizations", *Administrative Science Quarterly*, 55 (4): 673-76.

Leca B., 2006, "Pas seulement des 'lemmings'. Les relations entre les organisations et leur environnement dans le néo-institutionnalisme sociologique", R*evue Finance Contrôle Stratégie*, 9 (4): 67-86.

Lévesque B., 2016, "Économie sociale et solidaire et entrepreneuriat social : vers quels nouveaux écosystèmes ?", *Revue Interventions économiques*, 54, <https://interventionseconomiques.revues.org/2802>, consulted on 16 November 2016.

Lévesque B., 2002, "Développement local et économie sociale", *in* D.G. Tremblay *et al.* (dir.), *Développement local, économie sociale et démocratie*, Québec, Presses de l'Université du Québec, p. 41-68.

Lévesque B., Fontan J.-M., Klein J.-L., 2014, *L'innovation sociale : les marches d'une construction théorique et pratique*, Québec, Presses de l'Université du Québec.

Lounsbury M., 2007, "A Tale of Two Cities: Competing Logics and Practice Variation in the Professionalizing of Mutual Funds", *Academy of Management Journal*, 50 (2): 289-307.

Mandell M.P, Keast R., 2007, "Evaluating network arrangements: toward revised performance measures", *Public Performance and Management Review*, 30 (4): 574-97.

Monnet J., 2010, "Le territoire réticulaire", *Anthropos, (Nuevos territorios e innovación digital)*, 22: 91-104.

Musso P., 2003, *Critique des réseaux*, Paris, PUF.

Ndiaye A., 2011, "Économie sociale et solidaire : animation et dynamiques des territoires", *in* A. Ndiaye (dir.), *Économie sociale et solidaire : Animation et dynamiques des territoires*, Paris, l'Harmattan, p. 15-29.

Painter J., 2009, "Territoire et réseau : une fausse dichotomie ?", *in* M. Vannier (dir.), *Territoires, territorialité, territorialisation : controverses et perspectives*, Rennes, PUR, p. 57-66.

Pecqueur B., Itçaina X., 2012, "Économie sociale et solidaire et territoires : un couple allant de soi ?", *RECMA – Revue internationale de l'économie sociale*, 325: 48-64.

Richez-Battesti N., Gianfaldoni P., 2005, "Gouvernance territoriale et réseaux : une illustration par l'accompagnement à la création d'entreprises en France", *Annals of Public and Cooperative Economics*, 76 (4): 621-44.

Richez-Battesti N., Gianfaldoni P., 2008, *La gouvernance partenariale des banques coopératives françaises*, Report to DIIESES, Paris, <http://www.univ-avignon.fr/fileadmin/documents/Users/Fiches_S/Gouvernance-partenariale-des-banques-cooperatives.pdf>, consulted on 18 September 2015.

Scott W.R., 1995, *Institutions and Organizations*, Thousand Oaks Ca, Sage.

Seo M., Creed W.E.D., 2002, "Institutional Contradictions, Praxis, and Institutional Change: A Dialectical Perspective". *Academy of Management Review*, 27 (2): 222-47.

Tessier É., 2005, "Le premier Guide d'analyse des entreprises d'économie sociale", *Revue interventions économiques*, 32, <http://interventionseconomiques.revues.org/898>, consulted on 16 November 2016.

Théret B., 2003, "Institutionnalismes et structuralismes : oppositions, substitutions ou affinités électives ?", *Cahiers d'économie politique*, 44: 51-78, <http://www.cairn.info/zen.php?ID_ARTICLE=CEP_044_0051>, consulted on 15 September 2015.

Thornton P.H., Ocasio W., 2008, "Institutional Logics", in R. Greenwood, C. Oliver, R. Suddaby, K. Sahlin (eds.), *The Sage Handbook of Organizational Institutionalism*, Los Angeles, Sage, p. 1-46.

Trouvé H., Couturier Y., Saint-Jean O., Somme D., 2010, "L'organisation en réseau dans le champ gérontologique : à la recherche d'un nouveau mode de gouvernance ?", *Géographie, économie, société*, 1 (12): 31-52.

Vaillancourt Y., 2013, "The Co-Construction of Public Policy: The Contribution of the Social Economy", *in* Bouchard M.J. (ed.), *Innovation and the Social Economy*, Toronto, University of Toronto Press, p. 127-57.

Vienney C., 1994, *L'économie sociale*, Paris, la Découverte.

Chapter 2

Cooperative Banks and Territories

When Anchorage Improves Performance

Nadine Richez-Battesti & Béatrice Chauvin

University of Aix-Marseille, LEST-CNRS UMR 7317

The increasing financial globalization and the development of the prudential requirements on the European and international scale, the growing banking concentration movement and the evolution of cooperative banks obliged them to find a point of balance between offensive strategic positioning and searching performance and keeping up value and these "added values" or spiritual enrichment and these social values supposed to be only found in cooperative banks. These organizations have specific property rights corresponding to a system of democratic governance. The organization based on members rather than on shareholders and the collective property which is its consequence as well as the attribution processes of the results intentionally limited, thus the use of an economic democracy in the decision-making processes illustrates this system.

If in spite of these rules and under the influence of statutory requirements, some people stress the risks of deterioration of the large cooperative organizations, however original dynamics which tend to reaffirm a strong link of cooperative banks with their territory and with their members can be observed.

The central point of its article is about the links between cooperative banks and territory in France by considering territory a social construction. We have chosen to lay the stress on an experiment: the itinerant banker at the NEF, the most recent banking cooperative in France.

As far as methodology is concerned, this paper comes from a combination of collective studies conducted for about ten years about the network of cooperative banks (Richez-Battesti, Gianfaldoni, 2006; Richez-Battesti, Gianfaldoni, 2008) as well as from the doctoral research about the NEF (Chauvin, 2015), very recently considered as an ethical bank. All our information has been found thanks to interviews conducted in regional or national offices concerning the stakeholders of French cooperative banks wage earners, members, customers and to different documents (papers or the Internet) produced by the banks. In the study of the NEF more precisely, analysis and figures are the result of an intervention study whose purpose was to find an original response to the subject of strategic development of the NEF with restricted financial resources. In this context, the researcher's status is very special, since he/she is involved in the construction of artefacts which are operating for stakeholders having to give strategic responses, a mediating role leading to the mental construction of reality. The experiment of the itinerant banker is its consequence.

The object of this experiment consisted in expanding the NEF in a given territory, without opening any branch, with a twofold mission: maintain the social project and the democratic dynamism of the cooperative while increasing the economic activity.

In the first part, we illustrate the links between cooperative banks and territory, at first by putting in perspective the question of territory, then by characterizing the cooperative banks in France and by showing the double aspect of the links they have with territory in terms of governance and of economic activity. Then we focus our analysis on the NEF, the most recent French banking cooperatives and on the experiment of the itinerant banker conducted since 2009. We describe the construction of this anchoring process to the territory which relies upon an itinerant banker who coordinates the territory and we study its impact. Then, we show how releasing the experiment reduces its impact by changing the itinerant banker into a staff member in charge of decentralized credit.

1. Characterizing cooperative banks in France and their links with territory

It is quite complex to deal with the subject of links between territory and organizations, and especially when you are interested in the social solidarity economy enterprises, a sector in which cooperative banks find their place. These organizations, referring to their values and principles at the roots of their creation, often consider themselves as naturally belonging to territory: the importance of the collective project at the basis of their activity, the running of a democratic governance, the rules which are the framework of their field of intervention, for the cooperative banks and for the agricultural cooperatives as well, or moreover the principle of double quality, clearly mark this link to territory. This link to territory is both a link to the members who are part and parcel of territory and link to territory as such. Does this double aspect of this link contribute to create specific resources and owing to what process, both for territory and the cooperative bank?

1.1. Territory as a social construction

The regional development literature lays the stress upon the difficulty to define and make the notion of territory operational. We come back to the definition of territories by Pecqueur and Itçaina (2012: 48) as a contribution of development actors, in a determined spatial context whose aim is to raise a societal or a shared production problem and then to try and solve it under environmental constraints. This definition insists upon the committed and collective dynamics which spread in a specific context and which tend to transform the existing habits thanks to their action. Territory is implicitly considered as a social construction based on multiple interactions which contribute to the emergence of common representations and conventions. Thus, territory has an impact on the relations between the actors, who through their interactions reciprocally act upon their environment and consequently give territory its structure. So, territory has a geographical and administrative concrete dimension, which can be identified in terms of distance, area or morphological characteristics. However, it is not limited to this. It is also the result of interactions and shared representations which are at the roots of this territory and which can be measured in terms of intensity of common interactions and of common vision. The works about proximity (Pecqueur, Zimmerman, 2004) would make a distinction between geographical proximity, which can be identified in terms of distance and organized proximity focusing on interactions and their effects.

The analysis of links between firms and companies lies on two central points: the resources – which can be specific or generic – and the coordination between the actors (Colletis-Wahl, Perrat, 2004; Colletis-Wahl, 2008; Pecqueur, 2005). The local resources are not static allocations. In the contrary, they can be activated and transformed by collective and individual actors who work on them and rearticulate them in an original way. For instance, the works on local productive systems, the industrial districts, the innovative environments or the territorial system identify three aspects of theses interactions between firms and territories (Torre, Tanguy, 2014): they are based on specific anchorages in the territory and so on the influence of the environments in which activities develop, on solid relations between heterogeneous groups of actors and on the predominant horizontal relations of cooperation more than on vertical relations of subordination (Richez-Battesti, 2008a). So, anchorage to territory finds its expression in the multiplicity of interactions between actors based on commercial and non-commercial links, the territory becomes an asset for the firm whereas the cooperative is here to bring prosperity to the territory. This mutual commitment brings force to the social capital and to the confidence on territory: these ones being at the root of the strengthening cooperations.

This double dimension of interactions and territory anchorage can be found in a part of studies dealing with cooperatives. Draperi and Le Coroller (2016) show how cooperatives strengthen social links in territories. They show the influence of cooperatives regulations on the bonds of citizenship (p. 56) by emphasizing the development of an inter cooperative meso-republic (p. 64). For his part, Filippi (2014) describes the role of territory as an economic and governance tool, in the framework of an analysis of agricultural cooperatives. She shows that French cooperative strategies transform their localization into territorial advantages by enhancing the value of local resources, reinforcing the members' loyalty and interdependence between members and consumers. More widely, Demoustier and Richez-Battesti (2010) jointly analyze the transformations of the productive systems and of the frameworks of public action that the actors of ESS are likely to contribute to produce. They also show how ESS is an actor of territorial regulation "as a mode of interaction and coordination of the activities, jobs, and capital flows which enable to guarantee the regularity of the productive system." They also show how it can act on the territorial governance defined "as framework and institutional modality on the decision-making process, on the territorial development through public debates, public action and more precisely the production of public policies." These socio-economic and socio-political commitments of the ESS actors, and consequently of the cooperative banks, also described by Draperi and Le Coroller (2016) contribute to create a dynamic ecosystem in which public and private actors cooperate in an overall dynamic.

1.2. Cooperative banks in France

Even today, the originality of cooperative banks in France consists in their being composed of several networks in wider cooperative groups, unlike in the other European countries where one network is the leader. Cooperative banks in France, actually combine the Banques Populaires and Caisse d'Épargne grouped in BPCE in 2009, the Crédit Coopératif being a very independent subsidiary of the Banques Populaires, the Crédit Agricole, the Crédit Mutuel, as well as the most recent one the tiny NEF on which we will focus our study. These banking cooperatives which belong to their members (more than 22 million members in France in 2015) offer intermediation services to economic actors and households.

Table 1: Key figures for cooperatives and mutualist banks

LES CHIFFRES-CLÉS DES BANQUES COOPÉRATIVES ET MUTUALISTES

	Crédit Agricole	Crédit Mutuel	BPCE dont :	Crédit Coop.
Caisses régionales	39	18	35	12
Caisses locales	2 477	2 131	-	
Agences	11 300	3 167	8 000	117
Administrateurs	31 150	24 200	255	3 334
Sociétaires	8,2 millions	7,6 millions	8,9 millions	85 924
Salariés	140 000	83 650	108 000	2 021
pnb (groupe) en M€	30 200	15 400	23 300	0,41

Source : Panorama sectoriel des entreprises coopératives, édition 2016, CoopFR.

They represent nearly two thirds of detail banking activity. If cooperative banks have not been spared from the financial crisis (Richez-Battesti, Leseul, 2016), they were not the cause, and have been better able to resist due to the importance of retail banking activity, a diversification into other activities (insurance, electronic surveillance, real estate transactions, etc.) and less of a dependence on networks concerned with financial markets. They have thus maintained a good level of activities, especially in lending, resulting in deposit/lending ratios that are declining and the challenge of winning new deposits, which indicates a "resilience in the cooperative model in a time of crisis." (Birchall, Ketilson, 2009).[1]

In a context of financial globalization on a European and international scale, the transformations which have affected cooperative banks are largely due to evolutions in the national or international environment (Pastré, 2007). The French financial system reform, introduced by the banking law of 1984, supplemented by another law in 1996, was devoted to the de-specialization, de-compartmentalization, and de-intermediation ("the three D's") of banking activities in order to boost competition between financial intermediaries. The introduction of the term "credit institution" in view of European financial integration and harmonization, covers not only the former "registered" banks but also cooperative banks, Caisses d'Épargne (that the lawmaker legally transformed into cooperatives in June 1999 through an operation of "mutualization" designed to bestow an "owner" on all Caisses d'Épargne), financial companies and specialized financial institutions. The specialization of cooperative banks is being challenged as well as most of the advantages that they enjoy. Thus, these institutions have sought to form large competitive entities, not just in terms of the number of customers but also of the size of their workforce, resources or equity.

The maturity of the banking system and the growing competition leads to growth strategies used differently by banking organizations for enhanced competitive results. Some organizations choose the option of scaling up by merging regional authorities widening what made their original territory. Others re-buy in priority competing banks in the framework of strategic alliance bringing hybridization. As a result, these last years, the decentralized characteristic of the regional banking networks has reduced because of a regional merging movement. Let us take the example of the group BPCE, the regional banks tend to merge faster and faster. In 2011 we witnessed the merging of Banques Populaires du Sud-Ouest with the Centre Atlantique one, in 2014 les Banques Populaires d'Alsace with the Lorraine-Champagne one, whereas the Caisses d'Épargne from North-pas-de-Calais and Picardy announce their fusion in 2016, and the Banque Populaire des Alpes, de Loire and Lyonnais and du massif Central decide to merge. The aim is to

1 For more details on cooperative banks in France, see Richez-Battesti and Leseul (2016).

increase the size of regional banks so as to reach a critical size, achieve economies of scale and accelerate the transition to the digital economy. A hybridization of cooperative banks also developed under the control of Banque Indosuez, Sofinco and Crédit Lyonnais by Crédit Agricole, or CIC and Cofidis by Crédit Mutuel, etc.

In this context how are the links of banking cooperatives with territories reconstructed?

1.3. The double dimension of links with territories

Whatever strategy is chosen, the subject of links to the members of the territory they belong to stays essential; it conditions the efficiency of the governance and thanks to it the effective strategic choices, and in the same time takes part in a differentiation strategy of the products or in the improvement of their quality.

Historically, cooperative banks develop on a specific territory in the march to independence like regional branches as soon as the running of business, generates sufficient net banking products. A large part of the deposits received is re-invested locally and the predominance of retail activities leads to financing the activities of craftsmen, of small and medium sized companies and households. As essential actors of the financial running in a given territory, they adapt their offers to the needs of territory. So, in an area with a high rate of Portuguese immigrants, the Crédit Mutuel Méditerranéen chose to devote a branch to this specific clientele, or near a training institute for teaching students, a branch is reserved for teachers and teaching students. They also decide to develop local branches for young people and with young people: As a result, in the end of 2015 the Crédit Agricole Toulouse opened a local office for the 18/35 year-old and citizen "coffees" for members.

Since the early 1990s, the managers have reaffirmed the anchorage in the territory by re mobilizing their members to societies, then by using their foundations when they exist to select and back projects linked to local development. Banking cooperative networks can at last choose to support actors and projects specific to territory. As an example, the Crédit Mutuel de Bretagne organizes "initiatives for territory challenge" to support 32 enterprises which propose innovative actions in the employment and sustainable development sector. With the introduction of the banking card *member* the Crédit Agricole Rhône Alpes has proposed special funds to finance solidarity initiatives in the region. Today digital development has not only become the stake of their changing structures, but also a tool to establish links between actors of territory and members and of supported local projects.

At last a part of the link to territory goes directly *via* the members banking cooperatives, those who are shareholders and more precisely administrators (Richez-Battesti, 2008b). They bring business to their branches. The deep knowledge they have of a territory on which they live gives them the capacity to evaluate risks and to find pertinent opportunities. At last the networking they contribute to establish between their banks and the actors of territory consolidates the bank's presence on territory and creates proximity between members and the people who are granted loans.

It is unclear whether these actions can radically influence the cooperative banks' strategies. However, they express a will to support territory which is, after all, their core business. But when the geographical territory gets larger, the expression of proximity is more and more complex, and it is more often a tool of communication rather than the object of renewed practices. Beyond that point, regulations through the recommendations of the European banking authorities risk to make this construction more fragile if they wish to reinforce the evaluation of the directors' and managers' competences to perform their duties and by making sure that the independent director, has no business or personal relation with the bank so as to avoid any risk of conflict of interest. Yet, as the administrator is not independent in the framework of the double quality principle, i.e. both a capital owner and a customer of the bank, he is capable of taking part in the integration process of his banking cooperative to territory.

2. The NEF itinerant banker: between territorial innovation and isomorphism

We present now the itinerant banker's experiment at the NEF. This experiment, illustrates in an original way links to territory, but also shows its limitations when you try to get this model widely adopted.

2.1. A small cooperative bank

The NEF, recently set up, is the very last French banking cooperatives. First it is created as an association, the new fraternal economy in 1978 and is given a cooperative status which enables it to become a financial company in 1988, the financial association of the NEF, with a commercial partnership with the Crédit Coopératif. Its aim is to give innovative projects the opportunity to develop. As such, it grants credits and term accounts for professionals, but it cannot manage current accounts directly. From a banking point of view, it relies on the Crédit Coopératif *via* the BPCE group. It has been a fully-fledged bank since April 2016, i.e. it is entitled to open accounts for professionals with the services included in the package, and for individuals in the middle'17. Since 2015, it has also developed a participatory financial body with a platform for donations and a platform for collecting savings devoted to specific projects. These products should be completed by an investment platform in 2017.

The NEF, as a solidarity and ethical bank, have two main characteristics. Firstly, the objective of achieving a positive impact on the collection and use of money. The NEF give the opportunity for savers to exercise their responsibility on their money by orienting them towards financing solutions for general interest projects characterized by a social, ecological or cultural utility. Indeed, for 25 years, the NEF has developed a real expertise in financing organic farming, biodiversity, fair trade, renewable energies or work integration. Particularly oriented towards social and environmental innovation, it strongly supports the creation of activities and new forms of entrepreneurship based on short circuits and citizen participation. In this sense, the NEF is *deeply rooted in the territory* in which it operates, and in its socio-economic networks. Secondly, beyond the value of participation, transparency is a fundamental value for the NEF: transparency in the origin and in the use of money, in credit and business management especially towards customers.

In 2016, the NEF is a banking cooperative with almost 38,000 members with a capital in a dramatic increase – about 38 million €. It grants nearly 40 million credits on a basis of collection on savings accounts directly, on term accounts, and since 2016 on saving books. The loans are granted for special projects: more than 28% for social matters with a financial support for work integration projects, 60% for agriculture and energy and between 2 and 4% for cultural projects. Among these 38,000 members, 248 active shareholders distributed in 28 appointed groups take part in animations, fairs, and organize events in order to promote the "NEF" among the territory they live in. These events can have different forms: visiting projects, discussions, information meetings, pre-annual meeting brainstorming, etc. Too few referring members, badly distributed in territories were the basis of the essential representation of the NEF so far in territories.

The 84 wage earners are distributed in operational headquarters at Vaulx-en-Velin and 5 commercial delegations in Lyon, Paris, Toulouse and Nantes. One of the delegations runs the individual customers and their savings and their savings and terms accounts proposed by distance sale, whereas the 4 other delegations deal with professionals' activities (loans and opening accounts). The member of staff in charge of credit receives the project initiator' application in his delegation by post, phone or *via* internal forms. He studies the project and determines if it is, eligible in terms of field of intervention (ecology, social aspect, insertion, culture) and if it is economically feasible.

The NEF's main characteristics consists in a rather centralized organization with a reduced commercial network since there is no local office, and it has to develop innovative strategies to make sure the client base will extend. Then how is it possible to reinforce its presence in territories without local branch, without large financial resources? How to gain market shares on project financing?

2.2. The itinerant banker's experimentation

So, in 2009 the idea of the itinerant banker was born and experimented in the south of France in a first phase. Then in 2012 it began to extend progressively on a part of the French territory with the recruitment of 3 wage earners in 2013/2014 and two more in 2015.

How to characterize this itinerant banker? At root he is a banker without office, not considered in his only commercial mission, but more widely as a territory animator. He represents the NEF on a territory he tries to "canvass": make people familiar with the NEF, identify the projects and the savers, meet actors of ESS and public actors who could conclude a partnership with the NEF. This itinerant banker, who has to know perfectly the territory where he intervenes, bases his action at first on the network of shareholders that he contributes to mobilize and widen. These shareholders, often committed, were little mobilized so far.

The itinerant banker makes allies of them, prescribers, who sustain the development of the network, favorable to gaining of new market shares.

Consequently, the shareholders take an active part in the life of the cooperative which formalizes the framework of a professional agreement. This agreement is a combination of a financial help from the cooperative to repay the shareholders' expenses and also all the running and intervention rules. He especially includes a confidentiality clause: the shareholders can actually have access to sensitive data. He manages to organize training sessions "How to speak about the NEF" whose aim is to construct a common language more than to get them to learn technical data. Then the members receive training and information. Occasionally they have exchanges about the learning methods and with the NEF increase their knowledge of the strategic stakes for cooperative and territory.

By motivating and training his members, the itinerant banker builds his territorial anchorage and contributes to boost initiatives on territory thanks to all the interactions he contributes to create. So, the commercial development is consequently regarded as the result of a mobilization of the territory whose main actors are the members. The itinerant banker is supported in his action by a relaying person in the delegation who organizes the administrative part of the financing files and the essential part of his activity consists in creating, spreading and reinforcing the local network. This is what his commitment means.

2.3. The results of the experiment

These effects are analyzed in terms of view point and of members' involvement and of its effects on governance (better understanding of the stakes and constraints of the cooperative; larger involvement in the activity), on the better understanding of the environment and the safety brought to the financed projects, and on the number of activities carried out. The double dimension of anchorage to territory is clear once again in terms of governance and of economic activity.

The results of the interactions – itinerant banker- active members – have been measured essentially in the 2 alpine departments (Alpes de Haute–Provence 04 and Hautes-Alpes 05) and also partially in the Var department (83). Among the 28 active local groups referenced in France, 3 are referenced in the itinerant banker's territory. They emerged thanks to the animation of territory, and they organize about 15 event every year (so a little less than 10% of the total number of animations in France).

The organization and the animation by active members and the itinerant banker of the 2016 preparation meeting of the annual meeting express the members' will to reach a better knowledge of financial techniques by devoting the necessary time to organize thorough exchanges on the economic model of the cooperative, read and analyze counts and stakes linked to the resolutions which have to be approved at the general annual meeting (statutory meeting). Meeting regularly and constructing confidence in the case of such a regular collaboration also foster exchanges and mutual understanding.

This process of members' involvement has also a deep impact on the economic development of the cooperative as shown on table 1. Before 2014, this territory was characterized by non-active members, without local group, no correspondent for more than 5 years, average saving deposit but a credit volume not far from "0". But for the NEF the main stake consists in changing of the savings collected by certain people into loans for the others. If loans are not increased, the economic model of the banking cooperative will be fragile. After 3 years of members' mobilization thanks to the itinerant banker, the number of loans has dramatically increase, even if it is still limited, the volume of loans equals now the volume of the Isère department (38) with a population 4 times as large as this territory. The number of members on this territory is also very high compared to the departments considered. Their saving efforts in the 2 departments are very large since they are 80% to those of Var (83), a border department having however a larger number of members. So, keeping in mind that the territories in which the itinerant banker's experiment was conducted are rural, rather poor territories and whose levers for economic growth are agriculture and tourism it is obvious that departments 04 & 05 have both very positive dynamics for the NEF.

Table 2: Economic activity of the NEF in 5 territories, Year 2015

Departments	04-05	13	38	84	43
Population at 31-12-2014	301,195	1,993,177	1,235,387	549,949	226,203
Number of members	593	1,294	1,613	645	181
Number of loans	44	63	49	32	6
Term accounts	80	58	243	39	22
Saving counts	96	162	236	49	55

Source: B. Chauvin on the basis of internal statistics of the NEF

Another way of analyzing the size and the impact of members' mobilization consists in observing it through the projects.

Among 17 projects financed these last months (2016) in the 2 departments chosen for the experiment, only 2 were made on line. The others were sent directly from the territory, brought by the members themselves either by prescription or *via* the network itself. As a rule, a vast majority of the projects are received by the delegation, except the new loans applied by former project leaders.

The role of members as business providers is part and parcel of the help brought in setting up and following up the projects. 1/3 of these 17 projects were visited by local members or were given an evaluation. In a rural and mountain territory this support of members enables to feel nearer each other and to have easier access to the information about the environment of the loan for the itinerant banker, even if the member has no real role in the economic analysis (balance, previsions, etc.). The members' support may be technical. The itinerant banker may request their help according to their personal skills which can help him have a clear appreciation of the projects, above all, when the project concerns territories seldom explored and for which risk analysis is complex. Anticipating the difficulties of the company can also be made easier and the firm will be in a better position to meet the needs. Last but not least, members take part in the follow up of the projects leaders by visiting the companies which receive financial help, with or without the itinerant banker. These visits of companies can be the opportunity to take part in long range "NEF walks…" which gather members around a luncheon on the day of the visit. This sort of approach makes the links between savers and borrowers still closer and helps have a clear answer to the question "How do they use my money?" and also have a concrete vision of the real mission of the cooperative. At last, movements in support of these activities appear thanks to "useful addresses" whose aim is to help these new activities, and which are widely spread in the territory. Active members actually use the whole network of members to highlight projects and even mobilize funds on the donation platform.

Consequently, in rural areas, the itinerant banker, expands the credit volume in the medium term by putting the emphasis on the creation of groups of active members.

2.4. The misuse of the experimentation: the weight of isomorphism

However, keeping banking intermediation at the current level is difficult in a context in which interest rates stay at a low level for a long time and brings along a fast increase of loans. This strategy is difficult to combine with the time needed to canvass a territory, establish links and help skills match with projects. Making this experimentation known means its founding principles should be carefully adapted. The role of itinerant banker is actually affected. He becomes a member of staff in charge of decentralized credit. The suitable profile of applicants will show they have a good knowledge of the territory they expect to enter, but commercial skills prevail over animation skills. The essential objective becomes the fast increase of the credit files, building files, release of funds, and so increasing the net banking product of the NEF and supporting its economic model. Mobilizing members is no longer the keystone on which the link to territory is built in the long run.

The articulation of the itinerant employee banker's commitment with the members is reduced. The member's low level of commitment leads him to become a member of another organization's member, so reducing the resources available to the NEF. The degree of mutual enrichment and learning opportunities is reduced.

Coming back to the priority given to commercial job undoubtedly shows that the aspect of territorial animation has not been really recognized as legitimate; this would have made this position more common in the company. This reminds us of the choice cooperative banks had made in the late 1980s and during the 1990s in response to the 1984 banking law which had caused their versatility and made necessary the increase of their market share. This tendency also led them to their uniformity. From this viewpoint, it seems difficult to avoid a form of normative isomorphism when you try to develop in a highly competitive market.

Conclusion

What are the essential points of this analysis? The links between cooperatives banks and territory find their expression thanks to their members in priority. Embedded in their territories they are also the actors of an informed governance, adapted to the local issues. But they also ensure that the service offers meet exactly the local needs. Thanks to their members, cooperatives transform the territories they belong to, but the territory becomes both a competitive advantage and a differentiation tool (Filippi, 2014). These territorial mobilizations led to confidence and loyalty on a territory in which organizations deeply depend on each other. They are also provided joint-learning and versatility. The resources generated thanks to this process are often intangible and are given little value by the actors of territory themselves. Then, once the cooperation decisions are made concretely, they are considered as an ordinary process rather than the result of a collective commitment. The stress is laid more often on their time-consuming aspect, than on their results, sometimes slow to come and on the fact they are not directly quantifiable; that tends to weaken the recent embedding attempts as shown by the itinerant banker's experiment. In this sense and in the current context of merging processes in the regional branches of cooperative banks, the link to territory is clearly seen as an *issue* but not a *priority* whereas it is, as we have stressed it, at the heart of the identity and of the cooperative performance.

References

Birchall J., Ketilson L.H., 2009, *Resilience of the Cooperative Business Model in Times of Crisis*, Genève, BIT.

Chauvin B., 2015, "L'émergence du banquier itinérant : influence d'une réorganisation territoriale au sein d'une coopérative financière en termes d'isomorphisme et disopraxisme. L'expérience de la NEF", Thèse de doctorat, LEST, Aix-Marseille Université.

Colletis-Wahl K., 2008, "Micro-institutions et proximités : quelles lectures des dynamiques territoriales ?", *Revue d'économie régionale et urbaine*: 251-64.

Colletis-Wahl K., Perrat J., 2004, "Proximités et dynamiques spatiales", *in* B. Pecqueur, J.-B. Zimmermann (dir.), *Économie de proximités*, Paris, Hermès-Lavoisier.

Demoustier D., Richez-Battesti N., 2010, "Les OESS : gouvernance, régulation et territoire", *Géographie, économie, société*, 12°(1): 5-14.

Draperi J.-F., Le Coroller C., 2016, *S'inspirer du succès des coopératives*, Paris, Dunod.

Filippi M., 2014, "Using the Regional Advantage: French agricultural cooperatives' economic and governance tool", *Annals of Public and Cooperative Economics*, 85 (4-Agricultural Cooperatives in Europe).

Pastré O., 2007, *La guerre mondiale des banques*, Paris, PUF.

Pecqueur B., 2005, "Les territoires créateurs de nouvelles ressources productives", *Géographie, économie, société*, 3 (7): 255-68.

Pecqueur B., Itçaina X., 2012, "Économie sociale et solidaire et territoire : un couple allant de soi ?", *RECMA – Revue internationale de l'économie sociale*, 325: 48-64.

Pecqueur B., Zimmermman J.-B., 2004, *Économie de proximités*, Paris, Hermes/Lavoisier.

Richez-Battesti N., 2008a, "Innovations sociales et territoires : une analyse en termes de proximité ; une illustration par les banques coopératives", *Marché et organisation*, 7 (Le développement durable des territoires : Économie sociale, innovation et territoire): 36-50.

Richez-Battesti N., 2008b, "Gouvernance coopérative et sociétariat : une reconquête inachevée ?, Une illustration par les banques coopératives en France", J.-F. Draperi (coord.), *Défis coopératifs : alimentation, crédit, démocratie, développement, Les Cahiers de l'Économie sociale*, No. 6, Paris, l'Harmattan, p. 199-220.

Richez-Battesti N. Gianfaldoni P. (dir.), 2008, *La gouvernance partenariale des banques coopératives en France*, Recherche financée par la DIIESES.

Richez-Battesti N., Gianfaldoni P. (dir.), 2006, *Les banques coopératives en France : le défi de la performance et de la solidarité*, Paris, l'Harmattan.

Richez-Battesti N., Leseul G., 2016, "Cooperative credit banks in France: Emergence, change, and challenges", *in* S. Karafolas (ed.) *Credit Cooperative Institutions in European countries*, Springer, p. 55-82.

Torre A., Tanguy C., 2014, "Les systèmes territoriaux d'innovation : fondements et prolongements actuels", *in* Boutillier S., Forest J., Gallaud D., Laperche B., Tanguy C., Temri L. (dir.), *Principes d'économie de l'innovation*, Bruxelles, Peter Lang.

Chapter 3

The Social Economy in Borderscapes

The Changing Cross-Border Dynamics of the Social Economy in the Basque Country

Xabier Itçaina
Centre Émile Durkheim, CNRS, Sciences Po Bordeaux, University of Bordeaux

Marc Errotabehere
CREG-Université de Pau et des Pays de l'Adour

Introduction

The use of sub-national regions and smaller areas is a useful starting point, and a variation to the customary methodology, for improving our understanding of the dynamics of Europeanization: how territories adapt to the new regulations, trends in public policy, beliefs and norms that are initially determined at the European level (Radaelli, 2003: 30). This sub-state perspective is indispensable to an analysis of the dynamics of cross-border and transnational cooperation, which is one of the most tangible effects of European integration. Although a large number of studies have addressed these relationships from the perspective of inter-institutional relations, only a few (Sanchez-Salgado, 2007) have focused on the role of civil society and the social and solidarity economy (SSE) in configuring and operating these schemes.[1] This viewpoint is even more indispensable in cross-border regions that are characterized by a cultural identity that transcends state frontiers. This cultural variable

[1] The terms *third sector* and *social economy* refer here to "organizations producing goods and services that are not founded on the principle of maximizing profits" (Laville, 2000: 8).

complicates the nature of cross-border relations and the uses made of EU policy instruments, which consequently cannot be restricted to technical and depoliticized procedures (Malloy, 2010; O'Dowd, McCall, 2008). In this regard the Basque border region, located in both France and Spain, can be considered a "borderscape", in the sense meant by McCall:

> Borderscapes are border landscapes displaying cultural and political complexity, contested discourses and meanings, struggles over inclusion and exclusion, and involve multiple actors (Rajaram, Grundy-Warr, 2008: IX–XL). However, borderscapes are also important landscapes for inter-cultural dialogue that advances conflict amelioration. Borderscapes signify the fact that these multifarious dynamics stray well beyond the borderline. (McCall, 2013: 199).

This complexity comes into full play in the Basque border region. The task here is thus to assess the involvement of the social economy in the emergence of a cross-border "governance network", a term which refers to "public policy making and implementation through a Web of relationships between government, business and civil society actors" (Klijn, Skelcher, 2007: 587). Such governance networks are intended to go beyond formal state-led models of negotiation, allowing for more flexible and more transparent processes of agenda-setting and of devising and implementing public policies. With this in mind, this chapter addresses three sets of questions. First, how does the participation of SSE actors contribute to the truly cross-border nature of a cooperative endeavor that goes further than direct "one-to-one" and functional forms of cooperation? Does this form of cooperation strengthen national borders or transcend them (O'Dowd, McCall, 2008)? Second, what is the role played by territorial identities, sometimes in mutual conflict, in fostering or impeding the engagement of the SSE in cross-border cooperation (CBC)? Third, what is the role of market constraints in this cross-border activism: are the internal tensions specific to SSEs also visible here?[2] Did the 2008 economic crisis, which was particularly pronounced in Spain, present an opportunity or a constraint for alternative economic spaces such as those promoted by SSE organizations in their cross-border activities?

---

2 For Defourny and Nyssens (2006) there is an initial tension between those SSE companies that put all their production onto the market and organizations whose activities have only a limited economic dimension and which are based on non-market resources. A further tension may emerge between organizations that are intended to satisfy the mutual interests of their members and organizations whose aims address the wider public interest.

In order to address these questions, we draw on evidence from 32 interviews conducted in 2013 within 24 third sector projects involved in CBC in the Basque border region.[3] The projects identified were partly or totally funded by cross-border interregional and EU funds: 17 were funded between 2006 and 2012 by bilateral agreements between Aquitaine and Euskadi, 7 between 2007 and 2012 by the Aquitaine-Navarre fund. 6 of the projects were eligible for POCTEFA funding.[4] All of them involved at least one partner from the third sector and social economy. Interviews were conducted on both sides of the border, but there was a particular focus on French Basque actors in view of the fact that this territory has to date been neglected by the literature on Basque mobilization, albeit with some exceptions (Jacob, 1994; Ahedo, 2008; Bray, 2006; Itçaina, 2017). The cases selected covered diverse sectors: language and culture, minority media, agriculture, health and social issues, job creation, the environment and sustainable development, women's rights, small-scale industry and specialist businesses, and sustainable tourism. Interviews were also conducted with representatives of public institutions involved in CBC: the regional council of Aquitaine, the government of the Basque Autonomous Community or Euskadi (Spain), the government of the Chartered Community of Navarre (Spain), the Aquitaine-Euskadi Euro-region, the inter-municipal federation of Garazi-Baigorri (France), and the municipality of Banca (France).

It is evident that there is no discernible clear and consistent set of principles; the multiform nature of the SSE is apparent, here as elsewhere. It is analyzed here from two perspectives. In the section that follows, we examine the relatively recent formation of these cross-border relations: having developed at the edges of dynamic civil societies which broke new ground in this area, they then became linked to a new public policy framework which eventually became favorable to CBC. Subsequently, we examine the current involvement of SSE organizations in cross-border relations under this legacy, with their contrasting forms of operation. In particular, SSE actors involved in CBC need to address four asymmetries in order to establish effective cross-border governance networks: *institutional* asymmetries between contrasting levels of decentralization;

---

3 The interviews were conducted as part of the research programme *Vers une gouvernance transfrontalière en réseau ? Expériences transfrontalières du tiers secteur en France et au Royaume-Uni*, Sciences Po Bordeaux-Région Aquitaine, 2010-2014.

4 "POCTEFA" refers to the EU programme for cross-border cooperation involving Spain, France and Andorra, financed by the European Regional Development Fund.

political asymmetries between functional and politicized conceptions of cooperation; *organizational* asymmetries between different SSEs; and finally, *market* asymmetries. An added complication was the risk, increased by the 2008 crisis, that funding bodies would perceive proposed ventures as opportunistic cooperation that was not genuinely integrated.

1. A proactive role for the SSE in cross-border relations

1.1. The SSE and cross-border relations: a role as initiator

SSE organizations were largely ahead of policy-makers in matters of CBC. This was above all due to their social embeddedness within their respective territories. The importance of the social economy in the Basque Autonomous Community is well known. The Observatorio vasco de economía social (Basque observatory of the social economy) distinguishes between the traditional social economy, consisting of cooperatives (56,231 employees in 2010) and *sociedades laborales* (workforce-owned companies, 9,177 employees), and more recent forms (OVES, 2011: 19-20). The social economy is marked by a strong presence in the industrial sector, although it is increasingly undergoing a process of tertiarization. Much, but not all, of this dominance by industry is due to the Mondragón group of cooperatives (83,859 employees – both within and outside Spain – in 2010, 81,320 in 2014). The Spanish Basque social economy also includes new types of multi-member cooperatives which bring together public, private for-profit and private non-profit partners within the social sector (Enciso Santocildes, 2001).

A comparison is yet to be made between the French Basque Country and Spanish Basque territories, partly because of differences in demography and national history.[5] However, two dynamic forces, one associative and the other cooperative, have also been characteristic of the French Basque Country at the regional level since the 1970s, and have contributed towards the establishment of a specific "territorial regime" for the SSE in this particular area (Itçaina, 2010). The components of this environment include producer cooperatives, micro-finance, fair

[5] The population of the French Basque Country is 300,323 (in 2014), as against 2,175,819 (in 2017) in Spain's Basque Autonomous Community and 642,797 (in 2017) in Navarre, and the processes of state-building and nation-building in France and Spain have been very different.

trade, peasant agriculture, and, since 2013, a local social currency (*euskal moneta*). In 2011 the Basque Country was the leading French area for the presence of *Club locaux d'épargne pour les femmes qui entreprennent* (CLEFE –local savings clubs for women entrepreneurs), and the Soule district, specifically, led France in *Comités locaux d'épargne pour les jeunes* (CLEJ –local savings committees for young people) (Brana, Jégourel, 2011). All these ventures were promoted by a local social movement in favor of local economic development, with the significant, but not exclusive, involvement of *abertzale* (Basque nationalist) activists.

However, not all sectors within the SSE are based on this particular territorial regime with its highly politicized features. Initiatives that can be described as "social integration through economic activity", in particular, are based on distinct developmental practices and governance models. In his comparative study of this sector in the Basque Autonomous Community and French Basque Country, Manterola (2013) has identified two distinct regional models. In the former area, where small social integration enterprises have often come together in larger business units and regulation by the Autonomous Community's government has been streamlined, the sector is based on competition and exposed to market fluctuations. In the French Basque Country, by contrast, there is decentralization but more regulation by the public authorities, which have higher expectations about engagement with competitive markets. The impact of the market, whether chosen or imposed, threatens the economic viability and social aims of these enterprises.

In the 1970s various SSE actors in the Basque Country began to initiate contacts between operators on both sides of the border. At this point the intention was to avoid depending on public policy, which during this period was ambivalent towards this type of venture, and to transcend the border by constructing a cross-border territory in bottom-up fashion. A shared cultural identity was the essential basis for cross-border initiatives. These dynamics were particularly visible in two sectors: Basque language and culture, and producer cooperatives.

In regard to language and culture, the end of the Franco dictatorship allowed bodies within the Basque movement to take various forms: some were associations, some cooperatives, and some governmental, located within the regional and provincial institutions of the Autonomous Community. On the French side of the border the first *ikastola* (Basque language schools) emerged in 1969, as non-profit organizations. With the Spanish transition to democracy, a large number of joint initiatives were organized on a cross-border basis. However, these ventures very quickly came up against an institutional asymmetry between the two sides of the border, especially following the establishment in 1980 of Autonomous Communities in Spain, where the Basque language was granted official status both in the Basque autonomous community and in Navarre; by contrast, it still has no official status on the French side. Most importantly, the forms of organization that the cross-border cultural movement adopted during this period were based on values very close to those of the SSE: most *ikastolas* south of the border were set up as cooperatives, and cultural and linguistic associations proliferated.

The cross-border dimension of the SSE has been just as strong in the producer cooperatives sector. The worker cooperative movement that emerged after 1975 in France's Basque Country was directly inspired by the Spanish Basque Mondragón experience. This was more than just a theoretical reference point: several future founders of French worker cooperatives were trained at Mondragón, and with the training came financial and logistical support. For many Spanish Basque nationalists, supporting the French Basque cooperative movement was a way of providing assistance to what they perceived as a politically and economically neglected territory. In 1982 the French Basque movement set up the *Lana* (work) association with the objective of involving cooperatives, on the Mondragón model, in order to industrialize the interior of the region as had been done in the valleys of Gipuzkoa. This cross-border influence was an intrinsic part of this first and predominantly activist-led phase of the cooperative movement in the French Basque Country (Itçaina, 2007).

1.2. The changing political opportunity structure: a favorable new environment for CBC

In the 1970s initiatives by civil society had been ahead of government-sponsored CBC, which was then in its faltering initial stages. The stabilization of Spain's new democratic regime and its accession to the European Community in 1986 slowly altered this state of affairs. European integration was a factor favoring CBC, which took two contrasting forms in Basque areas during this period (Letamendia, 1997). Firstly, inter-state cooperation over border controls was strengthened by European anti-terrorist and immigration policy. Secondly, European integration helped to establish a framework that encouraged the involvement of regional and local authorities in cooperation, whereas previously this had been the exclusive preserve of states (Harguindéguy, Hayward, 2014).

In 1983 the French Aquitaine region and Spain's Basque Autonomous Community were among the nine border regions that founded the *Communauté de Travail des Pyrénées* or *Comunidad de Trabajo de los Pirineos* (Working Community of the Pyrenees). Spain's entry into the Common Market saw a proliferation of cooperation schemes supported at the different levels of government. Cooperation between the Basque Autonomous Community and Aquitaine developed in the period after 1989, encouraged by the reform of the European Structural Funds and the impetus given to regional policy by the Single European Act. The identity-based cooperation of social networks was now supplemented by formal governmental cooperation, stimulated in particular by funding from the European Territorial Cooperation (INTERREG) programs from 1990 onwards. In the Basque Country, INTERREG funding took over from the existing collaboration between local authorities. The Basque Autonomous Community and Aquitaine added to the numerous bodies already in existence by setting up a joint body to fund research, development and training initiatives; Navarre joined this in 1992 but withdrew in 2000 because of political tensions with the Basque Autonomous Community government. As a result, Aquitaine maintained separate agreements with Euskadi, Navarre and Aragon until 2015.

Among other developments, creation of the "Basque Eurocity" established cooperation in planning matters between the urban areas of Bayonne and San Sebastián.[6] The Bidasoa-Txingudi "Eurodistrict", established in 1992, brought together the Spanish towns of Fuenterrabia and Irun with the French Hendaye in one organizational structure, and this was taken a step further with the creation in 1998 of the Bidasoa-Txingudi *consorcio transfronterizo* (cross-border consortium), which became an exemplary success story of Pyrenean cooperation (Harguindéguy, 2007). The Treaty of Bayonne, signed by France and Spain in 1995, strengthened the legal framework for cooperation by giving a freer hand to local authorities. Small-scale experiments in local cooperation between the border municipalities and valleys of Navarre and the French Basque

6 An initial agreement between the *Diputación Foral* of Gipuzkoa and the Bayonne-Anglet-Biarritz conurbation was signed on 18 January 1993. A permanent agency for cross-border cooperation was set up in 1997 as a European Economic Interest Group.

Country flourished (Conseil de développement du Pays Basque, 2003). The Aquitaine-Euskadi Euroregion, a European Grouping of Territorial Cooperation formally initiated on 12 December 2011 by the regional presidents Alain Rousset and Patxi Lopez (both members of their respective Socialist Parties), represented a new stage in the establishment of a framework for CBC, this time at inter-regional level. Finally, the General Council of the Pyrénées-Atlantiques department and the Regional Government of Navarre renewed their cooperation agreement in April 2012.

It can thus be seen that the establishment of CBC as a policy issue currently has three distinguishing features. First, far from being the preserve of *abertzale* (Basque nationalist) parties, cross-border policies are promoted by heterogeneous coalitions of actors who may have perceptions of the border that are pragmatic, or identity-related, or both. Second, the formal establishment of the French Basque Country as a "*pays*" (see below) after 1997 has helped to strengthen CBC. Third, the partial Europeanization of public policy (in the sense that the French national and local authorities have made use of European schemes for cooperation) has not necessarily entailed a Europeanization of norms and values, even within the border territory as formally defined (Bray, 2004). The new public policy framework, which encourages cross-border collaboration, has provided the context for the more recent initiatives by SSE actors.

1.3. A potential relationship between CBC and conflict amelioration

The pragmatic approach that government bodies developed towards CBC needed to address the issue of identity in the Basque border region. With the reduction in political violence after ETA's definitive ceasefire in 2010, some actors in the political conflict – for the most part from the *abertzale* side – saw cross-border relationships as having the potential to contribute to conflict transformation. The promotion by *abertzale* activists, from both sides of the border, of new peace forums on the French side such as Bake bidean (On the road to peace) illustrates this wish. From the *abertzale* perspective, the involvement of socio-economic actors in CBC was seen as a contribution to conflict amelioration by engaging grass-roots civil organizations, rather than political parties and movements, in peace-building.[7]

Outside the peace movements themselves, Northern (French) and Southern (Spanish) Basque third sector actors were clearly constantly engaged in CBC in their respective sectors without aiming to contribute directly to the peace process. Some pursued functional outcomes of economic cooperation, while action by others had a more political orientation. For *abertzale* activists, however, strengthening cross-border relationships represented a further step towards the unity of the Basque people. Small projects, even if their applications to the various official cross-border funding schemes were depoliticized, were seen as contributions to *eraikuntza nazionala* (the nation-building process). Irrespective of these contrasting interpretations, the increase in CBC from the 1990s onwards, in particular through the processes and mechanisms of knowledge diffusion and shared learning (Radaelli, 1999), assisted the normalization of cross-border relations: institutional asymmetries were by-passed, and a positive contribution was thus made to conflict amelioration. In this respect, we would agree with Bray and Keating's cautious conclusion on the potential for interactions between the peace process and cross-border relations: "As the peace process evolves, the projection of the Basque community across the border could be one element that will reconcile the conflicting French/Spanish and Basque nationalist conceptions of political community. The Basque community, however, will remain a work in progress, interpreted differently by various actors on either side of the border" (Bray, Keating, 2013: 151).

We need to view the potential relationship between bilateral or EU-sponsored CBC and conflict amelioration with this degree of caution. In an instructive comparison between the role of the EU in conflict resolution in Cyprus, Northern Ireland and the Basque Country, Bourne relates CBC to the third of four possible ways in which the

---

7 In addition to "conflict resolution" and "conflict transformation", McCall proposes "conflict amelioration" as an intermediate concept: "it is now generally accepted by peace-building theorists that the engagement of the 'grassroots' is an essential component of a peace-building endeavour. This is particularly the case in border conflicts where borderlanders are, more often than not, on the periphery of the state and geopolitically remote from the central government. Accordingly, conflict amelioration, as used here, attempts to capture a peace-building effort wherein political violence has largely abated, competing ethno-nationalist political elites have entered into an agreement on governance and, crucially, local borderland "grassroots" communities have been engaged in an on-going peace-building effort" (2013: 206).

EU may encourage the resolution of conflicts, "subversion",[8] which is the most relevant to the focus of this chapter and to the "conflict amelioration" perspective:

> In a process that mirrors the classic 'community method' of EU co-operation, parties to a conflict may be encouraged to co-operate with each other or make conciliatory moves as part of their compliance with the technical requirements of EU membership or as a consequence of *functional objectives* [our emphasis] otherwise unrelated to the politics of conflict. (2003: 400).

In the Basque case, European integration encouraged conciliatory moves by the Spanish and French central governments that partially satisfied certain Basque cultural and political aspirations. Given the emphasis on the removal of physical borders between member states within the single market program, "French and Spanish governments overcame some of their reluctance to support more extensive cross-border collaboration" (*Ibid.*: 402). EU funds supported various programs, including some with a clear cultural content such as Basque language projects. Bourne goes on to say that "[p]erhaps more importantly, market integration in the EU has helped justify the need for more permanent institutionalized co-operation among these authorities" (*Ibid.*: 403). The progressive consolidation of a framework of cooperation between sub-national authorities since the 1980s illustrates this trend.

As mentioned earlier, the progressive construction of this framework of cooperation had contrasting effects on conflict amelioration. Facilitating CBC "provide[d] some important symbolic and material gains for Basque nationalists" (Bourne, 2003: 403) by bringing the seven provinces together.[9] The Spanish government reinforced this politicized interpretation when it initiated legal action against the Basque Autonomous Community government over the latter's legal authority in CBC after the Treaty of Bayonne (*Ibid.*: 404). As Letamendia (1997) observed, promotion of the Southern model of political autonomy as a by-product of the development of CBC put additional pressure on the

8 The four ways that the EU may stimulate conflict resolution, as described by Bourne (2003), are the "sticks" of exerting pressure on the parties in conflict to pursue compromise, the "carrots" whereby the parties are encouraged rather than pressurized, "subversion", described here, and the "post-modernist" strategy, described later.

9 Historically, the Basque Country encompasses seven provinces, three in France (Labourd, Lower Navarre and Soule) and four in Spain (Biscay, Gipuzkoa, Alava and Navarre).

French authorities to grant some degree of self-government to the French Basque Country.

In other words, "subversion", Bourne's third way in which the EU can stimulate conflict resolution, was probably the most developed effect of European influence on the Basque conflict. In addition, differences can be seen between the initial aims of EU-driven policy and its effects, as there were shifts in meaning, if not a change in the policy paradigm, during the phase of implementation. Bray and Keating (2013: 144-45) shed light on the multiple understandings of the EU CBC policy in the Basque case. There was a disparity between the initial aims of CBC as promoted by a European Commission stressing economic and functional considerations, thus downplaying the cultural and political elements, and its implementation by Basque activists whose intention was to consolidate their pre-existing Basque Country networks. Bray and Keating note that "the idea that European subsidiarity provides minorities in control of their own regions with new opportunities to explore constituting cross-border political communities with their co-nationals needs to be qualified, since power relations are conditioned by state controls to varying extents (2013: 145).

However, it was also the case that some local actors used EU CBC schemes in a functional way, and not in relation to nationalist aims. Localized engagement in individual projects was effective in the practical creation of CBC networks: "Practical work at the very local level on specific projects also follows the logic of localism, of personal and partisan networks, and of micro-politics rather than grand visions of nation building. This is because on this level actors can manage to achieve concrete results. (Bray, Keating, 2013: 147)".

Bourne describes a fourth way in which the EU may stimulate conflict resolution: "European integration, as a manifestation of broader processes of globalization, may transform and 'moderate' national identities"; according to post-modernists, she says, "the reconfiguration of borders and other key features of 'modern' political order as part of the processes of European integration and globalization opens up new possibilities for less antagonistic forms of identification" (2003: 405). The Ibarretxe plan, put forward in 2002 by the president of the Basque Autonomous Community, proposed a "model of co-sovereignty, freely and voluntarily shared" (2003: 408), and included a reference to the strengthening of CBC.[10] However, this "post-modernist" approach did not help to eliminate or de-emphasize differences and thereby reduce the grounds for conflict. The Ibarretxe plan drew particular criticism for its aspirations to full Basque sovereignty.

Bourne's overall conclusion is that although the EU has become part of the landscape of conflict in the Basque Country, Northern Ireland and Cyprus, there is very little clear evidence that it has had a significant role in the resolution of conflict in these regions. Discussing the Irish and other European contexts, McCall has observed that there is "some disjuncture between the theoretical advocacy of 'peace-building from below' and difficulties in developing practical ways of engaging people at the grassroots in conflict amelioration activities" (2013: 206); this is also the case in the Basque Country, and perhaps even more so here because of the absence of a political agreement involving the state authorities.

The role of the third sector can be assessed in relation to the emergence of cross-border governance networks that may have an indirect impact on conflict amelioration. We need to understand how the participation of SSE actors contributes to the truly cross-border nature of a collaborative effort that goes beyond pragmatic cooperation, and what role territorial identity plays in this process. In the section that follows, we address these questions by means of our case study.

2. Pragmatic or identity-based cooperation? The social economy, cross-border cooperation and conflict amelioration

In this section we give some empirical substance to the earlier discussion by analyzing the main results of the qualitative survey that we conducted with third sector organizations and with other actors and political institutions involved in CBC.

---

10 The Ibarretxe plan proposed alteration of the Basque Autonomous Community's constitution to allow for an open political partnership between the Basque Country and Spain, instead of a mere devolution of power from the center to the regional authorities. The plan was approved by the Basque parliament on 30 December 2004 and rejected by the Spanish parliament on 1 February 2005.

2.1. Persistent asymmetries as potential obstacles to CBC

In a previous survey undertaken in the early years of the adoption of CBC by different tiers of government (Itçaina *et al.*, 1997), it was observed that CBC in the Basque country had to overcome the political and institutional asymmetries that still existed between the regions north and south of the state border. More recent observations (Itçaina, Manterola, 2014) and the series of interviews we draw on in this chapter confirm that, more than 15 years later, these asymmetries are still present, despite the development of a governmental framework that is more favorable to CBC.

Institutional asymmetries are still reflected in disparities in financial resources between the Aquitaine Region and its southern counterparts the Basque Autonomous Community and the Chartered Community of Navarre: in 1997, Aquitaine's budget was only a tenth of that of the Basque Autonomous Community, for example (Letamendia, 1997: 37). However, these disparities did not prevent any of the regions from investing equivalent sums in their bilateral agreements. A more significant problem was caused by differences in the fiscal powers of the Basque Autonomous Community and Navarre and their provincial Deputations, which were extensive in comparison to those of the French regions and departmental General Councils. Finally, the central role of the Prefect as the representative of the French state had no real equivalent on the Spanish Basque side of the border.

The way that political elites on either side of the border have perceived cross-border cooperation has often been indicated by the different approaches they have taken. Since 1986 the Aquitaine region has been governed by administrations on both the right and left that have had a functional perception of cooperation, relating this to collaboration on transport, infrastructure and the economy, rather than an identity-based one. South of the border, the Basque Autonomous Community was governed from 1980 to 2009 by the Basque Nationalist Party (PNV), either on its own or in coalition; during this period the PNV saw cross-border cooperation, like the Basque diaspora (Totoricagüena, 2005), as an opportunity to strengthen ties between Basques while sidelining the role of the central state (Ithurralde, 2002; Bourne, 2008). A third entity, the government of Navarre, has had conservative or socialist majorities that have favored a functional approach to cooperation, carefully distancing themselves from the discourse of the Euskadi government. As a consequence of the Lizarra-Garazi Accord and the pursuit of greater sovereignty that followed the ceasefire by ETA in 1998-9, Navarre withdrew in 2000 from the trilateral cooperation agreement with Euskadi and Aquitaine, but continued to maintain bilateral agreements with the latter. In the same vein, Navarre did not initially participate in the Aquitaine-Euskadi Euroregion established in 2011. In 2015, however, Navarre's new government announced its intention to join this.[11]

This characterization of contrasting positions, which held sway during the 1990s, needs to be modified for the period after 2010. The "Euro-enthusiasm" of the Basque government, as of other minority nationalist parties in Europe (Elias, 2008), has gradually given way – starting before the change of government in 2009 – to a form of "Euro-pragmatism", in response to the lack of positive movement towards creation of a genuine "Europe of the Regions". The long-standing PNV strategy had been to use the EU to make the role of nation-states redundant (Letamendia, 1997: 37). However, nationalists quickly realized that the EU could be used, in particular by the Spanish state and other Autonomous Communities, for diametrically opposed strategic aims: disputes about the Basque tax regime, for example, could be shifted to the European level (Bourne, 2008).

Prior to the mid-1990s, the lack of proper governmental bodies for the French Basque Country acted as a brake on the development of cross-border cooperation at the level of the Basque Country as a whole. This situation changed with the establishment, on the French side, of the Conseil de développement du Pays Basque (Basque Country Development Council), the Conseil des élus du Pays basque (Council of elected representatives for the Basque Country), and the Institut culturel basque (Basque cultural institute). In 1997 the French Basque Country was recognized as a *pays*, in the sense determined by the law of 1995.[12]

---

11 "La Navarre prête à intégrer l'Eurorégion Aquitaine-Euskadi", *Sud Ouest*, 30 October 2015. After the Autonomous community elections of 24 May 2015, a new majority arising from a coalition of left-wing and Basque nationalist parties replaced the conservatives in the regional government of Navarre.

12 Neither an administrative unit nor a local authority, the *pays* (as defined by the 1995 *Loi d'Orientation pour l'aménagement et le développement du territoire* or "Pasqua law", amended by the 1999 *Loi d'Orientation de l'aménagement durable du territoire* or "Voynet" law) is an area that has a geographical, cultural and economic coherence, within which municipalities work on a shared development plan. The *pays* can generate development agreements with the state, the region, and other sub-state authorities.

The new institutions are seen as compromises between nationalists, civil society and the state, partly intended to compensate for the latter's refusal to create a new *département* (Letamendia, 1997). Within France the Basque experience was seen as a commendable example of coherent local development and was one of the inspirations behind the wider implementation of policy for local areas (the "*pays*"). The joint expertise of the Basque Country Development Council and the Council of Elected Representatives informed the content of two contracts between local and regional authorities and the state, covering all sectors (economic development, social welfare, language and education, and planning for balanced land use). Cross-border cooperation was one of the three broad aims announced by the Development Council in the "Pays Basque 2020" consultation exercise launched in 2005, along with the equitable distribution of resources (between the coastal zone and the interior) and sustainable development.

Our research interviews revealed that actors within the social economy had to overcome two other asymmetries, one structural and one cyclical, alongside the general institutional and political asymmetries discussed above. The first of these was an *organizational* asymmetry between the northern and southern social economies. The Réseau transfrontalier de l'économie sociale et solidaire project (Social and solidarity economy cross-border network), funded by the POCTEFA program, published an analysis that revealed the very different nature of the social economies in the three regions: while a culture of industrial cooperatives remained strong in Euskadi, agrarian cooperatives were prevalent in Navarre, and in the French Basque country, and Aquitaine as a whole, the focus of the social economy was more on services and on small and medium-sized enterprises. The small-scale cooperatives of the French Basque Country, and of Aquitaine as a whole, could not really be compared with the cooperative giant of Mondragón in the south, supplemented by those cooperatives that were outside the Mondragón federation.[13] Legislation and fiscal conditions also generated differences: similar activity could be

---

13 The Mondragón cooperative federation, on its own, included 289 businesses and cooperatives, and collectively had 81,320 employees in 2014, both in the Basque Country and abroad <http://www.mondragon-corporation.com/fr/>, consulted on 4 June 2014. In Aquitaine, the federation of worker cooperatives (URSCOP) accounted for 134 cooperatives with 1,900 employees in 2014 <http://www.scop-aquitaine.coop/sites/fr/unions-regionales/les-scop-aquitaine/qui-sommes-nous/Missions.html>, consulted on 4 June 2014).

undertaken by a cooperative in the South and an *association* (non-profit organization) in the North.[14] In specific areas such as fishing, the Spanish Basque *cofradía*, an association like a medieval guild that governed the economic and social aspects of the sector (Hess, 2009), had no real counterpart on the French Basque side. Within France, the legal and tax system was more favorable than its southern counterpart towards features of the small-scale social economy such as micro-finance (for example CLEFE, CLEJ and Herrikoa)[15] or the small worker cooperative. In the cultural sector, French government policy created the category of publicly-funded *intermittents du spectacle* (casual employees in the performing arts), which had no equivalent in Spain. Generally speaking, however, social economy actors on both sides of the border consistently shared a perception of the asymmetry in size between third sector organizations in the different countries, as expressed by this French Basque activist working on a cross-border cooperative project for job creation by women:

> We took part in meetings with southern women, aged between 55 and 60. They all said that this was impossible. A worker cooperative has to be constituted by 50 people. Not by two. It's something collective. And we told them that a cooperative can be founded by two people. Here [in France], it's possible. Values are important. Numbers do not matter. Of course, it's better to be many. But you can start with two people, and then you see what happens.[16]

A fourth sort of asymmetry, a *cyclical* one, emerged with the global crisis of 2008, which hit Spain particularly badly. This initiated an unexpected market asymmetry between the north and south of the Basque Country. While Euskadi was far less badly affected by the crisis than any other Spanish region, the consequences were still more damaging there than in Aquitaine. In 2012, unemployment was as high as 14.9 per cent in Euskadi (25 per cent in Spain), against 10 per cent in Aquitaine (10.3 per cent in France) (Bihartean-Eurorégion, 2014: 7). The crisis created new fragilities in the South both for the most market-oriented sectors, illustrated by the bankruptcy of the Basque industrial cooperative

---

[14] The status of an association is defined by a French law of 1901.

[15] Herrikoa is a venture capital company, set up in 1980, which takes deposits of savings from the general public in order to support the creation of small businesses in the French Basque area.

[16] Interview, Andere Nahia (French Basque women's organization), 2013, translated from French.

Fagor and its European subsidiaries (Errasti *et al.*, 2016), and for sectors dependent on public resources. In 2013 the government of Navarre decided not to fund the cross-border cooperation scheme with Aquitaine, due to the depletion of its resources.[17] The crisis had the knock-on effect of undermining the public institutions themselves, thus downgrading CBC as a policy priority. The scarcity of resources had two contrasting effects. On the one hand the crisis stimulated the development of many third sector organizations, which had to look inward and secure their own survival before launching new partnerships. On the other, the crisis prompted some southern actors to turn to cross-border projects with the precise intention of gaining access to bilateral or European funds that would compensate for the decline in their own resources. Northern actors saw southern actors coming to them in order to build some sort of advantageous partnership. This was the case for a local television station in the Basse-Navarre, a cooperative, which had originally been approached by television stations from Gipuzkoa with a view to developing a joint audiovisual project based on their shared Basque culture and common use of *euskera* (Basque language). Subsequently, with the Spanish economic crisis, the nature and balance of the motivation shifted. As one of the French Basque cooperative members observed: "Now they don't have enough money to work. As a result, they approach us because they see that there are resources in France and in Europe. So now they are approaching us, but it's because they need it."[18]

In this case, a cross-border project that had initially been motivated by shared cultural aims was transformed into a functional and pragmatic partnership whose primary objective was the capture of CBC funding. It also gave more leverage to the northern actor, unlike in the more usual situation where the French Basque partner would have been the weak link in the partnership.

---

17 The Aquitaine region, however, chose to continue to support the project partners from Aquitaine in order to maintain a minimum level of cooperation, thus relying on the self-financing capacity of the partners from Navarre (interview, Aquitaine Region, Bordeaux, 2013).

18 Interview, SCIC Aldudarrak Bideo (local television station), French Basque Country, 2013, translated from Basque.

2.2. The silent politicization of the social economy: contrasting styles of implementing CBC

Despite these persistent asymmetries, there were steady advances in the process whereby CBC by SSE actors became incorporated into governmental strategy and action moved steadily forward, with at least three distinct types of motivation and styles of implementation.

CBC as an instrument for nation-building. In this first situation, funding from public CBC programs (whether interregional or EU) came to strengthen and supplement pre-existing CBC networks. This was particularly the case for networks that were clearly oriented towards a Basque nation-building process. As discussed earlier, CBC with a nation-building orientation had established cross-border networks in various sectors from the 1970s onwards, prior to the state-sponsored cooperation schemes. Over the years, these civil society networks developed the ability to use the new schemes in order to consolidate their partnerships. The federation of French and Spanish *ikastola* (schools using the Basque language) set up a European Cooperative Society in 2009 with this in mind. The Society for Basque Studies (*Eusko Ikaskuntza*), which was structured on a cross-border basis but had a different legal status on each side (a public interest body in the South and an *association* in the North), also regularly used CBC funding schemes to develop cross-border cultural projects. Basque-speaking non-profit radio stations in Navarre and the French Basque Country also used this funding, as did the cross-border radio station *Antxeta irratia* in the Txingudi border area.

All these initiatives oriented towards nation-building had to overcome two sorts of difficulties. The first was the recurrent problem of institutional equivalence. In the late 2000s *Hemen* ("Here"), the French Basque association for local development, wanted to launch a cross-border job-finding scheme but was turned away by the Spanish state employment service, which only wanted to work with its French state counterpart and not with an organization with no official status. The second difficulty, which was seldom publicly expressed even within the *abertzale* milieu, related to the risk of a Basque type of centralizing Jacobinism, whereby CBC decision-making was located and concentrated in the Spanish Basque Country to the detriment of the French partners.

Sector-based CBC, with a reference to shared Basque identity. For a second category of CBC projects it was a shared Basque *cultural* and *territorial* identity, rather than Basque *national* identity, which was part of the motivation for cooperation, although sector-based goals were the essential element. This was especially the case for the CBC projects that related to social movements, such as women's organizations, small farmer associations and environmental groups, whose aim was to build or strengthen cross-border networks on specific issues. For these projects a shared Basque identity overlapped with sector-based interests; an example of this is EHKOlektiboa (EHKO), the cross-border association of organic farmers from the French Basque Country, Euskadi and Navarre that was founded in 2014. Its aim is to create a cross-border system of organic certification, intended to be "private, but collective". For *Biharko lurraren elkartea* (Association for the land of tomorrow), the French Basque association promoting the project:

> The members are the farmers. Farmers from the whole Basque Country. But our goal is not the Basque Country as a *herri* (people),[19] it's not the Basque Country for the Basque Country. There is, also, a national vision. But our philosophy consists of saying that most of the people are positive about identifying themselves with, or subscribing to, a name that would cover the whole Basque Country. I identify with this. This *lurralde* (territory) has a cultural reality, and they all agree on this.[20]

Similarly, the French Basque women's association *Emazteek diote* (Women's voice) began its relationship with its southern counterparts in 1998-1999, during the period of the Lizarra-Garazi Accord, when the ceasefire declared by ETA created an environment that encouraged cross-border projects aimed at strengthening all kinds of links between the two territories. Although it was focused on women's issues rather than motivated by Basque identity, this feminist CBC project benefited from the climate that was directly related to the political process.

Functional and non-identity-based CBC. For a third category, CBC was based on new partnerships between actors who did not necessarily know each other before a project was set up, nor base their cooperation on reference to a shared Basque identity. This absence of identity-based common ground did not prevent these projects from achieving positive results in terms of network governance. This is illustrated by two specific projects in the field of cultural and industrial heritage: one, on the iron mines of Banca, brought municipalities and valleys from the Basse-Navarre

19 The Basque *herri*, like the Spanish *pueblo*, has many meanings, and depending on the context can be translated as "people", "country", "village", or "nation".

20 Interview, *Biharko lurraren elkartea*, 2013, translated from Basque.

(in France) and Navarre into partnership; the other, on maritime heritage, linked together associations from both the French Basque coastal area of Labourd and Gipuzkoa. This category of projects also includes some with more functional aims. A CBC project regarding migrant integration was promoted by AIFRISSS, a French organization whose officer described himself as being "*très jacobin*" (very French centralist) and suspicious of Spain's devolution of power to its autonomous communities. This attitude did not prevent AIFRISS from developing substantial skills in acquiring European funds for cross-border and transnational projects. However, cases also emerged of opportunistic and unintegrated cooperation that had generated unwarranted windfalls for enterprising applicants, an effect feared by the governmental promoters of CBC. Finally, in some specific sectors of the social economy, such as "social integration through economic activity", CBC has to date remained weak due to the very different institutional arrangements on the French and Spanish sides of the border (Itçaina, Manterola, 2014; Manterola, 2013).

2.3. Politicizing against depoliticizing CBC: conforming to institutional expectations

Assessment of the "success" or "failure" of CBC must relate to its initial stated objectives. In reference to the Basque case, Bray and Keating make the following observation:

> Cross-border cooperation has, then, been successful in some ways but not in others. The verdict depends on what we are talking about: the romantic unification of people without frontiers, the unification of the 'Basques', institutional unification, or the pragmatic solving of social and health services, transport infrastructure, or taxation. However, it can well be argued that one cannot be effectively carried out without the other. (Bray, Keating 2013: 48).

Our fieldwork fully confirms this variety of interpretation. There can be a disparity between the declared objectives of some cross-border cultural movements, such as to contribute to Basque nation-building, and the declared policy objectives of CBC, for example to increase functional cooperation in pursuit of socio-economic aims. This variety is even more apparent when it comes to the impact of CBC on conflict amelioration. We can hypothesize that policy-makers, although they may not make it explicit, also see CBC as contributing to a general process of social reconciliation in the Basque country by disconnecting cooperation from the promotion of cultural and political identities. It can be argued that policy-makers have been attempting to depoliticize CBC and promote functional objectives, in the manner described by Jullien and Smith: "[o]ften also called 'technicization', depoliticization is a type of political work which downplays values in favour of arguments based upon 'expertise' and 'efficiency'" (2008: 21).[21]

However, it would be an oversimplification to contrast a depoliticized CBC led by policy-makers with a politicized use of CBC by social movements. The formal adoption of CBC by the various levels of government affected the behavior of identity-related social movements: in order to take advantage of these new opportunities, they had to depoliticize and "technicize" their discourse in order to make it acceptable within the official process. More precisely, they had to adjust their discourse to fit the priorities determined by the Euroregion, which conformed to EU priorities: social and territorial cohesion, structural change in energy systems, educational attendance, social and labor mobility. The discourse also had to be consistent with the Euroregion's overall goal, which was to rise above being just a financial resource for cross-border projects: "the Euroregion has not been established to manage the Aquitaine-Euskadi call for projects. It was created in order to develop a strategy of mobilization, of 'capture' as the Spaniards say, of European funds."[22]

Both Aquitaine and Euskadi clearly wanted to avoid the phenomenon of projects repeating their applications to the bilateral CBC schemes on an annual basis, and encouraged them to develop their approach and apply to other sources such as, in particular, the European Regional Development Fund. This generated particular difficulties for fragile small third sector organizations that lacked organizational and financial capacity, for example over their cash flow and coordination of different funding streams. Some former beneficiaries of these bilateral schemes felt that there was a contradiction between the authorities' hope for enduring strong cross-border partnerships and the cessation of bilateral funding after a few years in order to prioritize newcomers to CBC.

For their part, the third sector organizations that were based on Basque identity and the Basque nation-building process frequently

---

21 By contrast, "politicization occurs when actors explicitly employ values either to transform the meaning of an issue or in order to transfer its treatment to another site of negotiation" (Jullien, Smith, 2008: 21).

22 Interview, Eurorégion Aquitaine–Euskadi, Hendaye, 2013, translated from French.

applied double standards. They attempted to conform to the formal requirements in order to gain access to government-led CBC schemes, but if these attempts failed they could still activate the alternative CBC network that related to Basque social movements. This was the case in 2005 when the French Basque ELB farmers' union decided to found Euskal Herriko Laborantza Ganbara (EHLG), an alternative Chamber of agriculture for the Basque Country. This met hostility, and when EHLG faced legal action from the state and the main French farmers' union (Itçaina, 2011) it had no choice but to turn to Basque cross-border social movements in order to secure alternative resources. Support from the Manu Robles Arangiz Foundation, connected to the southern Basque nationalist trade union ELA, was decisive in acquiring office facilities for EHLG, and it also received support from the Udalbiltza cross-border association of local councillors. In 2006 EHLG also signed an agreement with Itsasmendikoia, a public agency for rural development linked to the Basque Autonomous Community government. Similarly, but in a less public manner, EHKO (the cross-border association of organic farmers mentioned earlier) applied to the bilateral interregional funding scheme, but this turned them down giving the reason that the Aquitaine region was implementing its own labelling for organic food. The EHKO organizers then turned to Udalbiltza. Local actors demonstrated that they had both the strategic ability and the ideological flexibility needed for dealing with both governmental and alternative resources in order to move their projects forward.

Finally, we should mention an unforeseen by-product of the adoption of CBC by governmental bodies: the generation of new competition *between* third sector organizations struggling to gain access to public resources. This was the case when French and Spanish Basque associations competed for public funding in regard to commemoration of the history of Basque whaling in Newfoundland. This type of competition could be based on both economic and ideological motivation. In the educational field, the three French Basque networks for the teaching of *euskera* (the *ikastola*, mentioned earlier, the Ikas-bi/Biga bai, public bilingual schools, and the Euskal haziak, private bilingual Catholic schools) cooperated in their demand for more official recognition from the French state, but competed with each other to gain access funding available from the South, and especially from the Basque Autonomous Community government (Harguindéguy, Itçaina, 2015). In this regard, the initial steps taken to establish a Basque language policy in the French Basque Country had an unexpected effect. The Office public de la langue Basque or Euskararen erakunde publikoa (Public office for the Basque language), created in 2005, included representatives from the Spanish Basque Autonomous Community government on its board alongside representatives of the French state and local authorities, and was intended to channel, rationalize and, in the state's interests, keep a check on the resources coming from the South. This led to a dispute over the redistribution of these monies between the three educational networks, which had until then maintained bilateral access to the southern institutions. These controversies provide an indirect illustration of the effectiveness of the initial steps to give the French Basque Country a more formal status that would mean more than just a "cosmetic decentralization" (Mansvelt Beck, 2005).

Conclusion

The involvement of Basque SSE actors in CBC has followed two tracks: an official governmental track that has attempted to establish a stable framework for functional and sector-based CBC, and an alternative track that has reinforced the Basque nation-building process by means of cross-border social movements. In our analysis of third sector organizations involved in CBC we found that both these tracks were used as alternatives, or even simultaneously, by various civil society organizations; this related to ideological factors, but also to more contingent and pragmatic considerations. SSE organizations developed new skills in order to consolidate their own resources and to overcome the four asymmetries we have identified (institutional, political, organizational, and market) between the two sides of the border. Although cross-border relations may not have had a direct impact on the peace process itself, their intensification led to improved mutual understanding, a reduced recourse to stereotypes, and a focus on shared practical issues. The increase in CBC certainly made an indirect contribution to the normalization of cross-border relations and, as a consequence, to a silent and sustainable process of conflict amelioration.

This case study was intended to emphasize the contribution of political sociology to the study of the territorial dynamics of the SSE. Far from being limited to uncomplicated socio-economic exchanges, cross-border SSE flows mirror the institutional, political and cultural issues peculiar to this territory. Beyond the Basque case, future research should scrutinize the political work undertaken by SSE actors at multiple governmental scales (local, regional, state, supra-state) in order to take their claims forward. Research should be particularly sensitive to the way SSE operators capture European policy instruments for CBC (Cross-Border Cooperation). The uses made of these instruments may be limited to their functional dimension. In contrast, their implementation may support political and/or cultural readings of the border. In this respect and as already suggested in this chapter, comparing the Basque case with the Irish border region would be particularly fruitful. Unlike in the Basque case, the EU became directly involved in the peace process in Northern Ireland. This involvement led, among other things, to support for cross-border relations between third sector organizations. Irish third sector organizations used EU Peace Programs to take their projects forward, albeit with mixed results, while, in the Basque case, a number of SSE actors tried to "translate" into identity-related terms EU and regional CBC programs which initially were totally disconnected from the Basque political question (McCall, Itçaina, 2017). As a result, a sort of secondary foreign policy that does not speak its name emerged in the Basque Country, led by an organized civil society aiming to build a shared territory. Beyond its singularity, the Basque case lends itself to comparisons between different territorial mobilizations around SSE, which are undeniably political in nature.

Acknowledgements. Earlier versions of this chapter were presented at the 5*th CIRIEC International research conference on social economy* (Lisbon, 14-18 July 2015) and at the 13*th National conference of the Association française de science politique* (Aix, 22-24 June 2015). The authors wish to thank all the participants and discussants for their comments and suggestions. Thanks also go to Stuart Oglethorpe and to Mike Fay for their help with the editing, and to the Aquitaine Region for its support through the research program *Vers une gouvernance transfrontalière en réseau ? Expériences transfrontalières du tiers secteur en France et au Royaume-Uni*, Sciences Po Bordeaux-Région Aquitaine, 2010-2014.

References

Ahedo I., 2008, *The Transformation of National Identity in the Basque Country of France, 1789-2006*, Reno, University of Nevada Press.

Bihartean-Eurorégion Aquitaine-Euskadi, 2014, *Eurorégion Aquitaine-Euskadi en chiffres 2013*, San Sebastián/Bayonne.

Bourne A.K., 2003, "European Integration and Conflict Resolution in the Basque Country, Northern Ireland and Cyprus", *Perspectives on European Politics and Society*, 4 (3): 391-415.

Bourne A.K., 2008, *The European Union and the Accommodation of Basque Difference in Spain*, Manchester, Manchester University Press.

Brana S., Jégourel Y., 2011, "La réalité de la microfinance à l'échelle régionale : l'exemple de l'Aquitaine", *Revue d'économie régionale et urbaine*, 2: 245-68.

Bray Z., 2004, *Living Boundaries: Frontiers and Identity in the Basque Country*, Brussels, Peter Lang.

Bray Z., 2006, "Basque Militant Youths in France: New Experiences of Ethnonational Identity in the European Context", *Nationalism and Ethnic Politics*, 12 (3-4): 533-53.

Bray Z., Keating M., 2013, "European Integration and the Basque Country in France and Spain", *in* T.J. Mabry, J. McGarry, M. Moore, B. O'Leary (eds.), *Divided Nations and European Integration*, Philadelphia, University of Pennsylvania Press, p. 127-56.

Conseil de développement du Pays Basque, 2003, *Les coopérations transfrontalières en Pays Basque. Rapport adopté au Conseil de direction du 15 décembre 2003*, Bayonne, Conseil de développement, <http://ns352889.ovh.net/~lurralde/uploads/media/Synth-cooptransf-B.pdf>, consulted on 1 May 2015.

Defourny J., Nyssens M., 2006, "Defining social enterprise", *in* M. Nyssens, S. Adam, T. Johnson (eds.), *Social Enterprise: At the Crossroads of Market, Public Policies and Civil Societies*, New York/London, Routledge, p. 3-26.

Elias A., 2008, "From Euro-enthusiasm to Euro-scepticism? A Re-evaluation of Minority Nationalist Party Attitudes towards European Integration", *Regional and Federal Studies*, 18 (5): 557-81.

Enciso Santocildes M., 2001, "Las cooperativas de iniciativa social", *Anuario de Estudios Cooperativos. Kooperatiba Ikaskuntzen Urtekaria*, 2001, p. 159-64.

Errasti A., Bretos I., Etxezarreta E., 2016, "What do Mondragon Coopitalist Multinationals Look Like? The Rise and Fall of Fagor Electrodomésticos S. Coop. and its European Subsidiaries", *Annals of Public and Cooperative Economics*, 87 (3): 433-56.

Harguindéguy J.-B., 2007, "Cross-Border Policy in Europe: Implementing INTERREG III-A, France-Spain", *Regional and Federal Studies*, 17 (3): 317-34.

Harguindéguy J.-B., Hayward K., 2014, "The Institutionalization of the European Internal Cross-Border Co-operation Policy: A First Appraisal", *European Planning Studies*, 22 (1): 184-203.

Harguindéguy J.-B., Itçaina X., 2015, "State Tradition and Regional Languages in France: The Case of Basque", *in* L. Cardinal, S.K. Sonntag (eds.), *State Traditions and Language Regimes*, Montreal/Kingston, McGill–Queen's University Press, p. 170-88.

Hess A., 2009, *Reluctant Modernization: Plebeian Culture and Moral Economy in the Basque Country*, Bern, Peter Lang.

Itçaina X., Manterola J.-J., 2014, "Towards Cross-Border Network Governance? The Social and Solidarity Economy and the Construction of a Cross-Border Territory in the Basque Country", *in* K. Stokłosa, G. Besier (eds.), *European Border Regions in Comparison: Overcoming Nationalistic Aspects or Re-nationalization?*, Abingdon, Routledge, p. 169-87.

Itçaina X., J. Palard, B. Vignes, 1997, "Politique institutionnelle ou mobilisation sociale ? Le Fonds commun Aquitaine–Euskadi", *in* J. Palard (dir.), *L'Europe aux frontières*, Paris, PUF/GRALE, p. 131-54.

Itçaina X., 2007, "Des entreprises politiques ? Les SCOP dans l'espace public basque", *in* X. Itçaina, J. Palard, S. Ségas (eds.), *Régimes territoriaux et développement économique*, Rennes, PUR, p. 67-82.

Itçaina X., 2010, "Les régimes territoriaux de l'économie sociale et solidaire : le cas du Pays Basque français", *Géographie, économie, société*, 12 (1): 71-87.

Itçaina X., 2011, "Mobilisation territoriale autour d'un projet agricole en Pays Basque", *in* S. Béroud, N. Dompnier, D. Garibay (dir.), *L'Année sociale 2011*, Paris, Syllepse, p. 175-89.

Itçaina X., 2017, "Multiple Sovereignties? Civil Society and Territorial Construction in Iparralde", *in* A. Kolås, P. Ibarra Güell (eds.), *Sovereignty Revisited: The Basque Case*, London, Hurst.

Ithurralde M.-A., 2002, *Le Pays Basque, la Catalogne et l'Europe : stratégies politiques des Autonomies basque et catalane*, Paris, l'Harmattan.

Jacob J.E., 1994, *Hills of Conflict: Basque Nationalism in France*, Reno, University of Nevada Press.

Jullien B., Smith A., 2008, "Introduction: Industries, Globalization and Politics", *in* B. Jullien, A. Smith (eds.), *Industries and Globalization: The Political Causality of Difference*, Basingstoke, Palgrave MacMillan, p. 1-28.

Klijn E.-H., Skelcher C., 2007, "Democracy and Governance Networks: Compatible or Not?", *Public Administration*, 85 (3): 587-608.

Laville J.-L., 2000, *L'économie sociale et solidaire en Europe*, Paris, CRIDA (Les notes de l'Institut Karl Polanyi).

Letamendia F., 1997, "Basque Nationalism and Cross-Border Co-operation between the Southern and Northern Basque Countries", *Regional and Federal Studies*, 7 (2): 25-41.

Malloy T.H., 2010, "Creating New Spaces for Politics? The Role of National Minorities in Building Capacity of Cross-Border Regions", *Regional and Federal Studies*, 20 (3): 335-51.

Mansvelt Beck J., 2005, *Territory and Terror: Conflicting Nationalisms in the Basque Country*, London/New York, Routledge.

Manterola J.-J., 2013, "Gouvernance des entreprises sociales d'insertion basques : le marché en guise de débat", *RECMA – Revue internationale de l'économie sociale*, 327: 43-62.

McCall C., 2013, "European Union Cross-Border Cooperation and Conflict Amelioration", *Space and Polity*, 17 (2): 197-216.

McCall C., Itçaina X., 2017, "Secondary foreign policy activities in Third sector cross-border cooperation as conflict transformation in the European Union: The cases of the Basque and Irish borderscapes", *Regional and Federal Studies*, 27 (3): 261-81.

O'Dowd L., McCall C., 2008, "Escaping the Cage of Ethno-National Conflict in Northern Ireland? The Importance of Transnational Networks", *Ethnopolitics*, 7 (1): 81-99.

OVES (Observatorio vasco de la economía social – Gizarte ekonomiako Euskal behatokia), 2011, *Informe de situación de la economía social vasca, 2010*, San Sebastián, GEZKI-EHU.

Radaelli C.M., 1999, *Technocracy in the European Union*, London, Longman.

Radaelli C.M., 2003, "The Europeanization of Public Policy", *in* K. Featherstone, C.M. Radaelli (eds.), *The Politics of Europeanization*, Oxford, Oxford University Press, p. 27-56.

Rajaram P.K., Grundy-Warr C., 2008, "Introduction", *in* P.K. Rajaram, C. Grundy-Warr (eds.), *Borderscapes: Hidden Geographies and Politics at Territory's Edge*, Minneapolis, University of Minnesota Press: ix-xl.

Sanchez-Salgado R., 2007, *Comment l'Europe construit la société civile*, Paris, Dalloz.

Totoricagüena G., 2005, "Diasporas as Non-Central Government Actors in Foreign Policy: The Trajectory of Basque Paradiplomacy", *Nationalism and Ethnic Politics*, 11 (2): 265-87.

Chapter 4

The "Farmers' Market" Phenomenon

A Survey on the Farmers' Market's Customers in the City of Cesena

Andrea Bassi & Sara Fabbri[1]

University of Bologna

Introduction

The globalization of markets and trade, together with modernization, have created new needs and new demands from different segments of the population. It is in this context that farmers' markets develop; they jump stages of the lengthy traditional supply chain by marketing and selling products directly to the consumer. "Industrialization tr[ies] to uphold the concept of mobility for which it is not important where you live and what you do. Instead it is important to stop, because, if nothing else, we understand that if we ruin the place where we live, we will live among the ruins" (Berry, 2009).

The real protagonists in this story are the people who act individually in everyday life by purchasing goods at these markets. The farmers' market is a space that nurtures the relationships between people and provides meanings and conveys meaning to the people who attend them.

The rise of such markets in our modern society is an effect of the development of a new type of consumer: an individual that has the need to regain control over social, economic and political processes that support the automation of food production.

---

1 The Introduction and Conclusions are the result of a common work; paragraphs 1, 2 and 5 are written by Andrea Bassi and paragraphs 3 and 4 are written by Sara Fabbri.

In practical terms, the benefits to consumers in direct sale are of two types: economic and qualitative. From the economic point of view, there is a reduction in prices due to a number of conditions such as the reduction of the steps of the traditional distribution system, less costs related to packaging, and less costs related to the transportation of goods. From the qualitative point of view, traceability and farmer knowledge allow individuals to buy a higher quality product in terms of freshness, wholesomeness, and safety. Additionally, farmers' markets create a new relationship between the individual and society, proposing an ideal of simplicity and sobriety, solidarity and responsibility towards themselves and towards others.

The article is organized in four sections. The first one is dedicated to the presentation of the definition of the term "farmers' market" and to the illustration of its principal characteristics. In the second section, we will analyze statistical data concerning the diffusion of the farmers' markets movement in the USA and in Europe, with a particular focus on the Italian context. In the third section, we will present briefly the history and the main developmental phases of the farmers' market in the city of Cesena (a medium size town in the North-East area of Italy). The fourth section is dedicated to presenting and commenting on the result of an exploratory survey with a sample of 50 customers of the Cesena's farmer market. In the conclusion, we summarize the line of thought developed during the article and present some final remarks.

1. Definition and analysis of "Farmers Market" movement

The industrialization and the subsequent change in production and consumption patterns have led to the expansion and growth of long supply chains. Globalization has meant that production and consumption have become standardized and increasingly removed from the local context.

Today, to reverse this trend, there are several growing alternatives in antithesis to this globalized market. For example, the "short chain" is a commercial formula growing fast in many industrialized countries. The idea of locavore markets exhibits new traits that have economic, social, cultural and territorial dimensions. The consumer, in fact, is now aware of "critical" and "sustainable" consumption, and thanks to the spread of farmers' markets, farmers complete the entire production cycle with direct sales of their products to the final consumer.

Before the industrial revolution, the only selling arrangement was the direct relationship between producer and consumer. However, industrialization and urbanization have changed the socio-economic relations with important consequences both on the structural and social aspects. On the one hand, *urbanization* has accentuated the gap, both physical and symbolic, between producers and consumers; on the other hand, *industrialization* has enabled the agro-food industry to develop and market its products, first with retail by third parties, and – at a later time – through the wholesale distribution.

Buying at the farmer's market is like starting again from our land, choosing to support our neighborhood, combining simplicity with quality. For the consumer, it is like shopping in a traditional market, only with the producer being right there, providing all the necessary information on the products and production methods. The consumer and the producer will easily establish a *relationship of trust* that makes the purchase not just an economic, but also a social act, significant from the human point of view.

The bond formed with the source, and consequently with our own land, socially satisfies the consumer. The farmers' markets are in fact places where it is pleasant to stop and shop, to observe the products, and to talk and discuss with the producers. The markets in which local products are exclusively traded are now well established around the world.

Small producers of the local area have the opportunity to sell to consumers food produced by their companies, avoiding intermediate steps and being able to meet the growing demand for freshness and safe products.

The positive externalities of the increasing development of farmers' markets involve multiple dimensions, including economic, social, and environmental, as shown in the following figure.

Figure 1: Positive externalities of farmers' markets

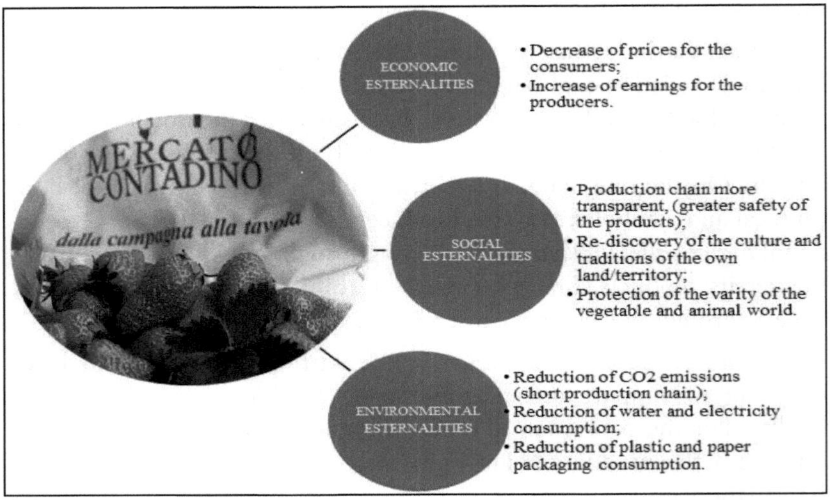

Source: the authors

The assumption of the "zero distance" (km0) movement means that the foods are transported only over relatively short distances, which reduces energy consumption and carbon dioxide emissions. Moreover, farmers cultivate following the rhythms of nature, and the products found in farmers markets are strictly seasonal. The rediscovery of the periodicity of fruit and vegetables is critical to the success of these markets and at the same time stands in stark contrast to the atypical seasonality of large retailers.

The cardinal principle is that of *proximity* between production and consumption, which is achieved through the meeting in a place specially dedicated to farmers and citizens of the same territory, favoring the creation of a system of two-way relations.

The families are now demanding to know more about what "you put on the table", trying to reconcile the requirements of food safety and hygiene with those of a higher quality, while still maintaining less environmental impact with an affordable price. Farmers' markets pursue the dual objective of increased profitability for farms and a greater purchasing power of consumers (the absence of intermediation inevitably leads to price reduction).

The added value created by pursuing "zero distance" (carbon neutral) with respect to the mass distribution is given by the greater transparency for consumers regarding the source, the freshness, and the quality of products.

Choosing to buy at the farmers' market also means supporting a universe of certain values, a non-globalized model of production and contributing to the rediscovery of ancient social relations.

In the next section, we will analyze statistical data concerning the diffusion of the farmers' markets movement in the USA and in Europe, with a particular focus on the Italian context.

2. The dimensions of the phenomenon

2.1. The International scenario

"Eating is an agricultural act." The aphorism is of Wendell Berry, who is a poet, essayist, farmer, and rural American prophet, as defined by the *New York Times*. He is the promoter of the experience of the farmers' markets, which were born in California in the 1970s.

The farmers' markets subsequently became popular in the 1990s, also in California, on the initiative of chef Alice Waters, vice president of "Slow Food International", and nowadays, they form an increasingly consolidated reality.

The development of farmers' markets is recorded by the data of the United States Department of agriculture, which in 2000 (Payne, 2002) carried out an initial investigation by counting 2,863. A second survey carried out in 2006 registered about 4,400 active markets nationwide, an increase of almost 150% since 1994[2] (the year of the first census, in which there were 1,755).

In 2014, there are more than eight thousand farmers' markets in the United States.[3]

2 See: <www.usda.gov>, consulted on 10 September 2014.

3 See: <www.usda.gov>, consulted on 10 September 2014.

Figure 2: Farmers' markets evolution in the USA, from 1994 to nowadays

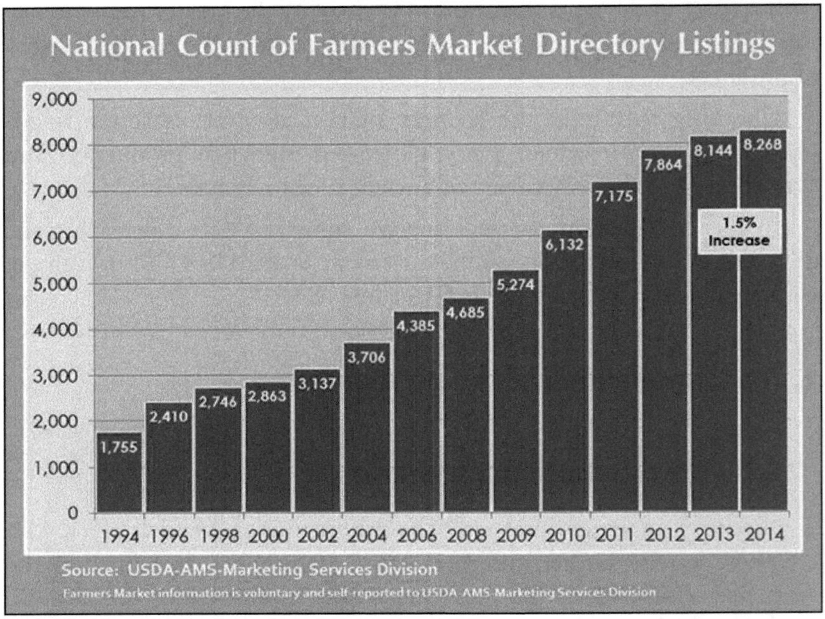

The European response to the Americans farmers markets did not take long to arrive.

In France, farmers' markets were born around the 1980s, and today the direct sale covers 15% of the French food market (Aguglia, 2009).

In Switzerland, in the *marché paysan*,[4] products for sale must comply with the rules on health and hygiene safety and must be obtained strictly through the use of raw material produced by local enterprises and by non-industrial transformation processes.

In Germany, the first *bauernmarkt*[5] was born in 1992 in Bavaria, and the tradition continues into the modern day, where the markets are managed by the German Ministry of food and consist of associations with its disciplinary regulations and statutes. An estimate of 2009 counts more than 5,000 *bauernmarkt* scattered throughout Germany (Aguglia, 2009).

4 See: <www.marchepaysan.ch>, consulted on 10 September 2014.

5 See: <http://www.muenchner-bauernmaerkte.de/>, consulted on 10 September 2014.

2.2. The Italian context

Farmers markets were born in Italy in 2007 behind the impulse of the Finance Law for that year which promoted the development of markets for farmers in direct sales (Article 1 paragraph 1.065 L.27 / 12/2006 No. 296).

The findings of the research "Italians and nutrition: adaptive strategies" conducted by Coldiretti in 2011 showed a steady growth of consumers buying directly from the manufacturer without intermediaries.

Figure 3: Direct purchases by the producer, 2011

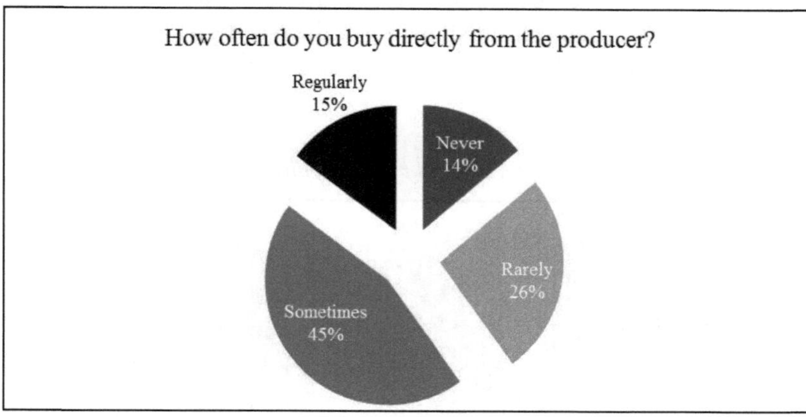

Source: Research Report: *Gli italiani e l'alimentazione: strategie adattive*, Coldiretti 2011, the authors

In 2011 the direct sale was recorded at a frequency that sees about half of the sample "sometimes" purchase directly from the manufacturer, while only 14% said they had "never put in place this practice" (figure 3).

In order to carry out a direct survey of one of the Italian farmers' markets, first it is necessary to analyze a reference picture of the phenomenon in Italy, of which there are unfortunately, until now, limited data available.

The growth of the farmers' markets in Italy is strongly supported by Coldiretti and the main Associations for consumer protection. The *Campagna amica* Foundation, founded by Coldiretti in 2008, has created the largest and most extensive network of direct sales in the Western world with a workforce of farms and markets involving 28,000 farmers throughout the Italian territory.[6]

In Campagna amica, markets and agricultural producers, all enrolled in Coldiretti and members of Campagna amica, organize themselves into an association Agrimercato (usually at the provincial territorial dimension) that has a regulation and a specification to which all members adhere.

According to the latest report prepared by the Campagna amica foundation for 2013, there are about 1,200 farmers' markets in Italy, and there have been 15 million Italians shopping, with an increase of 25% in just one year.[7]

If we consider the geographical distribution (figure 4), the Italian farmers' markets are concentrated mainly in the North (61% of the total), and the remainder (39%) are in equal measure in the Center and South (Franco, Marino, 2012).

Figure 4: Farmers markets by geographical area, 2011

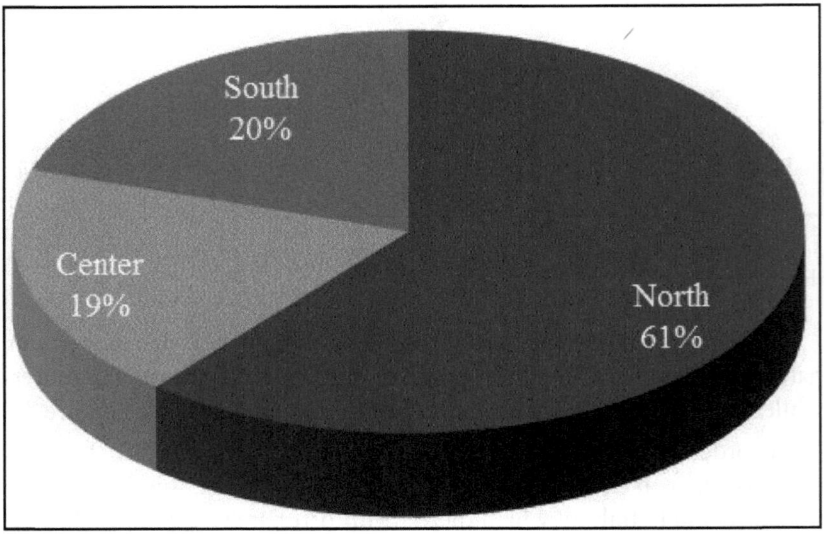

Source: Research Report: *Gli italiani e l'alimentazione: strategie adattive*, Coldiretti 2011, the authors

6 Coldiretti, Indagine 2013, <www.coldiretti.it>, consulted on 10 September 2014.

7 See: <http://www.campagnamica.it/Pagine/default.aspx>, consulted on 10 September 2014, Report by Campagna Amica Foundation, 2013.

Analyzing the data at national level, there are about 700 Italian municipalities served by the farmers' markets, which, considering all the Italian municipalities (8,057),[8] is still a rather small number.

The Regions with the highest presence of farmers' markets are Lombardy with 91 municipalities, the Emilia Romagna with 85 municipalities, Veneto with 80 municipalities, and Piedmont with 73 municipalities (figure 5) (Franco, Marino, 2012).

Figure 5: Number of Municipalities with farmer's market by Region, 2011

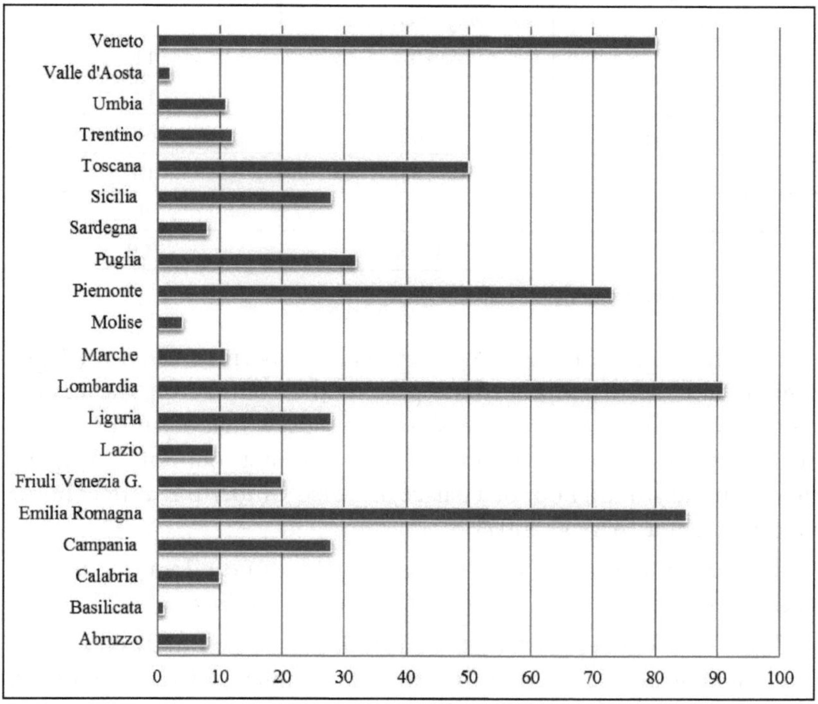

Source: Research Report: *Gli italiani e l'alimentazione: strategie adattive*, Coldiretti 2011, the authors

The most purchased products in the Italian farmers' markets, according to Coldiretti,[9] are mainly fruits and vegetables, then cheeses, meats, milk, wine, and preserves.

8 See: <www.istat.it/censimento-popolazione>, consulted on 10 September 2014.

9 See: <www.coldiretti.it/news>, consulted on 10 September 2014.

From the results of the *Monitor OrtoFrutta Agroter* 2013 on the frequency of purchase of fruit and vegetables, it is clear that 11% of the interviewees go "every day" to shop for fruit and vegetables (table 1.1). Another 11% "4-5 times per week", while the largest share (61%) has a frequency of purchase of "2-3 times per week". Around one fifth (18%) answers "once a week", while only 3 people affirm to buy fruit and vegetables "once every 15 days".

Table 1: Purchase frequency of fruit and vegetable products

Purchase Frequency	*Number of interviewees*	*%*
Every day	107	11
4-5 times per week	110	11
2-3 times per week	605	61
1 time per week	175	18
1 times every 15 days	3	0
	1,000	**100**

Source: *Monitor Ortofrutta Agroter*, 2013

In Italy, the first stable farmers' market was born in Taranto (Puglia Region. It is in the southeastern part of the country on the eastern peninsula that extends on two seas), one of the few that occur "on a daily basis" and one of the few indoors. It is located in a room of 200 square meters on the ground floor of a palace in Corso Umberto I, a street in the historical center (AAVV, 2001).

Farmers came from all over the territorial area near Taranto, and the market is devoted to fruit, vegetables, and dairy products.

The Corso Umberto Market is an initiative of Coldiretti of Taranto as a result of a serious crisis that strongly emphasized the discomfort of local agricultural companies, and this occurred at a time that saw – paradoxically – the increase in imports of fruit and vegetables from abroad, not always clearly indicated by a transparent labeling.

The first Italian farmers' market was thus born with the objective of allowing the consumers to have direct knowledge of local production, of contributing to the dissemination of local cultural traditions, and, at the same time, of safeguarding the purchasing power of consumers and the survival of the agricultural enterprises of the territorial (AAVV, 2001).

The biggest Italian farmers' market is the *mercatale* of Montevarchi in Tuscany, a region that boasts the largest number of "Short Supply Chain" initiatives in Italy (Noferi *et al.*, 2007). It is an experimental project for the enhancement of quality local production sponsored by the City of Montevarchi with the province of Arezzo, the public agency Arsia-Tuscany Region, and the Biodiversity Slow Food Foundation.

In the *mercatale* of Montevarchi Valdarno, the participation is open to individual or associated agricultural producers, producer groups (including non-professional), agribusiness craftsmanship trades, associative structures, and organizations of representation of economic categories.

In the next section we will present, briefly, the history and the main developmental phases of the Farmer Market in the City of Cesena.

3. The farmers market of Cesena

The Province of Forlì-Cesena is one of the most important agri-food centers of the region, and its specializations cover sectors such as fruits and vegetables, wine, poultry, seed, and the transformation connected to them. Based on the data of the Chamber of commerce (Economy report), the food industry sector employs 6,035 people and has a number of enterprises of considerable size.

The distribution of companies in the agri-food sector tends to be divided between lowland and upland areas. In fact, 70% of these enterprises is concentrated in the municipalities of the plains of the Forlì-Cesena Province.[10]

---

10 Cf. <www.provincia.fc.it>, consulted on 10 September 2014.

Figure 6: Concentration of the agri-food sector enterprises in Forlì-Cesena Province

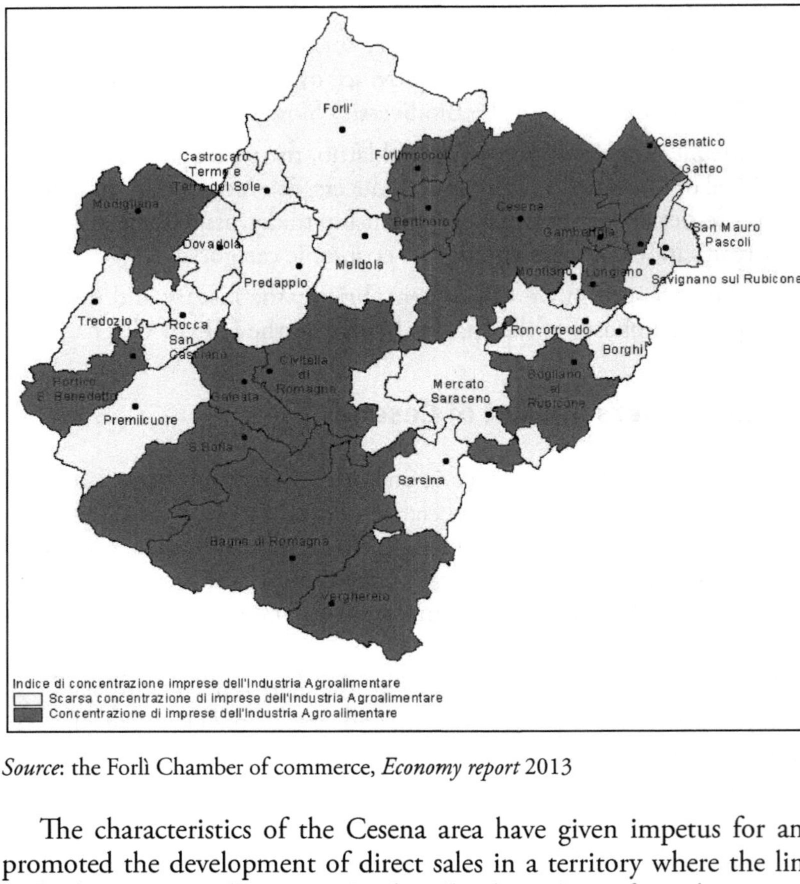

Source: the Forlì Chamber of commerce, *Economy report* 2013

The characteristics of the Cesena area have given impetus for and promoted the development of direct sales in a territory where the link with the past is still strong. In this "landscape", in fact, the peasant culture plays a central aspect.

The farmers' market of Cesena is one of those markets that throughout Italy adhere to the network of Campagna Amica Foundation. Going shopping at the "*Campagna Amica*" Market is convenient because:[11]

1. you can find only local products with low CO2 emissions;
2. you can buy fresh fruits and vegetables in season;

11 Cf. <http://www.campagnamica.it/la-nostra-rete/mercato/mercato-contadino-di-cesena/ >, consulted on 5 September 2014.

3. you can buy fresh milk and take it away in your glass bottle;
4. you can get the products delivered at home;
5. the shopping bags are "environmentally friendly" because they are biodegradable, made of cotton or corn starch;
6. organic waste is returned to the farm to become compost and/or fertilizer;
7. you can taste the typical products with biodegradable disposable utensils.

The farmers' market of Cesena was established institutionally as a result of Cesena City council resolution No. 35 of 25/02/2010: afterwards, the Italian farmers confederation Forlì-Cesena and the Provincial federation Coldiretti Forlì-Cesena promoted the initiative, taking on the burden of organizing and managing the agricultural market.

Like all agricultural markets set up by Italian municipalities, it must comply with the hygiene rules laid down in EC Regulation No. 852/2004. The food must be labeled in compliance with the regulations in force for the individual products and the indication of the place of geographical origin and the manufacturing company.

The municipality has allocated € 10,000 to implement the necessary work such as plumbing and electrical connections, in addition to the installation of a fountain.

Due to its flexibility in amount of goods purchased and the ensuing increased consumer freedom, the market area has been identified in Viale IV Novembre. Since this area is close to the historic center, it is within walking distance for those who intend to buy small amounts of goods, but for those who want to buy larger quantities, cars can easily be used.

After discussions with the promoters, the agricultural associations, the market demonstrated the feasibility of the market continuing throughout the year with products that ensure continuity and diversification of the offer, while also in consideration of seasonality. A presence of 15 producers is guaranteed (later increased to 20)[12] twice a week on Wednesday and Saturday mornings. The days and hours (8.00am to 1.00pm) correspond to those when the "street market" takes place in Piazza del Popolo; this

---

12 Resolution of Cesena Municipality Council No. 77 of 09/06/2011, see: <https://servizi.comune.cesena.fc.it/applicazioniweb/consultazioneAtti/documenti/home.0.3>, consulted on 10 September 2014.

street market attracts, in itself, a substantial number of citizens and also possible clients of the farmers' market.

Initially the Cesena farmers' market had been set up only on an experimental basis for one year from the date of first Municipal Resolution, but it was later made permanent after a positive opinion emerged on the first year of activity. A widespread satisfaction[13] had been measured both among producers and consumers who frequented the market, estimated at an average of about 500 people during the day.

It was emphasized that the direct relationship between the producer and the consumer represents an *added value* for the territory of Cesena, whose vocation is historically agricultural, and it has been highlighted that the producers involved in "direct selling" have found an interesting addition to agricultural income. It is therefore urgent to expand the market area in order to ensure that such opportunities can be accessible to a greater number of producers, precisely those producers who – despite having the requirements to participate – were not admitted because of the lack of places.

The next section is dedicated to presenting and commenting on the result of an exploratory survey with a sample of 50 customers of the Cesena's farmers' market.

4. The survey on the customers of the Cesena farmers' market

4.1. The research design

In a two-month period, we carried on a quantitative survey with 50 interviewees. The choice of the questionnaire as a tool for data collection has been motivated by the need to collect information on the main characteristics of the consumer-type of the Cesena farmers' market and her/his purchase motivations in an easy and quick way. The questionnaire was developed trying to maintain a basic structure, while leaving the interviewee to feel free to express him/herself (including both questions with closed and open answers).

The questionnaire was structured by taking into account four semantic nuclei:

---

13 Meeting of the Advisory Committee for Agricultural Activities of Forlì-Cesena, held the 27/04/2011.

- *Motivational aspects*: the questions in this section are investigating why people buy at the farmers' market;
- *Relational aspects*: questions of this group aim to understand what the relationship with the producer/seller is;
- *Environmental aspects*: this group of questions want to investigate the sensitivity towards environmental protection and resource crisis;
- *Link with the territory*: finally, this section aims to discover the territorial identity, in relation with the peasant tradition and culture.

4.2. The farmer market customer's identikit

Respondents were consumers of the Cesena farmers market with ages between 30 and 70 years. The survey was conducted in March-April 2014.

The intent was to detect the *purchasing behavior* of Cesena families in order to understand how – in an area characterized by a strong rural culture and a close relationship with the territory – these types of choices have been made. Additionally, the *socio-demographic characteristics* had the objective of outlining a "typical consumer" of the Cesena farmer's market.

The sample was composed of 64% of women and 36% of men (figure 7).

Figure 7: Sample by gender

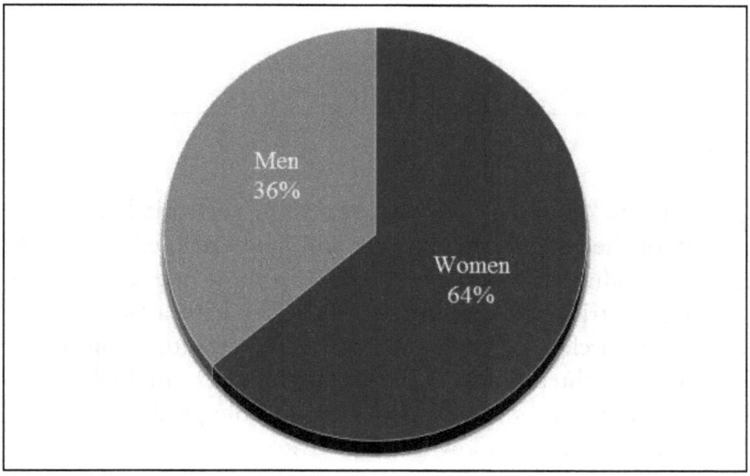

Source: the authors

These data show a higher presence of the female figure in the "act of purchase". In most cases it is the woman who takes care of the shopping and who pays more attention to nutrition with the aim to bring fresh and healthy products to the table. Even if there is an increasing attention to food quality also among men, the women still usually have the larger influence on what the family consumes.

Regarding the *age group*, the sample is divided as follows: one respondent in ten (10%) appears to be a young adult "between 30 and 39 years"; a quarter of respondents (26%) falls within the range of adult from "40 to 49"; just over a third (36%) is between "50 and 59" and a further quarter (28%) is included in the group of young-old between "60 and 70" (figure 8).

Figure 8: Sample by age classes, %

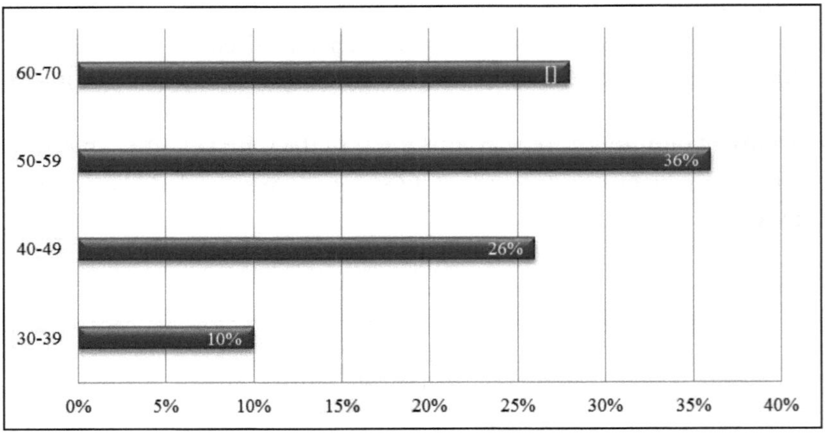

Source: the authors

People between "50 and 59 years" appear to be particularly attentive to the quality of the goods they purchase and more inclined to directly purchase from producers. Younger consumers are more oriented towards buying in large distribution centers; they also may have a lack of time to devote to the search for greater quality. The more mature consumers – distributed in the three most significant class of age – are looking for – besides genuine foods – the direct contact with the producer and the possibility to rediscover the link with their territory.

The profile of the *level of education* (figure 9), of course, turns out to be in close connection with the distribution by age group. The prevailing level of education is that of the High school diploma (upper secondary education) with little less than half of the sample (46%), followed by one-fifth of respondents (22%) with the Middle school; 14% have an elementary License. Finally, a substantial percentage are graduates (18%), significantly higher than that found in the Italian population (12.3%, as stated by the National statistic institute – ISTAT).

Figure 9: Level of education

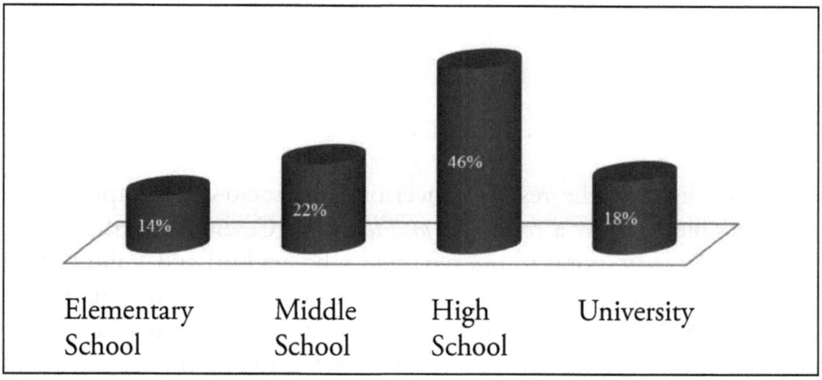

Source: the authors

In summary, it can be said that the consumers of Cesena farmers market are mostly people of average education, driven by motivations of "healthiness" and "localism" rather than by "moral" and "ethical" factors.

The last type of personal data we have taken into account concerns the *professional position* (figure 10).

The farmer's market of Cesena appears to be attended by two main groups of people: "employees" and those who are "no longer in active working position", each representing 40% of the respondents; the remaining fifth is represented by the "self-employed".

The first group, "the employees", can be divided into those who perform "office tasks" (26%), those who perform "manual activities" (8%), and "teachers" (6%). The second group consists of "pensioners" (24%), "housewives" (12%) and "unemployed" (4%). Finally, the third group consists of "self-employed" and "professionals" (10% each).

Figure 10: Occupational typology

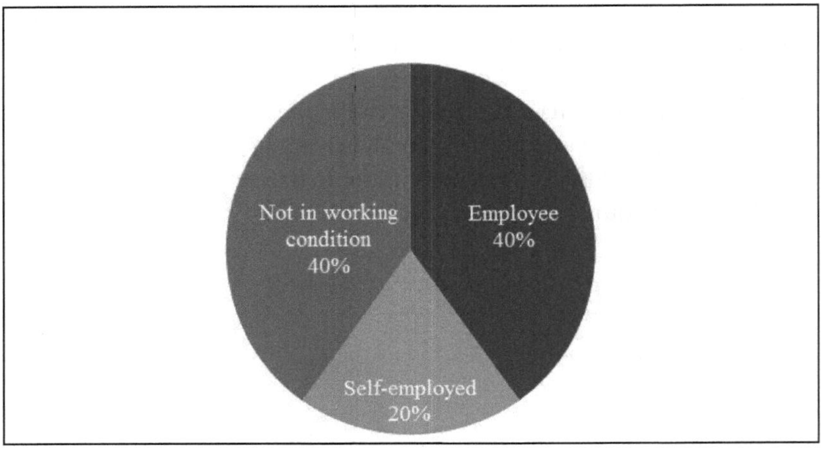

In the light of the results concerning the socio-demographic data, it is possible to draw a *consumer profile* of the Cesena farmer's market. They largely correspond to the type that scholars Lori and Volpi (2007) indicated by the term: "Traditionalist consumers suffer the marketing chaos of the third millennium, and automatically tend to decline the communication complexity of *consumer goods* through the 'use value' and 'exchange value': two criteria which obviously require less cognitive effort" (Lori, Volpi, 2007).

We have seen, in fact, that the "consumer type" of the Cesena farmers' market is predominantly female, aged between "50 and 59 years old" and has not continued their education beyond "high school graduation".

The farmers' market is at the same time old and new. It is an "old" phenomenon because it has its roots in the tradition of the local rural culture, and it is a "new" one because of its innovative arrangement (like involving a network of stakeholders). It is a "space" in which consumers seem to adapt to a clear and explicit tendency to re-evaluate and enhance the "tradition" that – in a sense paradoxically – is manifested as "innovation".

4.3. The origins of a choice: how, when and why

We analyze below the various ways in which consumers have approached the Cesena farmer market. 60% of respondents replied they knew about it through “friends and acquaintances”, 24% “directly from the manufacturers”, the 12% “thanks to job colleagues”, and only 4% through “the local press and television” (figure 11).

Figure 11: How did you know about the farmer market?

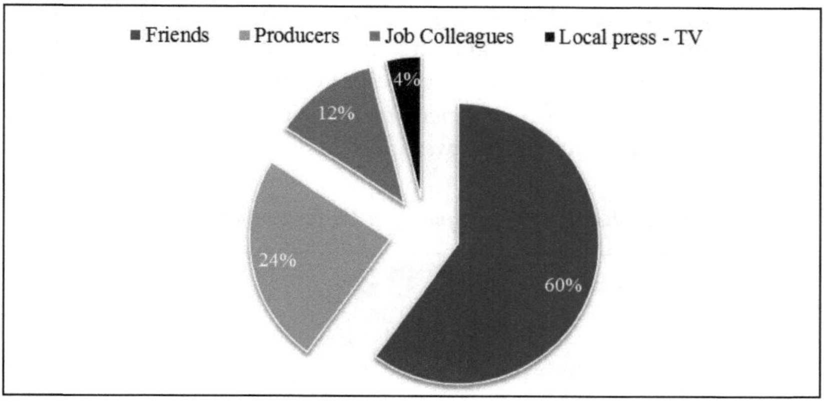

Source: the authors

The first mode that has encouraged a large proportion of consumers to go to the farmers’ market (72%) is the “word of mouth”. It is through the advice of friends, relatives, and co-workers who have attended the Cesena farmer market that the interviewees have known its existence. The “purchase satisfaction” and the “trust relationship” with the producer seem to be the reasons that drive people to recommend this type of consumption. The “word of mouth” is an information dissemination process; it is through the word that social cohesion develops. It is thanks to the opinion shared by the group in which one identifies him or herself and because of his/her personal motivations – such as that of a more responsible style of consumption – that the consumer approaches the farmers’ market.

Also, because of the medium-small dimensions of Cesena (about 97,000 inhabitants),[14] a quarter (24%) of respondents said that it was the farmer that recommended buying the goods from the “market along Savio” (nick name for the local farmer market). Farmers, who for years have sold their products to agricultural cooperatives (for the big retailing chain of distribution, such as supermarkets) and to friends

14 See: <www.comune.cesena.fc.it>, consulted on 10 September 2014.

and acquaintances, may reevaluate their profession and sell freely their products without other intermediaries, thanks to the new regulation[15] of "direct sales".

The Cesena farmers' market is run (organization and management) by two representative organizations: the CIA – Italian farmers confederation and the Provincial federation of coltivatori diretti of Forlì-Cesena. These organizations promote and encourage direct sales in the province. Nevertheless, only two of the fifty respondents (4%) said they were aware of the existence of the farmers' market through advertising: "local television" or articles in "local newspapers".

Figure 12: Purchase frequency at the farmers' market, %

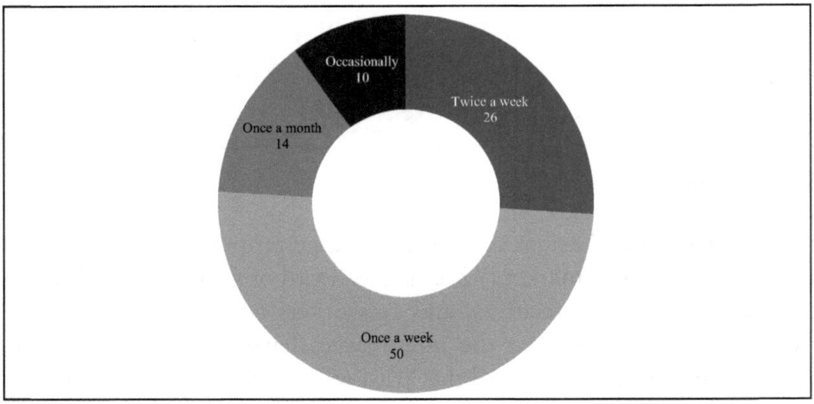

Source: the authors

The consumer purchasing frequency in Cesena farmers' market shows a clear trend: People who frequent in the vast majority of cases do so in "constant manner". Purchasing at the farmers' market, in fact, is not an isolated case dictated by random factors, but instead is determined by well-established reasons.

As many as 50% of respondents said they go there to buy vegetables, fruit, fresh dairy products, and meats "once a week". A quarter (26%) even go "twice a week", while 14% buy "once a month", and only one in 10 does "occasionally" (figure 12).

15 Resolutions of the Cesena Municipality Council No. 35 of 25/02/2010, and No. 77 of 09/06/2011. See link: <https://servizi.comune.cesena.fc.it/applicazioniweb/consultazioneAtti/documenti/home.0.2>, consulted on 10 September 2014.

The advantages of *short chain* occur along three main dimensions:

1) *Economic* – lower food prices for consumers and more profitable for producers;
2) *Environmental* – the offer of "carbon neutral" (km0) reduces energy consumption and pollution associated with the transportation and storage of food in refrigerators;
3) *Social* – a better freshness and healthiness of perishable products, the development of trust in relationships, and exchanges of information without intermediaries between producers and consumers.

It is not only the search for a satisfactory "price-quality" ratio that adds value to the commodity, but also the search of typical local products, to which are attributed a number of values.

The key question for understanding the origins of purchase in Cesena farmers' market concern the "purchase motivations".

Many of the respondents identified a plurality of purchase reasons; the most frequent is undoubtedly "the quality and freshness" of the products (see graph below). It is interesting to note that none of the respondents are motivated merely by a "cost savings" motive. Figure 13 shows consumer preferences of the Cesena farmers' market in respect to the five "reasons to buy" included in the questionnaire.

Figure 13: Purchase motivations

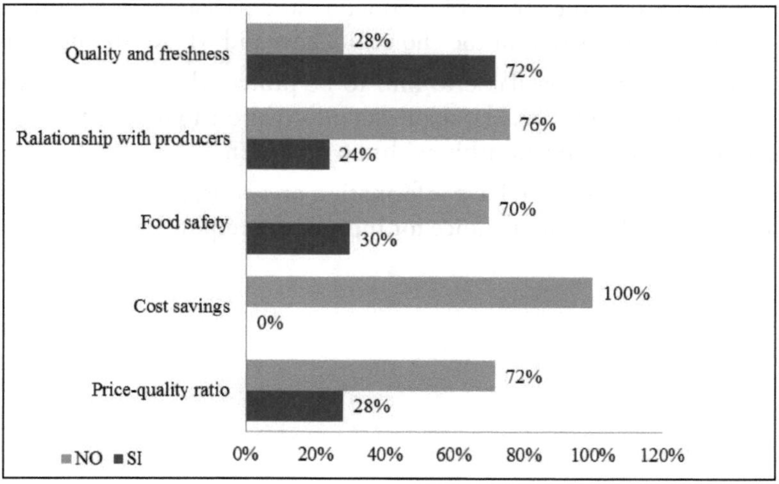

Source: the authors

The attention towards "quality" is one of the finest examples of a *responsible consumer* behavior. Today's consumer is increasingly aware and informed on the issues of *quality* and food *safety*, on nutritional properties of food, and on the ethical aspects of *sustainability* in a context of globalization of markets; he/she tends to be critical of the products, especially in the food industry, considering they are not in line with the quality and safety requirements. As noted by Fabris (2003):

> In the transition to the *post-modernity* the protagonist is a new consumer who has little in common with the traditional figure that we know. Not only he has now completed his novitiate as a consumer and has become more demanding, cunning, selective, proactive, unfaithful to the brand. But it is radically rewriting our knowledge on consumption. That, in addition to its tangible meanings, it is increasing its aspects of "sign", "communication", "social exchange". A new language, that of consumption, with its own grammar and syntax, which are essential to be learned. A new consumer who changed skin in search of *experiences* rather than products, *emotions* and *sensations* rather than use values. (Fabris, 2003).

The direct relationship with the producer – which disappeared with industrialization and globalization – is recovered just by buying in farmers' markets.

The distance created between producer and consumer with the elongation of the chain implies a loss of control by the consumer in terms of quality and safety, especially for the health. He can no longer have direct control over the phases of production and packaging of foods, but he can assert his position in the choice of "how and where" to buy food.

The only defense available to him to be protected from the risks in alimentation is *knowledge*, like acquiring information about products and establishing a direct relationship with the producer.

Being able to speak, to have information on goods, and to know their history is a valid reason of choice for most of the respondents.

Figure 14: Relationship with the producer, %

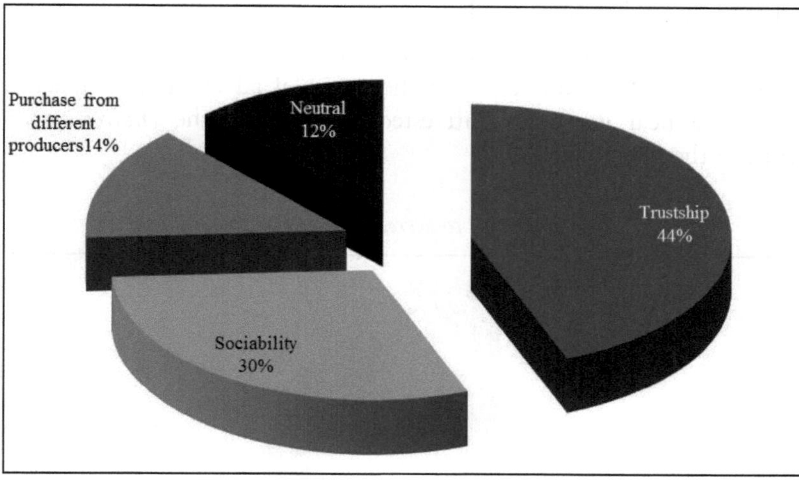

Source: the authors

Buying at farmers' markets means giving the food a meaning that goes beyond that of simple consumer goods; instead, it is assigned a *relational value*. In fact, 44% of respondents (figure 14) believe that the "trust relationship" that is established with the manufacturer is an essential factor.

The "face to face" relationship creates *sociability* between the consumer and the producer, and the continuity in purchasing creates the opportunity to reinforce this relationship.

From the encounter between the producer and the consumer stems excellent results:

a) the producer sells his/her merchandise – typical of the territory in which he/she operates – at a price that allows adequate remuneration;
b) consumers buy fresh and guaranteed goods, which have not experienced price increases and alterations due to transportation, and he/she became aware of the "typicality" of local products, becoming an *informed (conscious) consumer*.

The mere economic aspect is not important to the farmers' market customer, and the centrality of the relationship with the producer is a proof. The *short chain* has the aim of bringing the consumer to the "source" of the product, and this tends to naturalize an economic process as that of the exchange of goods.

The "careful and responsible consumers" are sensitive to product information and do not represent the target of advertising campaigns, but they appear genuinely interested in knowing the *environmental impact* of the goods they buy.

Figure 15: It is important to decrease the environmental impact?

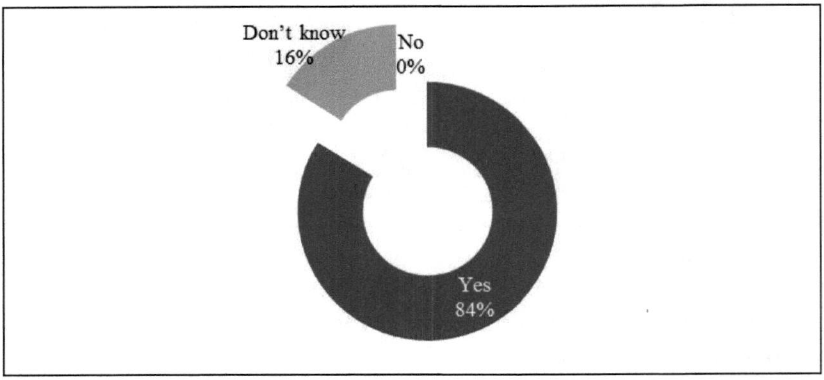

Source: the authors

A striking 84% of respondents (figure 15) argue that they are interested in reducing the "environmental impact" as a result of the purchase of "zero kilometer" products at the farmers' market.

Consumers of the Cesena farmers' market are convinced that with their small daily gesture they can reduce waste and, in the long-term, have a positive impact on the environmental system.

The increasing air pollution and un-sustainability of urban areas impose choices that cannot be postponed any longer; these also are involved with the activities of daily consumption.

Individuals with an ecological sensitivity are increasingly pushed to revise their *way of life*, beginning from "alimentation style" and moving towards a more critical and sustainable style of consumption.

More and more often, we speak of "food kilometers" as an index to measure the environmental impact of the food that arrives on our tables. The more kilometers a food has traveled, the more energy it has consumed, the more fossil fuels have been burned, and the more greenhouse gases it has produced.

The classic example are the vegetables or fruits that we eat "out of season" and that often come from distant continents, transported by airplanes, but also from seasonal products coming from other countries that compete with local ones.

Shopping at a farmers' market means supporting the development in a social and ecological way, choosing local products – which do not require transportation with an environmental impact –, and not wasting paper and plastic for packaging.

Nowadays behind the act of "eating" hides the rediscovery of our own territory, of our rural world, too long forgotten and abandoned.

Just in the Province of Forlì-Cesena – a territory largely rural and with a wide agricultural and alimentary cultivations sector –, several aspects are increasingly getting attention: 1. the local dimension; 2. the characteristics of products; 3. the folklore (local culture); 4. the various elements that characterize an area that has always been distinguished for its genuine flavors and its peasant traditions.

One of the questions asked to the Cesena farmers' market consumers concerns precisely the "weight" that had the fact that with their purchase the *local agricultural production* is promoted and sustained, enabling them to keep alive the relationship with the territory.

As we can see in figure 16, more than half of the respondents (52%) say that they give a "very high weight" to the fact of being able to purchase products from local farmers while keeping alive the relationship with their own territory. Only one respondent in ten (10%) declares to be "little concerned" about it, and even a smaller group of people answers "do not know" (8%).

Figure 16: Importance of the relationship with the territory, %

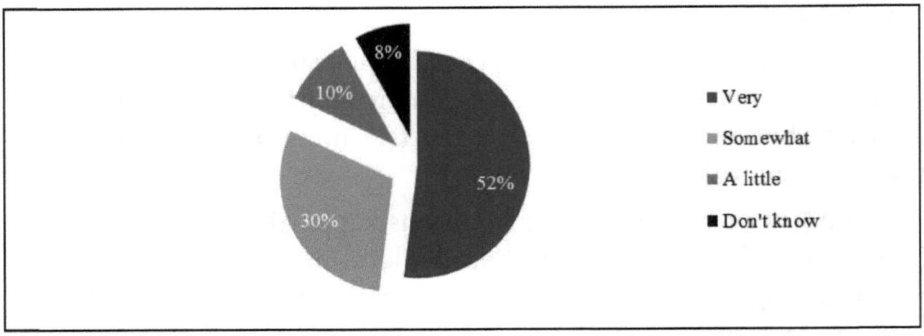

Source: the authors

5. The social impact of the farmer's market

There is a large debate among opinion makers, policy makers, managers of social enterprises, and service providers on how to evaluate (measure) the social impact of a given policy, action, program, or project in the social sphere.

As has been noted by several parties (Bassi, 2012), that measurement (detection) is particularly difficult for a number of reasons, related both to the intrinsic characteristics of the field of intervention: "the social", which by its nature involves the production, the exchange, and the consumption of goods and services that are by large "intangibles"; both for the discrepancy between the evaluation time and the time at which presumably the most consistent effects of the analyzed program (time dimension) will occur; and, finally, the difficulties related to the allocation of causal effects to the intervention in question (given the multi-causality presents in the social sphere).

For these reasons, we have put in place a multiannual program of research aimed at the development of a *conceptual framework* that provides a solid scientific basis for the preparation of a *social impact assessment system* that is more extensive and detailed than those currently existing and that use – in the majority of cases – "management type" conceptual models. The conceptual framework has been called SAVE i.e.: Social added value evaluation (Bassi, 2014).

The idea/concept of social added value is wider and deeper than that of social impact as it takes into account all stages of the value creation chain that a social enterprise, or a network of non-profit organizations, puts in place during the realization of a particular action, service, policy, or program (Bassi, Vincenti, 2015).

The SAV is the result of a series of *virtuous circles* that are activated – consciously or unconsciously, directly or indirectly – from the activity of an NPO or SE whenever they act as subjects of civil society that is responding properly to the values, norms, cultural orientations peculiar to them and constitute them as intermediate bodies, as actors of the capacity for autonomous self-organization of the citizens, or even in societal arrangements of the high (post) modernity or advanced (late) modernity.

In the specific case analyzed here, the farmers' market example, the following actors/social subjects emerge:

- Citizens as consumers;
- Small local agricultural producers;
- The level of local government;
- The public administration agencies;
- Associations representing farmers;
- Environmental and consumers organizations.

Usually the *process of activation* of a farmers' market follows a common pathway, that can be summarized in the following phases:

1. In the first place, a group of civil society organizations (environmental, consumers, slow food movement, etc.) (Forno, Graziano, 2014) puts in place an advocacy campaign, pushing the local administration (municipality) towards the adoption of deliberation in order to activate a farmers' market;
2. After a long period of bargaining, the Municipality council enacts a resolution that establishes the institution of a farmers' market as an experiment (for a limited period of time, usually 6 months or one year);
3. There are counter-powers as well. For example, usually the big umbrella association that represents the interest of small and medium retailers (merchants, shop keepers) opposes the opening of a farmers' market; that is why (as a compromise) the Municipality council adopts the deliberation of activation with several restrictions (such as: days of opening; hours of activity, etc.) and as a temporary concession;

4. After a certain period of activity (three to four months), the farmers' market results to be a very successful policy, and the Municipality is obliged to extend the period of experimentation (usually to another year) or, more often, to adopt the initiative as a permanent policy;
5. Also the retailers' interest representation associations should recognize the success of the idea and, unable to obstruct (block, impede) it, they start a strategy of imitation and replication in the shops of their members;
6. Once the farmers' market becomes a permanent activity, usually, the citizens as customers and the small producers (local farmers) – individual or associated (Guidi, Andretta, 2015) –, are able to obtain an extension of both the days and the times of opening.

By research and analysis outlined above, it is possible to observe the activation of, at least, the following "virtuous circles" (taking into account the three dimensions of social action: micro, meso and macro).

A] at the micro level:

1st – citizens have access to wholesome seasonal food that triggers a virtuous circle that leads them to reflect on the "practice of consumption", to develop a "critical and responsible attitude" towards alimentation, and to adopt a healthy life style;

2nd – the rediscovery of typical fruits and vegetables that disappeared as a result of the industrialization process of the agro-food sector. This triggers a virtuous circle that leads people and families to promote the cultural identity of their territory and to rediscover traditional recipes from the past; this also favors the intergenerational exchange, for example between grandparents and grandchildren (educational dimension);

3rd – the position in an area easily reached on foot by people of all ages. Additionally, this allows people with limited mobility to retain or re-acquire some independence in managing their daily lives, regarding a central element such as "food supply" (grocery shopping), while also encouraging residential areas of elderly and/or not completely self-sufficient people next to the historic centers. This allows the specific urban area to be kept alive and not having it turn into a high-density area of offices that is sparsely populated and frequented outside of working hours;

B] at the meso-level:

4th – occupation, revitalization, and social control of an urban space abandoned or under-used and therefore at risk of social degradation (urban petty crime, drug dealing, prostitution, etc.). The measures put in place by the city administration to adequately "equip" the area in order to accommodate the producer/vendor stalls, have improved street furniture and lighting, making this space usable also in other times of the day to the inhabitants of the place, especially to families with small children;

C] at the macro level:

5th – the farmers' market allows small farmers to achieve economic integration, however limited but significant, which allows them to stay active, not to having to close the agricultural enterprise, and to continue their presence on site. This territorial settlement qualifies itself as a real "presidium" of maintenance of the territory. It in fact counters the depopulation of the countryside and hilly areas (foothills), and it lets small farmers continue to treat the soil, keeping the forested areas clean, guaranteeing the channeling and drainage of rain water, and thereby reducing the risk of landslides and floods that for decades have been ravaging – on a seasonal basis – our country;

6th – the fostering of a commercial outlet for local products (km0), has a positive effect in terms of reducing pollution and urban traffic, and thus – indirectly – it produces a significant impact in terms of "quality of life" and individual and collective "wellbeing".

The six aforementioned *virtuous circles* (but constitute only one example and many others could be found by a more in-depth analysis or using different points of observation) show in a simple and immediate way that even though it may seem to be trivial politics in the decision to grant a public space in some moments of the week for the conduct of a farmers' market, the farmers' market has a number of beneficial effects and positive outcomes on the surrounding community and on the involved stakeholders, which go far beyond the intentions of the promoters of the initiative. And that it is possible to do "good policy" without necessarily requiring the use of huge economic resources and long-term investments.

6. Final remarks

If until a few years ago the main tendency was to have fruits and vegetables from every place and every season, nowadays the attention to *food source* – meat, dairy products, fruit – is pushing more and more towards a rediscovery of respect for *cycles of nature*, seasonality, and consequently of preservation of the places where the goods are cultivated.

For those who frequent the farmers' market in Cesena, there is a close link between product and territory, and this link is to be considered as an *added value* of the product itself. It is an expression of authenticity and food safety.

The link with the "source" allows us to rediscover the relationship with the earth and the real relationship, unmediated, with those who cultivate the fields and harvest the products. To valorize the tradition and the specific characteristics of local products, to rediscover the relationship between seasonality and food, to highlight the work of the farmer in respect of the environment, to encourage biodiversity-farmers' markets have contributed towards the rise of these new components in modern culture. The quality and safety of products, a more *responsible consumption*, the rediscovery of their own land, and new kinds of relationships are the motivations (reasons) shared by the farmers' market consumers.

They are the key features that refer to the image of a "rural world" from which our roots arise. A world of small and simple things. In a sense paradoxically, this rediscovery is made possible in the most advanced stage of post-modernity and globalization process.

References

AAVV, 2001, *I farmer's market di Taranto, la città dei due mari*, <http://sapori-italia.it/it/blog/i-farmers-market-di-taranto-la-citta-dei-due-mari>, consulted on 10 September 2014.

Aguglia L., 2009, "La filiera corta: una opportunità per agricoltori e consumatori", *Agriregionieuropa*, giugno, 5 (17), <http://agriregionieuropa.univpm.it/content/article/31/17/la-filiera-corta-una-opportunita-agricoltori-e-consumatori>, consulted on 10 September 2014.

Bassi A., 2012, "How to measure the intangibles? Towards a system of indicators (SAVE) for the measurement of the performance of social enterprises", *in* F. Hans-Werner, J. Howaldt, J. Hochgerner (eds.), *Challenge*

Social Innovation. Potentials for Business, Social Entrepreneurship, Welfare and Civil Society, Berlin, Springer, p. 326-50.

Bassi A., 2014, "The Social Added Value of Third Sector Organizations", *in* L. Boccacin (ed.), *Third Sector, Partnerships and Social Outcome: The Cases of Italy and Ireland*, Vita e Pensiero, Milano, p. 76-108.

Bassi A., Vincenti G., 2015, "Toward a New Metrics for the Evaluation of the Social Added Value of Social Enterprises", *Revista de Economía Pública, Social y Cooperativa*, 83: 9-42.

Berry W., 2009, *Intervista con Wendell Berry, il guru del km zero*, <https://www.gdoweek.it/intervista-con-wendell-berry-il-guru-del-km-zero/>, consulted on 10 September 2014.

Coldiretti, 2011, "Gli italiani e l'alimentazione: strategie adattive".

Fabris G., 2003, *Il nuovo consumatore: verso il verso il postmoderno*, Milano, Franco Angeli.

Forno F., Graziano P.R., 2014, "Sustainable community movement organisations", *Journal of Consumer Culture*, 14 (2): 1-19, <http://joc.sagepub.com/content/early/2014/03/19/1469540514526225>, consulted on 10 September 2014.

Franco S., Marino D., 2012, "Il mercato della Filiera Corta. I farmers' market come luogo di incontro di produttori e consumatori", *Gruppo 2013 Working Paper*, 19, <http://www.gruppo2013.it/working-paper/Documents/WEB%20Working%20Paper%20n.19%20-%20Gruppo%202013.pdf>, consulted on 10 September 2014.

Giarè F., Giuca S. (a cura di), 2012, *Agricoltori e filiera corta. Profili giuridici e dinamiche socio-economiche*, INEA – Istituto Nazionale di Economia Agraria, Roma, <https://flore.unifi.it/retrieve/handle/2158/778958/24184/2012%20-%20INEA%20-%20Agricoltori%20e%20FilieraCorta.pdf>, consulted on 10 September 2014.

Guidi F., 2009, *Filiera corta: percorsi di innovazione tecnici, organizzativi e sociali nella gestione strategica delle nicchie. Esperienze in Toscana e in Provenza*, Tesi di Dottorato, Università di Bologna, <https://core.ac.uk/download/files/330/11012267.pdf>, consulted on 10 September 2014.

Guidi R., Andretta M., 2015, "Between resistance and resilience: how do Italian solidarity purchase groups change in times of crisis and austerity", *Partecipazione e conflitto*, 8 (2): 443-77, <http://siba-ese.unisalento.it/index.php/paco/issue/view/1290>, consulted on 10 September 2014.

Lori M., Volpi F., 2007, *Scegliere il "bene". Indagine sul consumo responsabile*, Milano, Franco Angeli.

Noferi M., Panichi C., Scarpellini T., 2007, *Il Mercatale del Valdarno*, Montevarchi, <http://www.regione.toscana.it/documents/guest/Documenti/Pubblicazioni/Mercatale>, consulted on 10 September 2014.

Payne T., 2002, *U.S. Farmers Markets – 2000: A study of Emerging Trends*, US Department of Agriculture.

Chapter 5

Social Economy and Territorial Development in Romania

The Challenge of Clustering Coops and New Social Enterprises in the Post-Communist Re-Construction of Rural Production and Trade Chains

Cristina Barna & Ancuţa Vameşu

Laboratorul de Solidaritate – Solidarity Laboratory

Social economy can be considered an alternative meso-economic model for many territories in Romania, a determinant of sustainable territorial development, especially in poor rural areas affected by economic downturn following the post-communist transition. A strategy of strengthening of social capital and s building-up of social enterprises could lead to the re-construction of viable territories with new competitive advantages, able to meet local needs in an innovative manner, and thus acting locally, to contribute to solving some of Romania's major socio-economic challenges: big gaps in living standards between rural and urban areas, poverty and social exclusion, unemployment and substantial informal and black economy.

This paper has three main research objectives. In the first part we analyze the stage of re-creation of social capital (first objective) and re-configuration of social economy in Romania at national level after the communist fall (second objective), considering theoretical clarification of the terms "social capital", "social economy", "territorial/local development" and an analysis of the inter-relations social enterprises – social capital – territorial development (third objective).

The second part is a case study which analyses the re-configuration of social economy at the level of an integrated rural territory placed around a market town assessing the role of social enterprises in the local production chains in Horezu. This case study includes the elaboration of a local socio-economic profile of the territory, a profile which contains an analysis of social economy development and, an insight into existing production chains. The case study answers the third objective of assessing the potential for collective action in the form of cooperatives and other new social enterprises, their role in re-thinking production chains in Horezu, and their contribution to the re-construction of the territory. The choice of the territory starts from the hypothesis that given the fact that the socio-economic conditions following transition from communist, state controlled economy in particular in the agriculture and forestry sectors in rural areas are similar in some respects with the historic conditions which have led in the 19th century small farmers in Europe to networking, cooperation and creation of cooperatives, in order to survive during difficult economic circumstances the strategy adopted by locals could be similar (Svendsen, Svendsen, 2004).

The purpose of the case study is to assess the evolution of social economy organizations and of social entrepreneurial development strategies of various stakeholders in a traditional mountain rural area. We look in particular at social economy types of strategies for consolidation of small farmers and the sustainable management of natural goods (forests and pastures) through commons – re-instated traditional, centuries old, collective ownership and management organizations drawing from the general landscape of the social economy in the given territory.

1. Recreation of social capital and reconfiguration of social economy in Romania after the communist fall

1.1. Back to a new "old" resource – social capital

1.1.1. Social capital: theoretical approaches

Social capital is defined in terms of norms, networks and trust, and the way these allow individuals and communities to be more effective in achieving their objectives (Schuller, 2002). The social capital, understood as a tool of adaptation, can be of key importance in contributing to a wide range of positive outcomes, including higher educational achievement, higher income, life satisfaction and social cohesion, and, finally, economic growth and sustainable development. As such, it has become a concept increasingly present in debates about local economic and social development and social economy.

The core idea regarding the social capital is very simple: social networks have value. In scientific literature, three basic types of social capital have been identified (Woolcock, quoted from Côté, 2001): *bonding social capital* which refers typically to relations among members of families and ethnic groups; *bridging social capital* which refers to relations with distant friends, associates and colleagues and *linking social capital* which refers to relations between different social strata in a hierarchy where power, social status and wealth are accessed by different groups.

Robert D. Putman in his famous book *Bowling alone: The Collapse and the Revival of American Community* (2000) looked to whether social capital is bonding (or exclusive) and/or bridging (or inclusive). A step forward in the conceptualization of social capital was proposed by Michael Woolcock who introduced the third type of social capital: *linking social capital*. In his opinion "social capital also has a vertical dimension, which can be called 'linkages'. […] The capacity to leverage resources, ideas and information from formal institutions beyond the community, most notably the state, is a key function of linking social capital" (Woolcock, 2002).

Social capital allows individuals, groups and communities to resolve collective problems more easily. Collective action involves use of norms and networks in situations when individuals might otherwise be reluctant to be socially engaged. In this way the norms of reciprocity and networks help ensure compliance with a collectively desirable behavior. For example, better social connections can help to solve the "free-rider" problem in providing public goods, or they can create trust between individuals in the absence of explicit contracts (Glaeser, 2001: 4).

CONCISE project[1] proposed a working definition of social capital that encapsulates the key elements we are discussing: social capital consists of resources within communities which are created through the presence of high levels of trust, reciprocity and mutuality, shared norms of behavior, shared commitment and belonging, both formal and informal social networks, and effective information channels, which may be used productively by individuals and groups to facilitate actions to benefit

1 CONCISE, "The contribution of social capital in the social economy to local economic development in Western Europe", funded under the Key Action "Improving the socio-economic knowledge base" of FP 5 (1998-2002).

individuals, groups and the community more generally. These maybe grouped into three categories: trust, social networks and reciprocity/mutuality are about relationships between individuals and organizations; shared norms of behavior and shared commitment are about more than one individual and/or organization sharing values, sharing a way of thinking; and effective information channels which permit individuals and organizations to access information from outside and within their community (Kay, 2006: 163-4).

David Skidmore synthesized four main pathways through which social capital enhances economic performance, which, in our opinion, can be applied also for the case of establishing social economy organizations and to local economic development: 1. High levels of social trust and strong traditions of generalized reciprocity reduce transaction costs (Fukuyama, 1994; Putnam, 1993; Narayan, Pritchett, 1999, quoted from Skidmore, 2001: 59). Societies with high levels of trust and reciprocity rely less heavily upon formal institutions for enforcing contracts and thus pay less for the overhead costs such institutions generate; 2. By providing individual members with sources of support during times of trouble, social networks spread risk and allow the group as a whole to engage in overall higher levels of innovation and risk-taking (Narayan, Pritchett, 1999, quoted from Skidmore, 2001: 59); 3. Social networks facilitate the rapid dissemination of information and innovation among members and reduce the asymmetries of information that can otherwise discourage profitable transactions (Narayan, Pritchett, 1999, quoted from Skidmore, 2001: 59); and 4. Social networks allow members to solve collective action problems more easily with less fear of defection and free riding (Putnam, 1993, quoted from Skidmore, 2001: 59).

Considering all four pathways described above, it is clear that social capital could be a determinant in the appearance and evolution of social economy organizations – associations and cooperatives – and of the local development process, especially in time of (post)crisis, when reduced transaction costs, new sources of support for affected people, new innovative models and social involvement are required for recovery.

There are yet no commonly agreed indicators to measure social capital. Therefore, in most cases proxy indicators are used such as: membership in local associations and networks, indicators of collective action, of trust and adherence to norms.[2] Associational involvement is one such

[2] CONCISE, *op. cit.*

indicator – various forms of participation in voluntary organizations, membership, participation in activities, donations, voluntary work (Scrivens, Smith, 2013). Associations and cooperatives result of mutuality and reciprocity and are formal networks that can be considered important sources of social capital. Although criticized for being an indirect measure of associational involvement, the use of administrative data on the density of associations is useful when accurate survey data are not available.

1.1.2. Romania: low level of social capital after communist fall; a long process of social capital re-creation

Totalitarian regimes tend to destroy social capital through excessive control of social life and over reliance on state for delivery of public goods. Romania's social capital and social economy were heavily affected by the communist period characterized by no social and civic participation, lack of trust, and forced volunteer work. After the communist fall, from 1990 Romania faced and is still facing the challenge of re-creation of social capital.

Trying to briefly assess the level of social capital in Romania, we can have a look at *volunteering*. After 1990, volunteering had a positive trend, with the first steps of citizens' involvement in NGOs, changing the negative image of forced work from communist period, with a variety of initiatives such as of promoting volunteering of employees in corporations and foreign NGOs, the development of organizations and centers dedicated to or based exclusively on volunteering. Though, Romania is still below the EU average when speaking about population involvement in voluntary activities. According to Special Eurobarometer 75.2 "Volunteering and intergenerational solidarity" (2011), on average in EU 27, close to a quarter of respondents currently undertake a voluntary activity (24%), while in Romania only 14% of the respondents carry out voluntary activity on a regular basis or occasionally. When asked about the two main benefits of volunteering, on average in EU 27, respondents primarily mentioned maintaining and reinforcing social cohesion (34%), while in Romania the percentage was 23%.

Trying an exploratory assessment of *trust* level, and in particular trust in institutions, we can observe different trends after the communist fall: a positive trend of the trust in NGOs, which could be considered an important determinant of social economy development (considering the fact that social economy emerged from NGO sector – to be explained later), a low level of trust in public institutions (with higher percentages of trust for local institutions, potentially an asset for local, territorial development approach), in the context of a considerable negative trend of the turnout at national elections (which can be considered as evidencing indirectly population's need for another type of socio-economic model).

More specifically, according to a national representative opinion survey conducted in 2010 by the Civil society development foundation, the level of trust in NGOs in 2010 was 32% in the context of a relatively small number of organizations, and many respondents not being yet aware of their existence (rate of "don't know" answer is quite high for these institutions) still reduced as absolute value, but on a positive trend from 1998 when the percentage of the respondents with high and very high trusts in NGOs was only 19% according to Soros Barometer 1998-2007 (quoted from Lambru, Vameşu, 2010), and in the general context of lack of trust in public institutions, which continues to date. In 2014, according to a INSCOP Research, the level of trust in institutions (% of respondents with high and very high trust) was: Municipal councils (42.1%), County councils (32.1%), Government (30.6%), Constitutional court (28.7%), Presidency (22.6%), Parliament (19.5%), political parties (11.7%). This low level of trust in institutions is correlated with the negative trend of the turnout at the elections, which dropped with approximately 50% in 2012 comparative with 1990 (for example, the turnout at parliamentary elections evolution was: 1990: 86.19%, 1992: 76.29%, 1996: 76.01%, 2000: 65.31%, 2004: 58.51%, 2008: 39.2%, 2012: 41.72%). The loss of public interest for parliamentary elections is more pronounced than for local elections (1990: approx. 65%, 2008: approx. 50% [Alexandru *et al.,* 2009: 10-1]), which may suggest, in this respect, stronger social capital in local territories.

A good indication of the rhythm of re-creation of social capital in Romania post-communism may be given by *the annual rates of registrations for associations after 1990.* Membership in an association means besides a form of involvement, also networking, a shared mission and objectives, volunteering, so generally – social capital. As it is seen in the bellow table, the evolution of the associations recorded in NGOs Register – Ministry of Justice in the period 2000-2012 is characterized by a growth rate of the number of organizations, in 2012 Romania having a total of 55,596 recorded associations, and 16,504 foundations.

Table 1: Annual rates of registration 1990-2012 for associations in Romania

Year	*No. of New Associations Registered annually*	*Year to year comparison of registration rate of new associations, %*	*Total No. of associations registered Cumulative*
<1990	5		
1990	1,186		1,191
1991	809	-31.8	2,000
1992	742	-8.3	2,742
1993	1,138	53.4	3,880
1994	1,492	31.1	5,372
1995	1,897	27.1	7,269
1996	2,208	16.4	9,477
1997	2,360	6.9	11,837
1998	1,338	-43.3	13,175
1999	1,395	4.3	14,570
2000	2,251	61.4	16,821
2001	2,801	24.4	19,622
2002	3,938	40.6	23,560
2003	2,242	-43.1	25,802
2004	2,225	-0.8	28,027
2005	2,687	20.8	30,714
2006	**3,330**	23.9	34,044
2007	**3,432**	3.1	37,476
2008	**3,014**	-12.2	40,490
2009	**3,481**	15.5	43,971
2010	**3,671**	5.5	47,642
2011	**4,028**	9.7	51,670
2012	**3,925**	-2.6	**55,595**

Source: Barna, 2014: 29-30

Analyzing annual registration rates for associations, we can observe peaks in 1993, 2000 and 2002. The year 2000 peak coincides with the new legislation for associations and foundations/NGOs-G.O. 26/2000, 10 years after Revolution which liberalized conditions for forming an association: reduced minimum number of members from 20 to 3, lifted the requirement for an administrative approval before court registration. The previous law dated since 1924 (Law 21/1924 – known as Marzescu Law, considered at the time one of the most modern laws in Europe) and miraculously not repelled during communist regime and re-activated after 1990, was used until 2000, when, after a significant practice, issues that were necessary to be changed were identified.

This brief analysis shows a generally low level of social capital in Romania, but also some positive trends that could constitute the basis for a strategy of social capital strengthening especially in local areas. The low level of social capital is an important reality which must be taken into account in the current process of social economy development, a barrier to overcome, a challenge for practitioners and policy makers.

1.2. Discovering, re-discovering, and development of social economy

1.2.1. Reconfiguration of social economy in post-communist Romania: from history to present

In Romania social economy is still a relatively new concept, mainly embedded in NGO sector and in civil society. Despite the fact that Romania has a long tradition in social economy, this was unfortunately interrupted by the communist period, which affected the essence of volunteering and cooperative movement, and created in this way some barriers that we need to face and to struggle to overcome even nowadays. We can speak about social economy in Romania starting with the year 1835 (see table 2).

Table 2: History of social economy in Romania before 1989 Revolution

1835	• The agronomic and manufacturing society (*The Phalanstery from Scaieni*) – one of the first forms of SE in Romania
Since 1845	• 1851 – First popular bank is established in Transylvania in Bistrita almost simultaneously with the credit coops in Germany Schul Delish and Raiffaieisen models • 1855 – In Brăila, the first credit, savings and mutual loan associations being established. A precursor of todays' credit unions • 1860 – Ion Ionescu de la Brad, a famous agriculture professor and rural development promoter establishes the first popular bank in a village Brad, Roman • 1873 – first consumer cooperative • In 1886 first rural popular bank "*Frăţia*" is established in Domneşti – Muscel and first rural consumer coop "*Economatul*" in Retevoieşti

1903-1935	• First Cooperative Law – already 700 popular banks in existence at the time – in 1903. The Law on popular rural banks and their Central Caisse, which through later modifications will regulate all other types of cooperatives • Romanian King Ferdinand attends the Congress of Cooperatives 1925 • 1929 – "Law for organization of cooperatives", which is revised several times. In 1935 the Law is revised to allow for various forms of cooperatives: credit cooperatives and popular banks, agricultural land purchase or lease, agricultural cooperatives, worker coops, agricultural machinery coops, marketing coops, housing coops, forestry and fishing coops • Development of the cooperative movement • In 1,938 worker cooperatives were providing work places for 1,150,000 workers
1921	• The first Romanian regulation on associations and foundations
1947-1948	• The civil society and associative structures susceptible of conflict with communist interests were dissolved (1,000 local and national organizations)
1948	• Disabled workers' cooperatives were set up
1948-1989	• Despite democratic appearances, the remaining organizations were an ideological tool • Forced membership; forced volunteering

Sources: 1. *Research Report on Social Economy in Romania from a Compared European Perspective*, MLFSP, Bucharest 2011, p. 35

2. <http://www.centrocoop.com/istoric/evolu538ia_coopera538iei_de_consum_in_538arile_romane-53-996-ro.html>, consulted on 1 September 2015

3. "Ce este cooperatia?", 2010, <http://emiliacorbu.ro/2010/05/ce-este-cooperatia/>, consulted on 1 September 2015; "REZULTATELE COOPERAŢIEI", 2010, <http://emiliacorbu.ro/2010/05/rezultatele-cooperatiei/>, consulted on 1 September 2015

The period after the 1989 Revolution can be divided into two different periods: 1989-2005 from the beginning of post-communist transition to the launch of a first national support program for social economy development and the period 2006-to date. The sector of social economy, the part of the economy grouping cooperatives, mutuals and credit unions and non-profit sector had no common identity as social economy in Romania prior to 2005. In the period 1989-2005 in Romania we had a declining cooperative sector (number of members of cooperatives going down from over 1 million to below 30,000), a stagnating credit union sector and a thriving non-profit sector which grew exponentially getting in 2012 to approximately 40,000 active organizations over 130,000 employees, the three sectors with distinct identities enjoying limited to no visibility. The legal framework for associations has a number of ambiguities related to the possibility of non-profit entities to conduct economic activities (associations may carry out any direct economic activities, if they have accessory character and they are closely related to the main aim of the association, but the "accessory character" is not clearly defined), and the legislation for cooperatives has been reformed in 2005 turning cooperatives closer to commercial companies – the cooperatives may distribute part of the profit generated in proportion to the capital contribution of the cooperative members while the sector itself only partially enforces in practice the internationally recognized traditional principles of cooperatives. Also, during the years after the change of political regime, when most state property companies were privatized, coop membership has dramatically declined, small members being bought out generally by the members of managing bodies – property/assets have been concentrated and the social purpose having thus been lost. Previously Romania had an important network of rural consumer coops which served two functions: on one side as retail shops for underserved territories and on the other side as marketing of agricultural products from small farmers. Most consumer coop retail shops have been leased by the "privatized" coops to one of their members or to entrepreneurs on the local market now running private shops in the same locations. Although in some aspects, the cooperative operational model is similar to that of a commercial company, the mechanism of democratic governance (one person, one vote) make the decision rights not to be in proportion to the capital contribution of cooperative members like in commercial companies case, and their mission to serve the common interest of the members makes them be part of the social economy (Barna, Vameşu, 2014).

The social economy concept has gained more significant public attention in Romania following support given through the European Social Fund, Operational Programme for Human Resource Development (OPHRD) following a lobby campaign by the NGO Sector representatives involved in the programming debates in the period 2005-2006. Previously there were initiatives of "enterprising non-profits" (around 10-15% out of total non-profits had reported income generating-economic activities during 2000-2009) and income generating projects in poor rural and some Roma communities and of social service providers such as Caritas and a number of protected workshops that could fall under the broad definition of social enterprise, as well as a significant credit unions and mutual financial help movement of the old age. As a consequence of these debates the OPHRD has designed a Major area of intervention the development of social economy allocating €600 mil. for grants. Around 200 projects have been financed in the period 2007-2013. In this way, EU funds have played an important role for the visibility of social economy, having financed numerous initiatives with a variety of approaches which provided information/awareness raising, training, start-up advice, created local/regional resource centers and, in rather few cases, direct financial support for enterprise start-ups. According to the Annual Report for 2012, this program created 261 new social enterprises with €150 million. Regarding the number of jobs created by the program, this indicator has registered a spectacular growth in 2012 compared to 2011, increasing the number of jobs created approximately 17 times. The total number of jobs created by social economy structures in this program (2007-2012) was 4,684 jobs in 2012, a 129% increase from 3,630 expected by the program with only 35% of the funds allocated (Barna, Vameşu, 2014).

These initiatives gave a lot of visibility to the social economy concept and generated debates around the various concepts such as social economy and social entrepreneurship. At present there is still no common understanding around the concepts of social economy and of social enterprise, many approaches co-exist. As stated in SEFORIS Romania Country Report 2014 (Etchart *et al.,* 2014), in Romania, currently social enterprises are seen by the general public and key stakeholders as a way to promote economic and social inclusion. There are several definitions of social enterprises and related concepts of social economy, social entrepreneurship inspired from international definitions or other European legislative models. For example, the project *Making Social Economy Visible in Romania* financed by European Commission, DG Enterprise & Industry, of the Institute of social economy – Civil society development foundation that included also the first-time calculation of the social economy satellite accounts in Romania for 2011 and 2012 used the definition of social economy proposed by CIRIEC[3] that is adapted to the concepts used in the national accounts systems:

> The set of private, formally-organized enterprises, with autonomy of decision and freedom of membership, created to meet their members' needs through the market by producing goods and providing services, insurance and finance, where decision-making and any distribution of profits or surpluses among the members are not directly linked to the capital or fees contributed by each member, each of whom has one vote, or at all events take place through democratic and participative decision-making processes. The Social Economy also includes private, formally-organized organizations with autonomy of decision and freedom of membership that produce non-market services for households and whose surpluses, if any, cannot be appropriated by the economic agents that create, control or finance them.

Other papers and reports, for example *Atlas of Social Economy 2014* issued by Institute of social economy-CSDF, embraced also EU definition from Social business initiative:[4]

> a social enterprise is an operator in the social economy whose main objective is to have a social impact rather than make a profit for their owners or shareholders. It operates by providing goods and services for the market in an entrepreneurial and innovative fashion and uses its profits primarily to achieve social objectives. It is managed in an open and responsible manner and, in particular, involves employees, consumers and stakeholders affected by its commercial activities.

In July 2015 a Law of Social economy was adopted, which partially responded to one of the challenge perceived by stakeholders in the previous years – the lack of a clear legal and regulatory framework for social enterprises.

We can speak in present about a visible early development of social economy sector in Romania, an increasing public recognition of the sector, and a genuine early circulation of social economy models and

---

3 CIRIEC-Centre International de recherches et d'information sur l'économie publique, sociale et cooperative, 2012, Luis Monzon Campos, Rafael Chaves Avila, *The Social Economy in the European Union*, p. 21.

4 European Commission, 2011, Communication from the Commission to the European Parliament, the Council, the European Economic and Social Committee and the Committee of the Regions, *Social Business Initiative. Creating a favorable climate for social enterprises, key stakeholders in the social economy and innovation*, COM(2011) 682 final, Brussels, 25 October 2001, p. 2.

practices with specific phenomena of a beginning: debates, refining and improving operational models, mistakes and also outstanding results.

1.2.2. Social economy in Romania 1990-2012: general statistics and territorial aspects

But what is the stage of reconfiguration of social economy in Romania in figures? The most recent statistics, *Atlas of Social Economy 2014*, has shown a number of 39,347 active organizations, from which 33,670 associations and foundations, 2,228 cooperatives, 2,767 credit unions and 682 social economy groups for 2012.

The report elaborated by National Center of Training in Statistics in the framework of the project *Making social economy visible in Romania* in 2014 has shown the weight of the gross added value of the social economy in the national economy was in 2012 of 1.9%. According to *Atlas of Social Economy 2014*, the social economy sector employed 1.9% of the total number of employees in 2012.

The same publication has shown that social economy sector was characterized in the last 3 years by positive trends. During the period 2010-2012 all main indicators of social economy organizations registered accelerated growth tendencies: the number of organizations increased in 2012 by 25.62% compared to 2010, the fixed assets increased by 40.32%, the revenues increased by 59.27%, and the number of employees increased by 30.35%. All these encouraging trends show a moderate-sized, but dynamic sector, changing rapidly, more and more accepted by people and communities, which, through bottom-up processes may generate possible models for socio-economic local development.

Trying to have a complete picture of the evolution after the communist fall, we provide bellow a time series of data of the social economy sector (in number of organizations):

Figure 1: Evolution of active associations and foundations and of associations and foundations with economic activity, 2000-2012

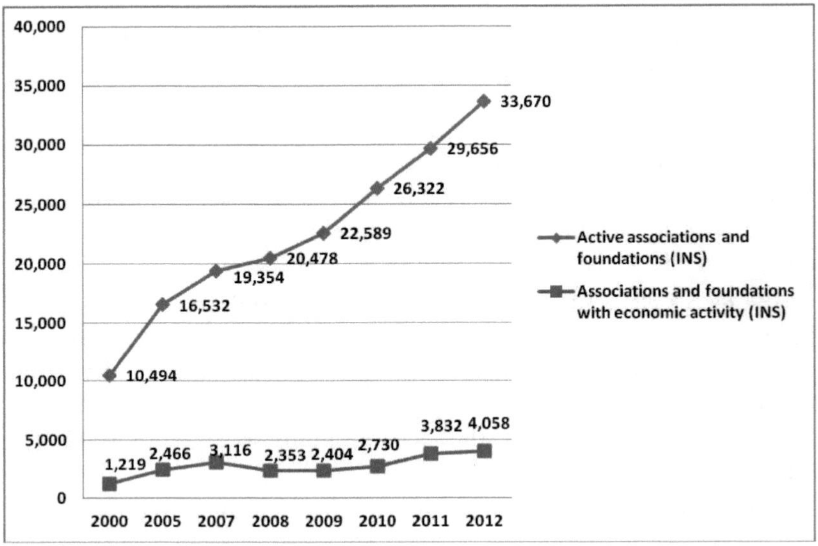

Source: Barna, 2014: 16

Figure 2: Evolution of number of crafts cooperatives, 1989-2008

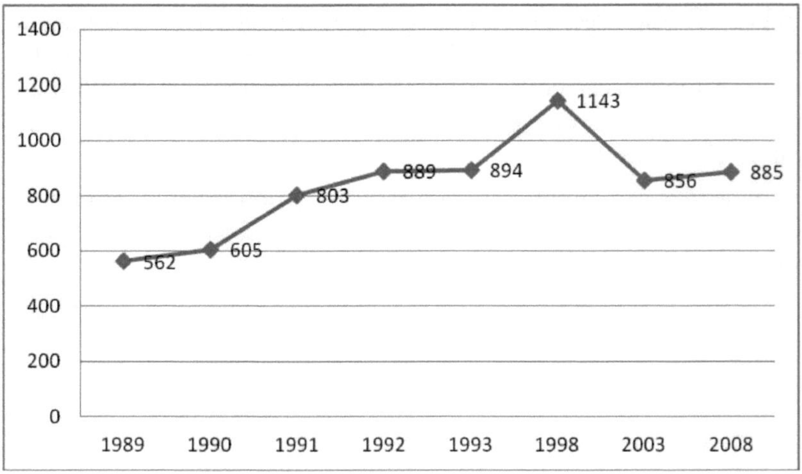

Source: UCECOM 2011, quoted from Petrescu, 2013, p. 83

The growth in numbers of crafts cooperatives in the period 1989 to 1998 maybe due to splits rather than start-up of totally new cooperatives.

Figure 3: Evolution of number of consumers cooperatives, 1989-2008

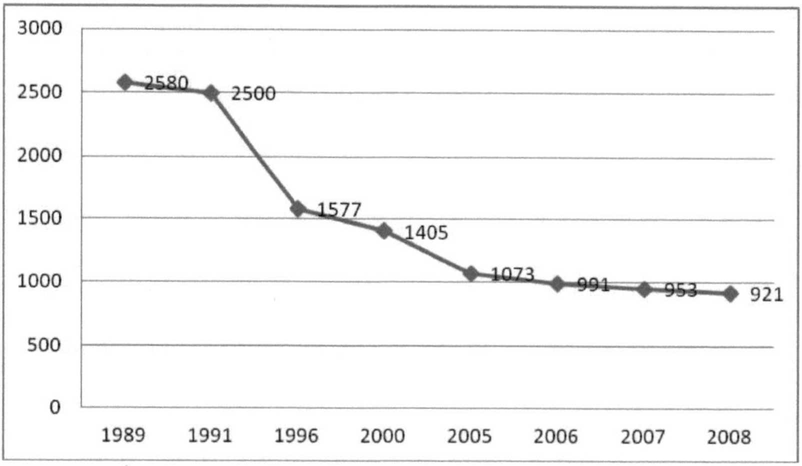

Source: Crisan, 2010, quoted from Petrescu, 2013, p. 81

The fall of the consumer coops after 1989 was caused by the problems of the transition to the market economy: the shift of economic paradigm from a centrally planned economy to an ultraliberal economy – privatization of state enterprises, land and property restitution which led to problems regarding the property of lands and buildings by cooperatives, galloping inflation and the fall of some banks which reduced access to credit, and the fall of traditional supply chains specific to a centralized/planned economy. Cooperatives were part of this chain which, with the fall of communism, was dismantled. Although Romania had a tradition of consumer coops from before the war, and some of the communist cooperatives inherited this tradition, during the communist period they have enjoyed a monopoly position in rural areas in commerce and services people were forced to become members in order to benefit from industrial products (Petrescu, 2013: 79, 81).

Cooperatives in Romania recorded an involution particularly pronounced in 1990-2000; almost one of three consumer coops having disappeared during the period. After 2000, the number of cooperatives, the worker/crafts and the consumers ones, has remained relatively constant;

788 handicrafts cooperatives and 894 consumers' cooperatives have filed balance sheets for the fiscal year of 2009 (Constantinescu, 2011).

Since 2009 the same evolution persists with few new cooperatives being registered, mainly in the agriculture sector.

Figure 4: Evolution of number of cooperatives by type, 2009-2012

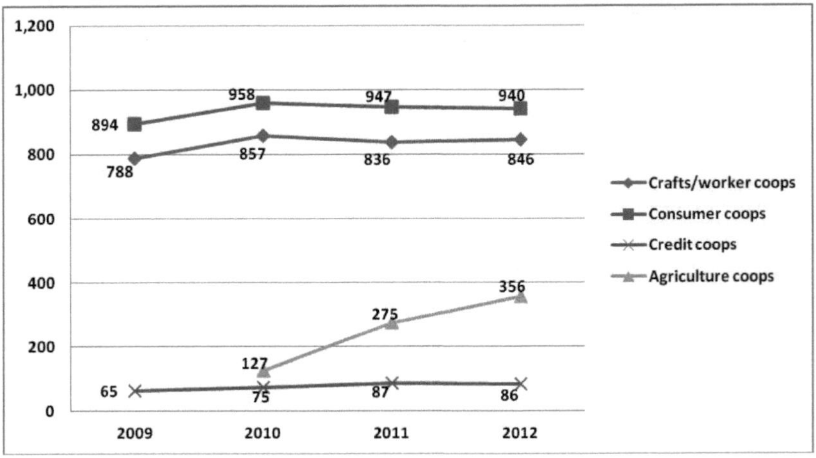

Source: Barna, 2014, p. 69

In terms of economic and social results of cooperatives, the fixed assets of cooperatives have registered an upward trend between 2000 and 2009; growth was more pronounced for consumer cooperatives, by the end of 2009, on average, handicrafts coops had fixed assets of four times larger compared with those of consumer cooperatives (Constantinescu, 2011).

Social economy organizations can contribute to local development, they can reconcile economic and social development. They can use the existent social capital in a territory, and also build social capital. Creating social enterprises and strengthening social capital in the same time, could lead to effective local development. As stated by Xavier Greffe (2007: 96), generally, there are three main processes through which social economy organizations can contribute to local development: they can consider the external costs resulting from a split between the economic and social dimensions and act as a lever for integration; offset information asymmetries and stimulate new productive behavior; and reduce moral hazards and create trust and social capital. The further case study is an illustration of social economy development at local level considering the particular context of the low level of social capital in Romania in the context of a declining rural economy; it is the story about a process of territorial re-construction in the light of the holistic strategy to link economic and social dimensions by creating social enterprises, the role of social economy in job creation and further reinforcement of social capital through entrepreneurship and networking, strengthening community ties and collective action through associations and cooperatives

Both in terms of economic development and development of social economy there are significant differences within Romania among regions and among rural and urban spaces. For example, considering indicator "density of social economy organizations" (number of social economy organizations/1,000 inhabitants), the highest density in 2012 was met in Central Region (3.07), and the lowest density (0.24) in South Region. South-West Region (where is located Horezu territory, subject of the case study presented in the second part) has a density of 1.44 of social economy organization at 1,000 inhabitants, which is slightly below the national average of 1.78.

Considering differences in distribution rural – urban, we can notice that in general only 25% of the active associations and foundations are in rural area, phenomenon due to many causes such lack of financing, lack of information, organizing models with high costs etc. Considering different types of social economy organization, there some predominantly rural. For example, handicraft cooperatives are an organizational form exclusively urban, whereas consumer cooperatives are predominantly rural, 74% of the total number activating in rural areas. In total, 19% of the total number of social economy associations develop their activity in rural area, the most representatives being the commons and agricultural associations from the nongovernmental sector and consumer cooperatives, the latter one representing an organizational reality predominantly rural.

2. Case Study: social economy and territorial development in Horezu

The territory chosen is Horezu, a rural market town in South West Romania, mountain region. The South-West Region is the second poorest region in Romania, with a GNP per inhabitant of 4,258 Euro in 2012.

This region generated the lowest level of revenues in the social economy and generated the fewest jobs (7,798 employees) in this sector.

For this territory we have developed a local socio-economic profile, an analysis of social economy – evolution of main indicators for these organizations, an analysis of existing production chains for dairy farms and forestry and the feasibility of cooperatives in these sectors; and generate ideas for re-thinking production and trade chains, while re-constructing the identity of the territory. The research methods used to develop this case study were: 1. A local data profile constructed from existing available data sources about the area. This included information about demography, the economy – enterprises and social economy organizations; 2. Survey of farmers involved in cattle rearing on their associative attitudes used by the project team in testing up the feasibility of a milk collection and processing cooperative conducted in 2011; and 3. In-depth assessment – including interviews of a sample of social enterprises in the territory conducted in 2011.

Our reflection lends from a research approach proposed by Concise project, starting from the hypothesis that via co-operation and mutual support local social enterprises generate a form of social capital characterized by the development of a local social economy.

The purpose of the case study is to assess the evolution of social economy organizations and of social entrepreneurial development strategies of various stakeholders in a traditional mountain rural area. We look in particular at social economy types of strategies to answer particular economic constraints including the resilience of existing, surviving cooperatives, consolidation of small farmers in dairy cooperatives and the sustainable management of natural goods (forests and pastures) through commons – traditional, centuries old, collective ownership and management organizations drawing from the general landscape of the social economy in the given territory.

The period covered is from the fall of the communist regime, the nineties to the current period of post – EU accession. Unlike other parts of the country – lowlands where intensive agriculture could be performed on large scale properties, farmers in the mountain areas, Horezu included, have kept most of their land property rights up to the 20th century and during communist period, not going through forced communist cooperative system during the 1950s, and have been subject only to nationalization of pastures and forests hold in communal property and small parts of the agricultural land-orchards Land and forest individual/ family property sizes here were rather small. During the 1970s the area has undergone an industrialization process, which included, given the availability of local farm products (milk and fruits) and natural resources (timber), dairy processing and furniture production plants, and fruit collection and primary processing unit – drying and some bottling. As elsewhere, after 1989 the area was affected by rapid dismantling of state owned enterprises and decline of the state-controlled crafts and consumer cooperatives and credit unions and property restitution to owners from before 1945 (when communist regime started) of land, including forest and alpine pastures given back in common property. The area was thus affected by growing socio-economic difficulties. Various local development approaches have been tested in the period 2004-2009. Since 2009 social entrepreneurial strategies have been used in attempts to re-establish local economic cycles destroyed by the changes of political regime.

The economic handicaps specific to such a relatively remote, although well connected rural area in the above described context, make a situation in which private profit-oriented businesses can hardly prosper, and the public sector, given the emphasis on privatization and withdrawal of the state from the economy after 1989, is unable to play a role in economic recovery. Therefore, third types of enterprises, social entreprises may prove a viable option (Birkhölzer, 2009).

2.1. Horezu – local profile summary

Its territory is mainly highland with mountains. A territorial pole settlement around which a network of localities evolved, Horezu has a population of approximately 7,000 living in an area of 118 square kilometers. The name of Horezu is linked with the Monastery of Hurez, which is a monastic complex erected at the end of the 17th century, and which is listed in the UN World Heritage Site, a masterpiece of orthodox religious architecture, and also a cultural center that influenced the development of crafts in the region. The area is rich in natural resources – significant surfaces covered by forests, beautiful mountain landscapes. The market town Horezu is an administrative center of a network of villages, being focal location for health services – hospital care, education with high school and vocational training, justice court, banks and traditional markets. The territory is a combination of urban and rural habitat within the same administrative unit, with the market town taking a leading role in generating ideas for economic development.

Mountain areas such as this face many challenges: decreasing and dispersed population, a mainly rural character, a reduced capacity of endogenously generating "businesses" and jobs given a relatively low level of education and the small number and limited capacity of the local entrepreneurs.

The area faces a dramatic decrease of the population which reached 4% over 20 years in the period 1992-2012.

Figure 5: Evolution of the population Horezu 1992-2012

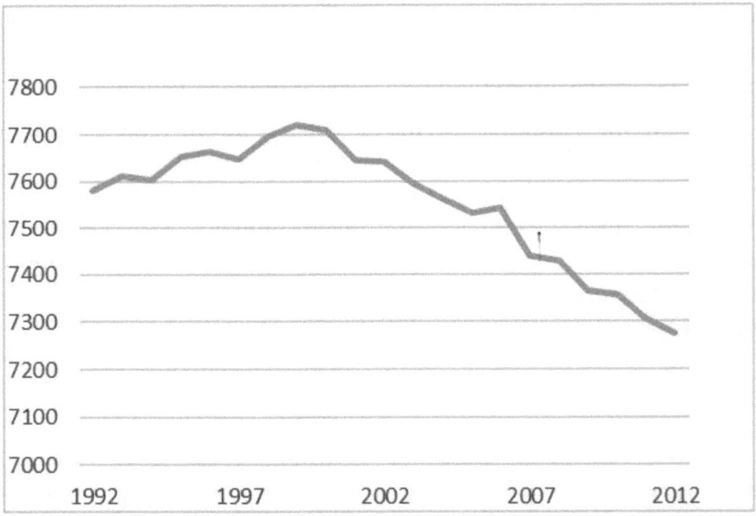

Source: National institute of statistics, Tempo on-line database

The territory is covered in its Northern part with alpine grasslands, as well as semi-natural meadows, most valuable ecosystems used for traditional agricultural activities (cattle and sheep rearing, haymaking, grazing, beekeeping). The area has important surfaces of *forests*, covering over 6,620 ha, representing 60% of the entire micro region.

The transition from a centralized economy when Horezu, during the second half of the 1900s, was a center for processing local products, to a market economy meant that industrial activities were mainly closed, the number of jobs decreasing to almost half, in 2011 being registered only

1,554 employees, many of the local citizens having to go back to their traditional way of living through farming to survive. The local economy and life is now based to a significant extent on *natural resources and traditional occupations.*

Figure 6: Evolution of employment in Horezu 1992-2011 – number of persons employed

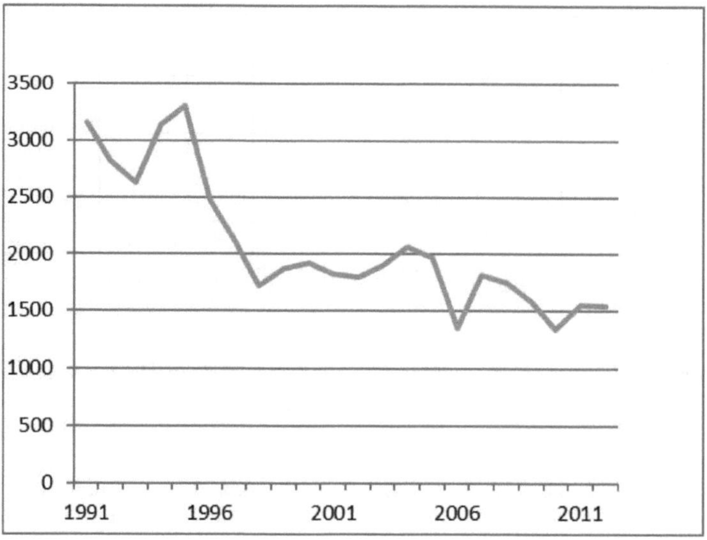

Source: National institute of statistics, Tempo on-line database

2.2. Social economy in Horezu area

2.2.1. Main indicators

In the area we identified a significant number of social economy organizations: 32, with a total of 117 employees, representing almost 7% of the total employees, above the national weight.

Most of the organizations were associations and foundations. Most of the cooperatives were registered before 1993, no new cooperative was registered since 1999 until 2010.

Table 3: Main indicators of social economy organizations in Horezu municipality 2010

Social economy organization by legal form	*No. of organizations*	*Personnel*	*Assets (lei)*	*No. of organizations with assets >0*
Associations	13	8	169,669	3
Foundations	10	9	63,361	6
Credit unions	1	4	668,457	1
Cooperatives – consumer, worker – crafts, credit	4	62	2,140,926	3
Commons and affiliated forestry services	4	34	492,282	3
Total	***32***	***117***	***3,534,695***	***16***

Source: Data from public registries – Ministry of Finance on-line database of tax payers

Figure 7: Number of SE organizations registered yearly in Horezu region since 1992 active in 2010

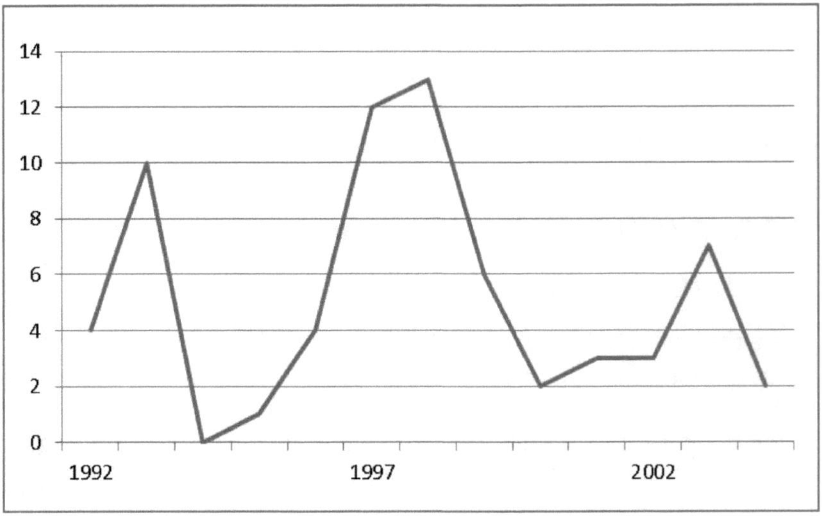

Source: National registry of NGO Ministry of Justice, Ministry of Finance database on taxpayers

Cooperatives are the biggest employers in the social economy providing 62 jobs, namely 53% of all the jobs in the sector, having also the most sizeable assets. They are followed by commons which have also a significant number of jobs but less assets, due possibly also to poor accounting registration of the land and forest assets. With 14% of companies, social economy organizations provide 7% of the employment in the territory.

2.2.2. Farming – the role of social economy organizations in the production chain

Numerous families in the region conduct subsistence and semi-subsistence farming activities, and several farms are engaged in farming activities for the market. In 2011 there were 825 cattle breeders in the municipality of Horezu and neighboring municipalities registered with the Agency for agriculture payments holding 4,613 of dairy cows, each between 3 and 42 cows. The rich alpine pastures held in common property are used to provide food for cattle during the summer seasons, the locals engaging in seasonal agricultural practices like other traditional mountain communities in Europe (Ott, 1993). As can be seen Fig. 8 the number of livestock is decreasing, with the exception of bees – bee-keeping growing as an occupation and pigs generally grown for own consumption and not for the market.

As observed by a study of the European Commission on Farmers Cooperatives in Romania (Calinescu, 2012) the subsistence agriculture hides in fact the lack of opportunities, real unemployment and poverty.

Figure 8: Livestock in Horezu farms, 2002-2010

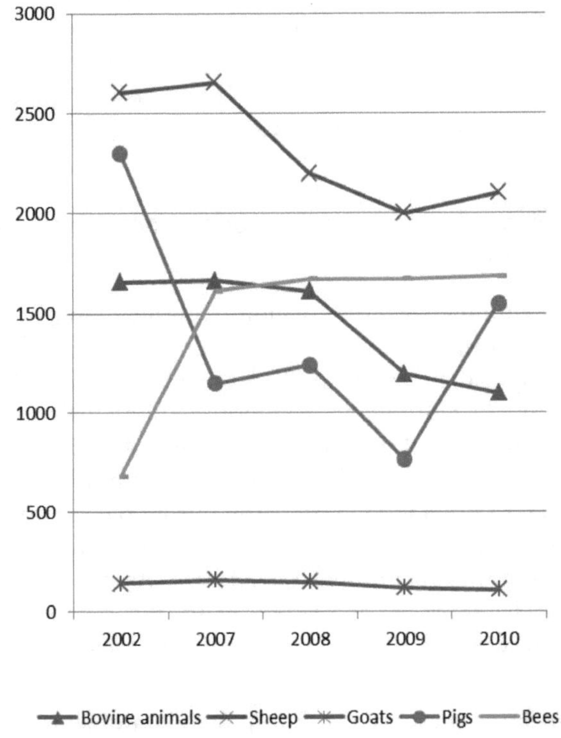

Source City hall - Agriculture Registry

The few local associations of farmers were not able to play a significant role in the dairy production and distribution role so far due to a lack of expertise and managerial capacities. The cattle breeder associations were used only as a vehicle for paying minor government subsidies and their role has declined. In 2011, two groups of young farmers, one of cattle farmers and one of goat farmers launched the initiative of forming marketing – processing cooperatives mainly for dairy products. We have assisted the farmers in conducting a survey to assess the interest of the farmers in joining an association, this being a measure of the trust and quality of community networks within the world of farmers. Of the 100 cattle farmers surveyed, 72% said they would join a cooperative. Finally, a number of 80 farmers have formally applied for membership in the cooperative of which 48 were willing to expand their farm, currently having on average 6.3 cattle. The cooperative had difficulty in starting-up its operation though. To run its business operations, a cooperative needs financial capital who can be built up based on social capital originating in one way or another from the members who, for instance, may voluntarily abstain from some patronage refunds. The financial capital is hence a kind of conversion of social capital (Nilsson *et al.*, 2012). Creation and operation of such a cooperative depends on social capital of people in the territory such as trust that leads to improved sharing of information, reciprocity and coordination reducing transaction costs in case of collective procurement for instance.

2.2.3. Forestry – the wood chain

Most of the forests (52%) are held in common, traditional property – restituted after 50 years of state management during communist times. Commons have been re-established starting with the year 2000 through a land and forest property restitution process and are legally registered as associations. Like in other similar regions, a large portion of forests, meadows and pastures were communal property (over 50%), while only small portions of arable land were communal property.

Figure 9: Weight of forest communal ownership in Horezu

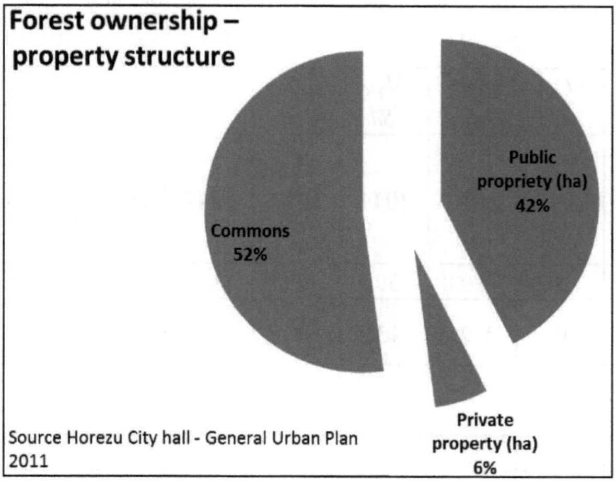

Although the inhabitants own in common important surfaces of forest and pastures, the members of the commons do not have the information, knowledge and habit, exercise of controlling the commons governing bodies on the administration and exploitation of their natural resources (wood, pastures). We have looked into the current economic and social role of the commons. Forest and forest resources (wood, landscape) are managed by a community board, the wood cropping and processing being entrusted to a specialized company according to forestry regulations. The board plays a critical role in proposing and pursuing local development plans on the land of the commons. So far it has planned a touristic development of the respective highlands – a lease contract for 49 years to private owners from outside the region. The commoners have not been consulted on this decision. It is not clear what the long-term implications of this long-term development plan on the community and on the common management of the respective land will be (Casari, 2000). The area faces a continuous process of deforestation caused by a complex of factors that often manifest in an aggressive manner. Forestry furnishes the firewood necessary for the heating of most dwellings.

Even so the commons provide an adequate legal and economic framework for acting as development catalysts but given their limited technical, managerial capacity, lack of social control exercised by members and lack of accountability by executive and governing bodies, their social and economic impact remains limited to job creation.

Table 4: Main economic and social results of commons and their forestry services companies (2010-2012)

	Ocolul silvic privat Buila		*Obştea Sătească Sărdăreasca*		*Obştea Buila*		*Obştea Horezu*	
Balance sheets Indicators (thou Lei)	**2011**	**2012**	**2011**	**2012**	**2011**	**2012**	**2011**	**2012**
Fixed Assets	0.0	10.8	39.5	39.5	72.6	68.2	480.3	944.1
Current Assets	246.5	239.2	13.7	1.5	97.0	28.6	2,095.4	1,863.4
Turnover	611.1	578.2	113.3	69.2	593.6	373.7	1,165.5	1,125.0
Personnel								
Non-profit	25	23	2	2	3	3	0	0
Economic	0	2	0	0	0	0		8
Total	**25**	**25**	**2**	**2**	**3**	**3**	**0**	**8**

Source: Ministry of Finance Database of balance sheets of taxpayers

Of the four commons registered we observe that number of jobs created varied depending on the size of land held in common between 2 and 25 jobs, all commons registering continuously growing turnover figures over the period studied.

2.2.4. Resilience of cooperatives from before 1989 in other sectors (crafts-workers, consumers)

During the assessment of the territory in 2011 we found 4 cooperatives still operating on the territory which is a better survival rate than the one found at national level.

The social indicators of these cooperatives were declining in terms of jobs offered – this may be seen as a decrease in the weight given to the social mission, in particular in the case of crafts – worker cooperative, over the economic results, correlated with improving economic results towards the end of the period. Thus, Ceramica Coop had a stable turnover in the period 2005-2009, following a period of bad financial results during 1999-2004 of adaptation to new economic conditions. The number of employees had constantly decreased. Data on membership is not available but it is likely, given the general pattern, that membership has decreased.

3. Conclusion

Following a change of political regime in the 1990s, Romanians are rediscovering the potential of freedom to associate and entrepreneurship. Cooperatives and credit unions were the only forms of quasi-private enterprises that existed during the post-war communist times and some of them prove remarkably resilient. Although with somehow poor results and partially de-mutualized, some cooperatives manage to survive unlike most of the state-owned companies. Also, the credit unions, following a period of decline are currently witnessing an upsurge. As Romania is a predominantly rural country with a delayed process of modernization of these areas, social economy can play a significant role in modernizing and improving the quality of life in rural areas while preserving the social fabric still persistent mainly in its mountain part. The case study shows the growing role of the sector in an economy that has undergone a rapid change in ownership structure, production and distribution channels and labor force. Considering the low level of social capital, social entrepreneurship in the form of cooperatives and commons seems to take root more slowly than the other forms of enterprises, but are looked at with hope in a context of poor and declining human capital and lack of financial capital. The case study shows that it is necessary to allot time and facilitating efforts in the local community in order to re-create the social capital lost because of the communist experiences, and build bridging and linking social capital. On the other hand, although the area is characterized by stronger social capital compared to the national average – if we consider for instance intensity of association in terms of number of associations and cooperatives for 1,000 inhabitants – this is though not enough for such collective strategies as social enterprise start-up to emerge.

Horezu territory, like other Romanian rural and poor territories but with a lot of natural and cultural resources, is facing the process of reconfiguration of social economy. Even in a small number, social economy organization can contribute to local sustainable development and also, they can build social capital. Pre-existing cooperatives although declining following the transition property reform processes, with many members being bought out by the management, had better survival rates than the national averages, and social and economic results within the national averages, showing the existence of the social capital necessary for the formation and operation of such organizations and the resilience of the business model for which this type of social economy organizations are known. Their social role is though limited to job creation at this stage.

The newly instituted, top down commons with membership bases far more than the cooperatives (most families belong to such commons) had social and economic results in line with those of pre-existing cooperatives. Their social and local economic development remains limited to their strict mission, and even though they had significant assets, these are rather captured and used more for private than group interests, given the lack of social norms to guide the public/community interest functioning of these organizations, therefore breach of trust within the social networks. The rate of new social capital formation through this top-bottom approach is disappointing. Therefore, although we can see signs of social capital and operating social enterprises, the missing linking type of social capital may lead to rather poor results and limited impact of social economy initiatives on local economic development and social capital development.

References

Alexandru V., Moraru A., Ercus L., 2009, *Declinul participarii la vot in Romania*, Friedrich Ebert Stiftung, Institutul de Politici Publice, Bucuresti, Romania, p. 10-11.

Barna C., 2014, *Atlas of Social Economy 2014*, Institute of social economy, Civil society development foundation, Bucharest, Romania.

Barna C., Vameşu A., 2014, "Reviving Social Economy in Romania – between emerging social enterprises in all sectors, surviving communist coops, and subsidiaries of globalization actors", *Working Paper*, CIRIEC (International centre of research and information on the public, social and cooperative economy), No. 07.

Birkhölzer Karl, 2009, "The Role of Social Enterprise in Local Economic Development", *EMES Conferences Selected Papers Series*, Interdisciplinary research group local economy, Technical University of Berlin, Germany.

Calinescu D., 2012, *Support for Farmers' Cooperatives*, Country Report Romania, Wageningen, Wageningen UR.

Casari M., 2000, "Emergence of Endogenous Legal Institutions: Property Rights and Community Governance in the Italian Alps", *Working Papers from California Institute of Technology*, Division of the humanities and social sciences.

"Ce este cooperatia?", 2010, <http://emiliacorbu.ro/2010/05/ce-este-cooperatia/>, consulted on 1 September 2015.

CENTROCOOP, <http://www.centrocoop.com/istoric/evolu538ia_coopera538iei_de_consum_in_538arile_romane-53-996-ro.html>, consulted on 1 September 2015.

Constantinescu St., 2011, *The Atlas of Social Economy*, Civil Society Development Foundation, Institute of Social Economy, Romania.

Cộté S., 2001, *The Contribution of Human and Social Capital*, ISUMA.

Etchart N., Iancu D., Rosandic A., Mocanu V., Paclea I., 2014, *The State of Social Entrepreneurship in Romania*, SEFORIS Country Report, NESsT, April.

European Commission, 2011, Communication from the Commission to the European Parliament, the Council, the European Economic and Social Committee and the Committee of the Regions, *Social Business Initiative. Creating a favourable climate for social enterprises, key stakeholders in the social economy and innovation* {SEC(2011) 1278 final}.

Fukuyama F., 1994, *Trust: The Social Virtues and the Creation of Prosperity*, New York, Free Press (quoted from Skidmore D., 2001).

Glaeser E.L., 2001, *The Formation of Social Capital*, OECD, <http://www.oecd.org/innovation/research/1824983.pdf>, consulted on 1 November 2015.

Greffe X., 2007, "The role of social economy in local development", *in* A. Noya, E. Clarence (eds.), "*The Social Economy: Building Inclusive, Economics*", OECD.

Institute of social economy – Civil society development foundation, <http://www.ies.org.ro/info-stiri/vrs/IDstire/980/t/finantarea-posdru-pentru-economia-social>, consulted on 1 September 2015.

Kay A., 2005, *Social Capital, the Social Economy and Community Development*, Oxford University Press/Community Development Journal.

KLM, Inc. Management Consultation, Social Capital and Economic Growth<http://www.klminc.com/intellect_cap/social_capital.html>, consulted on 1 September 2015.

Lambru M., Vameşu A. (coord.), 2010, *Romania 2010. NGOs Sector – Profile, Trends, Challenges*, Civil Society Development Foundation, Bucharest, Romania.

Narayan D., Pritchett L., 1999, "Cents and sociability: household income and social capital in rural Tanzania", *Economic Development and Cultural Change*, 47 (4) (quoted from Skidmore D., 2001).

National Center for Training in Statistics – Romanian National Institute of Statistics (2014), Report *Satellite Accounts of Social Economy in Romania 2011-2012*.

Nilsson J., Svendsen G.L.H., Svendsen G.T., 2012, "Are Large and Complex Agricultural Cooperatives Losing Their Social Capital?", *Agribusiness*, 28 (2), Spring: 121-240.

OECD, Directorate for Education, <http://www.oecd.org>, consulted on 1 September 2015.

Ott Sandra, 1993, *The Circle of Mountains: A Basque Shepherding Community*, University of Nevada Press.

Petrescu C. (coord.), 2013, *Cooperativele din Romania. Actori ai dezvoltarii socio-economice*, Polirom, Romania.

Putman R.D., 2004, "Education, Diversity, Social Cohesion and 'Social Capital'", *Meeting of OECD/Education Ministers: Raising the Quality of Learning for All*, Dublin, 18-19 March.

Putman R.D., 2000, *Bowling alone: The Collapse and the Revival of American Community*, New York, Simon & Schuster.

Putman R.D., 1993, "The prosperous community: social capital and public life", *The American Prospect*, 13, spring, (quoted from Skidmore D., 2001).

"Rezultatele Cooperaţiei", 2010, <http://emiliacorbu.ro/2010/05/rezultatele-cooperatiei/>, consulted on 1 September 2015.

Schuller T., 2001, *The Complementary Roles of Human and Social Capital*, ISUMA.

Scrivens K., Smith C., 2013, "Four interpretations of social capital: an agenda for measurement", *Working paper No. 55, OECD Statistics Directorate*, Paris.

Skidmore D., 2001, "Civil Society, Social Capital and Economic Development", *Global Society*, 15 (1): 53-72.

Special Eurobarometer 75.2, October 2011, "Volunteering and intergenerational solidarity", carried out by TNS Opinion & Social at the request of the European Parliament; survey coordinated by the Directorate-General for Communication.

Svendsen G.L.H., Svendsen G.T., 2004, *The Creation and Destruction of Social Capital: Entrepreneurship, Co-operative Movements and Institutions*, Cheltenham UK, Edward Elgar.

Woolcock M., 2002, "Social capital in theory and practice: where do we stand?", *in* J. Isham, Th. Kelly, S. Ramaswamy (eds.), *Social Capital and Economic Development. Well-being in Developing Countries*, Edgar Elgar Publishing House.

Chapter 6

Venezuela: An Outlook on SSE, Water for People and Related Public Policies

Benito Díaz, Angel Higuerey, Leonardo Argüello
Universidad de Los Andes

Mario Fagiolo
Universidad de Oriente

Fernando Aponte
Lawyer and social researcher, Venezuela

Introduction

This chapter is aimed at the presentation of an overview of the current situation of social solidarity economy (SSE) and the local management of water industry related to public policies and their performances by means of showing some SSE case studies and the performance of local water enterprises. A broader framework is outlined, showing main trends supported by evidence collected in two regions of Venezuela: the Andean (Trujillo State) and the Caribbean Sea coast (Sucre and Nueva Esparta States).

After the National Bolivarian Constitution was passed in the year 2000, several SSE have emerged, some of which and their links to local development are portrayed here: cooperatives, Technical roundtables of communal water (*Mesas técnicas de agua en comunidades locales*), Nucleus for endogenous development (NUDE), Communal councils and communes, all of which in turn would become the basis of the communal system of the Bolivarian revolution towards the so called socialism of the 21st century.

We are aware of the ongoing debate about the definitions of social and solidarity economy. Until today, there is no consensual agreement on the definition of social economy and this has implications for public policies and programs (Diaz, 2008). In the opinion of some authors, the concept of social economy must include only economic organizations while others propose to include non-profit voluntary organizations. From our point of view, the Technical roundtables of communal water, communal councils, communes and communal banks could be included within the definition of social economy if they comply with the principles of these autonomous community organizations, especially with the principles defined in the cooperative associations Act and the principles set by the International cooperative alliance. Hence, we will present as case studies some experiences from living SSE organizations, regional water enterprises and Technical roundtables of communal water working with organized community support and helping to organize the efforts of people to meet their common needs while building up a better world.

So far, this chapter is organized in the following way. It begins with an overview of social economy organizations and related public policies in Venezuela at the beginning of the 21st century. Two case studies are then portrayed: a successful one and a failed one. Further details are shown by means of, firstly, the case of a Nucleus for endogenous development (NUDE) in Trujillo State and, secondly, the Technical roundtables of water and communal councils. Later on, challenges to improve SSE public policies and performance of SSE actors are presented, mainly related to organizations providing water services to people. From this overview, some concluding lessons and challenges for further research are shown as recommendations.

1. Main features of SSE organizations in the Venezuelan 21st century

1.1. An overview of social and solidarity economy organizations and related public policies in Venezuela at the beginning of the 21st century

Early in the 1960s the Venezuelan State promoted cooperatives as instruments of social control to minimize conflict and against the Socialist preaching of left-wing parties. By that time, the government of the United

States of America promoted public policies aimed at Latin American governments that promoted cooperatives in a welfare perspective of small reforms within the so-called Alliance for Progress (Fals Borda, 1976). That was a part of an overall strategy of response to the impact of the Cuban revolution of 1959 in the Latin American subcontinent. So far, in 1998 in Venezuela, there were about 800 cooperatives formally registered and regulated by a National superintendence of cooperatives (SUNACOOP). The cooperative movement maintained a relatively low profile, although there were nationally integrated services and agencies (14 regional cooperative centers covering the 20 states of the whole country and a national central of cooperatives).

At the end of 1998, President Hugo Chavez Frias won the elections. When he took office, Chavez made a call for a National Constituent Assembly to draw up a new National Constitution. Many public inquiries were made to formulate the project of the new National Constitution of the Bolivarian Republic of Venezuela (CNRBV), which was approved by a popular referendum at the end of 1999, which had never happened before in the country. Civil society organizations could submit proposals that were incorporated in the CNRBV (particularly articles 70, 118, 184 and 308), in areas related to the promotion and consolidation of the social economy organizations, mainly cooperatives.

In April 2002, new programs supported by public policies with massive subsidies to the population began. Some of them were related to the promotion and creation of cooperatives. These programs, called Missions, in parallel to the traditional state provide care services to citizens, especially in matters of health, education and employment rights. For instance, the Mission *Vuelvan Caras* aimed at creating one million jobs in less than two years by means of the promotion and creation of cooperatives as part of a broad training program covering widely the country.

In this context, between 2000 and 2015, public policies for promotion of SSE were mainly addressed from the three national plans for social and economic development. In the first national plan (2001-2007), the cooperatives were the fundamental organizational form used to achieve the goals of development, to build an economy productive, competitive, with export quality, socially inclusive and to defend the Bolivarian revolution (Diaz, 2006). Cooperatives were perceived as an essential instrument for developing the productive economy. In order to achieve this goal, the Plan considered six specific sub-objectives, one of which was to "develop the social economy". Three main guidelines were identified in that respect: strengthening micro-enterprises and cooperatives; organizing the system of microfinance; and democratizing land ownership. Through a massive and accelerated process of state promotion, around 200,000 cooperatives were created between 2002 and 2007, which is far superior to the number of cooperatives that had been created during the 20th century, when they had never been more than one thousand (figure 1).

Figure 1: Registered cooperatives at the national level (1966-December 2007)

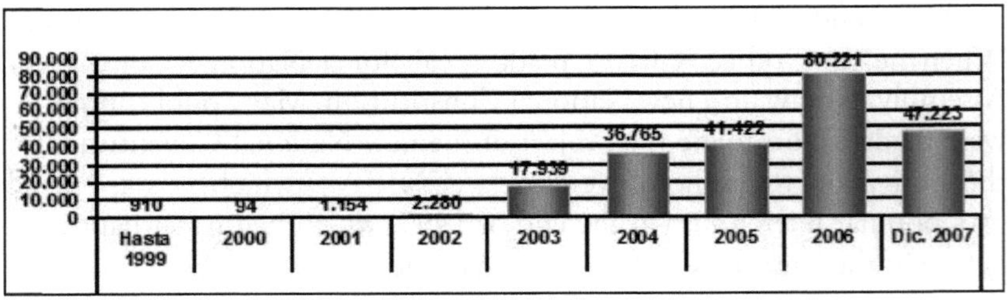

Source: <www.sunacoop.gob.ve>, consulted on 24 May 2015

In general, during the 2001-2007 period, cooperatives were concentrated in the most densely populated states of the country. Moreover, several empirical studies conducted during this period found the existence of different social representations about cooperatives. These representations varied according to the actors and to the vast regions of the country, which could adversely affect the implementation and the results of cooperative education programs carried out during this period (Hernandez *et al*, 2008), as well as the performance of the SSE created by the state-promoted cooperatives. In fact, around 90% of the cooperatives created by that program failed and disappeared once the subsidies finished, however they still are quite an important number. If just 10% survived out of the around 200,000 coops created, they remain as an important asset of the social solidarity economy, which deserve to be studied and served as well.

The second Plan of the nation (2007-2013) was declared itself as the *first Socialist Plan*. In this plan preferential treatment was given to the forms of SSE related to the Law on popular economy. However, they were soon abandoned, and preference and prominence were given instead to SSE forms included in the *Ley orgánica del sistema económico comunal* (Organic law on the communal economic system, Asamblea Nacional, 2010). Between the seven components of the Plan, cooperatives are only mentioned twice in the new productive model, while formerly coops were promoted in every possible way by public sector institutions.

The third Plan of the nation (2013-2019), self-proclaimed also as *the Plan of Homeland*, continued to downplay the importance of cooperatives and classical forms of SSE, and gave preference instead to new forms of SSE within laws for communal economic system. Main goals for this period include the following:

> the creation of 3,000 socialists communes, with an approximate annual growth of 450 communes, according to the demographic characteristics of the axes of territorial development. These communes will have grouped 39,000 communal councils, where 4,680,000 families will make life representing 21,060,000 citizens. As a result, about 68% of Venezuelans in the year 2019 will live in subsystems of aggregation of communes.

That will also include the making of 30,000 direct social owned enterprises.[1]

In that context, over one and a half million of spokespersons work for the Popular power voluntarily, which is described in the official speech as "a success of the political revolution" (Godoy, 2013). Nevertheless, many of those volunteers are unemployed, or have precarious jobs, or they do not enjoy a decent job, or have the illusion of getting incorporated into the communal enterprises promised within the National Plan. Even many of those who live in communes currently complain that resources do not come promptly to fund and implement projects within their Local Community Development Plan; as for instance, in the commune Tiuna el Fuerte, in Caracas, (López, Tabuas, 2012).

1.2. The case of a Nucleus for endogenous development (NUDE) in Trujillo State

The exponential growth of cooperatives was reinforced by the *Vuelvan Caras* mission, which aggregated thousands of cooperatives under the state protection. This mission was transformed and continued with the

---

1 <http://www.minci.gob.ve/2013/09/mas-de-40-mil-consejos-comunales-y-1-401-comunas-registradas-en-censo/>, consulted on 30 October 2014.

name of *Che Guevara* mission and continued doing training on technical matters, jointly with ideological views supporting the making of the Bolivarian socialism of the 21st century. Nowadays, on a lesser scale, this kind of approach has been continued by the *Saber y trabajo* (Knowledge and work) mission.

The objectives of the *Vuelvan Caras* mission were to train a sector of the population in specific trades. As part of this training, they were instructed about how they could create cooperatives, which guaranteed the financing, through projects, in order to put into practice the acquired knowledge and to practice a profession independently, thus contributing to the development of a social economy with local projects and national guidelines. Later on, the cooperatives that had been created separately were required to be integrated into a new social institution, the so-called Nucleus of endogenous development (NUDE).

Several NUDE were created in the Trujillo State, among them the NUDE Agua Santa. The Agua Santa NUDE was comprised of seven cooperatives, all of which were created with the *Vuelvan Caras* mission. The type of productive activity of the cooperatives that comprised the NUDE Agua Santa was as follows: five cooperatives associations carried out different activities; only two were engaged to carry out the same activity, such as civil construction. This is because the idea of creation of the nucleus of endogenous development, seeks to diversify the activities to be carried out with people without triggering competition between them but complementarity.

All the training courses had a technical component referred to the particular trade and another component on partnership, organization of cooperatives and ideological learning. The ideological component was common to all courses and technical variations were specific to every trade. At the end of the training course, participants had to create a cooperative and to develop a project in order to access funding through any of the several state funds serving cooperatives and micro-enterprises. However, as participants often did not know how to write projects, the trainers of the courses wrote projects for each one of the cooperatives that they had trained. They also drew up the statutes and recorded them legally, following models of statutes delivered by the same SUNACOOP.

These cooperatives began to have delays in their projects, delays in payments of loans and problems in their management processes. As a consequence, many of them failed and others had serious cash flow problems and lack of management skills that did not allow them to develop, grow and be competitive on the market. In order to tackle that situation, we were asked by SUNACOOP to conduct a research, looking at the financial, accounting and administrative aspects of cooperatives located in the NUDE Agua Santa, whose results and lessons learned are offered here.

Methodology

The study we carried out in the NUDE was a diagnostic evaluation and focused on the financial dimension. It initially consisted of meetings with staff and the SUNACOOP Regional representatives who had been involved in the organization and the training courses of the *Vuelvan Caras* mission. After that, field trips helped identifying key informants and organizations. Later on, a focus group was organized, which involved six out of the seven cooperatives of the NUDE. Furthermore, each one of the seven cooperatives in their productive premises were visited in order to collect further information by means of structured observation and applying a semi-open questionnaire to the treasurers, presidents, secretaries and other members of the cooperative associations that were present when the several scheduled meetings took place. At the beginning, some officials from SUNACOOP were present during the interviews, but later on just university researchers attended the scheduled visits in the seven cooperative premises. Moreover, further interviews between the cooperative members and the university researchers took place when the matters were clear enough. By this way, the freedom of speech of the people involved was preserved, and so was the principle of independence of the cooperative. Beside this procedure, the accounting books of the cooperatives were carefully reviewed.

Features of the NUDE Agua Santa

The NUDE was comprised of seven cooperatives, which performed different tasks and are briefly described as follows for an overview of what a NUDE is. The cooperative Luz y Paz, R.S. dedicated to civil construction, manufacture and sale of materials for building in general, was made up of 17 partners. The cooperative Fase 15-14, R.L. was devoted to civil construction, manufacture of materials for the construction, and was made up of 41 partners. The cooperative Trusfil, R.L. was formed with 42 partners engaged in agricultural and livestock production.

The cooperative Mujeres Emprendedoras 1541, R.L., constituted with 11 partners, provided computing services, internet, transcription of texts and everything related to the branch of service with a Cyber cafe. The cooperative Coarven 1448 was dedicated to the manufacture and repair of furniture upholstery, bags and backpacks, and was made up of 26 partners. The cooperative La Verdadera Felicidad 1147, R.L. was formed with 18 partners and was engaged in the manufacture of clothing, curtains and works related to the textile industry. While the cooperative Guerreras Revolucionarias 151, R.L., provided services of restaurant, bakery, and was made up of 23 associated women. The Agua Santa NUDE was originally made up of 178 associated, and when the evaluation took place, most of the cooperatives were not operational and most of the workers had dropped out of the cooperatives. Many of these casualties seemed to be due to cultural and economic factors.

1.3. Challenges to improve SSE public policies and performance of SSE actors

Public policies and promotion programs for the social and solidarity economy were successful in terms of social inclusion. However, there some ventures failed. Therefore, public policies related to social and solidarity economy and social economy organizations promoted by the state have many opportunities to improve. The state has invested significant amounts of money in cooperatives that made up the NUDE, but most of them are declining, with a tendency towards bankruptcy. In the majority of cases, partners were trained to work in projects that were different from the established enterprises. Some projects were not underway, and therefore the NUDE contributed very little to local endogenous development. The NUDE in the region and in the country should be assessed as part of the review for the correction of public policies and their sustainability (Higuerey *et al*, 2008).

Given its operational modalities, the policy of cooperative promotion imposed costs of management of state programs that, in fact, constituted a threat to the principle of freedom of association in the cooperatives. For example, promoters of cooperatives, following specific guidelines, decided on the size of the cooperatives and the number of their associated workers. Although the Cooperative associations act establishes that five is the minimum number of associates to form them, in the *Vuelvan Caras* mission, they pushed cooperatives to have a predetermined number of associates in a cooperative (initially 20 members, then 30). By this way, the cooperative does not decide with how many people it works. This affects the structure of production costs and puts the cooperative at a disadvantage in its competition with other companies in the market. This also brought about a new kind of organizational matters, as associates did not know well each other and were forced to become a member of a cooperative and to undertake a collective loan, which had to be paid jointly with people who had not been trained enough to deal with this kind of risks and social interactions (Díaz, 2006).

2. Main features of organizations providing water services to people

2.1. National panorama on Venezuelan water industry

Venezuela has a large availability of water that is concentrated in less populated areas. These and other features make the action area of the water operating companies quite different. Some companies serve vast regions, while others are located in areas of high population density. There are also differences in altitude and temperature in the assigned area. Currently, the supply of drinking water and wastewater collection service is provided by 17 public companies. Nine of which are centralized, they depend on the central Government and are coordinated by the Compañía Anónima Hidrológica de Venezuela, HIDROVEN. Seven companies are decentralized: they depend on state or municipal governments. One of them operates under the figure of an entity of the State Department (Higuerey et al, 2013).

The provision of the services of supply of drinking water and wastewater in Venezuela is coordinated by the state owned HIDROVEN. This organization acts as a governing body in the field of drinking water supply, collection and treatment of wastewater and urban drainage. This company also dictates guidelines for the management, operation, maintenance and expansion of systems that are delivered by its affiliates. So far, there are centralized and decentralized regional water companies in Venezuela, all of them ruled by HIDROVEN guidelines.

The most prominent differences between centralized and decentralized water companies, according to Escalona et al (2009), are as follows. In the centralized ones, decisions within the Assembly of shareholders are taken by a single entity, HIDROVEN, as being the sole shareholder and while being involved in the decentralized regional and local governments. The decentralized water companies work with resources that manage their operations and some investments from the regional governments, while the centralized ones also receive contributions from the National Executive. The decentralized companies do not have any direct relationship with national entities while the centralized do. Centralized companies' employees are considered civil servants, while decentralized companies are ruled by the labor law.

According to current regulations, the supply of drinking water and the wastewater collection service have to be delivered under the criteria of quality, efficiency, reliability, fairness, non-discrimination and profitability. Efforts have been made to ensure that water supply services reach the entire population, leading to achieve broader coverage fees. Coverage is lower in the sewage disposal service. These differences are accentuated in less populated areas, thus becoming more severe in rural areas.

According to the National institute of statistics (INE), the structure of the water consumption of Venezuela differs from the rest of the world. On the one hand, while worldwide agricultural consumption reaches around three-quarters of the water, in Venezuela it does not reach one-half. On the other hand, domestic use of water in the country is four times higher than the world average. This is due to the following aspects: a) the price for the service is very cheap; b) the political guidelines of the current government aims to favor the population by providing economic services, not considering the costs of their production; c) low community awareness about water use; d) free distribution of the service in low-resource areas; and e) in some cases, the companies that provide the water service do not make the effort to collect the billing. All this affects the wasteful use of water by the community (Francisco, 2008).

Sources of surface water (rivers and streams) are used for drinking water supply. Companies capture directly from the source or stored in reservoirs. From here, with current drinking water and drinking water infrastructure a population close to 30 million inhabitants could be serviced (Ministerio del Ambiente, 2006). However, in the last few years water cuts have increased, especially in highly populated cities that, leading to important conflicts up to nowadays. Water is one of the most important and sensitive issue about population needs affecting communities, cooperatives and SSE.

There are several rules that regularize the services of water supply and wastewater collection. The main one is the CNRBV, which points out the competencies of the municipalities to the disposal of wastewater and drinking water service. Moreover, CNRBV established that the waters were public property of the nation and declared that water policy and legislation were a matter of national public power.

2.2. A portray of the regional public water enterprises in Venezuela

In Venezuela, drinking water supply was provided from 1874 by the Ministry of public works. The Instituto nacional de obras sanitarias (INOS), body dependent on the central power, was created in 1943 and acted as a water supplier for the municipalities. In his 45 years of service, the INOS got to serve 90% of the population, raising the coverage of services in different cities, extending water and sewer distribution networks in much of urban areas and building large systems of production, purification, and driving (Sandia, 2002). State investment in water services was never covered with the tariffs charged (which is the current situation). In the 1970s, the INOS emphasized more on the construction of infrastructure works, neglecting its role as an operator of aqueducts. This situation is reflected in the low quality of drinking water service and coverage levels are reduced up to 76% of the population.

In 1989, in the middle of the restructuring of the INOS, the anonymous company hydrological Venezuela (HIDROVEN) was set up with the responsibility of developing policies and programs in the field of supply of drinking water, collection and treatment of wastewater, as well as to establish guidelines for the management, operation, maintenance and expansion of hydraulic systems. Together with HIDROVEN, 10 subsidiaries of firms were created, under the figure of joint-stock companies with equity capital and whose largest shareholder is the Venezuelan state, through HIDROVEN. All these companies were carriers of water, with the exception of CVG-GOSH, and were constituted as corporations, with financial and functional autonomy, but taking care of HIDROVEN guidelines. These companies were Hidroandes, Hidrocapital, MDS, Hidrocaribe, Hidrofalcon, Hidrolago, Hidrollanos, Hidrosuroeste, Hidropaez and HidroOccidente, which were then reorganized (Higuerey et al, 2012).

2.3. Technical roundtables of water (Mesas técnicas de agua: MTA)

The Technical roundtables of water (MTA) are organizations promoted by the state which are constituted in accordance with the Civil Code in order to ensure the participation of users in the supervision of the quality, rate and coverage of services. According to the 2001 Organic law for the provision of the services of drinking water and sanitation (*Ley orgánica para la Prestación de los servicios de agua potable y de saneamiento*), its functions are: a) to represent communities and neighborhood groups alongside the service providers; b) to review the investments that will be carried out for the development of these services; c) to disseminate information on aspects related to the provision of services; d) to guide the participation of the community in the development and monitoring of the provision of services; e) to propose plans and programs that could be given to subscribers; f) to collaborate with service providers in matters referred to consideration and any other body enabling to meet properly the water needs of local communities. MTA must be part of the communal councils.

The MTA have a strong territorial reference and encourage stewardship and social control by the communities and transparency in accountability. Their performance seeks to respond to the needs of the community and to improve the quality of life at the same time that they constitute spaces to build up and to exercise responsible citizenship. In some cases, the MTA are not only dedicated to solve the problems with the drinking water service, but they also deal with other subjects. In this way, they take advantage of the experience and meeting space becoming in several cases the leader organization of the communal councils, which in turn are, by definition, the basis of the commune system, supposed to be the basis of the Bolivarian socialism of the 21st century according to the National development plan 2013-2019.

The MTA prepare community projects that are aimed to solve problems of their community and to obtain funding. This money was formerly directly spent by MTA building up the water projects, although nowadays the money for water project is put into the bank account of the communal council which is in charge of the water project and which controls the funds. However, at the same time there could be MTA projects with funds in either their own bank account, or in the bank account of the communal council.

For the year 2006 there were 2,783 MTA, almost three times more than in 2005. For 2010, there were 8,109 MTA, most of them in the centralized companies. MTA have had different results in terms of performance. However, many of these MTA lost their aims, and became engaged in other activities, especially related to the political control of the population in local territories and disputes of communal councils. Then, the participation of the members of the MTA stopped being on voluntary basis in many cases. Those who were not paid did no longer participated in running community projects.

After the experience of the several MTA, the Consejos comunitarios de agua (CCA) were set up. The CCA integrated a broader ecological area and allowed MTA to look at the social and environmental factors affecting water services. For instance, in Margarita Island, the CCA was created in 2005 and is still very active in working with MTA projects. They currently deal with cycles of delivering water to diverse local communities. They meet on Saturdays every three weeks.

In this sense, MTAs could play an important role in promoting water as a "common good" (Ostrom, 2009), and particularly as regards community irrigation schemes which are still in operation and those which have ceased to function. Among the best known, especially for support to farmers, are: the Guárico river irrigation system (in Guárico State – Central Region of Venezuela); the irrigation system of the Clavellino – which uses the waters of the Carinicuao river, in the State of Sucre – and serves both sugar cane growers and planters producing short cycle vegetables; in addition, the irrigation system San Isidro in the Falcón State (central-western region).

Unfortunately, in the perspective of a "tragedy of common goods" (Hardyn, as cited in Fagiolo, 2012), it is essential to point out how the Cumaná Irrigation System (Sucre State) has gradually been lost (Marín, 2015). According to the quoted author, this tragedy is due to the poor planning policies of the municipality and the city of Cumaná (capital of the municipality and of the Sucre State). Local organizations, such as the Mayor's office, as well as multilateral organizations such as the Inter-American development bank are to be blamed in this respect.

However, SSE organizations – such as MTAs – through the organization of communities can play a very important role in the recovery, maintenance and management of these recovered and rehabilitated irrigation systems, which remains as unfinished issue.

3. Results and challenges of public policies for water management and the social and solidarity economy in Venezuela

MTA may be considered as an example of solidarity economy provided that they comply with the principles of autonomous community organizations and with the other principles established by the International cooperative alliance in 1995, as regards the cooperative identity. The MTA is an example of community organizations trying to coordinate the efforts of people targeted to improve the drinking water services, administered by the public water enterprises; in the Venezuelan case by HIDROVEN and its affiliates. However, given the complexity of the water problem in Venezuela, a new administrative, financial, technical and scientific deal is required (Gabaldon, 2010). In order to achieve a truly sustainable development, it is necessary to include the active participation of organized communities "to improve the service, by using the principles of responsibility, co-management, volunteer work, solidarity, promoting access to drinking water as a fundamental human right, fighting poverty and social exclusion through active staring participation of people's power" (Coalición de Mesas Técnicas de Agua, 2016).

In some cases, the MTA are not only dedicated to solving problems with drinking water, but they also address other issues, drawing on their experience, in order to become, in several cases, the leading organization of the community, the communal councils. These councils, in turn are, by definition, the basis of the system of the communes, supposed to be the basis of the Bolivarian socialism of the 21st century according to the National development plan 2013-2019. The MTA prepare community projects that are aimed at solving community problems, to obtain financing. This money was previously spent directly by the MTA, mainly for the construction of water projects; although today the money for the water project is deposited in the bank account of the communal council, which is in charge of the water project and controls the funds. For instance, in January 2011, the MTA had been allocated a total of Bs. 481,052,043 for the execution of 1,556 drinking and sanitation water projects, of which 1,097 were culminated and 459 are running, benefiting a population of 1,526,339 inhabitants with completed projects. When all these projects will be ended up, it is estimated that a total of 2,973,935 inhabitants will get direct benefits of these projects (Coalition MTA, 2016).

The MTA had contrasted results in their performance. Some researchers claim (Lacabana et al, 2008) that due to the performance of the Bolivarian National Constitution and the MTA, the Millennium development goals of halving the population without access to water had been reached ten years ahead of time and with improved coverage of wastewater collection.

However, and based on the available data, it can be estimated that these projects have actually involved only 5% of the total population – estimated at 30,000,000 people. When the ongoing projects will be carried out, they are expected to reach 10% of the population, with an average investment of Bs[2] 161.00 per beneficiary. Nevertheless, if the target population of these projects are the poorest people without access to water, instead of the total population, the results may have a different meaning, with increased debate. Moreover, beyond the aspects of sociopolitical management – as pointed out by Gabaldon (2010) – the water problem is very complex and, recently, "the complaint that the water is dirty is repeated in several regions of Venezuela, especially at this time when drought has increased rationing throughout the country" (*BBC-Mundo* and *El Nacional*, 4 February 2016).[3]

In addition (Lopez, 2011) pointed out that many of these MTA projects had lost their objectives and that MTA had engaged in other activities, especially in relation to the political control of the population in the territories and disputes of communal councils. Therefore, participation of the MTA members stopped being voluntary in many cases, and when monetary compensation began to diminish, these neighbors stopped participating in the management of the community project.

The BBC report notes that "According to ENCOVI 2015 survey, in which three universities studied the quality of life of Venezuelans, 81% of households have aqueduct, while 38% do not have continuous access to water."

The government recognizes that the current water problem is a serious one, both in quantity and quality. However, they do not take full responsibility for the situation, and say that drought is caused by the

2 $37.44 at the official Exchange rate for the year 2011 (Bs/$ = 4.30).

3 ¿Por qué el agua en Venezuela llega "hedionda y amarillenta"? BBC-Mundo y El Nacional, <http://www.el-nacional.com>, consulted on 15 August 2016.

natural phenomenon known as *El Niño*. On the contrary, many engineers and environmental experts (Gabaldon, 2010) claim that, despite the problems identified by the managers of HIDROVEN, it is essential to rebuild the national hydrological service, basing this reconstruction on the planner spirit of the "Commission of the National Plan for Water Resources Utilization" founded in 1967 (Gabaldon, 2010). As a result of this situation, the recent statement of the BBC-World says that it has become very common to see in Venezuela street closure on national roads in protest against water service interruptions for days and even weeks.

4. Lessons and challenges for further research

These considerations require deepening, without ideological blinders, the performance evaluation of the MTA as complementary tools to solve the water problem in Venezuela.

In general, regarding the MTA, it can be said that the so-called 21st Century Socialism model has been successful in terms "to strengthen the dynamics of organization and mobilization generated from below, providing an intermediate body, articulating and coordinating base organizations in popular communities" (Lopez, 2011).

However, not everything can be considered positive or negative, it is necessary to consider the development of MTA in the field of promoting participatory democracy. Following the intervention of Vegas (2012) (Executive Director of CESAP social group) at the National meeting of social organizations – organized by the Catholic University Andres Bello (UCAB) –, it can be said that there has been "an extension of popular participation, but it is promoted in practice that this is passive, receiving and loyal to the official discourse and practices; extending the legal framework around new mechanisms and participatory possibilities, but some laws exceed the citizen and supersede the authority".

In addition, Vegas highlights "the social inclusion and political exclusion; social inclusion of excluded sectors: women, peasants, indigenous, disabled, elderly, but also dismantling of existing services and poor quality of today services."

The long period of the Bolivarian government system – from 1999 to the present – can be divided neatly into three stages. The first stage runs from 1999 to 2006. The leitmotif was the promotion of participatory democracy and the MTA and the Water community councils (CED) were among the first participatory innovations for co-management of public services (Lopez, 2011).

A second phase, from 2007 to 2010, might be considered as a transitional one. This period started with the re-election (december 2006) of President Chavez and was marked by the failed constitutional reform (2007) and the approval of the constitutional amendment (2008) for indefinite re-election of the president and all public officers. During this period, participatory democracy gradually became more directed, through the power of oil revenue managed by the state.

The third phase, currently underway, began in 2010 with the approval – by decree – of a set of laws on the formation of a new "communal state" which, as stated by Lopez (2011), is a "no Liberal state" which in the name of direct participation, moves on the contrary to the re-centralization of a "petro-state" instead of favoring the real empowerment of grassroots organizations and full citizenship of people.

In this context, financial resources for investment and maintenance of water infrastructure are becoming smaller and distant. Tariffs remained anchored in time and did not contribute enough to meet operational costs, inflation and lack of regulation affects expenditures and budget allocation in water projects. New funding mechanisms for community projects are channeled through the Federal government council (Consejo federal de gobierno) with slower response times and lesser efficiency. These problems must be on the research agenda, in order to build up sustainable solutions with more autonomous and efficient MTA and SSE organizations working in the field of water services while developing full citizenship of people.

This work sought to compare the services of supplies of drinking water and wastewater collection provided by the regional companies centralized and decentralized in Venezuela, emphasizing possible forms of community management of water in each case studied. In general, it can be said by now that the model of Bolivarian socialism of the 21st century, based on the CNRBV, has had successful outcomes in terms of social inclusion, reduction of illiteracy, and growth in the number of people educated or incorporated in programs of training and creation of many universities, which have been recognized by several institutions like UNESCO, UNDP and CEPAL. However, the model seems unsustainable, due to in the lack of efficiency and a declining participation in the MTA and in the different community organizations that supposedly should integrate communal councils, communes and the SSE organizations defined in the National development plan. Such failures must be addressed and corrected, in order to look for efficient solutions in the broader framework of the sustainable development for a better world.

Furthermore, current public policies for social and communal economy may be at risk of repeating the similar mistakes that occurred in the past with the massive promotion of cooperatives. Some weaknesses, that remind the failures of the *Vuelvan Caras* mission, can be observed. They deserve to be reviewed in relation to the current promotion of the social economy organizations. In this context the exercise of the social controller for the fulfilment of the so-called "communal cycle" of the projects, might be the tool that could handle organized communities to prevent relapse in errors. Still, there is not a regulation of participation for the exercise of the social controller. But if relevant government agencies fail to act diligently for budget allocation to scheduled communal councils works, this can seriously affect people's motivation to participate, thus lowering social commitment. Financial and non-financial resources for community projects and the construction of communal aqueducts for MTA, in most of the local cases we observed, kept coming at times with asynchronous rhythms, which affected the viability of projects (Díaz, 2014).

In general, the effectiveness of responses to technical solutions agreed between the MTA, HIDROVEN and water operators such as Hidrocaribe and communal councils related to water availability, and the quality of service, has been declining for several reasons that have been described above. Currently the NUDE have been faded away and new organizational forms have been pointed out as alternatives in the framework of the communal system and the homeland plan. NUDE seemed to have been organizations with reduced reach while communal councils could be a more satisfactory one, allowing a wide-range of experiences of citizens participation like MTA. However further research is required as citizen participation in diverse SSE and community organizations are in an ongoing process of a search for alternatives to the current situation.

References

Asamblea Nacional, 2001, "Ley orgánica del sistema económico comunal", *Gaceta Oficial*, No. 6.011, Extraordinario de fecha 21 de diciembre.

Asamblea Nacional, 2001, "Ley orgánica para la Prestación de los servicios de agua potable y de saneamiento", *Gaceta Oficial*, No. 5.568, Extraordinario de fecha 31 de diciembre.

Asamblea Nacional, 2009, "Constitución de la República Bolivariana de Venezuela", *Gaceta Oficial*, No. 5.908, Extraordinario de fecha 19 de febrero.

BBC-Mundo y El Nacional, *¿Por qué el agua en Venezuela llega "hedionda y amarillenta"?*, <http://www.el-nacional.com>, consulted on 15 August 2016.

Coalición de Mesas Técnicas Agua, "Aporte al examen periódico Universal Derecho al Agua. Combate a la Pobreza y la Exclusión Social", Participación Popular, <http://lib.ohchr.org/HRBodies/UPR/Documents/session12/VE/CMTACoalicionMesasTecnicasAgua-spa.pdf>, consulted on 10 August 2016.

Díaz B., 2006, "Políticas públicas para la promoción de cooperativas en Venezuela", *CAYAPA, Revista Venezolana de Economía Social*, 6 (11): 149-83.

Díaz B., 2008, "Reflexiones sobre la economía social en Venezuela", *SIC Revista del Centro Gumilla*, LXXI (709): 411-14.

Díaz B., 2014, "Las nuevas formas de organizaciones de economía social y solidaria promovidas desde el Estado en Venezuela", *Voces en el Fenix*, 37: 78-85.

Escalona L., Espitia M., García L., 2009, "Descripción y caracterización del sector agua potable en Venezuela", *CAYAPA, Revista Venezolana de Economía Social*, 9 (18): 9-32.

Fagiolo M., 2012, "El conocimiento como bien común", *CAYAPA, Revista venezolana de economía social*, 12 (23): 65-83.

Fals Borda O., 1976, *El reformismo por dentro en América Latina*, México, Ed. Siglo Veintiuno.

Francisco C., 2008, "Mientras más herramientas tenga el poder popular más cerca estaremos del autogobierno". *Vertientes, la Revista de Hidrocapital*, 8 (23): 20-2.

Gabaldon A.-J., 2010, "Principales Problemas del Agua en Venezuela", *Jornadas Nacionales de Derecho Ambiental y Desarrollo Sustentable*, Caracas, Universidad Simón Bolívar.

Godoy M., 2013, "Viceministra de Participación Comunal del Ministerio del Poder Popular para las Comunas y Protección Social", en entrevista en *Venezolana de Televisión*, Caracas, 31 de enero, <http://www.vtv.gob.ve/articulos/2013/01/31/mas-de-44-mil-400-consejo-comunaleshacen-vida-en-el-pais-5670.html>, consulted on 10 August 2016.

Hernández M., León M., Díaz B., 2008, "Representaciones sociales de la educación cooperativa en el movimiento cooperativo venezolano", *CAYAPA, Revista Venezolana de Economía Social*, 8 (15): 137-66.

Higuerey A., Díaz B., Carrero M., Araujo S., 2008, "Evaluación del financiamiento público en las cooperativas de un núcleo de desarrollo endógeno en Trujillo, Venezuela", *CAYAPA, Revista venezolana de economía social*, 9 (17): 65-83.

Higuerey A., González M., Trujillo L., 2012, "Situación actual de los servicios de suministro de agua en Venezuela", *CAYAPA, Revista venezolana de economía social*, 12 (24): 9-36.

Higuerey A., Trujillo L., González M., D'Elia P., 2013, "Una aproximación a la determinación de la eficiencia en las empresas de servicio de agua potable y residual en Venezuela", *ACADEMIA*, 28 (12): 337-55.

Lacabana M., Cariola C., La Rosa I., Maldonado A., Villasmil M., Vielma L., 2008, "Las mesas técnicas de agua en el contexto de los cambios institucionales, la democracia participativa y la participación popular en Venezuela", Informe final del Proyecto *Mesas Técnicas de Agua, proyectos comunitarios y análisis de los procesos de participación* Contrato Nº GPFFC-02-2007 (Cendes-HIDROVEN) (Versión Preliminar), Caracas, <http://www.hidroven.gov.ve/publicaciones/912560_MTA%20AutoresVarios.pdf>, consulted on 1 January 2015.

López E., Tabuas M., 2012, "La utopía de las comunas", *El Nacional*, Caracas, 28 de Octubre, <http://www.elnacional.com/siete_dias/utopia-comunas_0_70792974.html>, consulted on 1 January 2015.

López M., 2011, "Democracia Participativa en Venezuela. Orígenes, leyes, percepciones y desafíos (1999-2010)", *Temas de Formación Sociopolítica*, 50, Caracas, Centro Gumilla.

Marín S., 2015, "El BID generaría la muerte del sistema de riego de Cumaná", <https://www.aporrea.org/>, consulted on 15 August 2016.

Ministerio del Ambiente, 2006, *Recursos hídricos de Venezuela*, Caracas, Fondo editorial Fundambiente.

Ministerio del poder popular para la comunicación, 2013, Más de 40 mil consejos comunales y 1,401 comunas registradas en censo. 17/09/2013, <http://www.minci.gob.ve/2013/09/mas-de-40-mil-consejos-comunales-y-1-401-comunas-registradas-en-censo/>, consulted on 30 October 2014.

Ostrom E., 2009, *Governare i beni comuni*, Venezia, Marsilio Editore.

Sandia M., 2002, *Ley orgánica para la prestación de los servicios de agua potable y de saneamiento. Estudio sobre el régimen jurídico de la prestación de los servicios de agua potable y saneamiento (Una posibilidad cierta para disponer de servicios eficientes)*, Caracas, Editorial Jurídica Venezolana.

Vegas D., 2012, Intervención en *Mesa de Trabajo "Organizaciones Sociales y Participación" en "Encuentro Nacional de Organizaciones Sociales"*, Caracas, Universidad Católica Andrés Bello.

Part II

Towards new heterogeneous forms of territorial cooperations?

Chapter 7

Exploring the Conceptualization and Design of "IEP-Sites"

SSE Initiatives Aiming for an Inclusive Economic Participation within Flemish Urban Cities

Nathalie Vallet, Michelle Bylemans
University of Antwerp

Simon De Nys-Ketels
Ghent University

Introduction

When focusing on the relationship between the territory and the social and solidarist economy (SSE), urban territories generate interesting challenges. Given the territory definition[1] used by the CIRIEC workgroup "SSE and territories", an urban territory refers to a dense and heterogeneous spatial context[2] gathering "… players that seek to bring out, then attempt to resolve under environmental constraints, a shared societal or production problem" (Pecqueur, Itçaina, 2012). Within an urban context these problems are related to the particular features, evolutions and future challenges of an urban society. Consequently, the

1 The territory as a social construction, see: CIRIEC International Scientific Commission Social Economy, proposed working group SSE and Territories: between interaction and co-construction, <http://www.ciriec.ulg.ac.be/fr/telechargements/WG_ES-Territoire_programm.pdf>, consulted on 1 March 2015.

2 The dense and heterogeneous features are related to the closely intertwined relationships between multiple activities, functions and people of an urban territory.

associated definition of territorial governance refers to a complex urban network of numerous private, social profit and public organizations where the local urban government fulfils an important key-position or "nodal" role (Leloup *et al.*, 2005).

In relation to the scientific investigation of urban territories, our attention is drawn by one particular challenge that manifests itself within many Flemish cities: the considerable high and expanding amount of socially deprived urban citizens.[3] An important cause of their socially deprived position is their weak and insecure economic position (Coene *et al.*, 2011; Termote, Galand, 2012; Coene, 2013). Although there exist many Flemish, provincial and municipal initiatives to improve the economic position of socially deprived citizens, these initiatives are often poorly coordinated and geographically dispersed in nature. As such, these initiatives are scattered throughout Flanders and its many large, medium-sized and small cities. This geographical diaspora makes the road leading socially deprived citizens towards these initiatives very difficult to find. Because many of these socially deprived citizens move, live and reside in cities, a lot of Flemish urban governments are therefore confronted with the following challenge: how can socially deprived urban citizens participate economically as a provider of labor and as a consumer in a more solid i.e. sustainable and structural way? What kind of alternative policy solutions do there exist, and which of these solutions is focused on the remediation of the poorly coordinated and spatially dispersed initiatives?

Within the multi-disciplinary research setting of the Henry Van De Velde Research group (University of Antwerp, Faculty of design

---

3 The evolution of socially deprived citizens within Flanders has been investigated by the Service Platform to Combat Poverty, Insecurity and Social Exclusion (in Dutch: het Steunpunt tot Bestrijding van Armoede, Bestaansonzekerheid en Sociale Uitsluiting) <http://www.combatpoverty.be> as well as by the Centre on Inequalities, Poverty, Social Exclusion and the City of the University of Antwerp (In Dutch: OASES) <https://www.uantwerpen.be/en/rg/oases/>, consulted on 10 August, 2017. Within Flanders, several definitions and/or criteria are used to define the concept of socially vulnerable or deprived citizens. According to the Public Employment Service of Flanders (in Dutch: VDAB) for instance, socially deprived citizens are identified by means of the following criteria: nationality/language (i.e. non-native), education level (i.e. low skilled), physical/mental work ability (i.e. limited and/ or absent) and age (i.e. older than 50) <http://partners.vdab.be/kansengroepen.shtml> and <http://www.vdab.be/english>, consulted on 10 August 2017.

sciences),[4] we have formulated an answer by introducing the concept of a so-called "Inclusive Economic Participation (IEP)site". In line with the ideas of Manuel Castells (1989, 1996, 2010; Stock, 2011), we define an IEP site as a spatially concentrated "hub" or location in cities that accommodates public, (social) profit and profit organizations who jointly strive for a (more) solid economic participation of socially deprived citizens, both as a consumer and as a provider of labor. Consequently, IEP sites may for instance accommodate providers of public services (e.g. employment, social housing and child care support), SSE organizations (e.g. sheltered workshops, social restaurants and production co-operatives) and profit organizations (e.g. eco-design stores, recycling pop-up shops, training experts and co-working facilitators).

Given the objectives of the CIRIEC workgroup "SSE and territories", an IEP site can be (re)defined as a particular territorial network that accommodates partners who try to resolve under the environmental constraints of an urban setting, the challenge of an inclusive economic participation. In relation to the territorial governance, appropriate models, frameworks or blueprints are needed to manage these networks in an effective and efficient way. As the concept of an IEP site is however new, the detection, analysis and evaluation of already existing governance models is not self-evident. We can however find some inspiration in already existing IEP site "related" initiatives (see also paragraph 2: methodology). But even then, the major scientific challenge will be to construct these appropriate governance models ourselves.

Based on our multi-disciplinary expertise, we will focus our construction efforts on a particular kind of governance model, being the so-called strategic-spatial model or blueprint for IEP sites. In an initially elaborated working definition, the strategic part of such a blueprint is focused on (i) the strategic meaning of the IEP site i.e. the importance and relevance of an inclusive economic participation in relation to the long term challenges and priorities of the entire city and its partners, (ii) the strategic and organizational design of the IEP site i.e. the organizational network features including the strategic decision process and structure, and (iii) the strategic impact i.e. the degree in which the activities of the IEP site actually contribute to a (more) solid economic participation of socially deprived urban citizens. The spatial part of these

4 The team consists of researchers within the disciplines of public strategic management, social economy, urban planning, architecture and interior architecture.

models or blueprints is focused on (i) the spatial context i.e. the precise location of the IEP site within the city and the particular features of this location, (ii) the spatial design of the IEP site itself i.e. the composition and architectural features of the IEP site and its buildings and (iii) the spatial impact i.e. the degree in which the spatial design of the IEP site actually contributes to a (more) solid economic participation of socially deprived urban citizens.

Eventually, our final goal is to develop a set of alternative strategic-spatial models or blueprints for the installation and development of IEP sites. The alternative nature refers to the assumption that the diverse types of socially vulnerable citizens as well as the specifically needed economic participation and the particular urban setting, presumably demand for the identification of different types of IEP sites. Each alternative model or blueprint will then specify and clarify the associated and internally consistent governance-principles of that particular IEP site type. This can inspire and support all partners involved – and in particular the policy makers of local governments fulfilling a "nodal" role – to make more well-considered, consistent and explicit policy decisions on their shared inclusive economic participation ambitions.

This brings us to the goal and objective of this paper. Within this publication we will report on the first set of preliminary research results realized within two explorative IEP site projects in Flanders. The preliminary character is due to the phase-wise analysis that is typical for a qualitative research methodology (see also paragraph 2 on methodology). Gradually, the collected data are coded and re-coded in order to interpret and re-interpret the extensive and complex set of gathered insights. As mentioned before, the research results are obtained from two IEP site projects within Flanders. On the one hand there is the so-called STIMPRO research project financed by the University of Antwerp. On the other hand, there is the pilot research project realized in the former vagabond colony of Wortel-Merksplas[5] and co-financed by the University of Antwerp and the Province of Antwerp.

Given the previously described objective, the following research question will be answered within this paper: what can we "inductively" learn from both explorative research projects in relation to (i) the conceptualization of an IEP site and (ii) the elaboration of strategic-spatial (governance) models or blueprints?

[5] Located near the city of Antwerp, Turnhout and Hoogstraten.

The structure of this paper consists of a description of the research methodology, a summary of the research results and the answers to the previously defined research questions and some concluding remarks on our future research agenda.

1. A Grounded Theory and interdisciplinary research design

As we aim for the development of a non-existent or new concept, the overall research design is clearly explorative in nature. In particular, we choose for a qualitative research design according to the principles of the so-called Grounded Theory (Straus, Corbin, 1994; Charmaz, 2006; Morse, 2009; Stern, Porr, 2011; Birks, 2011). By gradually collecting and analyzing (inspirational) field data of IEP site "related" SSE initiatives (i.e. the so-called quick scan case-studies), we strive for the inductive development of strategic-spatial models or blueprints for IEP sites.

The identification of the inspirational population for our Grounded Theory ambition (i.e. IEP site "related" SSE initiatives) is certainly not obvious. When looking for relevant information it becomes clear that no overall, extended and systematized inventory exists – or has been made – in Flanders or Belgium. Therefore, we have contacted several local, regional and Flemish SSE platforms[6] as well as Flemish local governments[7] to construct such an inventory-list ourselves.

For the subsequent selection of the quick scan case-studies, we aim for a set of IEP site related SSE initiatives that reflect the uncovered diversity of the population inventory-list (see before). At first sight, this uncovered diversity mainly relates to the particular type of (i) economic activity/ sector, (ii) socially deprived citizens and (iii) geographical locations in Flanders. Given the manageability of both explorative research projects[8] we have selected a set of 15 SSE initiatives within the STIMPRO research project and 10 SSE initiatives within the pilot research project of Wortel-*Merksplas*.

---

6 E.g. IN-C or the Flemish Platform for SSE organizations, <http://in-c.biz/>, consulted on 15 August 2015.

7 E.g. VVSG or the Flemish Platform for Cities and Municipalities, <http://www.vvsg.be/>, consulted on 15 August 2015.

8 Both research projects lasted for max. 1 year and were realized by one senior and two junior researchers.

The data-collection is focused on the existing strategic and spatial features of the selected SSE initiatives. Although we have defined these features at the beginning of our research activities (i.e. see before: the initial "working" definition), we have further specified and adjusted them during the data-collection itself. This gradual, data-induced specification of central concepts and their respective features clearly fits the overall principles of the grounded theory methodology. Thus, the continuous interaction between the initial working definitions, the subsequent inductive discoveries and the intermediate (re)conceptualizations, eventually led to a list of data-collection items related to the topics specified in the paragraph "uncovered topics of a strategic-spatial blueprint" (see later: 2.2.1).

The data-collection itself has been realized by means of four complementary data-gathering techniques being (i) written or digital documents (e.g. brochures, internal policy notes), (ii) visual representations (e.g. plans, maps, photos), (iii) open and/or half-structured interviews[9] and (iv) observations (e.g. visits to the SSE initiatives by the researchers).

During the data-analysis we have used several visualization techniques (e.g. tables, schemes and figures). These techniques have facilitated considerably the making of a comparative analysis of all quick scan case-studies involved.

Finally, the intermediate research results have been discussed profoundly within the so-called "IEP-Reference-Platforms". These platforms have been set up at the start of each research initiative to guarantee the overall quality and practical use of the inductive conceptualization and the elaborated strategic-spatial models or blueprints. On the one hand these platforms consist of academic network-partners that safeguard the multi-disciplinary embeddedness.[10] On the other hand these IEP-Reference-Platforms also consist of partners who safeguard the added value for the "work field". It concerns representatives of local urban governments, SSE organizations and organizations representing socially deprived urban citizens.

---

9 1 to 3 interviews with mainly management representatives or directors of the SSE initiatives.

10 Amongst whom Oswald Devisch (ArcK Research Group, University of Hasselt), Hans Leinfelder (Faculty of Architecture, University of Leuven), Tinne van Regenmortel (Centre for Sociological Research, University of Leuven), Astrid Coates (University college of Heverlee, University association Leuven) and Barbara Sak, Christine Dussart and Fabienne Fecher (CIRIEC, Université de Liège).

As indicated in the title of this paragraph, the research design is also influenced by an explicit interdisciplinary research focus. The development of strategic-spatial models or blueprints clearly requires a simultaneous input from the disciplines of (i) SSE, (ii) strategic public management and (iii) architecture & urbanism. Although the concept is new – so that an elaborated, existing state of the art literature is presently absent – we can however uncover some similarities between our particular IEP site ambitions and some specific interests, methodological traditions and ambitions existing within the different disciplines involved. Notwithstanding the fact that a more profound and elaborate description of this state of the art will be the subject of a future – and thus separate – theoretical paper, we can already mention some interesting points of attention:

- Within the discipline of SSE, there exists a growing amount of literature on (i) the increasing amount and heterogeneous profile of socially deprived and/or impoverished citizens in our global society, (ii) the evolving and unique identity of the SSE sector, (iii) the importance of the SSE sector for public management and (iv) the strategic features of social entrepreneurship (Spear *et al.*, 2001; Moulaert, Ailenei, 2005; Certo, Miller, 2008; Monzon, Chavez, 2008; Bouchard, 2009; Conforth, Brown, 2014).

A remarkable hiatus however exists on the particular relationship of the societal interest and strategic features of SSE initiatives on the one hand, and its facilitating spatial morphology and architectural features on the other hand (e.g. is a particular type of location and/or particular – easy accessible – form of architecture required?).

Both the growing amount of literature and the apparent hiatus can be seen as relevant for the future elaboration of our IEP site concept.

- As far as the discipline of strategic public management is concerned, our IEP site ambitions can be related to the extensive and growing literature on so-called multi-actor and governance networks (Koppenjan, Klijn, 2004; O'Toole, Meier, 2004; Sorensen, Torfing, 2007; Bevir, Richards, 2009).

Within this literature however only a relatively small amount of publications refers explicitly to the needed or facilitating spatial features of these networks (Vallet, 2013). When considering these spatial features, they mainly focus on process- and management-related considerations. As such, multiple authors within the specific literature on strategic urban planning for instance, have argued that the process of "(citizen) participation" in urban spatial development and planning offers a viable alternative to the classical top-down approach that often fails to capture the various voices and needs of all urban actors and subjects involved (Bryson, Crosby, 1993; Healy, 1996, 1997; Innes, Booher, 1999). In more recent publications, some authors have also suggested practical guidelines to further or actually implement such participatory processes in different spatial contexts (Innes, Booher, 1999; Bryson *et al.,* 2012). Moreover, other authors stemming from the specific discipline of public (interior) architecture have suggested a similar approach (Peterson, 2008; Smith *et al.,* 2014).

In short, both the growing amount of literature on multi-actor and governance networks and the apparent hiatus on the needed or facilitating spatial accommodations of these networks, can be related to our particular concept of IEP sites;

- Within the broad discipline of architecture & urbanism, there is a striking lack of academic work and literature on SSE initiatives. Neither the historical development of SSE architecture and urban planning has been described, nor has the construction of a new canon of "good practices" been undertaken.

Nonetheless, some literature exists that might be relevant or can be at least inspiring for our particular IEP site ambitions.

A first type of literature concerns the scientifically valid ways of architectural knowledge production, being "design research" (Bayazit, 2004), and the specific literature on "architectural research" (EAAE, 2012). Two methodological views within this literature are of particular importance for the way in which we conduct our explorative research into IEP sites: the literature on research-by-design (Bowen, 2008; Borgdorff, 2011; Verbeke, 2013) and on the actor-network-theory (Latour, Yaneva, 2008; Yaneva, 2012). In the former, knowledge production is realized not only by means of the final design, but also, heuristically, as the "design process forms the pathway through which new insights, knowledge, practices or products come into being." (EAAE, 2012). In the latter, the analysis of spatial objects is done by charting or mapping the various actors that are related to the architectural object during its lifespan. Thus, our Grounded Theory research design clearly relates to an evolving research tradition within the discipline of architecture & urbanism.

A second type of relevant literature concerns recent publications on the relationship between architectural design and subjective well-being (Smith *et al.,* 2012; Desmet, Pohlmeyer, 2013; Stevens *et al.,* 2014; Petermans, Pohlmeyer, 2014). This new and emerging topic in architectural research is presumably relevant for two reasons. On the one hand, these publications aim to develop instruments to evaluate how and in which degree architecture contributes to the so-called subjective well-being of its users. On the other hand, and based on the previously gained insights, their future goal is to identify specific design principles that allow architects to develop buildings that support or increase the subjective well-being of its users. As our IEP site concept focusses on the well-being of socially deprived urban citizens in their quest for an inclusive economic participation, this type of publications seems to be quite interesting.

A third and last type of literature concerns the publications on other hub-wise architectural typologies and relevant spatial features. Thus, there is for instance the literature on school campuses (De Langhe, Lyppens, 2012), industrial sites (Mozingo, 2011), gated communities (Lang, Danielson, 1997; Eshuis *et al.,* 2011) and building blocks (Apostel *et al.,* 2008). Accordingly, there is the particular literature on relevant spatial features of such hubs as for instance the inclusiveness (Amin, 2002; Verschaffel, 2006), accessibility (Pasaogullari, Doratli, 2004), multi-functionality and interwoven character (Hooimeier *et al.,* 2001). Especially these features relate rather directly to the essence of our IEP site concept.

In summary, the lack of publications on SSE architecture and the growing amount of literature on research-by-design, the actor-network theory, the subjective well-being of architectural design and the features of (other) hub-wise architectural typologies, can be related to the concept and our research ambitions on IEP sites.

2. Inductively elaborating and fine-tuning the central concepts

In this paragraph we will summarize the intermediate research results of our explorative research efforts: what can we learn from the realization of both explorative research projects? How can they inspire us in the elaboration and development of our central concepts and their features (i.e. an IEP site and strategic-spatial models)?

2.1. Inductively fine-tuning the concept of an IEP site

On the basis of our inductive exploration we have gained in-depth new insights into the precise meaning of "a spatially concentrated hub" and of the "joint activities and ambitions" (see: features of the initial working definition).

2.1.1. The uncovered morphological diversity of a spatially concentrated hub

On the basis of our inductive exploration we find out that our initial assumption on a spatially concentrated hub being a clear demarcated, enclosed and identifiable physical location in a city, is too simple and homogeneous an idea to fit the uncovered existing morphological diversity of IEP site related SSE initiatives. Thus, our research results indicate that the spatial concentration of IEP site related initiatives clearly covers different and alternative morphological forms (i.e. types of spatial concentration).

This morphological diversity has been experienced most noticeably in the analysis of the 15 quick scan case-studies within the STIMPRO research project. Thus, the meaning of "concentration" and "intertwined" initiatives could be associated with a location (i) within one single building or premises, (ii) within a well-defined (industrial) domain or restricted area, (iii) within a particular urban neighborhood[11] and (iv) along a spatial and/or digital "track" of permanent and mobile settlements throughout the larger territory of the entire city.[12]

From a governance point of view, it is plausible that another morphological form or shape of an IEP site implies other governance challenges and solutions elaborated in alternative strategic-spatial models. Because of these governance implications, it clearly makes sense to construct a kind of "spatial" typology of IEP sites on the basis of the uncovered morphological diversity. A first attempt results in the following IEP site types (De Nys-Ketels *et al.*, 2015):

- The single-building IEP site: all organizations are located within one building;

---

11 E.g. the quick scan case-studies of "Zuurstof voor de Brugse poort" and "Bruggen naar Rabot" in the city of Ghent.

12 E.g. the quick scan case-studies of "Levanto" (city of Antwerp), "WEB" (city of Turnhout), "Spiegelfabriek" (city of Herentals) and repair cafés (in several cities).

- The campus IEP site: all organizations are located within a well-defined domain or restricted area;
- The neighborhood IEP site: all organizations are located within a certain neighborhood;
- The satellite IEP site: all organizations are connected by means of a spatial and/or digital "track" of settlements throughout the city.

Although the morphological diversity has been experienced most noticeably within the STIMPRO research project, the morphological awareness has also been triggered during the pilot research project of Wortel-Merksplas.

At the beginning it was apparent that the colony of Wortel-Merkplas was a well-defined territory or domain with clear, fence-and-wall-wise borderlines. When however further examining the precise features of this domain, it became clear that it actually consists of several public areas (e.g. lanes, meadows, grasslands) and buildings or premises of which not all will become a part of the intended IEP site experiment. As such, the morphological complexity gradually becomes apparent. After all, the ambitioned IEP site within the colony of Wortel-Merksplas is simultaneously a location (i) in one domain (i.e. a campus IEP site), (ii) in several premises but not with an exclusive IEP site destination (i.e. a semi- or partial campus site?) and (iii) on the territory of two rural municipalities situated in neighborhood of three Flemish cities (i.e. a semi-urbanized campus site?).

To conclude this paragraph, we can therefore say that the uncovered morphological diversity clearly emphasizes the need to differentiate the meaning of "a concentrated hub" and to identify varies types of spatial concentration that imply other governance principles within the strategic-spatial blueprints (see also later: 2.2.2).

2.1.2. The desired openness of a spatially concentrated hub

Regardless of the specific morphological form, we also find out that a successful – this means an effective and efficient – spatially concentrated hub is explicitly associated with an "open" profile. What this exactly means, does not only become clear throughout the analysis of the quick scan case-studies, but also and perhaps most apparently during the various debates of the two IEP-Reference-Platforms.[13] Let us summarize the uncovered conceptual meanings.

A first set of "openness" meanings refers explicitly to the *user side* of an IEP site:

- According to most participants of the IEP-Reference-Platforms, IEP sites may not be used or destined exclusively to socially deprived urban citizens. As such, IEP sites may not be associated with for instance (i) "gated" economic communities for deprived citizens only, (ii) "isolated fortresses" or (iii) socio-economic "ghettos". In contrast, IEP sites should be open to all urban citizens, regardless of their specific socio-economic profile. This will prevent an undesired stigmatization which is very likely to happen when the word "concentration" is taken too literally.

Simultaneously, other participants however emphasize the fact that a "mixed" use may eventually scare off or even exclude socially deprived citizens as they risk not to be served, helped or supported in a proper or tailor-made way. When being a minority within the mix, chances are high that their specific needs will not be met by organizations looking for scale effects realized in serving mainly the non-deprived majority. Additionally, socially deprived urban citizens may not feel themselves at ease in a mixed environment, what may prevent them from visiting a mixed IEP site.

- A second meaning of openness refers to a (more) dynamic, temporarily and voluntary use of IEP sites by urban citizens. This meaning of openness is suggested by many participants on the basis of a self-perceived or experienced changing profile of socially deprived urban citizens in Flemish cities associated with (i) the aftermath of the contemporary economic crises and (ii) some emerging contemporary societal trends.

When referring to the aftermath of the economic crises, participants emphasize the increasing (long term) unemployment of native-speaking and relatively young urban citizens with a high instead of a low education level. Additionally, a lot of attention is paid to the increasing amount of bankrupt self-employed citizens or small businessman. Both profiles

[13] In total, six debates have taken place (three meetings per IEP-Reference-Platform).

clearly do not match the traditional profile of socially deprived citizens.[14] But, according to the participants their economic participation is nonetheless seriously jeopardized.

When referring to important contemporary societal trends, the participants mainly focus on two phenomena. On the one hand there are the so-called work-stress related illnesses (e.g. burn-out, depression, mobbing related anxiety) that not only prevent a full economic participation but simultaneously increase consumption expenses (e.g. increased need for medical and household support). On the other hand, there are the so-called "modes of cohabitation" and family-related challenges (e.g. the care for elderly and financially deprived family-members, the consequences of aggressive divorces and the mental and financial constraints of one-parent families). As such, also urban citizens that do not fit the traditional profile of socially deprived urban citizens may "suddenly" and "temporarily" or even "definitely" become socially and economically deprived.

Although during the debates most participants argued on the basis of their daily professional experiences, it is interesting to further investigate whether and how these changing profiles are actually present in our contemporary urban society. Meanwhile and according to several participants support may be offered by IEP sites with the profile of a "creative (re)energizing spot", a "decompression zone",[15] or "a discrete, non-stigmatizing free port".[16]

A second set of "openness" meanings refers explicitly to the *supply side* of an IEP site:

- According to most participants, organizations situated on an IEP site should be prepared to collaborate with organizations and/or partners that are not located on the IEP site itself. According to them, remediating a complex societal phenomenon like an inclusive economic participation, can only be realized by joining a lot of mental forces and material means (e.g. to jointly realize scale effects and increase the overall efficiency). Additionally, some

[14] E.g citizens with a low or absent education level, a low-income level, leading a socially isolated life, being rather old, non-native speaking, and mentally or physically disabled.

[15] An idea that has been suggested in particular when it comes to the re-integration of ex-convicts as a particular type of socially-deprived citizens.

[16] For some "new" or non-traditional socially deprived urban citizens it is a taboo to openly recognize their deteriorated socio-economic position within society.

of them find it therefore important that IEP site organizations also cooperate and/or even set-up region-wise SSE initiatives that exceed the location and even the city itself in which the IEP site is embedded. As such, organizations active on an IEP site are explicitly associated by them with the role of region-wise "connectors" and/or "facilitators". The IEP site itself is then considered to be the "energizing hart" or "base-camp" of these region-wise SSE initiatives.

Given this particular meaning, the wide-range accessibility of an IEP site is then clearly of major importance.

Admittedly, this particular meaning of openness is strongly related to one particular spatial or morphological form of an IEP site (see also before), being that of a spatial "track" or "route" throughout the larger territory of the entire city and even far beyond. Nonetheless it is an interesting one, as the arguments of the participants supporting this particular point of view are clearly related to the popular (theoretical) trend of (public) regional networking and strategic alliances.

– A lot of discussion also takes place on the particular position of SSE organizations within an IEP site. For most participants it is quite obvious that given the working definition of an IEP site, SSE organizations (should) hold a dominant position within an IEP site. After all, the realization of an inclusive economic participation of socially deprived urban citizens is directly related to their strategic identity, core-business and expertise. As such, all participants agree that IEP sites certainly should accommodate SSE organizations.

Whether this position should be dominant or even exclusive is however another matter. The arguments "contra" are based on practical as well as more fundamental or principle considerations. The practical arguments refer to (i) the overall financial feasibility and (ii) the long-term survival of an IEP site, which demands for a considerable cash-flow and return-on-investments that cannot be realized by SSE organizations alone. The reason for this is not only due to the fact that the dominant focus of SSE organizations is on social goals and on the production factor of "labor" – instead of economic goals and the production factor of "capital" – but also due to recent public policy decisions made within Flanders that restrict the public (co-)financing facilities for SSE organizations (i.e. subsidies) and urges SSE organizations to look for "money on the free market" (i.e. specified within the future "Maatwerk" decree or legislation). The principle arguments rather relate to (i) particular ideological[17] point of views (e.g. the conviction that the economic performance of profit organizations and of a free market system is per definition superior), (ii) particular organizational thoughts (e.g. the conviction that there exist no fundamental differences between SSE organizations and profit organizations) and (iii) particular reflections on synergy and innovation (e.g. only mixed alliances between "regular" and SSE organizations can generate innovative management).

A third and final meaning of "openness" refers explicitly to the *spatial* and *architectural side* of an IEP-site:

- According to some participants the openness of an IEP site also refers to the presence of an easy accessible location or spatial embeddedness of an IEP site within the urban surroundings. As such, an IEP site should not only be accessible by "users" and "suppliers" of an IEP-site, but also by the entire urban population and especially by the urban citizens living in the nearby neighborhoods.

To conclude this paragraph on the desired openness we can say that when it comes to specifying "a concentrated hub", the various user-, supplier-and space-related meanings clearly emphasize the need to specify and elaborate associated governance principles within the strategic-spatial models or blueprints of IEP sites that actually stimulate and generate such an "open" concentrated hub (see also later: 2.2.2). Other or alternative meanings of this openness, clearly demand for other or alternative governance principles.

2.1.3. The uncovered diversity of intertwining activities and ambitions

When analyzing the 25 quick scan case-studies of both the STIMPRO research project and the pilot research project of Wortel-*Merksplas*, we can identify a wide range of "intertwining" activities and ambitions related to (i) the nature of the activities themselves (i.e. types of economic participation), (ii) the beneficiaries of the intertwined activities (i.e. types of socially deprived urban citizens) (iii) the suppliers of the intertwined

17 This ideological point of view is present within most Flemish local urban governments that are still highly influenced by the aftermath of New Public Management and additionally triggered by the neo-classically inspired rationalization trend.

activities (i.e. types and numbers of partners involved) and the particular urban setting of the intertwined activities (i.e. type of city).

Let us look at this diverse nature of these uncovered intertwined activities and how this has influenced the further conceptualization of an IEP site:

A first set of "diversity" meanings relates to the different types of economic activities of an IEP site:

– When we analyze the different types of *economic activities* within the 25 IEP site related initiatives, the research results uncover a very divers and rich set of interesting economic opportunities, including for instance the construction and maintenance industry (e.g. repair, laundry, cleaning), the (bio)agricultural and food industry (e.g. bio-production of fruit, horticulture and gardening), the creative industry (e.g. eco-design, recycling furniture and clothing, arts-and-craft activities), the mobility, logistics and distribution sector (e.g. bicycle hiring-repair-selling shops, packaging), the retail sector (e.g. social groceries, catering services), the consulting and education sector (e.g. job-coaching, buddy-services, co-working infrastructure), tourism (e.g. eco-lodging, farm-tourism) and care and wellness (e.g. child-care, social restaurants, services for seniors).

This wide range of economic activities suggests that the intertwining nature of economic activities can result in either (i) a very specialized IEP site joining different partners within a similar sector (e.g. a creative industry IEP site, a touristic and leisure IEP site, a care and wellness IEP site), or (ii) a very heterogeneous and more generalist IEP site combining complementary sectors and offering a broad range of products and services, and (iii) a unique or tailor-made IEP site that combines particular sectors in accordance to the specific needs of the city or urban neighborhood.

Additionally, it is interesting to notice that the intertwining initiatives of an IEP site can focus on (i) more traditional economic activities (e.g. maintenance, mobility, logistics and distribution) but also on (ii) rather innovative activities that have not been elaborated (yet) within the Flemish SSE sector (e.g. creative industry, tourism and wellness);

– Another interesting finding is that the different types of economic activities intertwine participation facilities for consumption as well as for employment. Thus, the supposed or suggested combination of both types of economic participation within an IEP site is on the basis of the collected data presumably feasible. We should however emphasize that the presence of this complementary combination is not always the result of a deliberate strategy, but often of a "fortunate" coincidence (see 2.1.4).

A second set of "diversity" meanings relates to the beneficiaries of the intertwined activities, being the different types of *socially deprived urban citizens*:

- In accordance with the many (theoretical) criteria used to describe and define the concept of socially deprived urban citizens, the analysis of the IEP site related initiatives also uncover the many ways in which socially deprived urban citizens are actually categorized and (re)grouped. In general, and notwithstanding this categorization exercise, few intertwined activities focus however on only one particular group. Nonetheless we could make a distinction between (i) a single versus (ii) a multi-target group related IEP site.

When reflecting on this particular research result, we notice also that categorizations and "priorities" are most often used by the public partners involved. In view of target-group related electoral ambitions, they can be most sensitive in "choosing" and favoring particular groups or profiles of socially deprived urban citizens above others;

- When categorizing, the (combined) criteria of (i) age, (ii) physical and mental state and (iii) income position are used most often within the IEP site related initiatives. In the "age" category much attention is paid to children, youngsters and senior citizens (i.e. + 65). In the "physical and mental state" category, an increased attention is paid to citizens enduring addiction, developmental disorders (e.g. autism) and work-, burn-out or anxiety related problems. In the "income" position category, a lot of attention is paid to poor urban citizens, low-educated unemployed citizens, seasonal unemployed workers and the reintegration of ex-prisoners;
- Another interesting finding is that not all intertwined activities are solely focused on and thus destined for socially deprived urban citizens (see also before when discussing on the "desired openness"). This is mainly true for the consumption-related economic activities, less for the employment-related activities that still focus predominantly on socially deprived urban citizens;

A third set of "diversity" meanings refers to the suppliers of the intertwined activities, being the amount and different types of *organizations* or *partners* involved:

- As far as the amount of partners is concerned, we notice a variation within the IEP site related initiatives between 2 up until maximum 5 organizations. At present, a higher number of intertwined partners is not that commonly found. When reflecting on these research results, the relatively limited amount of partners involved could relate to (i) the experimental phase in which these initiatives presently reside (… so that the joint initiative is still growing) or (ii) the high competitive institutional context in which mainly SSE organizations have to operate that moderates their initial enthusiasm to eventually join forces (i.e. they rather prefer a diversification strategy of their own than to cooperate with "rivalry" partners);
- When considering the different profiles of the partners involved, it is clear that in most IEP site related initiatives a public partner is involved who financially (i.e. by means of subsidies or financial investments) or spatially (i.e. by means of the disposal and/or rent of a public domain, location or building) facilitates and stimulates the joint SSE initiative. This however does not mean that the public partner is still present "once the stimulation job is done" or that its stimulation is realized in an active, dominant or even tangible way. Furthermore, the identity of the public actor is mainly local (i.e. urban local government), but also consortia with different public agents on various policy levels occur (e.g. the province, the Flemish community, the federal state or European funding agencies). Thus, the public facilitation role can become rather complex and multi-layered.

In some cases, there is no public actor involved, and the initiative is fully grass-rooted. Mainly in these particular cases diversification strategies of one partner can create the (virtual) impression of an IEP site: visitors may perceive the site as a joint initiative of many partners instead of only one organization.

As such, we could identify (i) a planned versus (ii) a grass-rooted and even (iii) a virtual IEP site.

- Beside the public actor or single partner there is also the dominant presence of SSE organizations (see also before) and some other social profit or even profit organization. When reflecting on these research results it is however important to emphasize that the limited presence of profit organizations may be influenced by the way in which we have reconstructed the population (see also before). In mainly consulting the SSE sector to uncover the population of IEP site related initiatives, it may be that collaborations with profit and regular organizations are missed out.

Thus, we intend to conclude that certainly the precise nature of the profiles and roles of partners involved should be more elaborated in-depth as they are very important within the construction of governance models. This will be done by means of subsequent and future research projects.

A fourth set of "diversity" meanings refers to the particular types of *urban setting* of the intertwined activities:

- Throughout the IEP site related initiatives, we notice that the profiles of the cities involved are quite different, not only in size (i.e. small, medium-sized or big city), but also in "historical tissue" including some socio-economic and/or target group-related "traditions" (e.g. textile industry, non-native blue-collar workers). This is for instance most obvious within the Wortel-Merksplas project. The former identity of the location (i.e. a former vagabond colony in which domestic shelter and employment facilities were offered within an agricultural and handicraft setting) in combination with the historical heritage of most buildings and public spaces (i.e. UNESCO heritage) have clear implications for the specific and sometimes rather (re)strict(ed) profile of an IEP site. Other examples are the location on a former industrial site (e.g. the UCO-site in the city of Ghent that used to be the settlement of an important company active within the textile industry) and the peripheral belt of a growing and expanding small city (e.g. the Spiegelfabriek in the city of Herentals).

When reflecting on these particular research findings, it is important to investigate why and how the profile of the IEP site should – or should not – respect a certain "historic tissue" or contextual setting? Certainly, from the perspective of the public partners involved, this can be an important issue. Thus, the creation of a so-called "historically embedded" or "heritage" IEP site comes into our minds;

To conclude this paragraph, we can say that from a governance point of view, all previously described "diversity" meanings can have implications on the concept and design of an IEP site. After all it is plausible that another type – or combination of – intertwined activities implies other governance challenges as well as other governance solutions elaborated in alternative strategic-spatial models that stimulate, facilitate and support the actual realization of these diversity choices (see also 2.2.2).

2.1.4. The uncovered coincidence and casualness of intertwined activities

Another important aspect of the intertwined activities concerns the explicit awareness, ambition and modelling of these intertwined activities. After all, an IEP site is focused on the realization of deliberate and joint efforts focusing on the inclusive economic participation of socially deprived urban citizens. Admittedly, these features could also have been treated in the previous paragraph (2.1.3). But, because of their crucial and fundamental role within the concept of an IEP site, we have decided to treat them separately.

The data of the quick scan case-studies give us a first impression of the mere existence of "joint" ambitions and efforts. The data of the IEP-Reference-Platforms provide us however with additional and more in-depth information on the joint ambitions and efforts, as well as on the reasons why they are present or not? And the data on the decision-making process of the pilot research project of Wortel-Merksplas provide us with supplementary information on the so-called threats and opportunities. In this particular research project, we have experienced how potential partners of an IEP site under construction negotiate and consequently raise "objections against" and "support in favor of" this joint initiative. Let us summarize the most interesting findings:

- According to the preliminary research results of the 25 quick scan case-studies, it becomes apparent that the precise nature of most existing intertwined activities is the result of a "coincidence", rather than of a well-elaborated and carefully negotiated decision process amongst all partners involved. Indirectly and implicitly, most partners – and especially the SSE organizations – share a common concern for an inclusive economic participation, but they have not deliberately chosen for each other and negotiated or elaborated for instance a complementary or mutually reinforcing set of activities. Thus, most partners are located "next to each other" without consciously and deliberately developing joint projects or initiatives.

We also find out that the most deliberate consideration is often that of the local public actor involved, who puts a (public or semi-public) spatial territory and building at the disposal of organizations that "fit" and support the realization of particular socio-economic policy targets, amongst which a (more) inclusive economic participation of socially deprived urban citizens. The development of joint and synergetic initiatives or alliances is however seldom a specified precondition or explicit demand of the local public actor to reside on the site.

In short, the intertwining nature of the investigated IEP site related initiatives is often the result of (i) a coincidental joint spatial location and (ii) a general, underlying ambition of the local public actor involved to "accommodate" organizations that support "in some kind of way" a SSE-related policy ambition;

- The previously uncovered casual nature of intertwined activities is indirectly confirmed during the debates of the IEP-Reference-Platforms. When reflecting on the causes of this particular research finding, some participants explain this situation by emphasizing the influence of the specific nature of SSE organizations themselves.

As such, they suggest for instance that the casual nature of intertwined activities is caused by (i) the minor and at least subordinate attention for – mainly economic? – strategic goals in favor of the – mainly societal? – operational goals in SSE organizations, (ii) the day-to-day survival of most SSE organization[18] and (iii) the use of a narrow-scale and individual instead of a large-scale and organization exceeding focus.[19] Other participants however emphasize the influence of recent and future policy measures taken by the Flemish government to (i) increase the internal competition between SSE organizations (e.g. by means of public tendering) and to simultaneously (ii) limit and change the public financial resources (e.g. a decrease of subsidies and the obligation and constraint to seek their financial resources *via* the free market). Therefore, strategic alliances are certainly not self-evident;

- Within the particular pilot research project of Wortel-Merksplas, additional opportunities and threats for joint ambitions and

[18] As profit-margins are rather small, daily cash-flow concerns overrule inevitably the more strategic thinking of most SSE organizations.

[19] This small-scale focus is related to the dominant individual focus on each socially deprived "client" separately.

> efforts can be identified. In general, we mainly encounter potential threats, as the initial enthusiasm of the public initiator supporting the creation of an IEP site is quickly "questioned" by the other partners involved, being especially the representatives of both local governments. Let us summarize the major challenges and difficulties.

A first important challenge is the complexity of the public actor scenery (see also before) in which at least three public partners are involved being the Province of Antwerp, the two rural municipalities of Wortel and Merksplas and the small city of Hoogstraten (administratively connected to Wortel).

On itself, this "triple" identity does not necessarily have to result in difficulties for defining consciously joint ambitions and efforts. But, during several debates at the IEP-Reference platform, it becomes clear that all three public actors – and mainly the political and not so much the administrative representatives – have different and sometimes quite opposite (political) ambitions with the destination of the former Wortel-Merksplas colony and the presence itself of an IEP site. Thus, the IEP site debate is constantly drawn and gorged into a much wider and tense political debate. In short, the IEP site concept is embedded in a complex, this means a rather turbulent and sometimes quite hostile (political) setting, which seriously jeopardizes the eventual identification of a committed and deliberate joint IEP site ambition.

A second challenge or difficulty is that the destination of the former colony, its functions, buildings and spaces had (partly) already been determined before the IEP site idea came into the picture. As such, the IEP site concept is seen by some partners as a sudden or unexpected "intruder" or even an "unwanted guest" in the midst of an ongoing policy process.

The previous challenge results in an additional difficulty, being that of an ever-changing context for the elaboration of the strategic-spatial blueprint. Sometimes buildings and spaces are free or available for the IEP site, and on later occasions they are not anymore, etc. or *vice versa*. Sometimes we are free as researchers in specifying alternative SSE functions for these buildings and spaces in view of an IEP site, and on later occasions we are not anymore, etc. or *vice versa*. In short, the IEP site concept is embedded in an unclear and ever-changing setting, which also hampers the elaboration of a clear and well-defined joint ambition.

As a result of these three challenges and difficulties, the joint ambitions of the IEP site under construction in Wortel-Merksplas will be coincidental in so far that they will have to match the negotiated result and strict frameworks within an ongoing project, instead of consciously looking for synergetic effects.

To conclude this paragraph, we can say that from a governance point of view, the coincidental and casual nature of the intertwined activities as well as the possible threats and challenges for the conscious identification of a joint ambition, can have its implications on the concept and design of an IEP site. It is clear that the strategic-spatial blueprints should stimulate and support more actively the identification and awareness of joint ambitions, efforts and synergetic effects amongst all partners involved (see also later: 2.2.2).

2.2. Inductively elaborating strategic-spatial models or blueprints for an IEP-site

It is clear that the nature of these strategic-spatial blueprints is closely related to the previously described concept of an IEP site. After all, the blueprints are needed for the further specification, operationalization and governance of an IEP site. As such, the conceptual features have their implications on subjects or topics that should be present within a blueprint and specific points of attention for each topic.

2.2.1. Uncovered topics of a strategic-spatial blueprint

As far as the topics of a strategic-spatial blueprint are concerned, the data-collection of the quick-scan cases and the continuous interaction between inductive discovery and intermediate mental (re) conceptualization, has led to the identification of the following relevant subjects or topics.

The uncovered *strategic* topics of an IEP site blueprint are:

A. The particular urban societal challenge(s) that lead(s) to the creation of the IEP site (i.e. inductive elaboration of "strategic meaning");
B. The type of (economic) activities that will be undertaken or realized by the different partners of the IEP site (i.e. inductive elaboration of "strategic meaning");
C. The (particular) target group(s) that will benefit from the activities at the IEP site (i.e. inductive elaboration of "strategic meaning");

D. The identity and particular role of each partner involved (i.e. inductive elaboration of "strategic and organizational design");
E. The strategic ambitions (e.g. mission, goals, actions) of each individual partner and of their collaboration at the IEP site (i.e. inductive elaboration of "strategic and organizational design");
F. The structure and organizational features of each individual partner and of their collaboration at the IEP site (i.e. inductive elaboration of "strategic and organizational design");
G. The synergetic ambitions and/or effects of the collaboration between the partners and with other partners "outside" of the IEP site (i.e. inductive elaboration of "strategic and organizational design");
H. The financial construction or features of the collaboration at the IEP site (i.e. inductive elaboration of "strategic and organizational design");
I. The (effective) realization of the strategic ambitions of each individual partner and their collaboration and its direct and/or indirect effects on the urban societal challenge … and thus the realization of a more solid economic participation of socially deprived urban citizens (i.e. inductive elaboration of "strategic impact");

The uncovered *spatial* topics of an IEP site blueprint are:

J. The precise location of the IEP site within the urban territory and its particular features (i.e. inductive elaboration of "spatial context");
K. The phase-wise or historic coming into existence of the IEP site within the urban territory (i.e. inductive elaboration of "spatial context");
L. The spatial lay-out and plan of the IEP site, including the footprints of all buildings and spaces involved as well as lay-out related changes or evolutions (i.e. inductive elaboration of "spatial design");
M. The façade and architectural identity and/or communication of the IEP site (i.e. representation within the streetscape), as well as façade related changes or evolutions (i.e. inductive elaboration of "spatial design");
N. The nature of the buildings (e.g. newly built, renovated, a combination) as well as nature related changes or evolutions (i.e. inductive elaboration of "spatial design");

O. The degree of (easy) accessibility and (inter)connectedness of the IEP site with the urban territory (e.g. a low threshold for the surrounding neighborhood and all of its citizens), as well as related changes or evolutions (i.e. inductive elaboration of "spatial design");

P. The contribution of the spatial design to the realization of the strategic ambitions at the IEP site, etc. or the realization of a more solid economic participation of socially deprived urban citizens (i.e. inductive elaboration of "spatial impact").

2.2.2. Uncovered points of attention for the topics of a strategic-spatial blueprint

When we subsequently identify particular points of attention for each uncovered strategic and spatial topic, we find a lot of inspiration in the previously described inductive elaboration of the IEP site concept. As such the central question of this paragraph is: when we reconsider the conceptual research findings on the morphological diversity, the desired openness, the intertwining activities and the coincidence or casualness of this intertwining nature (see also 2.1) what relevant points of attention for the strategic and spatial topics emerge?

The relevant points of attention for the strategic topics of an IEP site blueprint are:[20]

- From a governance perspective, the various meanings of *desired openness* (see also 2.1.2) clearly emphasize the need to specify governance principles within the blueprints that safeguard this openness. The following points of attention emerge: (A) an IEP site may not be exclusive for socially deprived urban citizens alone, but should nonetheless guarantee that socially deprived urban citizens are and remain the principle target group of the site, (C) an IEP site should respond to the flexible, dynamic and temporarily needs of "new" socially deprived urban citizens, (D) an IEP site is not only formed or run by SSE organizations, but the presence of SSE organizations is vital and necessary for an IEP site to exist, and (E; F) an IEP site should be the "energizing hart" or "base-camp" of a region-wise action-radius, and;
- From a governance perspective, the various meanings of *intertwined activities* (see also 2.1.3) clearly emphasize the need to recognize different types of IEP sites within the blueprints. On the

20 The associated strategic topic (2.2.1) is put between parenthesis.

one hand, these types can be considered to form a kind of overall typology in which each type will have mutually distinctive features on each strategic and spatial topic of the blueprints. On the other hand these types can be considered to represent particular points of attention for one or more strategic topics: an IEP site (B) can be *specialized* in one particular sector, (B) have a more *general* profile offering a broad range of products and services and combining complementary sectors, (B) can be *unique* or *tailor-made* when combining a particular selection of sectors in accordance to the specific needs of a city, (B) can be *traditional* when focusing on traditional Flemish SSE activities, (B) can be *innovative* when focusing on new SSE activities, (B; C) can be explicitly embedded in the "*historical tissue*" of the city including some economic and/or target group-related "traditions", (C) can be *single* versus *multi-target group* focused, (D) can be *virtual* when managed by one organization and (E) can be *publically or formally initiated* versus *grass-routed*;

- When considering once again the intertwined activities and in particular the findings in relation to the *target group*(s), additional points of attention can be identified: (B; C) an IEP site may be more exclusive or solely focused on socially deprived urban citizens in relation to the employment-related activities, but less or not in relation to the consumption-related economic activities of an IEP site, and (C; D) the use of target group categorizations and "priorities" for an IEP site are most often used by the public partners involved. Because of political engagements and target-group related ambitions they can be most sensitive in "choosing" and favoring particular groups or profiles of socially deprived urban citizens above others;
- When considering once again the intertwined activities and in particular the findings in relation to the *partners* involved, additional points of attention can be identified: (D; E) a relatively limited amount of partners involved in an IEP site may reflect a deliberate strategy. After an initial (experimental) phase an organic and/or consciously growth phase will follow and (D; E) in prospecting the possibilities and options for a joint consortium of partners it is important to be aware of potential obstructions (i.e. threats) and facilities (i.e. opportunities) created by the institutional context and legislative frameworks. As such, the high competitive institutional framework in which Flemish SSE organizations

have to operate today and in the near future, clearly seems to moderate their (initial) enthusiasm to eventually join forces. As such, governance principles should try to "counter" or remedy the possible obstructive effects of these overall institutional framework;

- From a governance perspective, the *coincidence* and *casualness* of intertwined activities (see also 2.1.4) clearly emphasizes the need to specify governance principles that safeguard a more conscious and deliberate joint ambition of the partners involved. The collected data uncovers the following points of attention: (D; E; G) in an IEP site, the nodal role of the public actor may be more than just "accommodating" organizations that support "in some kind of way" a SSE-related policy ambition. A more explicit stimulation and facilitation is recommendable, (D; E; G; H) in an IEP site, it is important that SSE organizations do not only focus on operational or "survival oriented" goals, but also on joint strategic ambitions, and (D; E) in prospecting the options for a more conscious and deliberate consortium of partners it is important to be once again aware of potential obstructions (i.e. threats) and facilities (i.e. opportunities) created by the institutional context and legislative frameworks. As such, the competitive and financially changing institutional context in which Flemish SSE organizations have to operate emphasizes the individual need for operational survival. As such, governance principles should try to "counter" or remedy these obstructive institutional effects;
- When considering once again the *coincidence* and *casualness* of intertwined activities and in particular the research findings within the pilot research project of Wortel-Merksplas, two additional points of attention can be identified. First, (D; E; F) a turbulent and sometimes quite hostile political setting demands for governance principles that explicitly stimulate consensus-building on the central concept of an IEP site. This hostile political setting is characterized by the presence of many public actors with many different and sometimes quite opposite ambitions. Matching all of their point of views (i.e. in accordance with their political priorities and ambitions) and matching these points of view subsequently with alternative formulas or blueprints for an IEP site is therefore a very difficult exercise. The IEP site debate risks to be constantly "drawn" and "gorged" into a much wider and tense political debate. Second, (E; G) the installation of an IEP site within an already existing and/or "destined" location, may demand for a

more flexible, less explicit and "to be tolerated" blueprint of an IEP site by the other residential partners.

The relevant points of attention for the *spatial* topics of an IEP site blueprint are:

- From a governance perspective, the uncovered *morphological diversity* (see also 2.1.1) clearly emphasizes the need to recognize different types of IEP sites within the blueprints. On the one hand, these types can be considered to form a kind of overall typology in which each type will have mutually distinctive features on each strategic and spatial topic of the blueprints. On the other hand, these types can also be considered to represent alternative particular points of attention within two *spatial* topics: (J; L) an IEP site can take the morphological form of a single-building, of a campus, of a neighborhood or of a satellite;
- From a governance perspective, the various meanings of desired openness (see also 2.1.2) clearly emphasize the need to specify governance principles within the blueprints that safeguard and guarantee the spatial meaning(s) of openness. The ingredients for these specifications are the following points of attention: (O; O; M) the entire set of buildings and spaces of an IEP site, should be easily accessible for citizens from the (entire) urban surroundings, and (O; O) an IEP site should pay explicit attention to (additional) logistics and mobility facilities (incl. public transportation means) that connect the IEP site to a larger region or territory;
- From a governance perspective, the various meanings of intertwined activities (see also 2.1.3) also emphasize the need to recognize different *spatial* types of IEP sites within the blueprints. On the one hand, these spatial types can once again be considered to form a kind of overall typology in which each type will have mutually distinctive features on each strategic and spatial topic of the blueprints. On the other hand, these spatial types can once again be considered to represent alternative meanings or particular points of attention: (J; L) an (historic) IEP site can be accommodated explicitly within the socio-economic "heritage" or historical tissue of a city. As such, an IEP site can for instance be located within a former industrial domain or brownfield, a desolated factory building or a re-destined public domain, and (J; N) It is important to investigate why and how an IEP site should – or should not – respect a certain "historic tissue" or contextual setting. Certainly, from the perspective of the

public partners involved, this can be an important issue for the (re) destination and renovation of certain buildings and spaces.

3. Conclusion... and an agenda for future research

In relation to the scientific investigation of urban territories, our attention is drawn by one particular challenge that manifests itself within many Flemish cities: the considerable high and expanding amount of socially deprived urban citizens.

In order to remedy their weak and insecure economic position, both on the production side as a provider of labor and on the consumption side as a consumer of goods and services, we have launched the concept of a so-called "Inclusive Economic Participation (IEP) site". Given the objectives of the CIRIEC workgroup "SSE and territories", an IEP site can be (re)defined as a particular territorial network that accommodates partners who try to resolve under the environmental constraints of an urban setting, the challenge of an inclusive economic participation. In relation to the territorial governance, appropriate models, frameworks or blueprints are needed to manage these networks in an effective and efficient way. As the concept of an IEP site is however new, the detection, analysis and evaluation of already existing governance models is not self-evident. We can however find some inductive inspiration in already existing IEP site "related" SSE initiatives.

This paper reports on the first research findings of both research projects. On the one hand, there are the inductive lessons learned on the conceptualization of an IEP site. As such, attention is paid to (i) the uncovered morphological diversity, (ii) the various meanings of the desired openness, (iii) the uncovered diversity of "intertwining" activities and ambitions, and (iv) the uncovered coincidence and casualness of intertwined activities. On the other hand, there are the lessons learned on the elaboration of so-called strategic-spatial (governance) models or blueprints for the implementation and management of IEP sites. Here, attention is paid to (i) the relevant subjects or topics of a strategic-spatial blueprint, and (ii) the uncovered points of attention for each strategic and spatial topic.

As indicated in the introduction of this paper, our concluding remarks will also reflect on the development of a future research agenda. It is clear that the nature of this agenda is directly related to the lessons learned. Thus, we would like to emphasize three major headlines.

First, there is the identification of (alternative) types of IEP sites. We can say that during the elaboration of the IEP site concept and the blueprints, we have found several features that can lead to the identification of (alternative) types of IEP sites. Although some initial attempts to (re) construct such overall IEP site typologies have been undertaken within one of the two research projects (De Nys-Ketels *et al.*, 2015), additional efforts within future research initiatives are still highly recommendable. Second, there is the further elaboration of governance principles within the strategic-spatial blueprints. During the elaboration of the IEP site concept and the blueprints, we have found several features that demand for governance principles that (should) safeguard or guarantee the presence of these particular features. On the one hand, a further in-depth and more detailed analysis of the first set of existing research data is necessary to uncover mainly the (alternative) specifications, meanings and/or implications of each previously identified point of attention. The extent and complexity of the existing data is too high, to be analyzed all at once. On the other hand, also new data and case-studies are needed as they generate an even more rich set of inductive inspiration for relevant governance principles. Third, there is the well-considered consultation of published research reports and literature. During the elaboration of the IEP site concept and blueprints, we have registered several assumptions, point of views, conditions and supposed (causal) relationships. As this can have considerable consequences for a better understanding, implementation and management of IEP sites, it is therefore once again advisable to undertake additional research efforts that further substantiate these preliminary findings in more detail. On the one hand this implies additional empirical efforts and on the other hand focused theoretical or literature study efforts (i.e. models and theories).

Taken together, these future research initiatives will hopefully generate a more in-depth and complete image of the essence of an IEP site, its alternative forms (i.e. typology) and the way in which these alternative IEP sites can be (successfully) implemented and managed.

References

Amin A., 2002, "Ethnicity and the multicultural city: living with diversity", *Environment and Planning*, 34 (6): 959-80.

Apostel K., Janssen D., Pittillion F. (eds.), 2008, *Bouwblokkenboek: over het bouwblokkenweefsel in Antwerpen, theorie en praktijk*, Antwerpen, University Press Antwerp.

Bayazit N., 2004, "Investigating Design: A Review of Forty Years of Design Research", *Design Issues*, 20 (1): 16-29.

Bevir M., Richards D., 2009, "Decentring policy networks: a theoretical agenda", *Public Administration*, 87 (1): 3-1.

Birks M., 2011, *Grounded Theory, a Practical Guide*, Los Angeles, Sage.

Borgdorff H., 2011, "The Production of Knowledge in Artistic Research", *in* M. Biggs, H. Karlsson, (eds.), *The Routlegde Companion to Research in the Arts*, London, Routledge, p. 44-63.

Bouchard M.J. (ed.), 2009, *The Worth of the Social Economy. An International Perspective*, Brussels, PIE Peter Lang.

Bowen G., 2008, "Grounded Theory and Sensitizing Concepts", *International Journal of Qualitative Methods*, 5 (3): 12-23.

Bryson J.M., Crosby B.C., 1993, "Policy Planning and the Design and Use of Forums, Arenas, and Courts", *Environment and Planning B: Planning and Design*, 20: 175-94.

Bryson J.M., Quick K.S., Slotterback C.S., Crosby B.C., 2012, "Designing Public Participation Processes. Theory to Practice", *Public Administration Review*, 73 (1): 23-34.

Castells M., 1989, *The Informational City: Information Technology, Economic Restructuring and the Urban-regional Process*, Oxford, Basil Blackwell.

Castells M., 1996, *The Rise of the Network Society*, Malden, Blackwell.

Castells M., 2010, "Globalisation, Networking, Urbanization: Reflections on the Spatial Dynamics of the Information Age", *Urban Studies*, 47 (13): 2737-45.

Charmaz K., 2006, *Constructing Grounded Theory: A Practical Guide through Qualitative Analysis*, London, Sage.

Coene J., Dierckx D., Vrancken J., van Haarlem A., 2011, "De relatie tussen armoede en arbeid", *Over. Werk Tijdschrift van het Steunpunt WSE*, 21 (2): 86-90.

Coene J., 2013, "Is er ruimte voor kansengroepen op de arbeidsmarkt?", *in* D. Dierckx *et al.* (eds.), *Armoede en sociale uitsluiting, Jaarboek 2013*, Leuven, Acco, p. 105-22.

Conforth C., Brown W.A. (eds.), 2014, *Non-profit Governance, Innovative Perspectives and Approaches*, New York, Routledge.

Certo S.T., Miller T., 2008, "Social entrepreneurship: Key issues and concepts", *Business Horizons*, 51: 267-71.

De Langhe K., Lyppens G., 2012, "De paradox van de stedelijke campus", *in* K. Apostel *et al.* (eds.), *School in de stad in de school*, Antwerpen, University Press Antwerp, p. 43-58.

De Nys-Ketels S., Vallet N., Bylemans M., 2015, *Development of Strategic-spatial Blueprints for Different Types of IEP Sites, Social Economy Organizations in Synergistic Networks*, Paper CIRIEC conference, 15-18 July 2015, Lisboa (Portugal).

Desmet P.M.A., Pohlmeyer A.E., 2013, "Positive Design: An Introduction to Design for Subjective Well-being", *International Journal of Design*, 7 (3): 5-19.

EAAE (European Association for Architectural Education), 2012, "EAAE Charter on Architectural Research", <http://www.eaae.be/wp/wp-content/uploads/2014/05/2012-09-03_EAAE-Charter-on-Architectural-Research.pdf>, consulted on 20 August 2014.

Eshuis J. *et al.*, 2011, "Privaat beheerde woondomeinen: beloftevol of beangstigend fenomeen?", *Beleid en Maatschappij*, 38: 30-46.

Healy P., 1996, "The communicative turn in planning theory and its implications for spatial strategy formation", *Environment and Planning B: Planning and Design*, 23: 217-34.

Healey P., 1997, *Collaborative Planning: Shaping Places in Fragmented Societies*, Vancouver Canada, University of British Columbia Press.

Hooimeier P., Kroon H., Luttik J., 2001, *Kwaliteit in meervoud*, Habiforum, Expertisenetwerk Meervoudig Ruimtegebruik, Gouda.

Innes J.E, Booher D.E, 1999, "Consensus Building and Complex Adaptive Systems. A Framework for Evaluating Collaborative Planning", *Journal of the American Planning Association*, 65 (4): 412-23.

Koppenjan J.F.M., Klijn E.H., 2004, *Managing Uncertainty in Networks*, London, Routledge.

Lang, R.E., Danielsen K.A., 1997, "Gated Communities in America: Walling out the World?", *Housing Policy Debate*, 8 (4): 867-77.

Latour B., Yaneva A., 2008, "Give me a Gun and I will make all buildings move: an ANT's view of architecture", *in* R. Geiser (ed.), *Explorations in Architecture: Teaching Design Research*, Basel Boston Berlin, Birkhäuser, p. 80-9.

Leloup F., Moyart L., Pecqueur B., 2005, "La gouvernance territoriale comme nouveau mode de coordination territoriale ?", *Géographie, économie, société*, 7 (4): 321-32.

Mozingo L.A., 2011, *Pastoral Capitalism, a History of Suburban Corporate Landscapes*, Cambridge MA, MIT Press.

Monzon J.L., Chaves R., 2008, "The European Social Economy: concept and dimensions of the third sector", *Annals of Public and Cooperative Economics*, 79 (3): 549-77.

Morse J.M., 2009, *Developing Grounded Theory, the Second Generation*, Wallnut Creeck Calif., Left Coast Press.

Moulaert F., Ailenei O., 2005, "Social Economy, Third Sector and Solidarity Relations: A Conceptual Synthesis from History to Present", *Urban Studies*, 42 (11): 2037-53.

O'Toole L.J., Meier K.J., 2004, "Desperately seeking Selznick: cooptation and the dark side of public management in networks", *Public Administration Review*, 64 (6): 681-93.

Pasaogullari N., Doratli N., 2004, "Measuring Accessibility and Utilization of Public Spaces in Famagusta", *Cities*, 21 (3): 225-32.

Pecqueur B., Itçaina X., 2012, "Économie sociale et solidaire et territoires : un couple allant de soi ?", *RECMA – Revue internationale de l'économie sociale*, 325: 48-64.

Petermans A., Pohlmeyer A.E., 2014, *Design for Subjective Well-Being in Interior Architecture*, Proceedings of the 6th Annual Architectural Research Symposium in Finland 2014: Designing and Planning the Built Environment for Human Well-being, p. 206-18.

Peterson J., 2008, "Mobilising Mainstream Professionals to Work for the Public Good", *in* B. Bell, K. Wakeford (eds.), *Expanding Architecture: Design as Activism*, New York, Metropolis Books, p. 84-9.

Smith D., Metcalfe P., Lommerse M., 2012, "Interior architecture as an agent of wellbeing", *Journal of the HEIA*, 19 (3): 2-9.

Smith D., Lommerse M., Metcalfe P. (eds.), 2014, *Perspectives on Social Sustainability and Interior Architecture*, Singapore, Springer.

Sorensen E., Torfing J. (eds.), 2007, *Theories of Democratic Network Governance*, Basingstoke, Palgrave Macmillan.

Spear R., Defourny J., Favreau L., Laville J.L. (eds.), 2001, *Tackling Social Exclusion in Europe: The Contribution of Social Economy*, Ashgate, Aldershot.

Stern P.N., Porr C.J., 2011, *Essentials of Accessible Grounded Theory*, Wallnut Creeck Calif., Left Coast Press.

Stevens R., Petermans A., Vanrie J., 2014, *Converting Happiness Theory into (Interior) Architectural Design Missions*, Proceedings of the 6th Annual Architectural Research Symposium in Finland 2014: Designing and Planning the Built Environment for Human Well-being.

Stock W.G., 2011, "Informational Cities: Analysis and Construction of Cities in the Knowledge Society", *Journal of the American Society for Information Science and Technology*, 62 (5): 963-86.

Strauss A.L., Corbin J., 1994, *Basics of Qualitative Research. Grounded Theory Procedures and Techniques*, London, Sage.

Termote H., Galand S., 2012, "Deeltijds leren en werken: een opstap naar de arbeidsmarkt voor maatschappelijk kwetsbare jongeren?", *Over. Werk Tijdschrift van het steunpunt WSE*, 3, p. 52-60.

Vallet N., 2013, "Becoming Partners in Urban Development. A Case-study Research on the Strategic Roles of Flemish and Dutch Public Libraries in the Future Development of Cities", *Library Management*, 34 (8/9): 650-63.

Verbeke J., 2013, "This is Research by Design", *in* M. Fraser (ed.), *Design Research in Architecture, an overview*, Farnham, Ashgate Publishing Limited.

Verschaffel B., 2006, *Van Hermes en Hestia*, Gent, A&S/books.

Chapter 8

New Responses to (not so) Old Problems

Local Innovation in Portuguese Social and Solidarity Economy (SSE)

Susana Bernardino, Deolinda Meira, J. Freitas Santos

Polytechnic of Porto

Introduction

In the industrialized countries, most of the Social and Solidarity Economies (SSE) have been growing in recent years, and Portugal is no exception to this phenomenon. This change signals the emergence of new forms of institutional policies that raised the size of budgets allocated to the SSE sector. Also, initiatives from the civil society and private sector (such as corporate social responsibility initiatives) have been developed to help solve or attenuate social problems.

These new strategies pursued by public, not-for-profit and private sectors center not only on national social problems but also, and largely, on local problems, where proximity is a critical factor to identify and evaluate the problems and to improve efficiency in the actions taken. These actions relate to the dynamism of the social system, the vitality of the formal and informal local social ecosystem and the emergence of new forms of intervention adopted by local governments.

Based on exemplary cases of social innovation, we discuss new responses for societal challenges, analyzing how institutions decide, act and behave in order to fulfill social demands. Our intention is to report new and more effective and/or efficient social practices that can be replicated for intervention in other areas and in an international context.

In this chapter, we first provide a brief survey of some of the problems that SSE are currently facing. Second, we describe the Portuguese institutional responses designed to attenuate the diversity of social problems. Third, we look at two exemplary cases of social innovation in the Portuguese SSE. We conclude our analysis with a synthesis of some lessons that can be learned from the two case studies.

1. Mapping social problems: A broad perspective

SSE emerged as an attempt of civil society to react to societal problems. One way to capture the diversity of these problems is to examine the Portuguese classification system (Economic Activities Classification – CAE Rev. 3), which is based on the Classification System of Economic Activities (NACE Rev. 2) adopted by the European Community (INE, 2007), as well as the Handbook on Non-profit Institutions in the System of National Accounts from the United Nations (UN, 2003).

The Portuguese classification system indicates twelve areas of social intervention: a) culture and recreation; b) education and research; c) health; d) social services; e) environment; f) development and housing; g) law, advocacy and politics; h) philanthropic intermediaries and voluntarism promotion; i) international; j) religion; k) business, professional associations, unions; and l) not elsewhere classified (Franco *et al.,* 2005; INE, CASES, 2013).

The Portuguese Social Chart (MSSS, 2010) identifies seven areas of activity by target population (beneficiaries): a) children and youth; b) children, youth and disabled adults; c) elderly people; d) family and community; e) people suffering from substance abuse; f) HIV infected people and their families; and g) others. An analysis of the social chart provides a detailed listing of the political concerns included in each area of activity, such as mental disorders, homeless people, domestic violence and people with disabilities.

Moreover, the analyses of different types of questionnaires used on surveys from research and public institutions (e.g., British Office of the Third Sector) identifies questions related to the identification of the fields of activity and the beneficiaries of those activities. The following table seeks to synthesize some of the key issues relating to the social areas of intervention.

Table 1: Main social problems

Social Problem	*Description*
Community development and mutual aid	Alternative forms of proximity or neighborhood services of all kinds (ranging from church and non-profit to private sector organizations) were formed to fulfill specific needs and to promote mutual aid (home-based services and provision of help to the elderly)
Cohesion/civic participation	This field support actions that increase cohesion and civic participation at different levels of society (national, regional or local)
Culture and leisure	The main goal is to promote leisure and recreation services, such as arts, music and sports among disadvantaged people
Economic well-being	Members of disadvantaged social groups are typically subject to higher unemployment rates than the rest of society. Most of the social support is oriented to attenuate poverty-related social needs, social exclusion and long-term unemployment and to promote economic development
Accommodation/housing	This field includes the satisfaction of basic needs such as adequate housing and accommodation for different groups of society
Education and lifelong learning	In this area of work, lifelong learning and education aspire to meet the needs of instruction in general or more specific (professional) education
Training	People who live in urban areas frequently experience poorly remunerated employment or work in the informal economy and often do not have access to vocational training
Environment and sustainability	Actions taken are oriented to environmental protection, prevention and repair, as well as long-term sustainability. Energy, transport, water supply and waste disposal are among the issues addressed
Equality/civil rights	This area addresses the inclusion of people into society and the formal labor market regardless of gender, race or disability
Heritage	The institutions' work stimulates local cultural activities, such as hand-made artifacts that improve the dissemination of cultural heritage
Health and well-being (e.g., health, sickness, disability, mental health)	Given the prevalence of poverty in disadvantaged communities, people are frequently confronted with the lack of health and education services, violence, substance abuse, human trafficking, suicides, conflicts or crimes

Social Problem	*Description*
International development	International NGOs provide overseas aid, famine relief and assistance in underdeveloped countries, situations of war or weather catastrophes
Religious/ faith-based activity	Most religious services are administered by Catholic-inspired churches that also provide and operate important social services, particularly at the local and community levels
Criminal justice	Most of the organizations that deal with these issues promote access to justice for poor people
Animal welfare	Provision of health, shelter and food to different kinds of animals are offered at the municipality level by public and private organizations

Source: the authors

2. The Portuguese institutional responses

The social sector in Portugal has its roots far back in the past, as can be seen, for instance, in the activities developed by the Mercies (Misericórdias) since the 15th century or in the movements of workers at the beginning of the 19th century, which inspired the appearance of many co-operatives and mutual organizations that still exist today (Namorado, 2013; Parente *et al.*, 2013). During the dictatorship established in Portugal in 1926, later called *Estado Novo* ("New Order"), several restrictions were imposed on the associative sector (Universidade Cooperativa Europeia [UCE], 2003), which resulted in an increase in the participation of the Portuguese State in the process of social value creation, as opposed by the reduction in the number of social organizations.

As a result of the revolution of April 25, 1974, freedom of association was reintroduced and the civil society's participation in public life was restored (Azevedo, Couto, 2010). Thereafter, as a result of increased civic participation in solving social problems, a large number of organizations were created (UCE, 2003; Meneses, 2010).

Beginning in 1976, the SSE was explicitly recognized in the Constitution of the Portuguese Republic (*CPR*), which refers to this sector as the "social and co-operative sector" and classifies it as a complete sector on an equal basis with the public and private sectors (articles 90 and 82 of CPR).

The European Commission, aware of the virtues of the social economy, recognized, through a resolution of the European Parliament in 2009, the need for a legal system which would be able to accommodate the specificities of the social economy in each country.

In line with this objective, on 15 March 2013, the Portuguese Parliament unanimously approved the so-called *Lei de Bases da Economia Social* (LBES) (Law No. 30/2013, of May 8th), becoming "the second country in Europe (right after Spain) to pass a framework law on the social economy" (Meira, 2014: 5).

This Portuguese framework law establishes the foundations of the legal regime of the social economy sector in Portugal. It should be noted that this is a generic law that lays a framework for a legal regime that the government will subsequently develop through more detailed regulations. The law defines the concept of social economy and lists the entities engaged in this sector, presents the guiding principles and the mechanisms for its promotion and encouragement, and describes the creation of a tax and regulatory regime that will take into account the specificities of the social sector (Meira, 2013). Thus, since it was approved LBSE has allowed the reform of the SSE in Portugal, having already supported the implementation of some public policies to promote the sector (such as, the Solidarity Sector Restructuring Fund as provided in Decree-Law 165-A/2013 of December 13 and in the Ordinance No. 31/2014 of 5 February).

This Portuguese framework law (LBES) includes an open list of the entities that belong to the social economy, laid out in art. 4, according to which

> the entities that integrate the Social Economy, as long as they are registered in the country, include: a) co-operatives; b) mutual societies; c) Misericórdias (mercies); d) foundations; e) private institutions of social solidarity not included in the aforementioned ones; f) non-profit associations operating in the areas of culture, leisure, sports, and local development; g) entities of the community and worker collective sub-sectors; h) other entities with legal personality and complying with the guiding principles of the social economy, as established in art. 5 of the LBES – these entities must be included in the social economy database (Meira, 2014: 9).

The LBES does not consider the entities' legal form as the sole criterion for subjective definition. Under Portuguese law, the legal forms that traditionally integrate the social economy (co-operatives, mutual societies, associations and foundations) and legal status (the statute of private associations of social solidarity – IPSS) are considered to integrate entities in the social economy sector.

Some aspects of the entities' legal regime that will be the subject of our case study should be highlighted-namely, private institutions of social security and cooperatives.

Portuguese private institutions of social security were created by the Decree-Law number 119/1983 of 25th February, recently amended by the Decree-Law number 172-A/2014 of 14th November. According to this legislation (article 1), these institutions are "non-profit institutions, created by private initiative, with the purpose of giving organized expression to the moral duty of solidarity and justice between individuals". They are "not administered by the State or a local government body and pursue their goals through the provision of goods and services". The IPSS can have an associative or foundational nature. Those with an associative nature are: a) associations of social solidarity; b) associations of voluntary social action; c) associations of mutual aid and d) Misericórdias (mercies). Those with a foundational nature are: a) foundations of social solidarity; b) social and parochial centers; and c) institutes of religious organization (Almeida, 2011; Lopes, 2009).

Co-operatives have always been the strongest branch of the social economy and are grounded in logic and criteria that are similar worldwide (Dabormida, 1989). In fact, social economy is historically linked to co-operatives, the latter being the backbone of the former, and co-operative principles were the reference for the guiding principles established for the social economy (Monzón Campos, 2010). Cooperatives are autonomous associations of persons, freely associated, of variable composition and capital, which, through cooperation and mutual assistance of their members, and in obedience to cooperative principles, aim not at profit but at satisfying the economic, social or cultural needs and aspirations of their members. The cooperative pursues a mutualistic scope, which means that its social activity is directed to its members, who are the main users of the economic and social activities that it carries out.

Regarding the studies and reports produced with the aim of providing an overview of the SSE in Portugal, six studies conducted to dates are highlighted: a) the study carried out by Franco et al. (2005), developed under the "Johns Hopkins Comparative Nonprofit Sector Project"; b) the study conducted by the Centre International de Recherches et d'Information (CIRIEC) (CIRIEC, 2000; Chaves, Monzón, 2005); c) the research of Carvalho (2010) built on the basis of the Portuguese Labor and Social Solidarity Ministry data; d) the study of Quintão (2011); e) the satellite account of the social economy; and f) the Portuguese map and study of social enterprise and eco-systems in Europe realized for the European Commission (Velden *et al.*, 2014). According to the comparative Nonprofit Sector Project conducted by Johns Hopkins University, SSE plays a major role in the provision of services and the creation of employment and wealth in Portugal. The study estimates that, in 2012, this sector represented approximately 4.2% of the nation's gross domestic product (GDP) and employed 250,000 people, 70% of whom were in paid positions (Franco *et al.*, 2005). The aforementioned study covers only nonprofit organizations and therefore excludes the co-operative and mutual sectors, which rely heavily on the market economy and have great importance for SSE. The study of Carvalho (2010) estimates revenues of approximately 5.64% of the Portuguese GDP for SSE in 2007, as well as more than 10,000 organizations with various legal statutes.

At the same time, it is worth highlighting the studies conducted in 2011, under a protocol of cooperation established between the Portuguese National Institute for Statistics (INE) and the António Sérgio Cooperative for Social Economy (CASES). The result of this cooperation was the creation of the satellite account for the social economy. The objective of this account was to provide a detailed analysis of the main features of SSE and its economic dimension. The creation of this satellite account was made possible by the support of the European Commission and the Portuguese government, and it is a statistical recognition of the importance of the social economy in the country and in the European Union (Graça, 2013).

The construction of the satellite account of the social economy was based on the definition of social economy proposed in the report "The Social Economy in the European Union". This definition is considered the most appropriate for the National Accounts System because it takes into consideration neither legal nor administrative criteria but rather focuses on the behavior of social economy players and on social economy values. Also, this definition enjoys a broad scientific consensus and allows for an aggregation of the entities belonging to the SSE in a far more homogeneous and internationally harmonized way (Graça, 2013).

A recent report produced for the European Commission (31 October 2014) presents a map of the Portuguese social enterprises and their eco-systems in Europe based on statistical information and interviews with a range of stakeholders (Velden *et al.,* 2014). One of the secondary sources used in the report was the Portuguese Statistical Institute and the satellite account of the social economy (published in April 2013), estimating that in 2010 the social sector comprised approximately 55,000 organizations and represented about 2.8% of the Portuguese GDP and 5.5% of the paid employment. The analysis of published data confirms the strong heterogeneity of this sector, both in number and in the type of activities undertaken. It should be noted that most of the organizations (48.4%) develop their activities in the areas of culture, sports and recreation; further, it should be noted that associations and other social economy organizations represent about 94% of the total, contributing around 54.1% of the gross added value (GAV), 64.9% of paid employment, and 62.7% of paid jobs (Graça, 2013).

In 2010, social economy involved over €14,177,900; of those resources, 62.8% came from production, 23.8% came from current transfers and subsidies, and the remaining 10.3% came from property income (Graça, 2013).

Quintão (2011), through a disaggregated analysis of the various components of the social economy, defines the limits and importance of the SSE in Portugal. Figure 1 shows that the most important component of the sector are non-profit associations, which comprise approximately 17,000 entities, including NGOs, local/regional development initiatives, volunteer fire brigades and emerging initiatives such as fair trade, micro credit and others. The number of Private Institutions of Social Security is about 5,000, including Misericórdias and other organizations of the Catholic Church. Co-operatives (of production and of social solidarity) number around 3,000, and foundations and mutuals number approximately 350 and 120, respectively.

Although Quintão's study was published in 2011, the estimation was based on the existing data for each of the categories of the SSE; therefore, the data used to construct the forecast are dated (some from as early as 2005).

It should be pointed out that data were collected from different sources; therefore, some limitations arose in identifying the characteristics of this sector (Parente *et al.,* 2012). The analysis of figure 1 shows that, as noted by Parente et al. (2012), SSE comprises a wide variety of organizations, some more traditional than others; moreover, it also suggests the emergence of new institutions created with the purpose of addressing new social challenges.

Figure 1: Limits and importance of the social and solidarity economy in Portugal

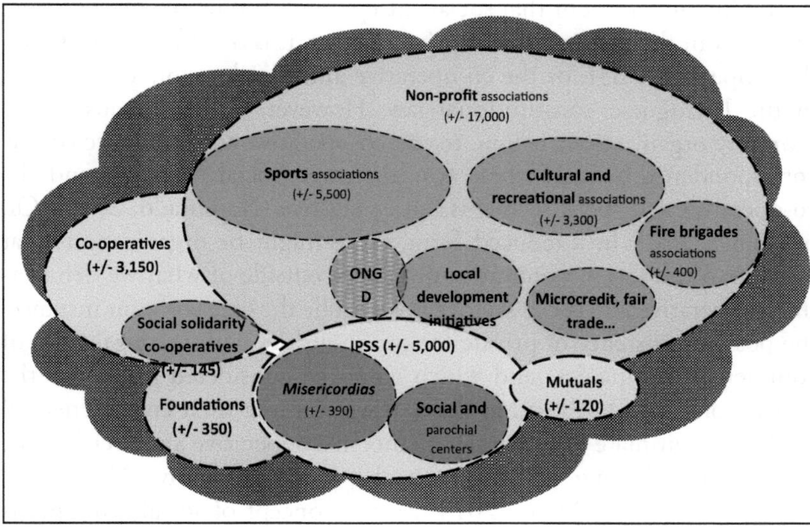

Source: Quintão (2011)

Dealing with SSE requires approaching the issue of social entrepreneurship in Portugal, which remains difficult to identify and quantify (Perista, Nogueira, 2009). This problem exists due to the lack of consensus on the criteria for assigning (or not assigning) the social entrepreneurial character to an initiative, which results in the persistence of a definition problem. We can also discuss to what extent social entrepreneurship should be restricted to the nonprofit sector or, conversely, if it could also occur within for-profit organizations. If we assume that this second hypothesis is possible, it is important to identify and list all the initiatives within the business sector, or even within the public sector, that are socially entrepreneurial. Furthermore, the non-existence of a legal figure for "social enterprise" in Portugal makes this task even more difficult.

Despite these limitations, several efforts have been made to outline an overview of social entrepreneurship in Portugal and to estimate its size and characteristics. Following the European tradition, social entrepreneurship is considered to fall within the domain of the SSE. In fact, in Portugal, the social entrepreneurial ventures are recognized as private initiatives, which are promoted by civil society, in a different sphere from the public and private sectors, and which perform their organizational activities with the purpose of achieving a social objective.

Taking into account that social entrepreneurship represents a distinct sphere from the public and the private sector, it is often analyzed within the scope of the SSE or the co-operative and social sector, as published in the Portuguese constitutional law. However, although most social economy organizations belong to the co-operative and social sector, the correspondence between these two elements (social economy and the co-operative and social sector) is not exhaustive (Namorado, 2006). On one hand, albeit in a reduced form, there might be organizations that belongs to the social economy and that are outside of what we define as the co-operative and social sector (as would be the case with, for instance, the possible existence of private for-profit entities with the legal form of commercial companies) and which could be considered as part of the social economy. On the other hand, if we consider their entrepreneurial level, it is legitimate to question whether all cooperative and social sector organizations belong effectively to the social economy (Namorado, 2006). As stated by Meira (2014: 7), the concept of social economy is "open and under construction, and, in legal writings, the difficulties in finding a precise and well-founded definition are more than obvious".

In the Portuguese study "A Map of Social Enterprises and Their Eco-systems in Europe" conducted for the European Commission, it is emphasized that social enterprise concept is not yet fully stabilized in Portugal and there is discussion about the meaning and the contents of this concept (Velden *et al.,* 2014). Namorado (2006: 13) states that, within the Portuguese legal regime, social enterprises are:

> (i) productive entities included in cooperative and the social sector; (ii) foundations and associations which act, directly or indirectly, as enterprises; (iii) enterprises owned by commercial companies, whose shares are held in full by cooperatives.

The National Institute for Statistics, in its conceptual delimitation of the satellite account of the social economy, advocates the possibility for organizations to act in two areas: (i) market or entrepreneurial (such as cooperatives, mutual organization, business groups controlled by cooperatives and other entities of the social economy); and (ii) non-market, such as associations charities, aid and assistance, trade unions, professional or scientific groups, consumer or religious associations, political parties, or social, cultural, recreational and sports clubs; foundations; entities whose production is mostly distributed for free or at prices that are not economically significant; or voluntary non-profit organizations for social intervention that produce goods of recognized social utility.

3. Methodology

The objective of the present study is to examine innovation in selected successful Portuguese social ventures that could be emulated and adapted to other social contexts and countries. To achieve this goal, we adopted a case study methodology to obtain valuable insights about different characteristics and strategies of social initiatives. Specifically, we intend to highlight the activities developed by social organizations in response to the needs of particular (micro) segments of society. The selected cases are expected to illustrate which key factors triggered the success of the examined social initiatives.

Case study research uses a qualitative methodology. In some areas, such as social innovation, where there is little theory available to serve as a guide, intensive study of selected examples is a very useful method of gaining insight about well-managed initiatives known for their abilities to innovate and execute (Eisenhardt, 1989; Ghauri, Gronhaugh, Kristianslund, 1995; Yin, 2013).

This methodology also gives the researcher great freedom, both in case selection and in the choice of information sources and analytical techniques. Such freedom makes it imperative for the researcher to clarify, from the beginning of the investigation, the main goals and structure of the research in order to avoid including unsuitable information.

The information used in the present case studies was taken from different sources. Previously, desk research was conducted based on the information contained in the site and statutes of the selected institutions. Then, to clarify some aspects of the analysis and enhance the content of the case study, interviews were conducted with the members responsible for the management of the social organizations. Also, previous academic works (students master's thesis supervised by the authors) were used to obtain supplementary information about the two case studies. Next, triangulation between those sources of information was examined in order to strengthen the validity of our research. By focusing on the behavior and performance of the selected social initiatives, we intend to identify the sources of innovation and the critical factors for their present success.

4. Social innovation in Portuguese SSE: Case study analysis

After identifying the social problems and the Portuguese institutional responses, we look more closely at existing social initiatives developed by institutions from civil society. Two Portuguese case studies were selected: the Bee Interpretation and Biodiversity Centre (Centro de Intepretação da Abelha e da Biodiversidade, Cooperativa Terra Chã), accepted in the Portuguese Social Stock Exchange, and the Production Cooperative of the Porto Masons Workers (Cooperativa de Produção dos Operários Pedreiros Portuenses).

4.1 Case study 1 – Portuguese Social Stock Exchange (PSSE) – Bee Interpretation and Biodiversity Centre (BIBC)

The first social stock exchange in the world was created in Brazil in 2003, on the São Paulo Stock Exchange (Bovespa). In 2009, the model was replicated in Portugal and integrated into Euronext. Later, the social stock exchange was adopted by the United Nations as a case study and recommended as an exemplary model to be followed by other stock exchanges, also receiving the Unesco endorsement (Grecco, 2010).

The Portuguese Social Stock Exchange (PSSE) is a social initiative that aims to reproduce, with some adaptations, the environment of a conventional stock exchange. The main objective is to mobilize resources for promising new social ventures. Despite the similarities, the PSSE is slightly different from a traditional stock exchange, since the concept of a social investor (used for individuals or entities that provide funds to the projects) corresponds to a donor. Likewise, following the logic of capital markets, social shares represent the unit of donation established by the PSSE (1€ each). The owners of the projects may issue shares that can be acquired by potential investors in order to generate funds for the social venture.

At present, projects listed on the PSSE do not have a "price" like their counterparts in the conventional stock exchanges. However, PSSE promotes the visibility of the selected projects, leverages the resources available for the project and facilitates the contact between donors (social investors) and civil society organizations with relevant work in the fields of education and social entrepreneurship.

In Portugal, projects carried out by nonprofit Portuguese civil society organizations are eligible to apply for the social stock exchange. The selection of projects is made by a specialized technical team, and the criteria for assessing these projects are, among others, the objectives of the project, its innovative nature, its scalability and replicability, the expected social impact and its technical and financial viability. Through the PSSE website,[1] the persons (or entities) interested in investing in social causes can access a brief description of projects that need funding. There are two thematic investment funds, one in the area of education and the other in the area of social entrepreneurship. The PSSE currently has 26 projects, 8 of which have gathered all of the necessary funding.

The existence of a mediator (PSSE), which tries to adjust the demand for grants with the projects of social entrepreneurs, increases the transparency and scrutiny of the whole process. These projects require a strong commitment in terms of their governance and accountability. Social investors may follow the projects and evaluate the social impact through the analysis of reports published in the Website of the PSSE.

One of the projects included in the PSSE is the Bee Interpretation and Biodiversity Centre. This project is carried out by Cooperative Terra Chã, an agricultural multi-sector cooperative, whose aim is to promote the local development of the village of Chãos. This is a small village with about 150 inhabitants, surrounded by mountains and inserted in the protected area of the National Park of Serras de Aire e Candeeiros, in the municipality of Rio Maior (in the central west coast of Portugal). Most of the families have one person that works outside the village, while the rest of the family are self-sufficient in small-scale agriculture.

Cooperative Terra Chã was founded in 2001 and started its economic activity by providing services and supporting local production. Currently, the cooperative's mission is to create opportunities for wealth generation by innovatively combining agriculture, environment, economy, tourism and culture. Its strategy is to stimulate the economic activity of the village to create jobs for young people. Specifically, the main aims are to create conditions for: i) maintaining the sustainable development of the region, through the conservation of nature, the management of complementarities in the use of the territory and the reduction of internal disparities;

1 "Bolsa de Valores Sociais", <www.bvs.org.pt>, consulted on 10 September 2014.

ii) enhancing its endogenous potential through meaningful actions conceived to improve the quality of life of the residents and to ensure the correction of severe environmental dysfunctions; and iii) generating multiplier effects and synergies to encourage the diversification of the region's socio-economic ecosystem.

According to its statutes, the cooperative has the following social purposes (Alves, 2012):

- To perform operations related to the products generated on its farms and to provide various services;
- To develop economic, social and cultural activities;
- To provide advice to local development projects;
- To support the production and marketing of handicrafts;
- To promote projects for environmental improvement and education;
- To promote gender equality;
- To promote and develop individuals' skills and competences;
- To enhance natural heritage;
- To contribute to the development of a new form of mountain farming, which combines landscape and production quality;
- To promote tourism based on nature as a way to enhance the characteristics of the protected area in which the cooperative operates.

The main beneficiaries are the population of the village, since about 30 individuals (in a village of 150 inhabitants) participate directly in the cooperative, although it also benefits, either directly or indirectly, the population of the nearby villages.

Through its activity, the cooperative aims to answer two main questions (It's our community, 2014): (i) What should be done to keep the village socially, economically and culturally viable, since agriculture is no longer the central activity of the people? (ii) What interventions can be made in a territory whose main competitiveness driver is its location in a natural park?

In order to address these social issues, the cooperative has developed several activities, such as catering and accommodation (of groups); tourism (tours in nature, observation of plant species), extreme sports (climbing, rappel and caving); forest activities; handicrafts (weaving); and training in weaving, information technologies and communication, and adult literacy (It's our community, 2014). Based on a diversified portfolio of activities, Terra Chã has sought to rebalance the biodiversity of the local ecosystem at the same time that generates the development of traditional activities with higher quality standards. Example of this strategy was the change of the agriculture and pastoral activities from own consumption to market orientation. Based on a partnership established with private entities, the cooperative decided to create a collective herd composed of autochthonous goats, adequate to the characteristics of the territory. Further, the range of activities developed has significantly increased the number of tourists in the village. As a result, the demand for local agricultural products has increased since they are sold at the Cooperative's restaurant or shop (and purchased from local producers).

An additional response to existing social problems offered by the cooperative Terra Chã was the development of a beekeeping activity. The implementation of a network of beekeepers and a honey Community Centre was a project presented for financial support under the national apiculture program in 2006. Also included in this project was the construction of an interpretation center of the bee and biodiversity. The main aims were to develop a set of actions that could improve the production and marketing of apiculture products; provide technical assistance to beekeepers through the monitoring and qualification of their production; and promote consumers' awareness about honey. The cooperative intentions were to add value to local products and to reinforce the attractiveness of the location as a tourism destination. Both goals contribute to the same purpose: to ensure the community's economic and social sustainability while, at the same time, increasing environmental preservation. The implementation of the project implies building an interpretive space (which includes an experimental apiary), where bees and their role in terms of biodiversity (through pollination) are presented to the public. The creation of this space aims to develop the knowledge and qualification of beekeepers and to stimulate the local economy.

The project intends to build a collective honey center, where its associates may extract honey in the facilities of the center that provides storage conditions and packaging in accordance with all the current legal standards. Furthermore, the project aims to promote the capacity for innovation, marketing and commercialization of honey and other apiculture products. Through this association, beekeepers do not need to invest in the creation of various infrastructures and their activities become (more) economically sustainable. The Interpretation Centre of the Bee also promotes the improvement of the apiaries, provides technical support, supports the qualification of beekeepers, promotes the adoption of sanitary measures and supports the achievement of diagnoses and treatments for bees. Currently, each beekeeper sells the honey production by its own, although some honey is purchased by the Cooperative to be sold, under the Cooperative's brand, in its shop. These activities are based on the exploitation of natural and cultural resources. Their purpose is to contribute to the creation of a sustainable economy, as well as to promote local economy through the support given to beekeepers, in order to create value while they are connected with activities of the village. It is expected that this project will generate new motivations for beekeeping activity, making it a more attractive activity for young people.

The development of BIBC has required a high financial investment. Therefore, at the end of 2009, Cooperative Terra Chã registered the project on PSSE, offering 229,765 shares of 1€. Since the project was listed on PSSE, it has obtained about €119,000. As the necessary resources have not yet been obtained, the project is not yet fully implemented.

Nevertheless, the association already offers several activities for beekeepers, including training on honey and beekeeping activities, information about bee pharmaceuticals and seminars. It also makes available the services of a veterinarian specializing in beekeeping, who provides technical support to beekeepers, focusing particularly on the best techniques for colonies and how to achieve the best results in terms of quality (Fagundes, 2014). This professional also helps with the proper distribution of the hives by territory, so that pollination is optimized.

The center already possesses the physical space (a former school) where the interpretative component will work; this location was provided through a protocol with the parish council of Terra Chã. The honey community center is already licensed, although it is still waiting for the financial support it needs. Some individual donations have also been gathered, and the cooperative intends to obtain resources through further project applications submitted to the Ministry of Agriculture.

According to the managers of the center, the conceptualization of the project was not difficult, since ideas emerged from the activities developed by the Cooperative Terra Chã (Fagundes, 2014). They believe that the revenue from its members' contributions, the price resulting from the sale of honey, the admission of new members and tourist activities related to the interpretation center will be enough to make the project self-sustainable.

At present, the cooperative is seeking to combine the generation of its own revenues with public funds resulting from the applications for the European and national programs (e.g., applications for institutions working in the social economy) (It's our company, 2014). The formal and legal establishment of the cooperative allows for the concession of some tax advantages and access to financial support offered by the Portuguese state, such as the Cooperative Development Program (PRODESCOOP). The cooperative is also incorporated in the Portuguese network of local development associations (ANIMATE).

The cooperative has created partnerships with various organizations, under the logic of corporate social responsibility, in order to increase its ability to create value and become sustainable. Examples of these include the environmental and forest grazing projects pursued through partnerships with organizations such as Quercus or the Vodafone Foundation.

4.2 Case study 2 – Production Cooperative of the Porto Masons Workers (PCPMW), Cooperativa de Produção dos Operários Pedreiros Portuenses

The Production Cooperative of the Porto Masons Workers (PCPMW) is a working production cooperative that was established in 1914 in order to respond to the problems of unemployment and assist masons and their families in illness. This centenary cooperative has received several national and international awards, due not only to its relevant services but also to the recognition of its social work and its impact on society. Therefore, PCPMW obtained the public utility status granted by the Portuguese Government.

At the heart of this foundation was a group of mason workers who faced problems of unemployment, disease and retirement, leading to the establishment of an institutional arrangement that could help to ensure their financial stability in adverse times. Thus, PCPMW arose from the membership of a group of workers who voluntarily joined to satisfy common economic and social aspirations through an institution that is democratically managed (based on the principle of "one member, one vote").

From the very beginning of the cooperative, work was considered the main source of income, as the workers felt these revenues would be sufficient for the economic viability of the cooperative. This group of co-workers obtained many projects for building construction and regeneration due to their commitment and professional knowledge. In fact, many emblematic buildings in Porto were constructed by the PCPMW, such as the Railway Station, the Town Hall, the Rivoli Theater, the Faculty of Law, the Portuguese Central Bank, and some churches and bourgeois houses in important locations in the city, among others.

To ensure the demand for its services, PCPMW focused on quality and innovation. It pioneered the introduction to Portugal of the industry of polished granite (1937), as well as new equipment and processing techniques. Cooperative facilities were endowed with advanced equipment, important for the execution of various works in ornamental rocks. Another of the organization's strategies was to invest in the qualification of its members. This commitment is expressed in its legal statutes. The financing of training is assured by part of the cooperative's surplus, which was generated by the work of its members and allocated to a reserve fund for education, training and information.

The benefits of the cooperative are distributed and used for paying its members, who receive a portion of the proceeds determined by factors such as workload or market conditions. The income the members will obtain is therefore a function of the quantity and quality of their work.

This surplus collectivization, based on the establishment and constitution of mandatory reserves, reinforces the cooperative's financial structure and guarantees members' social support when it is needed. A portion of the capital gains attained reverts to a pension plan for old age, disability of co-workers and assistance for unemployed members. The creation of this financial support helps to stabilize the members' income flows.

To strengthen social action and not be solely dependent on the results obtained in the construction activity, PCPMW's members decided to use the cooperative's reserve funds to construct buildings for rent, with revenues used to finance social assistance, such as unemployment in difficult times, healthcare aid and complementary pensions for its members and their widows. One example of this was the construction of one of the tallest buildings in the city at the end of the 1960s, in which a hotel, a restaurant and several apartments, as well as PCPMW's headquarters, are now located. It should be mentioned that the construction of the first building for rent took place in 1922, only eight years after the establishment of the cooperative.

The construction of these buildings allowed not only for the generation of additional income sources (not correlated with mason or construction activity) but also for the creation of new jobs for its members. In fact, a significant part of the cooperative work consisted in the construction of houses and now in the recovery and rehabilitation of buildings. These activities currently represent about 50% of the cooperative's work and have reduced potential fluctuations in the demand for construction work. Thus, when orders are smaller, the cooperative can use some of its members in the aforementioned types of activities and monetize the available human resources in improving PCPMW's collective heritage. Among the activities developed, those that should be highlighted include the ownership and working of quarries in various regions of the country, as well as the holding of an industrial stone factory on the outskirts of the city of Porto.

The cooperative has sought new sources of income through the creation of new business areas and the development of new working techniques. This has allowed for the pursuit of PCPMW's mission and the creation of a stable stream of income for its members. In recent years, new activities have been developed, such as coatings and application of granite and marble. Currently, PCPMW has more than 100 types of products in stock and has developed activities in more than 40 countries. Currently, its focus is on the transformation of ornamental rocks (urban furniture, garden pieces, thermal facade coatings, funeral art and sculpture of artistic value) and on the management of construction contracts and public works.

PCPMW's business has been negatively influenced by the economic crisis within the construction sector that has mainly affected the performance of construction contracts and the sale of components for customers. However, PCPMW has searched for new business that allows it to adjust to new market conditions, such as its recent focus on the repair and restoration market. Also, the cooperative has started training in the area of building rehabilitation, as the demand for work has increased in the city center of Porto.

PCPMW offers vocational training through various courses in its education centers, thus contributing to the dissemination of knowledge and the specialized training of individuals.

As we can observe, the cooperative's strategy has been developed based on self-financing and on the diversification of income sources. However, the development of activities also implies the use of bank financing and the financial resources established in the Cooperative Code (Almeida, 2013). The cooperative does not receive grants from the state; however, due to its social aim, PCPMW benefits from very significant tax advantages, such as the exemption from municipal property tax, value added tax (VAT), stamp duty and collective income taxes. PCPMW also has partnerships with various business associations and cooperatives, such as the Portugal Business Association (AEP) and the North Polyvalent Cooperative Union (Uninorte).

Within the activities developed by PCPMW, some social innovative practices should be noted. First of all, the cooperative created an innovative system of social support when a welfare stated did not yet exist in Portugal. From the income provided by renting buildings, it obtained resources required for creating a social security fund and providing support for its members who are in difficult situations.

To pursue the purpose of education, training and information, PCPMW created the Academy José Moreira da Silva (1989), at a time when there was no professional education in Portugal. Thus, the cooperative decided to provide a space for a nationwide education system for qualifying workforce. Moreover, an observatory was established in this Academy, aimed at creating local employment initiatives.

Another innovative practice was members' job rotation when there were no resources available to complete a construction. In this case, PCPMW shared the existent work among its members and used its funds to pay the wages of all members. Thus, since the cooperative was unable to keep all workers busy, it created working teams on a rotating basis, which is currently applied. Those who were unable to work continued to receive an income, supported by the cooperative's reserves, which also paid the wages of those who continued to work.

A century later, despite having adjusted its activities to the new market conditions, the cooperative maintains the same objectives, producing a social impact which makes PCPMW a unique institution in the city of Porto. The cooperative currently has about 200 members, 50 of whom are actively involved in activities related to the production of goods and provision of services, while the remaining 150 are inactive members or widows of former employees who belong to the cooperative's social solidarity branch. In the post-2008 crisis PCPMW has had an important role on the social protection of its members, since the adverse labor market conditions could expose individuals to a greater vulnerability. Currently some social protection is ensured by the Portuguese State. However, the public debt crisis has negatively impacted the budget allocated to support subsidies related with unemployment and other public financial resources available to disadvantages segments of the population. Herein, the contribution of the PCPMW remains highly relevant, particularly for people not covered by the State or as a supplement to the existing social programs. The PCPMW's strong resilience was due to its diversification strategy that cater incomes from different sources and the large amount of legal reserves that had been gathered over the years, as a result of the PCPMW' social and self-sustainability concerns.

5. Lessons learned from the two case studies

Social innovations can be defined as "new ideas (products, services and models) that simultaneously meet social needs (more effectively than alternatives) and create new social relationships or collaborations. They are innovations that are not only good for society but also enhance society's capacity to act" (European Communities, 2011: 9).

Social innovations usually happen by trial and error, learning-by-doing, and exchanging ideas within groups where exchange of opinions assures new ways of functioning. Innovative responses to problems and needs are imagined and initiated on the ground, led by practitioners, rather than by academics at the operational level.

The economic crisis has made it clear that today's challenges have taken on an increasingly social dimension. Among the most prominent societal challenges are the

> fight against unemployment, ageing and climate change. Increasing unemployment is often linked to increased crime and social exclusion, with long-lasting consequences not only for those losing their jobs, but also for their children who have fewer opportunities in society. Ageing of the population, and its associated health costs, was already a problem before the crisis, but is now even more problematic in view of the sustainability of public finances (European Communities, 2011: 8).

In order to draw some lessons from the two case studies presented here, we highlight the decisive characteristics of each case.

5.1. Development of economic activities for income generation

Social organizations aim to be economically and financially sustainable in the long term, which enables them to perpetuate the implementation of social activities and to continue fulfilling their mission. This mission is viable if an economic dimension is integrated in the social organization and if the cooperative adopts a proactive culture to search for new and innovative sources of revenue generation that depend on their own activities and public or private support. The diversification of existent sources of income is a concern in the case of PCPMW, which generates income based on the extension of the services offered to society and renting buildings to people. BIBC also created a broad portfolio of products and services related to its regional specificities.

5.2. Financial support

New social ventures are supported through grants given as gifts by donors and funds are borrowed from financial institutions (banks). However, donors retain the prerogative to provide grants according to their interests, which sometimes are not aligned with the objectives of the social entrepreneur. The PSSE offers a source of financing that could be sustainable in risky projects where financial institutions are not willing to participate.

The replication or extension of this financing system offers a customized instrument that corresponds with the needs of the social entrepreneur in the startup or pre-startup stage. The PSSE has also demonstrated a strong capacity to create constructive and lasting partnerships and networks between shareholders and entrepreneurs. The commitment to respond to community needs and the recognition of projects' contribution to local development is more visible when the initiatives are online.

5.3. Local development

Local economic development focuses on endogenous resources. It provides a means of identifying new opportunities by creating viable economic activities in a given location that could generate jobs and income for the local community. The distinctive feature of local economic development is that it involves participatory processes, in which both public and private actors are invited to take part. The effects of this social dialogue are measured not only in terms of new economic partnerships but also in terms of social cohesion and institutional transparency. The project of Cooperative Terra Chã is a benchmark for local economic development. The cooperative's aims are to contribute to social cohesion by attaching young people to economic activities developed in the village and to create jobs and decent sources of income that could deter emigration to the coastal cities of the country.

The case study describes how a significant number of inhabitants of a mountain village located in a national park founded a cooperative involving the municipality, public authorities and the PSSE. The economic activity developed by the cooperative is related to the production of honey, bringing together different experiences, knowledge, skills and other resources associated with the production of honey. Based on the principles of environmentally sustainable development, the cooperative created a center for bee interpretation and biodiversity oriented to attract tourists to the village.

The Cooperative of the Porto Masons Workers gave its members greater professional and financial stability (regardless of whether they were currently working), which greatly contributed to ensuring local social cohesion and preventing the emergence of social problems such as the development of informal economy, precarious working conditions, social exclusion and marginalization, not only for its workers but also for their families.

5.4. Unemployment and social protection

Cooperative structures can unite the economic and commercial concerns of workers in the formal and informal sectors and can also strengthen workers' actions and support their common demands of other economic actors (e.g., firms, government). They offer a variety of advantages for counteracting the difficult challenges in sectors that have been particularly hard hit by work instability and unemployment. Since 2008, the Portuguese market has been severely affected by the shortage of orders in the construction sector. The case of PCPMW is very illustrative of how a cooperative pursuing both social and economic objectives plays a major role in creating and securing employment and income for its members. The BIBC also reveals how employment can be promoted and created in almost deserted rural areas that have failed to attract the interest of traditional firms and have greatly suffered from the disintegration of the Portuguese economic sector. Our investigation reveals that the critical factor is to find a solution that will preserve and exploit the know-how of its population and its local resources. Older (and ancestral) activities have to be redesigned in order to attract new generations and deter migration to other central or coastal locations with better employment conditions.

Social protection is offered by the Portuguese state in case of unemployment, illness or poverty. However, the role of the PCPMW as a member-based social organization is to detect, in addition to economic and social problems, new needs faced by its members. The mason cooperative developed a social protection scheme that includes health insurance, as well as social transfer mechanisms for unemployed workers and widows (paid in cash or in kind), which will provide minimum income security and access to essential health care services and education.

5.5. Education and training

Education and training are key areas in which social organizations can play a specific role. PCPMW aims to address professional training problems faced by its members, running training courses to enrich the opportunities for workers to find jobs and to enhance the value of their work. Also, an increasing number of more general courses are offered that are geared to the economy as a whole, enabling professional training as well as training for individuals who may want to seek a practical position such as that of a mason (inside or outside the cooperative), for which the traditional education system does not give them the necessary preparation.

The development of activities by villagers of Chãos would not be possible without the support and training provided by the Cooperative Terra Chã. The beneficiaries of social programs are active players in the social response model. The social and economic value that is produced is to a large extent the result of the effort and value of their work (work in granite or stone [PCPMW] and grazing activities, commercialization of honey products and tourism, among others [BIBC]). Capacity building and empowerment of members is quite evident in both cases, in the support given for carrying out agricultural or beekeeping activities (BIBC) and training (PCPMW and BIBC). The technical knowledge and know-how promoted through these training programs are offered on the basis of local development initiatives, the preservation of local traditions and the protection of environment.

6. Conclusion

The main goal of this paper was to contribute to the identification of some of the innovative responses that has been developed in the SSE in Portugal.

New social ventures arise in response to severe social issues that remain unanswered in local communities. The intention to act arises from the awareness that those complex and multidisciplinary social issues will not be eliminated through social institutionalized national responses, either because they do not exist (such as in the absence of a social welfare state, as when PCPMW was created) or because they do not address the specific characteristics of local communities (such as regions with very specific locations and geographical features, as in the BIBC case).

We observe that individuals who are exposed to a social problem are usually drivers in the creation of new social ventures. The mason workers who were on the brink of being out of work were the main motivation for the creation of PCPMW. The contribution of BIBC to attenuate the local unemployment problem was to develop new businesses based on ethnic products sold outside the village, helping to create employment in small rural villages of the country, preventing the exit of the young people and keeping people in the community.

Although each social venture focuses on a range of social issues (e.g., unemployment and social protection in the PCPMW case), its social consequences are actually broader and have an impact in other social areas not explicitly recognized in its mission statement, such as social exclusion, civic cohesion, civil rights, promotion of human dignity and poverty. In the case of BIBC, the innovative response emerges from different activities: the combination of existing local resources (natural resources) in an innovative way to protect the environment and increase tourism; the identification of new sources of revenue; and the partnerships with other institutions (public or private) that shared common cultural and social values. As Okpara and Halkias (2011) suggest, the desire to innovate is not the result of one instance of creativity but is the *modus operandi* of social entrepreneurs.

A particular characteristic of the BIBC case is that managers have a deep knowledge of the existent social problems in the community. This awareness allows the institution to adopt an integrated and holistic approach to the problems faced by the citizens. The actions taken try to maximize the resources available in order to obtain synergies and expand the process of social value creation.

As stated by Witkamp, Royakkers and Raven (2011), the inclusion on the community of the social organization, the experience of the social issue and the strong involvement of the main stakeholders lead to the adoption of a response model that accommodates the characteristics of the target population. Most of the solutions mentioned above are not radical social innovations but rather derive from the knowledge of the reality of the situation and the combination of pre-existing elements (i.e., incremental innovation).

As we can see in the BIBC and PCPMW cases, understanding social problems allows for the design of holistic responses that explore in an integrated manner the resources and capabilities of the group or the region intended to be served. The creation of the two social institutions, in line with the specificities of the region (BIBC) or the group (PCPMW), is based on three cornerstones: (i) the social dimension; (ii) the economic dimension; and (iii) the cultural and/or environmental dimension. A virtuous combination of these three bottom lines, which reinforce each other, and is possible due to the deep local knowledge and the powerful motivation of their respective players to find a satisfactory and lasting solution to unemployment (PCPMW) and local development (BIBC). The two case studies demonstrate that the innovation and creativity of social entrepreneurs could facilitate the transformation of a social problem into an opportunity to create social and economic value in a lasting way.

References

Almeida V., 2011, *As Instituições Particulares de Solidariedade Social*, Coimbra, Almedina/CES.

Almeida P.C.A., 2013, A Cooperativa enquanto espaço do Empreendedorismo Social: o caso específico da Cooperativa dos Pedreiros, Masters' thesis, Instituto Politécnico do Porto-Instituto Superior de Contabilidade e Administração do Porto, Portugal.

Alves J.R.S., 2012, O desenvolvimento socioeconómico do sector cooperativo português: estudo de caso da Cooperativa Terra Chã e o projecto cotado na Bolsa de Valores Sociais de Lisboa, Masters' thesis, Instituto Politécnico de Lisboa/Instituto Superior de Contabilidade e Administração de Lisboa, Portugal.

Azevedo C., Couto P., 2010, "O desafio da sustentabilidade das OSFL e as finanças locais", *in* C. Azevedo, R. Franco, J. Meneses (eds.), *Gestão de organizações sem fins lucrativos*, Lisboa, Vida Económica, p. 371-407.

Carvalho A., 2010, "Quantifying the third sector in Portugal: An overview and evolution from 1997 to 2007", *Voluntas, International Journal of Voluntary and Nonprofit Organizations*, 21 (4): 588-610.

Chávez-Ávila R., Monzón-Campos J., 2005, "The social economy in the European Union, European Economic and Social Committee", *CIRIEC*, CESE/COMM/05/2005 – EESC, <http://www.ciriec.ulg.ac.be/fr/telechargements/RESEARCH_REPORTS/EESC2007_%20EnglishReport.pdf>, consulted on 20 September 2014.

CIRIEC, 2000, "The Enterprises and Organizations of the Third System: A strategic challenge for employment", *CIRIEC*– Directorate General V of the European Union, Liege, from <http://www.uv.es/uidescoop/TSE-DGV-CIRIEC-Full%20text-English.pdf>, consulted on 15 September 2014.

Constituição da República Portuguesa, 2011, *Constituição da República Portuguesa*, Coimbra, Edições Almedina.

Dabormida R., 1989, "Le legislazioni cooperative nei paesi della Comunità Europea", *Rivista del Diritto Commerciale*, 7-8: 451-97.

Decree-Law number 119/83, of 25 February, *Diário da República n.º 46/83 – I Série*, Ministério dos Assuntos Sociais, Lisboa.

Decree-Law number 172-A/2014, of 14 November, *Diário da República n.º 221/2014 – I Série*. Ministério da Solidariedade, Emprego e Segurança Social.

Eisenhardt K.M., 1989, "Building theories from case study research", *Academy of Management Review*, 14 (4): 532-50.

European Communities, 2011, *Empowering people, driving change: Social innovation in the European Union*, Luxembourg, Publications Office of the European Union.

Fagundes S.C.N., 2014, O empreendedorismo social como promotor da integração socioprofissional: um estudo exploratório, Masters' thesis, Instituto Politécnico do Porto/Instituto Superior de Contabilidade e Administração do Porto, Portugal.

Franco R., Sokolowski W., Hairel E., Salamon L., 2005, "O sector não lucrativo português numa perspectiva comparada", *Working Papers of the Johns Hopkins Comparative Nonprofit Sector Project*, Baltimore, The Johns Hopkins Center for Civil.

Ghauri P., Gronhaugh K., Kristianslund I., 1995, *Research methods in business studies*, London, Prentice Hall.

Graça E., 2013, "A Conta Satélite da Economia Social (CSES) em Portugal – 2013", *Cooperativismo e Economía Social*, 35: 213-21.

Grecco C., 2010, "Bolsa de valores sociais", *in* C. Azevedo, R. Franco, J. Meneses (eds.), *Gestão de organizações sem fins lucrativos*, Lisboa, Vida Económica, p. 99-104.

INE – Instituto Nacional de Estatística, 2007, *Classificação Portuguesa das Atividades Económicas*, Lisboa, INE, <www.ine.pt/ine_novidades/semin/cae/CAE_REV_3.pdf>, consulted on 25 September 2014.

INE – Instituto Nacional de Estatística, CASES – Cooperativa António Sérgio para a Economia Social, 2013, *Conta Satélite da Economia Social – 2010*, Lisboa, INE.

It's our community, 2014, "Cooperativa "*Terra Chã*" – Desenvolvimento Local, Artesanato e Serviços", <http://webcache.googleusercontent.com/search?q=cache:I01t2U2tyoAJ:www.itsourcommunity.eu/sites/default/files/documents/Portuguese%2520report.pdf+&cd=1&hl=pt-PT&ct=clnk&gl=pt&client=firefox-a>, consulted on 15 September 2014.

Law number 66/98, of 14 October, *Diário da República n.º 237/1998 – I Série A*. Assembleia da República, Lisboa.

Law number 30/2013, of 8 May, *Diário da República n.º 88/2013 – I Série A*. Assembleia da República, Lisboa.

Lopes L., 2009, *As Instituições Particulares de Solidariedade Social*, Coimbra, Almedina.

Meira D.A., 2013, "A Lei de Bases da Economia Social Portuguesa: do projeto ao texto final", *CIRIEC-España, revista jurídica de economía social y cooperativa*, 24: 21-52.

Meira D.A., 2014, "The Portuguese Law on Social Economy", *CIRIEC Working Paper*, 12.

Meneses J., 2010, "Liderança e gestão de OSFL", *in* C. Azevedo, R. Franco, J. Meneses (eds.), *Gestão de organizações sem fins lucrativos*, Lisboa, Vida Económica, p. 135-61.

Monzón Campos J.L., 2010, "La economía social ante los nuevos desafíos", *Estudios de Economía Social*, Universidad de Valladolid, p. 21-41.

Ministério da Solidariedade e Segurança Social – MSSS, 2010, *Carta Social: rede de serviços e equipamentos – relatório de 2010*, Lisboa, Gabinete de Estratégia e Planeamento.

Namorado R., 2006, "Os quadros jurídicos da economia social – uma introdução ao caso português", *Oficina do CES*, Coimbra, 251.

Namorado R., 2013, *O mistério do cooperativismo. Da cooperação ao movimento cooperativo*, Coimbra, Almedina.

Okpara J., Halkias D., 2011, "Social entrepreneurship: An overview of its theoretical evolution and proposed research model", *International Journal of Social Entrepreneurship and Innovation*, 1 (4): 4-20.

Parente C., Santos M., Marcos V., Costa D., Veloso L., 2012, "Perspectives of social entrepreneurship in Portugal: Comparison and contrast with international theoretical approaches", *International Review of Social Research*, 2 (2): 113-34.

Parente C., Costa D., Santos M., Amador C., 2013, "Empreendedorismo social: Dos conceitos às escolas de fundamentação. As configurações de um conceito em construção", *Work in Progress in Empreendedorismo social em Portugal: As políticas, organizações e as práticas de educação/formação*, <http://web3.letras.up.pt/empsoc/index.php/produtos/category/11-artigos>, consulted on 3 September 2014.

Perista H., Nogueira S., 2009, "National profiles of work integration social enterprises: Portugal", *EMES, European Research Network*, 2.

Quintão C., 2011, "O terceiro sector e a sua renovação em Portugal. Uma abordagem préliminaire", *IS Working papers*, 2 (2), <http://isociologia.pt/App_Files/Documents/is-wp-ns-002_110411025242.pdf>, http://isociologia.pt/App_Files/Documents/is-wp-ns-002_110411025242.pdfconsulted on 10 October 2014.

UCE, 2003, "Referencial europeu do empresário social", *Pensamento Cooperativo – Revista de Estudos Cooperativos*, 4.

UN – United Nations, 2003, *Handbook on Non-profit Institutions in the System of National Accounts*, New York, United Nations Publications.

Velden M.V.D., Alvarez N., Sá J., Meira D.A., Ramos M.E., 2014, *A map of social enterprises and their eco-systems in Europe – Country Report: Portugal*, European Commission, <http://ec.europa.eu/social/keyDocuments.jsp?ad

vSearchKey=socentcntryrepts&mode=advancedSubmit&langId=en&policyArea=&type=0&country=19&year=0>, consulted on 1 December 2014.

Witkamp M., Royakkers L., Raven R., 2011, "From cowboys to diplomats: Challenges for social entrepreneurship in the Netherlands", *Voluntas*, 22 (2): 283-310.

Yin R.K., 2013, *Case Study Research: Design and Methods*, 5th ed., London, Sage.

CHAPTER 9

A Delphi Study on the Cooperativization of the Social Services in the Province of Gipuzkoa

Enekoitz ETXEZARRETA ETXARRI, Eusebio LASA ALTUNA,
Anjel Mari ERRASTI AMOZARRAIN,
Juan Carlos PEREZ DE MENDIGUREN

GEZKI-Euskal Herriko Unibertsitatea, Universidad del País Vasco

1. Theoretical framework

1.1. Who is responsible for the provision of social services?

What is the State's role and what is that of the market with respect to the provision of welfare services? Should the State, as in the social democratic model, be the main provider or should these services be privatized and supplied by the market as upheld by the neoliberal thesis? Today, these are key questions in most European countries and the generalized reply in recent times points towards the gradual privatization of services.

However, neither of these two possible strategies deals appropriately with the question of public participation in the provision of these services. Or rather, each of them responds in a different way to this aspect. The social democrats situate public control in the use of the mechanisms of the representative democracy, and the neoliberals situate this control in the purchasing power of the individual on the market. However, neither of them considers the role that civil society must play as an active agent in the provision of the aforementioned services and not as a mere user of such. Nor do they bear in mind the collective dimension beyond the individual intention (regarding voting or purchasing), of civil society itself, which, articulated through various entities of the third sector, needs to be taken into account in these matters.

And the fact is that this third sector has always behaved in a highly integrated manner both with the State and with the market as far as the provision of public services is concerned (Brandsen, Pestoff, 2008). In countries where the third sector plays a major role, such as Germany or Holland, the third sector has been fundamental in the construction of the post-war welfare states. In others, the third sector has stood out as a result of the wave of liberalization of the last three decades, as is the case in the United Kingdom.

Furthermore, although the literature regarding public management has ignored it for a long time, initiatives based on direct citizen-based participation in the provision of basic services have always existed. As Ostrom concluded (1999), no market can survive without a government-based provision of public goods, but, by the same token, no government can be efficient and fair without a considerable input on the part of the citizens. This input, this greater implication of the "users", can be channelled through a democratic system of state supervision or through third sector entities (Walzer, 1988).

This strategy of providing more decentralized and participative social services brings the local dimension in territorial terms to the foreground, and the third sector or the social economy in terms of governance, as both spaces (in principle) have a tendency to democratize and re-socialize social structures.

In essence, the strategy is to rise to two challenges at the same time using the same tools: the democratic regeneration of the public structures on the one hand and the reform of the welfare state on the other, through greater participation from the social economy. Participation from the social economy is, therefore, considered to be able to "play a significant role in the renovation of the democratic political systems and of the configuration of the Welfare State" (Pestoff *et al.*, 2008: 593).

1.2. The "welfare mix" as the framework for action

Since the end of the 1980s and the beginning of the 1990s, a number of political policies were implemented in all European countries which still condition to a great extent the framework for action regarding public decisions. These policies sought to solve a problem which was raised in the following way: how to face the reality of new emerging social risks from the public institutions, taking into account the restriction imposed by a hypertrophic, inefficient public sector, with no possibility of organizational expansion?

At the same time, the nature of these new risks radically questioned the efficiency of the traditional mechanisms of income transfers offered by the welfare states (social security, for example, the pension system, etc.) and reoriented policies towards the priority of deploying a wide network of social services (Ascoli, Ranzi, 2002).

The solution to this dilemma was to adopt privatization policies which, as Ascoli and Ranzi pointed out (2002), ran in two directions: i) reorganization of the public system through the introduction of market mechanisms in public management (*New Public Management*), and; ii) the intense, direct incorporation of private, non-profit-making agents into the offer of welfare services. A second set of privatization policies, complementary to the aforementioned policies which have an influence on the offer, was oriented towards directly financing demand (*via* direct aid or tax incentives), offering a wider choice in the face of an ever more diverse offer.

All this is gradually giving shape to a new institutional framework, which is known as *welfare mix* (Evers, 1991; Evers, Svetlik, 1993), *mixed economy of welfare* or *welfare pluralism* (Johnson, 1999). These welfare systems, which, according to Johnson (1999), have always really been mixed, will reconsider the central elements of the European welfare systems: the State ceases to be the principal provider of services and delegates those functions to private lucrative and non-profit entities, while maintaining at the same time a central role in all that concerns the financing, regulation and inspection of these services (Evers, 2005).

Questioning the centrality of the State leads to the acknowledgement of a plurality of actors, two of which stand out and had barely been taken into account by welfare state theorists: the informal sector and the third sector (Johnson, 1999). Consequently, these new currents acknowledge the value of the work carried out both in the domestic environment and through non-profit entities in the provision of welfare services, explicitly recognizing the essential contribution made by these two sectors (Evers, Svetlik, 1993).

Lastly, as well as acknowledging the plural nature of the welfare systems, the theorists of *welfare mix* establish the role and influence of each of these agents in the welfare systems that have arisen as a result of the crisis in the welfare state. So, as a general tendency, they indicate that the State will gradually withdraw from its responsibility for the direct provision of services in favor of private entities while at the same time reinforcing its function as regulator, funder and assessor of the quality of the service offered. The public sector ultimately becomes responsible for the public service provided, no matter how little it has participated directly in any provision. And, at the same time, as a driving force and facilitator, it will also guarantee the user's "freedom of choice", opening up the provision of public services to competing private entities and endowing the user with solvency through demand policies.

Well beyond the discursive value of this plural or mixed character of actors, the fact is that this new reorganization has been resolved basically by a scheme to "roll back the state", where private entities, mainly of a profit-making character, have gained ground in detriment to third sector entities.

1.3. Alternatives to privatization: coproduction, governance and co-construction

The crisis of the welfare state and the progressive configuration of mixed models (or privatized models) in the public services have given rise to a profusion of literature on different ways of understanding this collaboration between public and private agents.

One of the first approaches was that which the American theorists adopted in public management in the 1970s and the 1980s under the concept of co-production (Parks *et al.*, 1999). At that time, the debate over the most efficient way of providing public services was largely dominated by those who proclaimed the need to create centralized and bureaucratic structures. However, through the proposal for co-production, these authors sustained that the most efficient system was one that enabled civil society to produce, at least in part, the services that they would later consume.

This first approach had a very limited vision, focusing only on the role of individuals or groups of individuals in the production of the aforementioned services (Brandsen, Pestoff, 2008). In the United Kingdom, though, co-production has been used more recently to study the role of voluntary or community entities in the provision of public services (Osborne, McLaughlin, 2004). And, from a more European standpoint, co-production has also referred to the growing organized implication of the citizens in the production of their own welfare services (Pestoff, 2005). They all conclude that the participation of the third sector (understood as groups of citizens or groups of organizations) transforms the manner in which public services are provided, at the same time as the third sector is also transformed by the very service that it provides (Brandsen, Pestoff, 2008).

But beyond conceiving this collective action on the part of citizens in the provision of services, there are those who analyze the participation of civil society before provision, that is, in the phases concerning planning, design or articulation of the services. Following the classification proposed by Osborne and McLaughlin (2004), at least three forms of cooperation between the third sector and the public sector should be distinguished:

- co-governance, where the third sector participates in the planning and provision of the service;
- co-management, where the third sector collaborates with the State in the provision of services;
- co-production, in the strict sense of the word, means that citizens produce their own services, at least in part.

This classification enables us to identify two analysis variables: the collective or individual nature of the relationship, on the one hand, and the policy cycle phase, on the other. Therefore, with respect to the former, co-production would signify participation of an individual nature, whereas the others signify interaction between organizations (both public and private). And as far as the phase is concerned, a distinction is made between planning and provision.

On the same lines is the contribution of the concept of co-construction as opposed to the concept of co-production. As Yves Vaillancourt established (2011: 40): "[…] All in all, the co-production of public policies develops at an organizational level (in the organization of products and services), whereas co-construction develops at an institutional level) in the establishment of general guidelines and founding elements of the policy" (our translation from Spanish).

This first notion of co-production is also very close to the notion of welfare mix or mixed economy of welfare, which has previously been analyzed (Evers, 1991; Evers, Svetlik, 1993; Pestoff, 1999; Johnson, 1999). The notion of co-construction, therefore, would go further, as Vaillancourt says (2011: 43): "Co-construction is related to public policies as they are drawn up and not only as they are implemented" (our translation from Spanish).

Vaillancourt (*Ibid.*) distinguishes four types or models of co-construction: a) the first, known as mono-construction, is that in which the State does not have a share but is the sole protagonist when it comes to decision-making; b) neoliberal co-construction, (now in fashion in many countries, notably with the popularity of the mainstream of *New Public Management*), where the State is motivated to create public policies in cooperation with the dominant socio-economic actors in the market economy; c) corporate co-construction, certain sectors of socio-economic activity and actors from the field of trade unions and management are included in dialogue and deliberations concerning the State, while others are excluded, and finally; d) democratic, solidarity-based co-construction.

This final model of co-construction is characterized in the following way: a) the State remains as a partner that is different from the others involved – it converses, interacts and deliberates with the non-State actors and, at the same time, is "over" but "close" to them; b) although the State is a partner of civil society, it does not stop being a partner of the market economy actors (it forms part of a general perspective of plural economy); c) it implies a deliberation between the best of representative democracy and participatory democracy, and d) it implies recognition of the participation of the social economy actors, as well as a partnership-based relationship between the State and the aforementioned actors (Vaillancourt, 2011).

As it considers social economy to be the principal ally, this model of "democratic and solidarity-based co-construction" fully coincides with the "partnership-based governance" model proposed by Enjolras (2008). This author contrasts this model with the current hegemonic model, which he refers to as "competitive governance", and which is based on the extension of market regulatory mechanisms (Enjolras, 2008: 19).

Over this model, previously referred to as *New Public Management*, Enjolras favors the partnership-based model, where the public sector does not play such a coercive role, but rather a role of coordinator between various agents of civil society and the State itself. Here, the local sphere appears as a privileged space, as it is the area where social capital makes it possible to develop institutional links and enhance the territory. In this network of agents, the social (and solidarity-based) economy plays a central role in the implementation of this model of governance as it enhances the local dimension in territorial policy and the democratic structure in organizational aspects.

Following the review of the theoretical models of relationship between the State and the economy, we present the results obtained in the case study carried out in the province of Gipuzkoa. This study endeavored to collate the opinion of a number of experts in matters of social policy regarding the strategy of cooperativizing the social services sector.

2. Case study: the cooperativization of social services in the province of Gipuzkoa[1]

2.1. The Basque welfare system

As established by Moreno (2009), the Spanish welfare system is characterized by three main elements: the decentralized structure of the design and application of social policy, the important participation of third sector institutions in the provision of services and the "over-exploitation" of family resources for the upholding of these policies. Therefore, the family and social environment is clearly the main support for social needs in Spain, while public policies reveal a decentralized territorial model and a management model based on coordination between the public and private sectors.

As far as the classification of welfare systems established by Esping-Andersen (1993) is concerned, the Spanish model follows a model of its own making (Mediterranean), which is based on the hybridization of characteristics of the three regimes referred to. The fields of health and education grounded on universalistic programs (the social democratic model) complement each other with a guaranteed income system within the social security system (the continental model), whereas, in the field of social assistance, that which prevails is the liberal one (Noguera, 2000).

The Basque Country falls within this context with full competence for the development of social policy (both for its financing and application) and with a social structure also rooted in strong participation from the family in the satisfaction of social needs.

---

1 This study has focused on the province of Gipuzkoa, which is one of the three provinces (or historical territories as they are called officially) that comprise the Basque Autonomous Community, which is at the same time one of the 17 autonomous communities belonging to Spain.

However, in comparative terms, the public sector and the third sector are significantly more developed in the Basque Country (Gallego *et al.,* 2003). Although there are significant differences between various subsectors (senior citizens, disabled people, children and social exclusion), it could be said that the management model of Basque social services is a public-social collaborative model.

This greater public performance in the Basque Country is supported by data that show the increasing scope of the public sector in the provision of social services. Between 1988 and 2006 the number of public workers in this sector has quadrupled while social spending per capita has multiplied by 8.7 points (SIIS, 2010).

Nevertheless, this important development in public intervention has rested on various policies which, ultimately, have increasingly limited the real scope of the public sector. Three main public policies have been developed over the last few years: a) increased social payments, derived largely from the opening of new benefits contemplated in the Dependency Law in Spain approved in 2006; b) financial support for the opening of private centers and; c) the opening of new state-owned centers managed, in most cases, by private sector entities (Arrieta, Etxezarreta, 2012).

These strategies have ultimately reinforced the greater contribution of the family circle and private entities in the provision of social services. The greater presence of private entities is reflected in the data referring to the evolution of social services centers between 2001 and 2009: the centers managed by private entities have increased by 57%. Nonetheless, this increase has also gone hand in hand with a significant increase in the management of centers by the third sector (42%) and by the public sector (31%) (SIIS, 2012).

Lastly, despite the recent tendencies towards privatization, the composition of all the centers still shows a clear public-social structure in the Basque Country: 49% of social service centers are managed by third sector entities, 39% are publicly managed and only 12% are privately run (SIIS, 2012).

2.2. Case study

2.2.1. Methodological aspects

The aim of the Delphi study below is to present the opinions of the various policy makers of the Department of Social Policy in the County

Council of Gipuzkoa with respect to the strategy of cooperativizing the management of the social services in their territory.

It has been chosen to apply the Delphi methodology because it is a technique used in social research which makes it possible, with a group of experts, to obtain the most reliable group opinion possible. It is a repetitive method (each expert is asked the same question at least twice) which respects the anonymity of the participants and includes controlled feedback, since the study coordinator is in charge of the return of the most important contributions and of omitting irrelevant information (Landeta, 1999). The ultimate aim of this technique is to try to narrow the initial differences between the experts, with a view to obtaining a group opinion with the greatest consensus possible while carrying out the survey in a personalized way in order to try to avoid group dynamics, which annul or exert a certain pressure on the opinion of each participant.

To this end, a panel of experts was created. The study was narrowed down to the province of Gipuzkoa due to the fact that the public institutions with the highest degree of responsibility in the management of social services in the Basque Autonomous Community are the County Councils themselves. After opting for the nearest Council, that of Gipuzkoa, contact was made with experts who, besides having a deep knowledge of the sector, have an influence on it as the majority of them are government policy makers. In this Delphi study, there were initially 16 participants, 11 of whom had a political profile (elected representatives, the majority playing a leading role or an advisory role in the main sections of the Department of Social Policy), whereas the remaining 5 had a more technical profile (all of them were area heads of services). Of the 16 experts who initiated the process, 13 finished the whole process satisfactorily.

The survey was based on a battery of 26 questions, classified in 5 sets and almost all of which were to be answered on a Likert scale of 1 to 5 (where 1 represents total disagreement, 5 total agreement and 3 neither in favor nor against). A great effort was made to formulate the questions in such a way that they were clear and comprehensible, adapting the language used from one academic register to another of more common usage. Each set of questions then ends with an open question which consists of a space in which the experts may write down any observation related with the previous questions.

The idea of this approach is to combine the quantitative results with the qualitative results. On the one hand, the answers have been objectified by means of averages and standard deviations, and the level of alignment between the first round and the second round has been analyzed through the comparison of these two variables. On the other hand, should the answers not show a clear consensus or there be no clear significant movements towards a convergence between the experts, analysis of the qualitative contributions will have led to a search for arguments that might justify the nature of the answers obtained.

The research process, the results of which can be seen below, took place in three phases. In the first phase, a focus group with the participation of various policy makers from the department together with social agents and researchers was organized, and it was here that the most significant variables and those which gave rise to more intense debate regarding the proposed object of study were detected. When the questionnaire which included these variables had been designed and the experts who were to form the panel had been contacted, in the second phase the experts were required to answer the questionnaire twice in two consecutive rounds, knowing in the second round the averages obtained in the first round for each question, and also the most significant contributions made by the experts (controlled feedback). The research process ended with a seminar organized by the authors of the study themselves in which the return of results (detailed below) was carried out before the participants.

2.2.2. Main results

a) Management model

A first set of questions analyzed the position of the experts as far as the ideal model of social services was concerned and allowed them to opt for a strictly public model, a strictly private model or a concerted model.

Three important aspects of the results obtained should be noted: a) an overwhelming majority showed themselves to be against the private model (92%); b) a solid majority (62%) supported the public model, and; c) a significant number of experts did not rule out the concerted model (38%), as they believed that this was the model that really prevailed nowadays in Gipuzkoa. However, the answers regarding the suitability of the concerted model showed a significant dispersion, as the experts were divided in the same proportion between those for and those against (31%), while a third part of the experts took no sides.

The process of convergence between experts did not change the initial answers significantly, the only aspect worthy of note being a greater concentration of views opposing the private model in the second round.

As far as the qualitative analysis is concerned, a good part of the contributions underlines the importance of keeping these services under public responsibility although, later, the management model may not be shared on the same level. There were experts who recognized the value of the contribution of the third sector entities in the management of these services and there were those who believed that the management model is not a determining factor in the final quality of the services.

b) The co-construction model

A second set of questions referred to the issue of the level of participation of the social economy in decision-making as far as the design itself of the social services was concerned. The questions covered three types of participation models: informative, consultative and decision-making models. In the informative model, the third sector is only taken into consideration when it comes to revealing the decisions adopted. At a consultative level, its opinion is included in the final decision as the third sector is regarded as an agent with a voice of authority in the sector. At the third level, the third sector is co-decision-maker together with the public administration, which could match the model of co-construction previously theorized.

The results obtained in this section are as follows: a) a significant majority (76%) is against the third sector being taken into account only at an informative level; b) the consultative model fully convinces almost nobody as practically the majority of the experts position themselves within the intermediate values, i.e., there is not a vast majority that supports it or rules it out; c) however, over half the experts (54%) look favorably upon co-construction, provided that the public administration has the final word. It must be noted that there also exists a significant percentage of experts who are against this last aspect.

The analysis of the degree of convergence between the experts yields some interesting results in this set of questions, as it can be clearly seen that the opinion of the participants has gradually veered towards the consultative model and moved away from the co-construction model.

This process may have been motivated by the contributions made, as many of them emphasize that the decision in case of difference of opinion or conflicting interests must ultimately fall on policy makers as they are ultimately responsible for the quality of the services provided. In this regard, it is worth noting that the participation of the third sector and other social agents also caused some experts to have misgivings when considering that this space may also accommodate a series of private interests which are not particularly compatible with the common interest.

c) Formalization of indirect management

The third set of questions refers to the way in which the relationship between the public administration as the contracting party (and responsible) for the service and the social economy as manager or provider of the same should be formalized. Three different formulas were considered: the establishment of concerted partnerships, in which the administration gives financial support to a private service; externalization, where the administration puts out to tender the management of a public resource to a private agent, and; a collective bargaining agreement, through which the administration establishes on a discretionary basis a financial commitment with a private entity to the provision of a particular service.

The general result of this set of questions is that the experts are not sure which of the three formulas should be the general norm. None of these three options achieved sufficient majorities either in favor nor against. More than half of the opinions are at an intermediate point in the three questions (54%, 62%, 54%, respectively), and there are hardly any opinions that can be found at either of the extremes (i.e., I totally agree, or I totally disagree).

The level of convergence between experts simply reinforces this indeterminacy: in the concerted model, as in that for externalization and collective bargaining, the variations appreciated between rounds all tend towards an intermediate point, moving away from totally favorable or unfavorable positions. There may have been a consensus when it came to moderate the initial answers.

This lack of clear positioning on the Likert scale makes the qualitative analysis essential for the understanding of these results. Most of the experts point out that the nature of the service to be provided is what determines the way of formalizing this relationship, whether that be through the concerted model, public contracting or collective bargaining. There is no perfect model which is valid for all types of service. However, there are those who hold that contracting is the formula that offers greater guarantees, although the social services law[2] favors a concerted model with respect to the future. According to another participant, collective bargaining should be reserved only for those services that are not covered in the catalogue of services (and, therefore, are not public responsibility). Lastly, there are those who play down this aspect and point out that the important thing is for the objectives and the catalogue of services to be well defined.

d) Positive discrimination measures

A fourth set of questions puts on the table the use of measures of a discriminatory nature to the advantage of the entities of the third sector as a whole and, more specifically, to the benefit of cooperative forms.

This question obtained perfectly clear responses: a) a vast majority (69%) was in favor of positive discrimination towards the third sector as opposed to the capitalist private sector; b) an even greater majority (85%) holds that "social clauses" are the most efficient tool for this type of measures, and; c) a consistent majority (61%) also believes that the cooperative formula is that which should be most particularly preserved, although this point also accounts for a significant percentage (31%) against this.

The analysis of convergence between the experts also reinforces this feeling of consensus in the three responses, as those positioning themselves in favor of the first two questions did not alter and, for the suitability of cooperatives, this partisan stance becomes stronger in the second round.

However, we believe that the experts' contributions in this case are of special interest as they give a more detailed insight into the apparent consensus reflected by the quantitative results. The majority of the comments point out that the important thing is the quality of the services provided, beyond the legal forms (for profit or non-profit) of the provider and, once the first is guaranteed, the use of discriminatory measures make sense. There are other comments warning that the legal form is not a guarantee of anything, nor is it a guarantee that the service

---

2 Law 12/2008 on Social Services of the Basque Autonomous Community was approved in 2008. This law points out among other aspects that for the development and maturation of the social services it is necessary to advance towards a concerted model, surpassing the inefficiencies created as a consequence of different contractual relationships between public administration and private providers.

is of the necessary quality, or that everything really works in a democratic, non-profit-making manner.

It may be concluded, therefore, that the majority position themselves in favor of discriminatory measures.

e) Cooperativization strategy

The last set of questions deals with the validation by the experts of the cooperativization strategy of the social services, proposed as a working hypothesis given that this strategy has not been implemented to a great degree in the territory yet.

This validation hinges on three fundamental questions: a) whether this cooperativization process is considered to be in favor of or in detriment to the public nature of the social services; b) whether cooperativization is valued as an objective in itself or an intermediate step towards a different scenario (or towards a public model or a privatization model), and; c) which model would be identified as the most suitable considering the cooperativization of the sector.

The global result of this set of questions is that the experts show significant doubts and disagreement with respect to these three questions.

Concerning the cooperativization strategy as a way of increasing public and social control, there are a wide variety of opinions, distributed almost equally among supporters, detractors and those who remain neutral. A similar distribution is obtained for the issue as to whether cooperativization is regarded as a way of privatizing social services, since a higher percentage of experts reject this hypothesis (46%), although a significant number support it (31%) or do not rule it out.

Neither are clear results obtained as to whether it is a desirable objective or not. Most experts believe that it could constitute an option (69%), though not to alleviate occasional problems of management (16%), or as an intermediate objective towards "publification" of the system as a whole (16%). Nor is it regarded as an end in itself or as a desirable model towards which social policies should be oriented, as only a third adopt a positive position on this aspect.

Lastly, as regards the model preferred for the cooperativization of the sector, a choice of four models was given: the creation of associated work cooperatives (with no additional characteristic); promotion of public utility cooperatives; encouraging social initiative cooperatives; or forming part of the social capital of mixed cooperatives.[3] The model with the greatest support is that of the social cooperatives (an average of 3.91 in the second round), followed by that of the mixed cooperatives (3.33), that of public utility (3.18) and finally that of normal cooperatives (2.16).

This order of preferences could indicate certain characteristics that the experts regard as being essential guarantees of the cooperativization process of the social services: a) that these cooperatives should be non-profit-making; b) that they should be compatible with greater public control, and c) that they should be regarded, like the educational cooperatives in the education sector, as integral parts of the public/concerted model of social services.

3. Conclusions

Through the literature review, it has been seen that the greater implication of the social economy in the design and provision of the social services could be regarded as being a valid strategy in the attempt to socialize (and not privatize) public services, i.e., in an endeavor to open them up to public participation and self-management. Thus, note has been taken of theoretical proposals which, beyond the individual nature of citizen participation (co-production), value the collective dimension of this action through social economy entities. The "democratic and solidarity-based co-construction" proposed by Yves Vaillancourt, or the "partnership-based governance" theorized by Bernard Enjolras, could be two theoretical reference points to be borne in mind in this sense.

Moving this concern to a specific territorial sphere, i.e., the Department of Social Policy of the County Council of Gipuzkoa, a Delphi study has been developed regarding the possibility of gradually cooperativizing the social services sector, the main results of which are as follows:

- The department is more inclined towards a public rather than a concerted model, with a perfectly clear ideological premise: that,

3 The first three options are purely private cooperatives, where the social capital is the exclusive property of the worker-members. The second and third are legal acknowledgements offered by the Basque Government to cooperatives that perform a public function and to non-profit cooperatives respectively. And, lastly, the mixed cooperative formula, although it is as yet unknown in the Basque Autonomous Community, would enable the financial participation of the public sector (as a collaborating partner or in whatever way may be determined) in the cooperative itself.

in the final analysis, the responsibility for the quality of the services provided is public and may under no circumstances be privatized;

- As regards the co-construction model, the department believes that the participation of the social economy in the design of the social services, albeit basically consultative, is very important as the public authorities reserve the right to exclusive decision-making power in the event of disagreement or conflicting interests;
- Where the manner of formalizing indirect management is concerned, the department believes that each type of service requires a different framework of relationships (concerted, recruitment or collective bargaining), which is why it does not decidedly wager for a generalization of any of them for the system as a whole;
- As far as positive discrimination measures are concerned, it is worth noting that the department values the incorporation of social clauses in public procurement very positively, although these clauses should be applied between entities which firstly certify sufficient technical capacity, the aim being to endeavor to encourage and preserve certain practices rather than specific legal concepts (such as non-profit-making or cooperative practices);
- As for the working hypothesis regarding the gradual cooperativization of the social services sector, it must be said that, nowadays, this strategy is not shared within the department. Although the majority would not put this process on a level with a privatization process, it is not interpreted as a valid way of expanding the public model. Moreover, it is believed that the strategy of cooperativization should go beyond solving specific situations, although this is not thought to be a final objective in itself. And, lastly, among the preferred models of cooperativization, support is given to those that encourage the non-profit-making nature of cooperatives and guarantee greater control on the part of the policy makers.

With respect to future lines of work, it would be interesting to continue looking into the strategic decisions taken by the department, as many of them are beginning to shape a horizon that is different from that outlined so far.

In a territory where collaboration with the third sector has usually been regarded as the most suitable model, the last government team advocated a re-publification of the services,[4] but the new elected government continues along the same bases of collaboration with the third sector. This is why the strategy of cooperativizing the management of social service centers does not appear at the moment to be the primary political objective of the Department of Social Policy although, as can be seen in the study, the favorable positioning regarding the inclusion of social clauses in public recruitment might well open up spaces that would accommodate both objectives.

References

Arrieta F., Etxezarreta E., 2012, "Análisis de la colaboración público-privada en el sector de los servicios sociales en Gipuzkoa: el modelo guipuzcoano de concertación con el tercer sector a debate", *Oñati Socio-Legal Series*, 2 (4): 130-43.

Ascoli U., Ranci C. (eds.), 2002, *Dilemmas of the Welfare Mix: The New Structure of Welfare in an Era of Privatization*, New York, Kluwer Academic/ Plenum Publishers.

Brandsen T., Pestoff V., 2008, "An Introduction", *in* V. Pestoff, T. Brandsen (eds.), *Co-Production. The Third Sector and the Delivery of Public Services*, Oxon, Routledge, p. 1-9.

Enjolras B., 2008, *Gouvernance et intérêt général dans les services sociaux et de santé*, Bruxelles/Bern/Berlin/Frankfurt am Main/New York/Oxford/Wien, Peter Lang.

Esping-Andersen G., 1993, *Los tres mundos del Estado de Bienestar*, Valentzia, Alfons el Magnànim.

Evers A., 1991, "Shifts in the welfare mix", *Eurosocial*, 57-58: 7-8.

Evers A., Svetlik I., 1993, *Balancing Pluralism: New Welfare Mixes in Care for the Elderly*, London, Avebury.

---

4 As testified by the recent creation of a regional autonomous body (Kabia) which will gradually take on the management of municipal residences. In the opinion of the political decision-makers, this body aims to be "an important instrument to advance towards a change in the model oriented towards the direct management of social services in Gipuzkoa" <http://www.noticiasdegipuzkoa.com/2014/07/14/sociedad/euskadi/diputacion-de-gipuzkoa-asumira-la-gestion-de-las-residencias-municipales-a-traves-del-organismo-autonomo-kabia>, consulted on 17 July 2014.

Evers A., 2005, "Mixed Welfare Systems and Hybrid Organizations: Changes in the Governance and Provision of Social Services", *International Journal of Public Administration*, 28 (9): 737-48.

Gallego R., Gomá R., Subirats J. (eds.), 2003, *Estado de Bienestar y Comunidades Autónomas: la descentralización de las políticas sociales en España*, Madrid, Tecnos, Universitat Pomepu Fabra.

Johnson N., 1999, *Mixed Economies of Welfare: A Comparative Perspective*, Hertfordshire, Pearson Education/Prentice Hall Europe.

Landeta J., 1999, *El método Delphi. Una técnica de previsión del futuro*, Barcelona, Ariel Social.

Moreno L. (ed.), 2009, *Reformas de la Políticas del Bienestar en España*, Siglo xxi, Madrid.

Noguera J.A., 2000, "Conclusiones. La reestructuración de la política social en España", *in* L. Adelantado (coord.), *Cambios en el Estado del Bienestar. Políticas sociales y desigualdades en España*, Bartzelona, Icaria.

Osborne S., McLaughlin K., 2004, "The Cross-Cutting Review of the Voluntary Sector: Where Next for Local Government Voluntary Sector Relationships?", *Regional Studies*, 38 (5): 573-82.

Ostrom E., 1999, "Crossing the Great Divide: Coproduction, Synergy, and Development", *in* M. McGinnis (ed.), *Polycentric Governance and Development: Readings from the Workshop in Political Theory and Policy Analysis*, Ann Arbor MI, University of Michigan Press.

Parks R.B., Baker P.C., Kiser L., Oakerson R., Ostrom E., Ostrom V., Percy S. L., Vandivort M.B., Whitaker G.P., Wison R., 1999, "Consumers as Co-Producers of Public Services: Some Economic and Institutional Considerations", *Policy Studies Journal*, 9 (7): 1001-11.

Pestoff V., 2000, *Beyond the Market and State. Social Enterprises and Civil Democracy in a Welfare Society*, Singapore/Sydney/Tokyo, Ashgate.

Pestoff V., 2005, *The Third Sector and the Democratization of the Welfare State: Revisiting the Third Sector and State in Democracy and Welfare Theory*, Östersund, Research Report.

Pestoff V., Osborne S.P., Brandsen T., 2008, "Patterns of Co-production in Public Services", *in* V. Pestoff, T. Brandsen (eds.), *Co-production: The third sector and the delivery of public services*, Oxon, Routledge, p. 99-103.

SIIS-Centro de Documentación y Estudios/Dokumentazio eta Ikerketa Zentroa, 2012, *II Informe sobre la situación de los Servicios Sociales en la*

CAPV, Consejo Vasco de Servicios Sociales, Eusko Jaurlaritza-Gobierno Vasco, Vitoria-Gasteiz.

SIIS – Centro de Documentación y Estudios/Dokumentazio eta Ikerketa Zentroa, 2010, *Gizarteratuz*, 7, August.

Vaillancourt Y., 2011, "La economía social en la co-producción y la co-construcción de las políticas públicas", *Revista del Centro de Estudios de Sociología del Trabajo*, 3: 31-68.

Walzer M., 1988, "Socializing the Welfare State", *in* A. Gutmann (ed.), *Democracy and the Welfare State*, Princeton NJ, Princeton University Press.

Chapter 10

Social Economy and Sustainable Territorial Development

The Inclusion of People with Disabilities in Labor in Southern Brazil

Maurício Serva & Júlia Graeff

Universidade Federal de Santa Catarina

1. Introduction

This study analyses social economy organizations located in Florianópolis, the state capital of Santa Catarina, Southern Brazil, which work on labor training for visually impaired people and people with intellectual disabilities. The study aims to point out how such micro-initiatives can contribute to sustainable territorial development (Andion *et al.,* 2006). According to the 2010 Census of the Brazilian institute of geography and statistics (IBGE), the majority of visually impaired people are living in the South of the country, and the employment rate for people with disabilities in the State of Santa Catarina is low in comparison to other States (Hammes, Nuernberg, 2015).

This study defends that the operation of these organizations presents characteristics of the sustainable territorial development approach, especially regarding the social dimension of development because of the possibility of inclusion of a portion of the population who is outside the labor market (Maccali *et al.,* 2015). Inclusion processes implemented by the analyzed organizations show evidence of special preparation in order to train the beneficiaries, as well as showing evidence of the creation of organizational environment and management practices that are appropriate for the inclusion of people with disabilities (Hammes, Nuernberg, 2015). Noteworthy is the importance of preparing those who live with people with disabilities in order to accept them and to establish interactions marked by respect and guarantee of rights. Therefore, the concept of inclusive development brought by Sachs (2004) meets the phenomenon studied here when it points out the need for education and assistance programs for people with disabilities, as central aspects for decent work. These programs can be provided either from public policy or from public-private partnerships.

Considering this context, two social economy organizations were selected for this study: the Associação catarinense para a integração do cego (ACIC) (State association for the integration of visually impaired people in Santa Catarina), established in 1977; and the Cooperativa social de pais, amigos e portadores de deficiência (COEPAD) (Social cooperative of people with disabilities, their parents and friends), established in 1999. ACIC was created by a visually impaired person who recognized the need and importance to enable and rehabilitate people with this disability, allowing them to be integrated into society and have a regular social and economic life. Relatives of people with intellectual disabilities created COEPAD, in order to allow them to work and participate in the economy through activities that are appropriate for their condition. It is important to say that these initiatives originated spontaneously from civil society, specifically from people with disabilities and/or their relatives. In the case of ACIC, for example, its creation preceded the laws tackling the specific issues for this public in the country.

Brazilian law concerning people with disabilities is comprised by Federal Law 8213/91, which regulates benefit plans in the Social Security System. The Federal Law establishes in Art. 93, that every company that has over 100 employees must have a quota of persons with disabilities and/or rehabilitated person on its staff. This quota is proportional to the number of employees, as follows: 100-200 employees, 2%; 201-500, 3%; 501-1,000, 4%; and above 1,001 employees, 5%. Other laws that regulate the access to employment are 7853/89, regarding the national policy for people with disabilities, and Decree 3298/99. In addition to these laws, there are two international standards signed by Brazil: Convention 159/83 of the International Labor Organization and the Organization of American States Convention, adopted in 1999.

According to the International Labor Organization, a person with a disability is a person who has permanent loss or abnormality of psychological, physiological or anatomical structure or function, resulting in incapacity to perform certain activities. The person in this condition is commonly framed in one of the following categories of disability recognized by Brazilian law: physical, mental, hearing, visual, multiple.

According to data from the IBGE, the 2010 Census identifies that of the 45.6 million people with at least one of the disabilities investigated (physical, visual, hearing or intellectual), 38.5 million lived in urban areas and 7.1 million in rural areas. The majority have visual impairment, which affected 35.8 million people in 2010, followed by physical disabilities (13.3 million), hearing (9.7 million) and intellectual (2.6 million). By analyzing the employment rate of these people, IBGE (2010) shows that 53.8% (23.7 million) were not employed. Regarding the rate of employment related to the type of disability, mental/intellectual disabilities were the most limiting to the insertion in the labor market for both men and women: only 17.4% were employed.

It is possible to observe the importance of these organizations, which are established with the objective to serve citizens who are not effectively benefited from public policies and, in many cases, do not properly access their rights.

This study uses as theoretical framework the sustainable territorial development approach and substantive conception of economy, highlighting the importance of the social economy nowadays. Summaries of these approaches are presented below.

2. Sustainable territorial development and substantive conception of economy

The concept of territorial development includes, among other things, the need for each territory to build their own development model, considering that a model successful in one territory may be inappropriate in another. Therefore, to avoid the reductionism of development models, it is important to recognize "creativity" as an added value to other values such as responsibility and – especially in the cases analyzed here – solidarity (Jean, 2010).

Sustainable territorial development (DTS) is an approach that is still under construction. According to Menezes (2011), this approach builds on two important dimensions of the theory of alternative development. The first is the territorial dimension, which analyses the contributions to development via innovations in socioeconomic and sociopolitical fields anchored in a given territory; the second has as its starting point the problems of social and environmental degradation and its relationship with long-term development strategies, together with the contributions of discussions on sustainability.

In recent decades, there has been an increasing theoretical and political debate on the need to integrate the territorial dimension in the analysis and planning of new development strategies (Gumuchian, Pecqueur, 2007; Pecqueur, 2000, 2006; Benko, Lipietz, 2000; Guesnier, Joyal, 2004; Bellemare, Klein, 2011). According to Pecqueur (2006), the concept of territory is closely related to its "construction" from the actions of its inhabitants. Thus, the notion of territory is used to designate a process of collective and institutional creation (Vieira *et al.*, 2010). In this sense, the analysis of the action of cooperative nature between organizations can help to understand processes of "territory building" which mobilize social actors sensitive to the identification of territorial resources (Vieira *et al.*, 2010; Gumuchian, Pecqueur, 2007).

Pecqueur (2006) argues that the actors associate to each other in order to solve production problems in a meso-economic scale, which is different from the individual and global scales. The group that actors form may have several reasons to act collectively, according to the benefits for each of the group members. The author states that "the meso-economic approach to economic space corresponds to the analysis of the building dynamics of an 'internal' in relation to an 'external'. The territory is a result of this discrimination process. A territory is a combination of abstract common space built by groups and a physical space" (Pecqueur, 2006: 96).

The territorial approach has obtained importance and diversity in social sciences. The comprehension of social innovations, for example, is improved with the use of this approach. For Bellemare and Klein (2011),

> For a large part of social sciences, whether fundamental or applied social sciences, the territory emerges as an important dimension of analysis [...]. The definitions, the theoretical perspectives and analytical tools are, however, very different from one research field to another [...] a question then must be asked: would it be appropriate to work towards a general territorial approach that allows observing the different dimensions of the territory? Such an approach would be especially important for the analysis of social innovation (Bellemare, Klein, 2011: 2).

Analysis of the territory as a scenario of actions aimed at development can be enhanced by considering the social innovation produced in this process. By mapping and examining the connections and interactions driven by the actors in the territorial space, the approaches of social innovation seem to meet the studies on the social dimension of territorial development. In this perspective, Andion (2014: 98) compiles the theoretical aspects of social innovation, noting that one of these aspects defines social innovation as "a new and long-lasting effect response to a poor social situation." The author also identifies other analytical options that "focus on understanding how social innovation is put into practice, emphasizing the role of social entrepreneurs, the social innovation system or network, and the links between different sectors of society in promoting it."

The approach to sustainable development is widespread scientifically and politically. Much of its spread is due to Ignacy Sachs. From the 1970s, he significantly contributed to the spread of the concept of eco-development, which, in his view, is an alternative concept for development that considers another pattern of relationship between society and nature, suggesting learning a pattern marked by a co-evolutionary symbiotic relationship with nature. The eco-development assumes this symbiosis based on three pillars: social justice, economic efficiency and ecological prudence.

According to Sachs (2007), all development planning effort should take into account five dimensions of sustainability featuring eco-development: social sustainability (understood as the creation of a development process that is supported by another logic of growth and subsidized by another vision of what a good society looks like); economic sustainability (made possible by more efficient allocation and management of resources, as well as a steady flow of public and private investments); ecological sustainability (which can be improved by promoting the use of resources of the several ecosystems with the least possible damage to life-support systems); spatial sustainability (aiming at achieving a more balanced rural-urban configuration and a better territorial distribution of human settlements and economic activity); and cultural sustainability (including the search for endogenous roots of modernization models and integrated farming systems, change processes that protect cultural continuity and to implement a plurality of solutions tailored to the specific needs of each social and ecological context).

Sachs (2004) presents a concept that extends this discussion especially with regard to the idea of development that balances two issues: mass unemployment and growing inequalities. The author suggests as a path "public policies that promote the necessary institutional transformation and affirmative actions favoring the weak and silent segments of the nation, the working majority devoid of decent work opportunities and livelihoods" (Sachs, 2004: 26). For Sachs, the "development aims to enable every human being to manifest potential, talent and imagination in the pursuit of self-actualization and happiness through individual and collective enterprises, combining autonomous and heteronomous work and time spent on non-productive activities" (Sachs, 2004: 35). Thus, the author discusses the concept of inclusive development based on decent work for all, as opposed to exclusive development. Sachs argues that inclusive development requires the guarantee of civil and political rights, especially as regards to access to assistance programs, public services, education, health and housing services to be provided directly by the government, by nonprofits or by private companies. These actions predate the creation of decent employment opportunities that generate income and provide a lasting solution to the social problem.

The communication of the two above-mentioned approaches raises in the scientific scene, the concept of sustainable territorial development. According to Lévesque (2010: 86), it can be assumed that the possible combination of territorial development approaches and sustainable development are the promising viewpoint of production of knowledge and mobilizing from the point of view of long-term actions. The author states that this construction, although in its beginning stages, allows to uncover the extent of empirical research in the field for this new perspective. On the same line, Jean (2010: 59) argues that:

> As many authors have noted, the major principles of sustainable development and those that support the new theories of territorial development are not so distant in terms of epistemological reflection. They converge in a fundamental point, namely the recognition of the capacity of the social actors who daily build territories where plurality of logical development is coherent.

In discussing the approach of sustainable territorial development (Andion *et al.,* 2006) add the importance of the social economy in the implementation of this alternative vision of development. These authors argue that territorial sustainability stems from a process of "social construction" in specific socio-spatial and historic contexts in which the general principles and norms are interpreted and reinterpreted by local actors. These actors create "solutions" that can be adapted to the problems raised by the environmental crisis at global and local levels. The challenge is then to analyze these solutions and their ability to cope with such problems innovatively. In the socioeconomic field, this analysis would require more than a simple superposition of the socio-political, socio-economic and socio-ecological dimensions of development. It is, above all, to build "bridges" between these dimensions, considering the inclusion of economic activities in the social and political relations and their interconnections with the socio-ecological dimension. Therefore, it is crucial to go beyond the narrow concepts established by neoclassical economics, seeking to redefine the traditional notion of economy. What is at stake is a new relationship between the public and private sphere and social economy, and the challenge of building new forms of connection and negotiation between these spheres. For the authors, "inserted in a context that increasingly demands the combination of technological and social innovations, organizations, whether private, public or linked to the social economy, give more value to the non-market factors or extra-economics involved in their operations" (Andion *et al.,* 2006: 213).

One of the most fruitful avenues for building such "bridges" or theoretical walkways including the social economy can be undertaken by the use of the substantive conception of economy, developed by Karl Polanyi. In the 1950s, together with of a group of researchers at Columbia University, Polanyi deepened his studies in the field of economic anthropology and laid the foundations of the substantive conception of economy. According to this concept, only in modern society with the advent of capitalism, was the idea that the market can be converted into the dominant principle of regulating the economy spread. In earlier stages, the market had never taken such a regulatory role because other principles, subordinated to the social institutions of the time, guided the economic regulation. According to a substantive conception, therefore, the economy was and is an institutionalized process, subject to social norms; the idea of the market economy as a self-regulatory process, separate from the social fabric, is a feature of modern society, and thus cannot serve as a reference for the historical analysis of economic processes.

According to Polanyi (1957: 250):

> The instituting of the economic process vests that process with unity and stability; it produces a structure with a definite function in society; it shifts the place of the process in society, thus adding significance to its history; it centers interest on values, motives and policy. Unity and stability, structure and function, history and policy spell out operationally the content of our assertion that the human economy is an instituted process. The human economy then is embedded and enmeshed in, economic and noneconomic

institutions. The inclusion of the noneconomic is vital.

Recognition of the importance of the non-economic dimension among the regulatory factors of economy implies considering and highlighting the action taken by the social economy organizations of today. In many cases, within a territory, these organizations operate the connection between values, goals and sociopolitical motives with economic related activities. Studies conducted in Brazil on social economy organizations point out the crucial importance of the noneconomic dimension to the economic survival of these organizations. Armani (2004) considers that the conceptual advances promoted in recent years have contributed to substantial cultural changes in the activity of civil society organizations in Brazil. One of the most important changes would be "the 'discovery' that the sustainability of an organization is also a function of how socially 'rooted' it is as well as its ability to connect locally and the credibility built with relevant actors present in the context that the organization operates" (Armani 2004: 4).

Pinheiro (2004) gives a significant step towards the development of the subject, working the concept of social sustainability. The author starts from the substantive conception of economy and deeply analyses the functioning of a civil society organization that promotes education of children with severe mental disabilities, the Associação franciscana de educação especial (AFECE). In his study, Pinheiro highlights the social relevance of AFECE activities, which transforms the purely economic and financial understanding of the issue, into a "perspective where the social dimension seems to show a greater importance as a key element of sustainability". Pinheiro (2004) argues that the importance of the social dimension in the process of sustainability is what defines the fundraising strategy. This assumption shows that the commercial exchange and the gains it may generate are not as important as the participation of those who make these processes possible noting the relevance of reciprocity, especially the relationship of people giving to the organization.

Regarding the actions taken by the organizations analyzed here, the strong motivation and social effects of these actions seem to make their economic activity embedded and enmeshed in non-economic institutions, contributing to their economic survival and social development of the territory. This is discussed in detail below.

The next section shows some information on the methodology used in the research and elements about the State of Santa Catarina. Following that, the organizations and the discussion of their actions based on sustainable territorial development will be presented.

3. Methodology and description of Santa Catarina and the organizations

This research used a qualitative methodology. The main instruments were the semi-structured interviews with managers and technical staff of the organizations, complemented by periods of non-participant observation of their overall operation. The research also used secondary data such as meeting minutes, statutes and the organizations' websites, as well as reports in the local media.

In February 2014, the researchers visited the organizations to introduce themselves and present the research proposal. Then, moments of direct observation and interviews were completed weekly and recorded over a six-month period. The interviews followed a script framework based on the sustainable territorial development approach and substantive conception of economy.

As mentioned above, the organizations are located in Florianopolis, Santa Catarina, Brazil. Santa Catarina is the smallest state in the South Region of Brazil and of the 26 states ranks 20th in area. According to IBGE data released in 2015, Santa Catarina occupies the eleventh position in population with about 6.8 million inhabitants, representing 3.4% of the population of the country. Regardless of its area and population, the impact of its economy is significant at national level. The IBGE reveals that the Gross domestic product (GDP) of the State ranks 6th among the States in Brazil (in 2015); its GDP per capita in the same year ranked 4th. Its Human development index (HDI) in 2010 was the third of the country. In the field of civil society, Santa Catarina's numbers are also impressive: according to the IBGE, in 2010 the State had 16,617 private foundations and non-profit organizations, corresponding to 6.7% of these types of institutions operating in the country. This socio-economic dynamic is due to the particularities of the State development, which is historically different from the general model present in Brazil. In Santa Catarina, an agricultural system was formed based on family polyculture farming and an industrialization pattern focused on small and medium enterprises. Unlike most Brazilian states, there is an economic and demographic decentralization, in which the urban centers do not constitute big cities. The IBGE confirms that in 2015 in all the 26 state capitals, Florianópolis (where the organizations studied here are based), ranked 22nd for population, with 421,000 inhabitants.

These characteristics can be explained in part by the particular features of its colonization by the dynamics of occupation of its territory and by the State's geographical characteristics.

A first step of the territory colonization began in the 17th century by the Portuguese. The occupation came from the coast, dominating the native indigenous population (Radin, 2001). A second colonization stage occurred in the second half of the 19th century, when the state received a large population of European immigrants made up of farmers, artisans, workers and traders who came mainly from Germany and Italy. These immigrants intended to build a new life in the country. They arrived in order to inhabit the new lands "turning the forest into productive fields" (Radin, 2001: 24) and settled in small family production units. This family polyculture system, spread over different regions, became one of the main pillars of production in the state and left a mark on its development path. Small family farms, in addition to defining particular features of the local production system, imprinted characteristics on the life style of the population in Santa Catarina. As pointed out by Vieira and Cunha (2002), this lifestyle is distinguished by sharing a culture and ethic centered on work, by community cohesion, close relationships between consumption and production and a significant autonomy from the state bureaucracy. In Santa Catarina several cities were created in the second stage of colonization and maintained for a long time by the communities, with virtually no support and/or government intervention; a series of public services such as education, fire brigade, road maintenance and others were created by local communities.

Today, evidence of these characteristics can be observed in organizations that stand out for the socioeconomic innovation they present. Some examples are: the first and still most important corporation of volunteer fire brigade in the country, Corpo de Bombeiros Voluntários de Joinville, founded in 1892 (Karam, 2014); the first and largest network of ecological family farming in Brazil, Rede Ecovida, founded in 1988 which is responsible for creating a participatory certification (Serva, Andion, 2008); the second community foundation established in the country, in 2005, Instituto comunitário grande Florianópolis (ICOM), an organization that provides financial and technical support to civil society organizations; the first association of ecological agritourism in Brazil,

Acolhida na Colônia, created in 1999, bringing together 184 families of small farmers. Thus, a dynamic associative and cooperative system, which shows a developed social economy as well as a large number of micro and small enterprises (making up 99% of the existing companies in the state), are specific to Santa Catarina.

The next section presents a summary of the social economy organizations analyzed.

3.1. Cooperativa Social de Pais, Amigos e Portadores de Deficiência – COEPAD

In 1998, a group of parents and friends of people with intellectual disabilities met in order to seek solutions to provide employment for those with intellectual disabilities. On 16 November 1999 the group founded Cooperativa social de pais, amigos e portadores de deficiência (COEPAD), which is established based on Law 9867 of 10/11/1999 that provides for the creation of social cooperatives aimed at social integration of citizens; COEPAD was the first cooperative in its sector created in Brazil.

According to one of its leaders, the objective of the cooperative "is to prepare its members (people with intellectual disabilities) to enter the labor market. They are over the age for basic school (literate or not), and through their work they can feel useful, gain self-esteem, and show society that people with disabilities can be fit for work with the right support."

During the period of the research, 41 people with intellectual disabilities were members of the cooperative, all of them over 18 and receiving monthly remuneration. The admission of a new member starts with a psychological evaluation by professionals of another civil society organization, the Associação de pais e amigos dos excepcionais (APAE), which operates in a network throughout the country. Then the prospective member works on a preliminary contract for 90 days, during which they experience all workshops in order to identify which type of production activity is most appropriate for them. In 2014, COEPAD had 35 volunteers who developed their activities at prearranged times and according to the need of production.

The board of directors is formed by 8 volunteers in the positions of president, vice president, secretary, commercial, production director, technical director, legal director and the director representative of parents and volunteers. Most of the directors are retired professionals, and some of them have relatives among members of the cooperative with disabilities. Two professional contractors who assist in the administrative and financial activities complement the staff.

The production is distributed in six workshops, coordinated by highly experienced professionals. The highlight is the adaptation of the production process to the specific conditions of the members of the cooperative; stages and the pace of the process are subject to the characteristics of those who run it. Over time the organization has created deep collective learning, allowing the production to be performed by people with intellectual disabilities with the quality demanded by the market and respecting deadlines. COEPAD has the support of educational psychologists through an agreement with the State University of Santa Catarina (UDESC), allowing students to do their internships in the cooperative.

In the handmade paper workshop, the cooperative recycles donated paper and the entire process is done by its members from chipping the paper, making paper mass, dyeing and drying. In two workshops, artisan papers are used to manufacture boxes and packaging for gifts, cover notebooks, binders, materials for events, gifts, and more. The graphic finishing workshop is specialized in packaging and specialized lines of stationery. The cutting and sewing workshop produces bags, purses and ecological packaging made in nonwoven fabric or cotton canvas; COEPAD develops customized models, which are completed in the screen-printing workshop, where office supplies, t-shirts, gifts, ecological bags and other customized products are printed.

COEPAD works with high quality products, commercialized at its headquarters and in other parts of the city, and according to the demand from various companies. The quality of products is guaranteed by the Federal University of Santa Catarina, which produces its branded products (clothes and stationery) exclusively through COEPAD, as well as other large companies that are well known clients of the cooperative. The organization is maintained almost exclusively by its commercial activity.

Institutional relations of the cooperative in the territory where it operates extend to various types of civil society organizations, companies and the State, such as Centro de Integração Empresa-Escola (CIEE), which is an organizations that connects companies and schools/universities for internships, APAE, the Federation of Industries of Santa Catarina, the Federal University of Santa Catarina, the State University of Santa Catarina, Casas da Água (large statewide company that sells building materials), Flex Contact Center (a large company in the area of IT).

3.2. Associação Catarinense para a Integração do Cego – ACIC

ACIC is a nonprofit organization that serves visually impaired people at all levels through the provision of services in the areas of habilitation, rehabilitation, labor training, culture, sport and leisure. A group of visually impaired people founded the association on June 18, 1977. Under Article 1 of its Bylaws, in addition to providing the above-mentioned services, the organization also implements study, research and work for the full development of citizenship of its beneficiaries. The mission of ACIC posted on its website is: "to promote actions aimed at social inclusion of visually impaired people contributing to their effective participation in society."

The history of how ACIC was founded was collected through interviews with some of its founding members. The development of the organization over its 39 years shows the ability of its members to face and overcome challenges. In 1977, the association's activities began in the house of one of its founders. Currently, ACIC has its own headquarters with 3,500 m^2 built on a large plot, which houses a Learning and Child Development Center, a Habilitation and Rehabilitation Center, and buildings with special facilities with 24 rooms to host disabled people from other regions that come to the organization to benefit from its services. At the time this research was conducted, ACIC was serving 219 people in these centers.

The Learning and Child Development Center serves children up to 10 years old through special techniques for inclusion in society. The main educational programs implemented are:

a) multisensory stimulation with activities that promote the development of perception through taste, hearing, touch and smell, enabling the child to perform various activities of their daily lives;
b) visual stimulation, promoting the development of attention, awareness and visual processing through sensorial-motor and psycho-affective function schemes;

c) physical education, for the acquisition of motor skills and increasing body and special awareness;
d) activities of daily living, aiming to work aspects of personal autonomy for hygiene, body care and food habits;
e) elaboration of concepts and literacy;
f) pre-soroban, initiating the use of soroban or abacus, an apparatus of mathematical operations invented in Japan especially for visually impaired people;
g) introduction to computing;
h) children's mobility.

For people over 10 years of age, the Habilitation and Rehabilitation Center offers the following services included in the Labor Training Program: occupational service (for people unable to enter the labor market and/or retired); workshop with recyclable products (offered through scholarships provided by private companies); labor training; vocational guidance; in-company training; loom weaving courses, tapestry, knitting, crocheting; two years internships in companies. Through the Habilitation and Rehabilitation Center, ACIC provides guidance and mobility services; activities of daily living; physical education; Braille literacy; basic computing, especially using internet; cursive writing; alternative communication; soroban; learning support and reading groups.

The board of directors is formed of 8 volunteers all of which are visually impaired. The staff consists of 61 people, 19 paid professionals working in the administration, 27 teachers paid by the city government and 14 teachers paid by the State government. ACIC counts on the support of 45 volunteers.

The financial statements published by the Association in 2014 showed that its financial resources come largely (about 80%) from contracts with the cities in the region (Florianópolis, São José and Palhoça) and the remaining 20% are donations from businesses and citizens.

ACIC is a member of several local, state and national participatory forums of public governance, such as the National Council on the Rights of Persons with Disabilities, the State Council of Social Services, the City Council of Children and Adolescents Rights, among others. These are spaces where it is possible to establish partnerships, advocacy, and control and monitor government and public policies.

4. Discussion

In the reported cases, both organizations work in the inclusion of people with disabilities in the labor market in the State of Santa Catarina, and were created by civil society. However, they work in different ways and these differences will be discussed below.

In Brazil, this field of activity is new. It is common to find experiences where people with disabilities are offered social services, but not assistance to access the labor market. In terms of sustainable territorial development, it is the inclusion in the labor market that will be highlighted in the cases. The two organizations analyzed, in addition to economically contributing to society through the generation of income for people often excluded from the labor market, are creating a socio-economic and existential space for people with disabilities through educating actors involved in their social environment. The organizations contribute to a significant change in the perception on people with disability in society; when creating opportunities for the protagonism of the person with disabilities in the labor market, they are no longer perceived as incapable, but as someone who can have a respectful and recognized role in society. In this sense, these organizations drive a cultural shift in the territory, from the workplace. According to Pecqueur (2006), in actions aimed at territorial development, the groups of actors have different reasons to act collectively; the social economy organizations examined in this research express social change as one of their main reasons, acting for change in the relationship of the people with disabilities in society. Even without entering the analysis of the social innovation undertaken by such organizations (as analyzing in depth this dimension would be out of the objectives of this study), it is possible to infer that these groups innovate in the territory. This is based on the fact that there was an unsatisfactory social situation – the exclusion of people with disabilities – and on the evidence that the organizations provided a new and lasting effect response (Andion, 2014): the organizations are the only ones in the country in their respective areas; ACIC is running for 39 years and COEPAD was founded 17 years ago. In ACIC it is possible to highlight innovations in teaching methods practiced in Brazil in the field of habilitation and rehabilitation of visually impaired people of all ages, preparing them for active life in society, or for the labor market, or providing occupational guidance for those that have retired. It is noteworthy that another innovative socio-economic aspect is that the organization was founded by visually impaired people and is managed throughout its history by the visually impaired; learning thus extends to the issue of the organization's management – often a very complex activity in civil society organizations.

In another perspective, when analyzing the dimensions of sustainable development indicated by Sachs, it is observed that social sustainability is the dimension that is most evident in the performance of both organizations in the territory. The contribution of ACIC and COEPAD is clear, from the reasons that drove the creation of the organizations, to the fact that most of the visually impaired people in Brazil are located in the Southern region, and that this region has lower rates of people with disabilities included in the labor market in comparison to the rest of the country. They promote development in the territory in an inclusive way, in favor of visually impaired people and people with intellectual disabilities, who are in great part devoid of labor opportunities. As noted above, Sachs argues that the dimension of social sustainability is an essential part of inclusive development, which is based on the idea of decent work for all.

In addition to the aspect concerning entering the labor market, Sachs also draws attention, as mentioned above, to non-instrumental aspects, namely, "the expression of potential, talent and imagination in the pursuit of self-actualization and happiness by individuals and collective enterprises." It is fair to say that people with intellectual disabilities members of COEPAD and visually impaired people served by ACIC would probably have less opportunities to express their potential during secondary socialization (socialization beyond family and those close to them) if they were not participating in collective initiatives such as those offered by the organizations, considering that these organizations are unique in their territory. This assumption is reinforced by observing the pedagogical action undertaken by ACIC in all its programs. The non-instrumental aspects of inclusive development also reach the field of guaranteeing civil and political rights. When obtaining better conditions for social participation, members of COEPAD and members (their managers are also visually impaired) and beneficiaries of ACIC are in practice conquering citizenship in a country where the administration of the State's bureaucracy has not adequately provided access to their rights. In both cases studied, the social economy collective enterprises and, in a broader perspective, organized civil society enterprises are the ones who provide access to rights and citizenship.

Social sustainability is interconnected with other dimensions, such as ecological sustainability and economic sustainability. In COEPAD, interconnection between these dimensions is more evident because it is a cooperative in which the recycling of materials, particularly paper, is the key to the production process as well as the basis of almost all of its products. The cooperative members perform all stages of recycling and reuse of materials. Its main revenue comes from the sale of their products; therefore, economic sustainability is directly interconnected to the production processes linked to ecological sustainability. In ACIC that ecological sustainability is not as clear and encompassing in its operations. It is noteworthy that ACIC's Labor Training Program offers a workshop of recyclable products, which is made viable by scholarships provided by private companies, reaffirming the connection between ecological and economic dimensions.

The analysis of the contribution of both organizations to sustainable territorial development brings out the crucial importance of social sustainability in the intertwining of the dimensions discussed above. Aspects of non-economic nature appear to be the essence of the origin, motivation, operation and the results achieved by each of the organizations. Confirming the argument put forward by Armani (2004), the social roots of the organizations base their economic survival.

ACIC has a number of volunteers almost equal to paid professionals, which indicates the credibility of the organization in the territory where it operates. The association is active in participatory forums of public policies related to its field of work, not only in the territory but also at the national level. ACIC is active at the National Council on the Rights of Persons with Disabilities, the State Council of Social Services, the City Council of Children and Adolescents Rights, among others, where it develops actions such as advocacy, establish partnerships, control and monitoring of government and public policies. Its political action, in a broad sense including the cause it defends, affirms its roots and gives it legitimacy and credibility to attract volunteers as well as the support and partnerships with the State and private companies, ensuring ACIC's survival over its 39 years of existence.

COEPAD also has a significant number of volunteers, which is a result of the credibility gained in the territory over time. At the institutional level, the cooperative has an extensive relationship with other civil society organizations, companies and the State, especially with the two large public universities in Santa Catarina. The relationship with the universities, for example, establishes a flow of resources and key opportunities for the economic survival of the cooperative. The Federal University of Santa Catarina granted its brand for COEPAD to establish a line of products for the students, and the organization has a place for commercialization inside the university's event center. This is an important marketing asset for COEPAD, a permanent distribution channel for its products. The institutional relationship with the State University of Santa Catarina enables qualified human resources in the field of educational psychology to be obtained at no cost.

Evidence observed in the action of the two organizations allows us to state that the cases present similarities with what Pinheiro (2004) conceptualized as social sustainability: organizational processes of deep interconnection between the social and the economic dimensions, with the first providing conditions for the second. In a broader analysis, it is possible to say that this empirical study illustrates the concept of "embedded" elaborated by Polanyi (1957) in the substantive conception of economy. These are examples where certain social economy organizations created within the civil society create jobs, capture, and move and transform resources in a perspective of ecological prudence. They, therefore, perform economic activities, but such activities are so embedded in non-market or extra-economic (social relations) factors, that these factors are the basis of the activities and define ultimately the economic survival of these organizations.

However, it is important to stress that the adoption of factors linked to social sustainability as the basis of survival entails challenging implications for these organizations. Ensuring the continuity of the enterprise, maintaining and improving the quality of the services, and achieving the objectives proposed without establishing the economic dimension as the main reason and purpose of collective action demands continuously improvement of the ability to overcome challenges. These are not organizations shaped by capitalism, which aim to profit and act competitively in a given market. These organizations need to ensure continuity working in areas characterized by the potential fragility of the main stakeholders towards the economistic productivism prevailing in society. The challenges are even bigger when one considers the instability of the State action in the social area in a country such as Brazil. Public policies in this area are insufficient and unstable, subject to the administrative discontinuity of the State apparatus, the excessive centralization of decision-making, the dominant technocracy among policy makers and the still recent process of democratization of the country. When adding to these factors the lack of knowledge the general public has about the nature, the real conditions and potential of visually impaired people and people with intellectual disabilities, it is possible to reach an understanding of the challenges that these organizations face in daily operations. The resources needed to operate both in the short term as well as to enable the continuity of operations in the long term are often scarce and obtained through a great individual and collective effort of its members. In the case of ACIC, for example, the organization's relationship with the State is marked by an unstable political system that underlies the State, which proves to be unable to democratically establish clear and durable public policies in the social area. As for COEPAD, among other operational challenges, there is the permanent need to overcome ignorance and prejudice about people with intellectual disabilities, fighting the lack of trust in the ability of these actors to fulfill professional commitments with high quality.

It is crucial to make clear that the day-to-day of these organizations is marked by significant difficulties both internally and externally. Therefore, the focus on social sustainability as the mainspring of an organization in its institutional environment requires coping permanently with highly complex challenges.

5. Conclusion

Returning to the ideas presented in the introduction, the objective of this study was to point out how certain social economy micro-initiatives can contribute to sustainable territorial development. The study focused on the situation of people with disabilities – in this case, those with visual impairment and people with intellectual disabilities – in the South of Brazil, and the need to increase the number of these people in workplaces and their inclusion in society as a whole. As empirical object, two social economy organizations were elected. They present unique characteristics in their respective areas of operation: COEPAD was the first to be created and is still one of the few social cooperatives to increase the number of workers with intellectual disabilities; while ACIC is the most complete organization (in the sense of the breadth of their services) of rehabilitation and integration of visually impaired people in the country.

It is important to emphasize that one of the particularities of this study – especially in Brazil – was to address the issue of development without considering the economic dimension as the center of the analysis. The decision to focus the action of organizations towards the labor market that privilege the social over the economic dimension, also shifts the theoretical framework of the analysis. This leaves aside the approaches of the economy traditionally used by development studies and focusing the basis to interpret on the sustainable territorial development and in the substantive conception of economy.

The uniqueness of both organizations is verified by a close examination of their actions from a broader point of view, showing that such ventures are carriers of social innovations in the territory in which they operate. COEPAD developed collective learning in production processes and in the concern for sustainability in the products made in its workshop, allowing its members to work appropriately to their specific conditions and produce for the market observing quality and delivery deadline specifications. ACIC has been creating and perfecting, throughout its 39 years of operation, pedagogical methods of preparation for life in society for visually impaired people of all ages, as well as for their inclusion in the labor market; its innovative characteristic extends to certain managerial aspects, where people with disabilities carry out activities autonomously.

The analysis of both organizations in this study presents evidence that the economic aspects of their practices are so embedded in the non-economic dimension that social sustainability stands out and guarantees the continuity of the organizations. The core of these processes is the ability to establish partnerships with other social economy organizations in the territory, with governmental organizations, companies and the community. All these relationships are based on the legitimacy and credibility built by ACIC and by COEPAD from their commitment to the causes they fight for concerning the context of visually impaired people and those with intellectual disabilities.

Together with the undeniable performance of the organizations' members, it is noteworthy the specifics of the territory as a factor favoring the creation and development of these enterprises. Both organizations were founded and operate in Florianópolis, capital of Santa Catarina, a State whose society has a unique history in comparison to the rest of Brazil. From the first stage of colonization in the 17th century, and especially after the second stage during the 19th century, the state of Santa Catarina has been influenced by an organization of society that presents a life style and productive system that are favorable for the type of organization studied here. As noted above, features like sharing a culture and ethic based on work, community cohesion and significant autonomy from the State bureaucracy are part of the reality of the State of Santa Catarina. The assignment of the importance of such historical and cultural aspects contributes to broaden the understanding of the mobilization of actors in the field of civil society, because it stresses the density and dynamic of the social fabric built over time.

Thus, despite being a relatively small State in Brazil, Santa Catarina has a collective protagonism in the social scene that can be considered as one of the most expressive of the country. As reported briefly above, in the field of social economy this protagonism is expressed in the action of several organizations that undertake social innovations with strong impact and that are replicated in other areas of the country. In this sense, it is possible to consider that the fact that ACIC and COEPAD are social economy organizations who are unique in their niche of operation and were founded in Santa Catarina, indicates and serves as evidence – together with many other successful collective experiences – of the dynamic of the social fabric of the territory.

This is a qualitative, non-positivist study. Within this perspective it is expressed the inference and not a direct causal relationship between the characteristics of the territory and the action of the analysed organizations. Nevertheless, sufficient evidence has been presented for the assertion of the inference: the cases of ACIC and COEPAD can be understood in part by the characteristics of the territory where they operate, ultimately by the social fabric that compose this territory.

Created within the civil society in Florianopolis, Santa Catarina, ACIC and COEPAD present originality in their causes and processes, especially in the field of inclusion in the labor market. Despite the material and subjective difficulties they face, these social economy organizations contribute significantly to sustainable territorial development. They contribute notably in the social dimension of development because both of them operate in areas (inclusion of visually impaired people and people with intellectual disabilities in the labor market) that national and local public policies do not reach with effectiveness; and contribute when establishing the social sustainability centered on legitimacy and credibility as base for their economic survival.

References

Andion C., 2014, "Inovação social", *in* R. Boullosa (dir.), *Dicionário para a formação em gestão social*, Salvador, CIAGS/UFBA, p. 98-102.

Andion C., Serva M., Lévesque B., 2006, "O debate sobre a economia plural e sua contribuição para o estudo das dinâmicas de desenvolvimento territorial sustentável", *Eisforia*, Florianópolis, PPGAGR, 4: 199-221.

Armani D., 2004, "Sustentabilidade: desafio democrático", *in Sustentabilidade: aids e sociedade civil em debate*, Brasília, Brasil Ministério da Saúde.

Bellemare G., Klein J. (dir.), 2011, *Innovation sociale et territoire : convergences théoriques et pratiques*, Québec, Presses de l'Université du Québec.

Benko, G., Lipietz A., 2000, "Géographie socio-économique ou économie géographique ?", *in* G. Benko, A. Lipietz (dir.), *La richesse des régions : la nouvelle géographie socio-économique*, Paris, PUF, p. 9-29.

Guesnier B., André J., 2004, *Le développement territorial : regards croisés sur la diversification et les stratégies*, Poitiers, Éd. ADICUEER/Faculté des Sciences Économiques Université de Poitiers.

Gumuchian H., Pecqueur B., 2007, *La ressource territoriale*, Paris, Éd. Economica.

Hammes, I., Nuernberg A., 2015, "A inclusão de pessoas com deficiência no contexto do trabalho em Florianópolis: relato de experiência no sistema nacional do emprego", *Revista Psicologia, ciência e profissão*, 35 (3): 768-80.

IBGE (Instituto Brasileiro de Geografia e Estatística), 2010, *Censo Demográfico 2010*, Brasília.

IBGE (Instituto Brasileiro de Geografia e Estatística), 2015, *Estimativas populacionais para os municípios e para as Unidades da Federação brasileiros em 01.07.2015*, Brasília.

Jean B., 2010, "Do desenvolvimento regional ao desenvolvimento territorial sustentável: rumo a um desenvolvimento territorial solidário para um bom desenvolvimento dos territórios rurais", *in* P. F. Vieira, A. Cazella, C. Cerdan, J.-P. Carrière, (dir.), *Desenvolvimento territorial sustentável no Brasil*, Florianópolis, Aped/Secco, p. 49-76.

Karam C., 2014, *Legitimando uma inovação social: o caso do Corpo de Bombeiros Voluntários de Joinville*, Tese de doutorado em administração, Universidade Federal de Santa Catarina, Florianópolis.

Lévesque B., 2010, "Comentários: as bases teóricas e metodológicas do enfoque de desenvolvimento territorial sustentável: convergências e aportes específicos", *in* P.F., Vieira, A Cazella, C. Cerdan, J.-P. Carrière (dir.), *Desenvolvimento territorial sustentável no Brasil*, Florianópolis, Aped/ Secco.

Maccali N., Kuabara P., Takahashi A., Roglio K. Boehs S., 2015, "As práticas de recursos humanos para a gestão da diversidade: a inclusão de deficientes intelectuais em uma federação pública do Brasil", *Revista de Administração Mackenzie*, São Paulo, mar/abril., 15 (2): 157-87.

Menezes E., 2011, "Epistemologia, gestão e meio ambiente: contribuições, conceitos e premissas da abordagem do desenvolvimento territorial sustentável", *I Colóquio Internacional de Epistemologia e Sociologia da Ciência da Administração*, Florianópolis, março.

Pecqueur B., 2000, *Le développement local*, Paris, Syros.

Pecqueur B., 2006, "A guinada territorial da economia global", *Eisforia*, 4: 81-103.

Pinheiro D., 2004, "Sustentabilidade social de uma organização da economia social: um estudo de caso na AFECE – Associação Franciscana de Educação ao Cidadão Especial", *Cayapa – Revista Venezolana de Economía Social*, 4 (7): 48-65.

Polanyi K., 1957, "The economy as instituted process", *in* K. Polanyi, C. Arensberg, H. Pearson, (eds.), *Trade Market in the Early Empires*, New York, Free Press, p. 243-70.

Radin J., 2001, *Italianos e ítalo-brasileiros na colonização do oeste catarinense*, Joaçaba, Ed. UNOESC.

Sachs I., 2007, *Rumo à ecossocioeconomia: teoria e prática do desenvolvimento*, São Paulo, Cortez.

Sachs I., 2004, *Desenvolvimento includente, sustentável e sustentado*, Rio de Janeiro, Garamond.

Serva M., Andion C., 2008, "Inovação e autonomia social numa rede de produção agroecológica: uma análise da certificação participativa na Rede Ecovida", *in* J. Cruz, T. Martins, P Augusto, (dir.), *Redes sociais e organizacionais em administração*, Curitiba, Juruá, p. 43-68.

Vieira P., Cunha I., 2002, "Repensando o desenvolvimento catarinense", *in* P. Vieira (org.), *A pequena produção e o modelo catarinense de desenvolvimento*, Florianópolis, APED, p. 289-310.

Vieira P., Cazella A., Cerdan C., Andion C., 2010 "Potencialidades e obstáculos à construção de territórios sustentáveis no estado de Santa Catarina", *in* P. Vieira, A. Cazell, C. Cerdan, J.-P. Carrière (dir.), *Desenvolvimento Territorial Sustentável no Brasil*, Florianópolis, Aped/ Secco, p. 289-328.

Chapter 11

Territorial Clusters of Economic Cooperation

New Levers for Local and Regional Regulation?

Danièle Demoustier

Sciences Po Grenoble

Introduction: Why clusters?

The revival of the Social and Solidarity Economy (SSE) since the 1970s has been broadly based on a proliferation of small-scale local, associative and cooperative organizations. This vitality has taken the form of a fragmentation of small-scale, often specialized organizations and increasing competition between them, aggravated by an increasing scarcity of public resources. This dynamic of renewal and development is reaching its limits, with the fragility of organizations and in the low territorial (local and regional) impact of their action, segmented as it is by activity or by public. The solution of concentration by merger and absorption, a model specific to the Fordist economy, is no longer the most effective response because of the need for SSE entities to have greater autonomy, for responses to be differentiated, for flexibility and for reactivity as well as because of the strength of commitment within small organizations. In numerous activities, economies of scale, access to multiple skills or the distribution of positive external factors result more from modes of mutualization and of cooperation than from processes of concentration.

This atomization of structures is a particular brake within certain business sectors: inclusion through economic activity has already begun a transformation through the creation of workplace integration coordination schemes and of "solidarity economy groups" (e.g. COORACE,

Co-ordination of organizations providing support through work to the unemployed). The cultural sector, through UFISC, the Federal Union for Intervention with Cultural Organizations, has been considering ways to achieve diversification and mutualization or pooling, often based on groups of employers and business and employment cooperatives, in order to preserve diversity in the face of a standardization of the cultural industry. Recycling, where the ESS used to be a pioneer, now sees the constitution of large-scale for-profit groups and needs to maintain its capacity for innovation. The food industry needs to be organized beyond short distribution circuits, which are very demanding in terms of individual initiatives and interpersonal relations, etc.

The atomization and sectorial specialization of SSE organizations also limit their local and regional impact: seen merely as instruments used by public authorities to help increase cohesion (between social action and the living environment) and the attractiveness of territories (services to people in cultural and sporting activities), they are not part of any strategic vision of regional economic development. Yet this kind of development is proving less and less responsive to the "ripple effect" rationale traditionally invoked to explain the priority given to for-profit companies. Directed more towards returns on financial investments, the creation of mercantile wealth is no longer transformed automatically, by market mechanisms considered "natural", or voluntarily, by public redistribution, into social development (DATAR, 2010), whether through the creation of employment and revenue or through the tax system. The task is thus to simultaneously encourage a re-localization of the economy and an internalization of the social dimensions of economic activity, without waiting for the social effects of individual economic enrichment to make themselves felt. The SSE, which is characterized by this internalizing of "externalities", thus has a new place in the scheme of things. But, as it has little presence in the industrial sector, it must perforce cooperate with other companies to bring the relationship dimension (social links, solidarity, workplace integration, etc.) back into a productive fabric which has increasingly externalized it.

One of the most emblematic forms of the revival of cooperation since 2010s has been the experience and recognition of Territorial clusters of economic cooperation (TCEC), initially promoted by a national network and then recognized by a new French law on the SSE and by two national calls for proposals. Article 5 of the Law defines TCECs as

> groupings on the same territory of companies within the voluntary and solidarity sector, associated with other companies, with links to local

> government and their associations, research centres, higher education and research institutions, and training bodies, which define a common and continuous strategy of mutualization, cooperation or partnership in the service of economic and social projects which are socially or technologically innovative and promoters of sustainable local development.

This national interest in a cluster-type dynamic is not a recent development: in the 1960s, DATAR promoted "poles of development" (*pôles de développement*, Perroux, 1964), and then in the 2000s, "clusters" in the shape of competitiveness clusters (*pôles de compétitivité*, 2004) and centres of excellence (*pôles d'excellence*, 2005). Poles of development were said to be constituted by "driver industries" able to generate "ripple-effects" through the income distributed within the region where they are present: both upstream, through the chain of subcontractors, and downstream through the income and the consumption of the employees whom they hire. The crisis of the 1970s moderated enthusiasm for these poles, with large companies opening hardly any new plant across the country, together with an internationalization of purchasing. Meanwhile the mobility of the best-qualified workers ceased to drive regional development, at the same time as concentration and specialization began to segment the industrial fabric. In response, clusters ("bunches" of firms, on the model of Italian districts) began to be promoted. These were followed by national or international competitiveness clusters (*pôles de compétitivité*) to stimulate and coordinate innovation between companies, linked to research and training centres. These developments placed great value on cooperation between businesses as a way to engender cluster effects, regarded as favorable to innovation and to companies' international competitiveness. These clusters were however relatively selective and targeted. They have therefore ignored certain less-favored regions and may even deconstruct others if their technological requirements effectively exclude an entire group of activities and segment of the population. To counter these processes, analyses of more endogenous regional development sought to stimulate "the activation of regional resources" (Gumuchian, Pecqueur, 2007) in local productive systems (LPS), while DATAR recognized that certain territories develop on an economic basis which is not productive but residential. TCECs are situated at the intersection of these two dynamics (clusters and LPS) and are based on SSE companies, initiating this movement towards regional economic structuring, in line with the hypothesis that regional cooperation may create synergies giving rise to positive externalities both for companies and for regions, in order to stimulate more socially – and environmentally –sustainable economic development.

Having analyzed the process through which clusters have emerged, starting from regional innovations very quickly taken up at institutional level and with a tendency towards standardization, we shall show that their modes of organization and intervention remain very diverse, signs of vitality but also of institutional fragility. The tensions inherent in the SSE as it seeks to combine the economic and the social thus seem to be exacerbated when the desire for internal cooperation extends to hopes for external cooperation.

1. Bottom-up development becomes institutionalized

Born from scattered country-wide initiatives, the TCEC concept was constructed at national level thanks to campaigns by various local and national SSE actors who sought recognition by the public authorities. While public authorities have sought to both support and standardize this mode of cooperation, they have neither allocated sufficient resources, nor succeeded in disseminating a single TCEC model. Regional dynamics remain the main driver creating and giving impetus to TCECs.

1.1. A renewal of inter-cooperation: cooperation between cooperatives

After twenty years of entrepreneurial vitality and service innovations, two forms of structural and organizational innovation have found a place within the SSE since the 2000s. On the one hand, there has been mutualization or pooling between SSE organizations, with the dual aim of making economies of scale and of accessing new resources, such as service platforms, or groups of employers. On the other hand, this period has seen the rise of more cooperative and less competitive forms of exchange (fair trade, short distribution channels, local currencies, etc.,) which integrate non-commercial dimensions within commercial exchanges. Certain local and regional authorities have encouraged these forms of organization which have been giving new life to modes of inter-cooperation which were widespread in the 1960s (such as relationships between agricultural cooperatives and consumers) and which had fallen into disuse due to the disappearance of some previous cooperatives and exacerbation of the competition during the 1980s.

The first initiatives linked the solidarity economy (the REAS network) with some public authorities through the creation of Local Solidarity Economy Clusters (*Pôles locaux d'économie solidaire*) as "resource hubs" to support project initiators (as in Dijon or Ramonville).

Next, the desire for decompartmentalization combined with an awareness on the part of certain companies of both their social responsibilities and their vulnerability to the financialization of the economy. TCECs thus emerged in areas which might be considered "in transition": demographic transition, with an ageing population or, conversely, an influx of new population (neo-rural or families distant from city centres), and economic transition, with the deindustrialization or the destructuring of attractive territories. The group of clusters identified at national level were the product of this kind of local initiatives which emerged in the 2000s.

Thus, in South Aquitaine the closure of the Forges de l'Adour metalworks in 1965 was followed by the creation of local committees for employment (*comités locaux pour l'emploi*) and then to a *comité de bassin d'emploi* (Employment Pool Committee). Local councillors, acting in an interventionist but not *dirigiste* way, made use of networking between SSE organizations to strengthen the substratum required if companies were to remain in the area (services hub, social and economic inclusion, training, accommodation, catering facilities, etc.). In the Drôme, the city of Romans saw the disappearance of the shoe industry, a great source of local pride. An association promoting inclusion was the basis for encounters between economic and social actors and led to action to relocalize some activities (leather, textiles, engineering). In the Arve valley in Haute Savoie, specializing in bar turning, the economic crisis led not only to the loss of automobile and aeronautical markets, but also by takeovers of local companies by foreign pension funds. A number of local entrepreneurs associated with the Innovales business incubator are working to retain control of development within the locality. Hard hit by the crisis of the steel industry, the zone between Metz and Thionvielle lost a lost a major part of its workforce while remaining relatively industrialized. Three organizations, Floranges, Écologie industrielle and Insertion, are supporting the revival of industry by managing and reclaiming waste from companies in four industry parks.

Nonetheless, these experiments have remained confidential and dispersed except in the case of specific workplace integration coordination schemes steered by the COORACE Federation.

1.2. Solidarity Economy Groups and the work of COORACE

Faced with the segmentation of their organizations due to public policy measures and an absence of opportunities for people needing placements on inclusion schemes, COORACE has encouraged through its research and innovation mission the foundation of Solidarity Economy Groups (*Groupements d'économie solidaire*, GES) involving an extension of the initial mission as an "airlock" leading towards the creation of sustainable jobs by actors within central government's Inclusion through economic activity framework (*Insertion par l'activité économique*). It was thus natural for COORACE to join the national inter-network, (*inter réseau*, network of networks) steered by the Le Labo de l'Économie Sociale et Solidaire (the SSE Lab). This currently coordinates two – now merged – "learning communities" at national level, which are managed across TCECs and focus on renewing the productive base and safeguarding career paths; in the Auvergne-Rhône Alpes region, it coordinates the working group shaping the regional TCEC community.

1.3. National networking and the presentation of landmark clusters by the SSE Lab

In 2009, on the initiative of Claude Alphandéry, at that time chairman of France Active, a collective bringing together hundreds of SSE actors met over the course of one year. Its work led to the drawing up of an ambitious strategy for developing the SSE based on 50 proposals "to change course". Among these proposals was the idea of economic cooperation clusters, the cooperative counterpart of competitiveness clusters, based on criteria such as local anchoring of economic activities, the social utility of what is produced, employment which is difficult to relocate, etc. Between January and June 2011, this thinking by TCECs fed into the consultative body the *États généraux de l'Économie Sociale et Solidaire* as it drew up proposals under the heading of "cooperating and mutualizing". Several of these sets of proposals drew upon cluster experiences and an initial debate was organized at the Palais Brongniart, the former site of the Paris Stock Exchange. This initiative resulted in the creation of the SSE Lab (Labo de l'ESS), a think tank tasked with promoting and thinking about the SSE as well as the constitution of a national approach to experimentation, a national network of actors to promote TCECs and challenge public authorities. This network, consisting of the ESS

Lab, national COORACE, the National Council of the ESS Regional Councils (CRESS), the Network of territories for a solidarity economy (Réseau des territoires pour une économie solidaire, RTES) and of the Solidarity Economy Movement (Mouvement de l'économie solidaire, MES), issued a call for proposals to be used as a basis for an analysis of their characteristics. Around a hundred responses, evidencing some very diverse forms of mutualization and cooperation, led to the selection of around twenty "landmark clusters", reference points providing support for lobbying from 2011 onwards. Two days of national study enabled the panel to be widened and provided an opportunity to discuss the fundamental characteristics of these innovative forms of organization, while the Lab set up a unit to analyze and increase understanding of the clusters. In this way, in less than five years, TCECs have become public objects presented to government as modes of consolidating the ESS, of exploiting and pooling resources, and as drivers of sustainable local and regional development.

1.4. Institutional recognition through the legal system and calls for proposals

While some regions had been previously involved in budding TCEC projects (in particular members of the RTES [Network of Local and Regional Authorities for a Solidarity Economy], such as the Lille metropolis, SICOVAL in the Midi Pyrénées region, the Greater Roanne council, etc.), national public authorities[1] reacted fairly quickly to the representations made by the network of national actors, both through official recognition under the terms of the SSE Law of 2014 and by two interministerial calls for proposals.

In its Article 9, the 2014 Law on the ESS recognizes the existence of PTCEs, defining them without however granting any seal of approval. One paragraph announced a decree setting out conditions for responses to national calls for proposals. An interministerial call for proposals requested applications from TCECs in 2013. About 200 responses were put forward, confirming the strong local and regional cooperation dynamic also the varied nature of the proposals. Arbitrating between the objectives of the various ministries concerned (Economy, Social Cohesion, Equality of Territories and Housing) was difficult, even if the main objective declared

1 Particularly the Delegated Ministry for the social and solidarity economy and consumption under Benoît Hamon.

was the sustainable development of territories, "based on cooperation between actors and social innovation." 24 clusters were selected, among which the control clusters become the most symbolic (as Pôle sud Archer in Romans, Pôle Sud Aquitaine, and Culture et Coopération in Saint-Étienne). A variance between responses led the government to ask for an evaluation by the SGMAP:[2] this body, in rather critical terms, noted "the difficulty of judging the potential of projects", "uncertainty concerning the strategic positioning of the TCEC", "vagueness about the sources of self-financing" with self-financing expected in 3 years, and finally "confusion between the simultaneous objectives of consolidation of structures and territorial development". This is why the application order for the law set out more precise selection criteria, in particular by requiring the creation of a structure dedicated to the TCEC which should include at least one SSE company, another for-profit company and one other actor. These requirements were applied to a call for proposals (CFP) in 2015 which went back to the idea that candidate TCECs should be exemplary, at the same time stressing the consolidation of members and the TCEC's economic model, relegating territorial development and innovation to a secondary position.

The autonomous economic viability of the TCEC "group" thus appears to be increasingly important for their institutional recognition, and as a greater priority than the general objective of sustainable development of territories. However, while this desire for economic normalization (linked to criteria of geographical and political distribution) was expressed when the 14 prize-winners of the second national CFP were announced, this is not so much the case in the local and regional effervescence to be seen in the studies focused on by the SSE Lab and in communications at RIUESS conferences.[3] In spite of an increasingly normative approach to public recognition, TCECs are not modelled on a single reference point: the model oscillates between that of the SSE Lab, inspired by the Solidarity Economy Movement (stressing networking, citizen initiatives, and campaigning for the development of the SSE and local and regional territories), and that of the second call for proposals, which stressed entrepreneurial principles and practices, creation of jobs and activities, and the quest for self-financing. This confrontation also affects the position of regions with a measure of autonomy: who are hesitating

2 Secrétariat général pour la modernisation de l'action publique (Secretariat general for government modernization).

3 See references.

between a role as an actor or as TCEC partners. Despite the signature of a charter during the 2nd National TCEC Day, a real formal "community" was not successfully established. This was on one hand because the diversity of these processes of territorial economic cooperation made it difficult to combine citizen, entrepreneurial and institutional dynamics (Matray, Poisat 2013; Podlewiski, 2014); and on the other hand because of the confused engagement of national federations: following neither a statutory nor a sectorial approach, and divided between the objectives of consolidating members and of territorial development, PTCEs have yet to find their place within existing institutional arrangements. Support for the SSE Lab as a think tank has been used to achieve recognition as significant innovations but not as a real means of organization and coordination, while clusters and competitiveness poles have achieved long-term inclusion within business strategies and public policy.

2. Shared foundations, but diverse patterns of local and regional cooperation

Given the nature and diversity of TCECs, several typologies accounting for their principal characteristics are possible:

- a typology based on the progress made in their construction process: initiative, emergence, form of organization, development;
- a typology based on area of operations and cooperation, or activity: a particular industry or sector versus a conglomerate, specialization versus cross-cutting, personal services versus business services, etc.;
- a typology based on type of economic model: community-based, entrepreneurial, territorial.

2.1. Based on the state of progress

To differentiate requirements in terms of results, the 2015 Call for Proposals distinguished between emerging TCECs and those engaged in consolidation. Meanwhile, another more finely-grained approach distinguishes between several stages: emergence, structuring and development, depending on the nature of the actors, the forms of coordination and organization, methods of mutualization and cooperation, and the strategic positioning of the cluster concerned.

2.1.1. At the initiative stage

Most often, initial championing of TCECs is carried out by a "mother" organization operating within the SSE. This can be a Solidarity Economy Group which has originated from a workplace integration coordination scheme. However, it may also be an SSE collective, one either specialized or territory-based, since some of these collectives are either affinity-based or an SSE network encouraged by the local or regional authorities. More rarely, local or regional government is the source of the project through having networked SSE actors together: examples of this are, Lille metropolis in the case of Unis Cité, and SICOVAL in the case of the Maison de l'économie solidaire (Solidarity Economy Centre). This shows the importance of a *driver organization* which has already set up partnership links with other actors within the local area or region and of a positioning as a *developer* (both innovatory and organizing) capable of finding people to share its diagnosis and prospects. Pole Sud Archer, Domb'Innov and Innovales were born from the unifying action of a charismatic leader, well-connected within the social and economic networks in his region and ready to take a chance on another mode of development. It may also result from a meeting between two developers with different backgrounds but united by the same desire to step out of established frameworks: as an example, Pole sud Aquitaine was born from a meeting between the organizer of the Employment Pool Committee and the director of a hostel for young workers, where each felt professional dissatisfaction by the opportunities offered within the region, especially to young people. In the cases most characterized by affinity groups, a group of campaigning "consumer-actors" may get together in a dedicated association (formalized to a greater or lesser extent) in order to promote the project (for example, short food distribution channels).

Very often these meetings crystallize on a particular occasion: a "trigger event" (for example a festival) or an "exemplary" action to crystallize interests and aims, and make a previously informal collaboration more visible.

A project to set up a TCEC in Drôme Provençale

On the initiative of the La Cigale association, promoting a cultural project, 15 organizations (13 associations and 2 businesses) met in December 2014, brought together by a wish "to innovate socially, to develop and endogenous economy and to cooperate in favor of local development" in a tourist region. A group of seven organizations formed a steering committee. This has overseen the drafting of a charter and set up an initial body funded by the National fund for the development of the associative life (*Fonds national de développement de la vie associative*, FNDVA). The first actions undertaken in common were drawing up a survey of the region and organizing a get-together for the SSE.

2.1.2. At the emergence stage

The question then arises of whether there is a desire for and interest in opening the cluster to include other businesses. Only some of the TCECs studied involved non-SSE businesses in their project beforehand: TCECs seeking to organize an industry or sector and quicker to resort to alliances than other types of companies; for example, the Village Documentaire de Lussas from the outset associated a number of production and broadcasting limited liability; recycling groups such as *TRI RA* at Pont Evêque and Écopole at Albertville included companies upstream or downstream of their social inclusion activity; Trivéo from its outset associated three plastics manufacturing SMEs in an Economic solidarity group (*groupe économique solidaire*, GES). For others, the task has been to transform bilateral partnerships into an associational relationship. The first approach often takes the form of a *business club or association* (either of craft workers or SMEs) or collectives of individual entrepreneurs (craft workers or farmers), due to the previous cooperative practices which these groups have already set up. In certain cases, SSE groups display reluctance or make difficulties, probably linked to the emergence phase, which may not necessarily lead to a fully-fledged TCEC due to gaps between sectional approaches and an integrated or peripheral strategy, or perhaps resulting from the difficulty of stepping away from strongly affinity-based practices. In other cases, the very term "other associated companies" seems ambiguous, because limited liability companies may be transformed into producer cooperatives when a TCEC is set up. Finally, there are rare cases of alliances with a large-scale multinational organization; these cases can be ascribed to historical links with the region or locality (for example Schneider Electric in Grenoble), or a relatively slow and gradual approach (there being several decision-making centres which are quite distant, and with the company preferring to control all resources internally).

There is also the question of whether to associate private individuals: volunteers from outside the circle of administrators may be called upon within certain clusters for purposes of networking, external relations, audits and expert assessments, etc.); the question of associating citizens or *civil society* still arises only rarely in spite of calls from the Solidarity economy movement; this rarely goes beyond the creation of new activities (business incubators, creation of social enterprises, etc.). Also called into question is the positioning of public institutions vis a vis the public service mission; some TCECs strongly supported by the public authorities seek to emancipate themselves, while others set up in more autonomous fashion seek their participation. Increasingly, local and regional government becomes a member of local TCECs, posing the risk of political hijacking, difficulties if there is political change, and conflicts of interest. One then sees the emergence of various affinity circles: the tight nucleus of driver organizations who define common strategy; the wider circle of partners associated with actions, some of whom will join the central nucleus; and finally, the "halo" of "as and when" relationships with relatively diverse actors.

2.1.3. At the organizational stage

Transforming the network into a lasting structure is an important stage in setting up at TCEC. The number of members in the central nucleus begins to stabilize; this is relatively low (around 5) in TCECs forming an integrated industry or sector, wider (around 15) in TCECs linking companies coordinated in a more cross-sector way, and much greater (around 50) in campaigning networks. One of the first common actions is devising forms of communication specific to the TCEC: the logo, organization chart, Internet site, etc. are identity markers which make the TCEC autonomous from its mother organization.

Le Bol
A resumption of an inconclusive TCEC project (Agri-Alim) in the Lyons region, aiming to build a locally-based food sector.
A group of organizations; creation of a dedicated association.
One annual unifying event: the Harvest Festival.
Public funding for a project to optimize members' logistical organization (procurement, transport, etc.).
Members offer their time (remunerated), intern present, but no long-term funding for organizers.

There follows the organization of a coordination function, to provide support for the leadership of the developer at that time concentrating more on strategy, then for the organization as a whole. The task is to maintain members' commitment, support development of new projects, organizing internal events and external communications. Governance tends to become more formalized, both through the setting up of an autonomous organization (in the form of an Association), a Cooperative society of public interest (*société coopérative d'intérêt collectif*, SCIC), an Economic interest group (*groupement d'intérêts économiques*, GIE), an Economic and social unit (*unité économique et sociale*, UES), or a Simplified Joint-Stock Company (*société par actions simplifiée*, SAS), and by the creation of bodies enabling activities at various levels: beyond the Management Board, steering committees, policy committees (to include external partners) and working groups (for operational activities).

In his study of modes of governance, Patrick Gianfaldoni (2015) distinguishes between "network entities" and "networks of entities". "Network entities" give structure to particular industries or sectors. TCECs assert themselves as "spaces for strategic pooling", a strategy which gradually turns into a challenge for cooperation. Managing a space which is common to all parties, while not a precondition, is nonetheless a factor favoring this type of identification: the geographical proximity which facilitates a mutualization of resources is a basis for confidence and for the construction of common, innovative projects. Other instances of mutualization are gradually put in place: jobs (groups of employers), administration and support functions, and even finance (accounts departments, etc.) Moreover, there increasingly emerges a function which pools responses to government procurement contracts (facilitating social and environmental clauses).

2.1.4. At the development stage

Once the outlines of a TCEC have been identified and stabilized, it is advisable to clarify its development strategy and specific directions of activity; while its launch stage pursues quite pragmatic objectives (potential business opportunities, support for the creation of new activities, structuring professional relations, etc.), if the TCEC is to make its presence felt (and justify itself externally), this means work must go into making its nature and its objectives explicit. Engaging in research and development, thinking through the economic model and support for training tools can be used to better characterize the TCEC and clarify the contributions it can make. Out of this may emerge activities specific to the TCEC above and beyond a strengthening of its members' activities.

Pôle Laine

In a rural region in difficulty, this TCEC resulted from an initiative by an Organization for inclusion through economic activity (*Structure d'insertion par l'activité économique*, SIAE) set up in 1992 which includes a training school for washing wool.

A recent organization but an old approach.

Association created in 2015 with four colleges: sheep raisers, transformers, promoters (culture, tourism, travel agency), and public institutions (municipalities, future regional park).

Two lines of development: providing renewed economic activity through promotion of quality wool; preserving the local heritage (skills and construction) by combining culture and tourism.

Initial funding by the Auvergne Regional Council from the regional Social Innovation Fund and made available to personnel by the Saugues municipality.

Often the process is considered, from a linear perspective, to be an indicator of the level of a TCEC's "maturation". But development is much less mechanical: there are numerous scenarios and overlaps between stages or leaps forward are possible. In addition, TCECs may experience drift from their initial projects, which may take the form of various breaks and forks in the road: breaks with the mother organizations, withdrawal by some members with others joining, redefinition of the project, relations between members, one actor taking over, etc. TCEC development follows more of a trial and error process, leading to a "plurality of pathways forward".

Table 1: TCEC development phases

Phase	*Funding*	*Partnerships*	*Governance*	*Objective*	*Purpose*	*Eco Model*	*Impacts*
Initiative	One SSE organization	One-offs	Autonomous	Transformations	One event	Own resources	On activity of mother organization
Emergence	A collective of SSE organizations	Within the SSE	Informal	Consolidation of members	Pooling of resources Specific common actions	Grant made available to members	On Member Organizations
Structure	SSE and companies	SSE public support exchange with companies	Organized	Structure of partnerships	Set up of activities in common	Mixed funding	Creation of activities and jobs within TCEC
Development		SSE companies training and research bodies	Formalized	Development of region or sector	Activities (collective and continuing)	Increase in Marker resources	in the region direct and indirect

Source: the author

2.2. Structure of activities

Outside industry- or sector-based TCECs (culture, recycling, etc.), the nature of the activity is often difficult to define because it is either cross-sector or innovatory, and thus habitual nomenclatures do not describe it well. It seems more apt to think in terms of the field of intervention. In 2014, the SSE Lab (CIGETO) identified three types of activities, some aspects of which are poorly defined:

- production activities (agriculture and food processing; renewable energies; construction and habitat, salvage and recycling);
- activities engineering local development (entrepreneurship, business services; management of social measures, training, personal services, citizen investment, green tourism);
- craft-based or artisanal activities (art and culture, music, the book trade, organization of professional networks).

We might thus think in terms of a sector (as a set of complementary activities which contribute either upstream or downstream to the production of a finished product or the response to a function: mobility or combatting energy poverty) or as a conglomerate (as a set of diverse enterprises united by certain links, which are generally legal and financial). Sectors are most often to be found in the culture industry (contemporary forms of music, the book trade, documentary films, etc.), the food industry (organic breads, perishable products), recycling (from collection to reuse), construction (ranging from eco materials to sustainable habitat *via* the fight against energy poverty), etc.

Alp'En

Combating energy poverty (*via* its SOLENI) service, the ULISSE Solidarity Economy Group has tried to decompartmentalize its partners' activities and strengthen cooperation, bringing together Accommodation and Social reintegration centres (Centres d'hébergement et de réinsertion sociale, CHRS), the Schneider Electric company, Gaz Électricité de Grenoble, EDF, the City of Grenoble (Sustainable City department), Grenoble Alpes Métropole (SSE and Housing departments) and the Municipal social action centre (Centre communal d'action sociale, CCAS). The collective was given a structure as an association in June 2015, in order to "construct a common offer of energy expertise services, providing a space for experimentation in order to innovate and promote the development of new skills." The approach is novel, bringing together SSE actors' skills in locally-based support and inclusion as well as the technical competence of private companies able to take a fresh look at their products and adapt them to a public exposed to job insecurity.

Conglomerates are more cross-cutting, to meet the diverse needs of the local area or region. However, TCECs are not regional development agencies; they need to be directly operational by coordinating and stimulating activities; amongst these, a clear line divides services to private individuals (social businesses) and to companies (service platforms, industrial logistics, etc.).

Domb'Innov

Constructed around a major social action association, in a region undergoing far-reaching demographic changes (receiving new families), this TCEC is intended to meet the population's needs by creating social businesses (subsidized stores, recycling, cinema, etc.) Their strength derives from the mutualizing of support functions; their dynamism is driven by "a festival of the economy of the third kind", which gives residents a chance to express their needs, to organize new collective enterprises and to support them through solidarity-based and participatory funding.

Pôle Sud Aquitaine

On the initiative of an Employment Pool Committee, in an industrial and port area, this cluster originated from a conviction about the role of cooperation in local and regional development. It is based on the activities of around twenty SSE companies (mainly in the form of Co-operative societies of collective interest) linked by multiple intersecting contributions (professional, economic, financial and above all strategic) to

- Step beyond the reception of young people to work towards inclusion and then the creation of activities;
- Provide services to businesses (inter-company restaurant, service hub, training, groups of employers, etc.);
- Support job seekers and new entrepreneurs in managing their daily life, promoting accommodation, mobility, access to local products, etc.

But there is crossover between these two dominant models: sectors are anchored in the region (e.g. recycling of mixed plastics in Plastics Vallée) and conglomerates have their own main lines of activity. They are thus located on a continuum between specialization and diversification: specialization in a sector of activity (for example, the cultural sector) or a function (energy expertise); there is diversification prompted by responses to needs (of the population or of companies).

Lussas Documentary Village: documentary films and images

The dynamic of the Lussas Documentary Village (Ardèche) began with the setting up of the Ardèche Images association in 1979 to produce art films (*films d'auteur*). In 1989, Ardèche Images organized the *États généraux du film documentaire*. This has become a major festival for documentary films. Ten organizations emerged from this dynamic. Starting in 2012 they decided to set up a TCEC. Today 13 associations and companies, ranging from production to distribution, employ 40 workers and generate nearly 3,000,000€ of consolidated budgets. Each year the TCEC takes on 18 university students as interns as well as 20 students doing in-service training.

Innovation concerns processes and practices more than products and services: accessibility, end-user participation (*maîtrise d'usage*), responsible consumption, taking ownership of economic activities, short distribution channels and reciprocity in exchanges, crowdfunding, etc. The TCEC sees itself as a "catalyst for community initiatives". It seeks to combine the relational capabilities of the SSE (inclusion, education, solidarity) and the technological capabilities of for-profit companies. All TCECs thus promote the creation of new activities, starting from a business incubation function, but some mostly outsource these new activities, while others internalize them. Still others try to support a relocalization of activities.

Pôle Sud Archer

Initiated by an intermediary association, in a city exposed to de-industrialization, this cluster was set up in 2003 following a realization that inclusion has its limits if no jobs are being created. Today, in the form of a simplified joint-stock company with 112 members (including two business associations), it is organized around four lines of development:

Mobilization of public service organizations in support functions and in training;

Get-togethers and exchanges between actors (social solidarity market, ethical store, mutualization of jobs, etc.);

Economic stimulus and organization within the region (purchasing cooperative, tourist circuit, entrepreneurship school, reactivation of shoe industry, etc.);

Economic action (relocalization, support platform for companies wishing to relocate their activity, maintenance of skills and know-how, launch of "regional start-ups", etc.).

Likewise, cooperation is more or less integral to the TCEC: some hold that the main task is to strengthen cooperative relationships between members: institutional, professional, commercial, payroll and financial relations, etc. Others think the priority should be to strengthen the TCEC as an autonomous entity by generating common activities (caretaking, advisory board, tasks which bring several members together, etc. As actors within regions and sectors in transition, the task is to promote new organizational forms at the same time as new skills; this is why almost everybody thinks in terms of training and career changes both as an internal activity and through links to training bodies.

Through the organizational innovations which are the very stuff of TCECs, collective expertise in development is what is most prized: expertise in regional development by entrepreneurs who wish to maintain or relocalize activities and jobs, redeveloping the region in more ecological directions; expertise in activities providing services to professionals or users no longer prepared to be elbowed aside from their own developing practices.

2.3. Types of economic models

Analysis of TCEC economic models needs to cover four scales or levels. The widest is the territorial (i.e. local and regional) economic model (Gaglio *et al.*, 2011) engendered by the TCEC's activity, required to account for all value added (both monetary and non-monetary) and the transformation of its distribution within the territory by ripple effects, knock-on effects and indirect effects. It is impossible today to construct this model, because of a lack, not of methodology, but of operational tools with which to measure these phenomena. Some rare TCECs have made the attempt, such as the Lussas Documentary Village which has estimated the multiplication effect of its activity on the local economy as a factor of three; as well as TCEC Sud Aquitaine which has estimated the leverage effect of public funding on the activity it generates as between one and twenty. Looking at the consolidated budgets of members is a more accessible approach: these amount to 2M€ at Lussas, at 7.2M€ for solidarity entrepreneurs in central Isère (around Grenoble), and 9M€ at Domb'Innov. The budget for the TCEC itself (organizing and activities) is fairly well available for inspection: between 80 and 150K€. Within it, the organizational function represents between 40 and 60K€.

If we look at their degree of organization and their type of economic activity, TCECs combine economic models which are mainly based on community, entrepreneurship or locality and region. They all face the challenges of consolidating their membership and the long-term continuation of the TCEC.

- *The community model*

The construction of an entrepreneurial "community" is based on the level of commitment displayed by its members: a great number of contributions in kind are required for TCECs to emerge: civic engagement, voluntary work by professionals within the organizations, resources made available by companies, donation of employees' skills and time by companies, etc. Without this initial non-monetary contribution, few TCECs would have seen the light of day. However, making an organizational function autonomous requires monetary contributions: intervention by public authorities (national CFPs, local programs, etc.) becomes indispensable to support and structure the process. This intervention requires a relationship of confidence in the promoters' experience and the risks being taken on by the project. It is mainly based on support by a mother organization and seeks civic contributions.

- *The entrepreneurial model*

The construction of integrated activities (sector-based TCECs) or new activities (local and regional TCECs) calls on the monetary resources of members and responses to more specialized calls for proposals (energy, construction, the food industry, etc.); as new projects are built up, part of the funding is allocated to the collective organization of the cluster. Cluster development is financed by a percentage levied on new productions and developments.

- *The territorial (local or regional) model*

Finally, to maintain local actors' capacity for innovation and mobilization, local and regional TCECs must find appropriate resources. Public funding is sought even if their assessment criteria make little allowance for long-term impacts; crowdfunding may also contribute, providing that citizens feel they are stakeholders in the project.

Beyond these ideal types, these economic models are always mixed but in varying proportions. Developments require greater involvement (financial and economic) from members, participation by public authorities (in kind, in grants, in calls for proposals, in markets), and involvement by civil society (new members, voluntary work, crowdfunding or solidarity funding, procurements, etc.) These "new entrepreneurial ecosystems" (Levesque, 2016), which seek to cut across multiple dimensions, are nevertheless caught up in tensions which may turn into real contradictions.

3. Tensions and issues

It emerges from a theoretical and practical analysis of TCECs today that after several years of operations (10 in the cases of Pôle Sud Archer and Pôle Sud Aquitaine), they are faced with three types of issue:

- Governance issues with respect to the objective of networking actors in a multi-partnership;
- Strategy issues with respect to the objective of innovation, mutualization and cooperation;
- Modes of territorial development issues with respect to the objective of the sustainable development of the region.

3.1. Governance issues

Governance issues concern the definition and participation of members (SSE, for-profit companies, public authorities, training and research bodies); the TCEC's mode of organization (autonomous or not, a network structure or a network of structures); relations with the mother organization (which may or may not remain a pivotal structure); its decision-making bodies (formalized or not, multiple or not); its modes of organization; its relationships with citizens (appeals, involvement, events) and with other SSE organizations (coordination, competition, selection). SSE organizations are always present at the birth of a TCEC: associations, Solidarity economy groups, more rarely cooperatives, which have already developed a culture of external cooperation.

At an initial stage, local and regional TCECs find difficulty in engaging with for-profit companies (sector-based TCECs share interests more directly); initial contacts are with SMEs or very small businesses, which are more conscious of common interests; large-scale companies, which are more autonomous, are more easily sensitized to local and regional cooperation by business clubs (which may be created for this purpose). When they realize the regional interest of these clusters, public authorities hesitate between direct participation and external supervision, between instrumentalization and disengagement. They may tend to use the cluster as a local development agency or as a substitute for local public services. These external alliances may thus lead to a redefinition of positions and powers within the TCEC; in some cases, the mother organization or the founders have been ejected from leadership of the cluster by their allies. This may feed into the legal structure of the cluster: the choice of becoming a simplified joint-stock company rather than an association or an SCIC (co-operative society of collective interest) indicates a shift in the balance of power. But within an association, the constitution of governing bodies may reveal a rebalancing of powers in favor of public institutions, for example. Conversely, adopting an SCIC structure in the early stages of a cluster may tend to close it off, with the diversity of the original members and the strength of their common culture seeming sufficient to maintain the cluster's dynamic. This explains why the place of the SSE may be thrown into question by the development of certain clusters: both in its driving and strategic role, and as an objective for the cluster's development. It may be easily transformed into an SME cluster, with their development as the sole objective.

This is also why the way the governance and action of TCECs is organized is also a sensitive matter: while initially, the challenge is to mobilize actors, the development of economic projects may quickly substitute for this coordination role; other actors in the region (residents, employees, associations, etc.), are then thought of not as active citizens but as recipients, customers, or even publics benefiting from the activity.

3.2. Strategy issues

Questions of strategy intersect directly with questions of governance. The first fault line, between regional industry or sector and conglomerate, is coupled with a distribution of very differentiated actors: in one case, a strong presence of companies, in the other, of public authorities. But the positioning and prospective strategy (Malo, 2001) is also thrown into question: positioning in a sector and a region; prospects for mutualization and cooperation. A straightforward positioning strategy to defend and increase the share of available business would tend to over-simplify the process to the sole benefit of entrepreneurial practices; conversely, negating it and merely concentrating on prospects or long-term innovation risks upsetting the initial balance and weakening the operation as a whole.

Some examples of strategic choices may shed light on this:

– A strategy of widening the circle of members and activities, starting with the mother organization: in the Drome department, Pôle Sud Archer has aggregated around the intermediary association a number of entrepreneurs who have given new dynamism to certain activities and been the impulse behind some "regional start-ups";

in the Dombes, Domb'Innov has led to the creation of one new social business per year; in Grenoble, Alp'En has widened its field of action by allying itself with distribution and electrical materials companies in order to renovate apartments and buildings;

- A strategic questioning about diversification (within or outside TCECs: Entrepreneurs Solidaires du Centre Isère hesitated between a strategy of providing business services (based around corporate social responsibility) and developing projects to provide services for their members (commercial development, spinning off new activities, etc.); in Haute Savoie, *Innovales* has been contemplating acting as a local economic development agency and refocusing on the sustainable habitat;
- A strategic change at the base: in Lyon, the structure of a food industry chain (from peri-urban market gardening to distribution) was the subject of a confrontation between one food processing project, Agri Alim, (which was setting up new intermediaries) and another, le Bol (less ambitious but associating citizen campaigning in the Fête des Récoltes [harvest festival] with a strengthening of the logistics of existing structures);
- However, some TCECs have been the victims of a strategic error: at Saint-Étienne, Culture et Coopération prioritized external innovation over services to founder members who felt ousted from their own project; in the Hautes Alpes, Éco-Matériaux 05 were too proactive in the development of eco-materials at a time when professionals (architects, craft workers, etc.) were not ready to use them.

Thus, pragmatism and a proactive approach do not always form stable unions. While TCECs very often make mutual arrangements for training (to develop skills), few of them mutualize other strategic functions: R&D and financial tools.

3.3. Modes of territorial development issues

While "sustainable regional development" makes an appearance in the law as the overall purpose of TCECs, the forms it takes locally and regionally may strongly diverge:

- For some, regional development still depends mainly on its capacity to attract companies from outside the local area; the TCEC should therefore help to improve the living environment, while offering businesses appropriate services and the population (especially new arrivals and managerial staff) favorable living conditions, or should even attract an external population (of tourists, retired people, etc.);

- For others, regional development is more endogenous and is based on the principle of the ripple effect of economic wealth becoming social development; the task is therefore to strengthen the economic dynamic by collective support for businesses, at the same time "greening" how growth is achieved;
- Still others, finally, think that this ripple effect, whether external or internal, is reaching its limits and the task is to promote more endogenous development, internalizing more the social dimensions (social and economic inclusion, training, employment, redistribution) within economic activity itself. From this perspective, the principles of the SSE linking economic activity and social integration are determining factors.

It is rare for a single approach to be expressed, but this confrontation between visions may run right through the TCEC itself, and above all regional actors (for-profit companies, public institutions, SSE actors), particularly because criteria for evaluating TCECs are still marked by a traditional vision. The economic activity of TCECs is relatively easy to identify from its direct impact in terms of innovation, creation of work, jobs, companies and revenues within the region; it is less easy in terms of knock-on effects (indirect, secondary, or what is termed externalities) and in changes in entrepreneurial behaviors. Environmental impact is also relatively visible: recycling, organic and/or local food, combating lack of job security, improving energy efficiency, eco-construction, alternative mobility, etc. It is more tenuous in terms of modes of exchange (short distribution channels, non-market relationships, cooperation, etc.) because some TCECs maintain internal and external relations which are wholly modelled on the market. Under the social heading, the impact claimed is often measured in terms of inclusion, training, access to employment, services to households, etc. It is less obvious in terms of changes in behaviors (both work and use) and of capabilities. This is why, despite the efforts made by the Solidarity economy movement (SEM), the economic democratization chapter has little value placed on it. It is rare to find TCECs which find room for these in their governing bodies (some associate local development councils); only "festivals" (of the economy of the third kind, harvest festivals, etc.) provide an opportunity to bring these together around the TCEC; and they are mostly sought out in their economic capacity as entrepreneurs, workers, interns or consumers that they are sought out. Conversely, it may be interesting to examine more closely how a TCEC enables new professional groups to gain access to local and regional governance.

We thus see a dialectical relationship between participation in governance, strategie and mode of regional development: we may find in TCECs, as in the SSE as a whole, a "reversal" effect, to use Claude Vienney's expression: the broad, diversified mobilization of the period of emergence may be reduced due to a polarization around the development of certain activities. For this reason, economic development (often tinged with environmental considerations) takes precedence over the social and over democracy. But this is not systematic: some TCECs organized in one sector may simultaneously diversify and combine other more social dynamics (particularly when a social or economic inclusion group is very active within it).

As a result, it is interesting to track the nature and place of SSE organizations within a TCEC because purely entrepreneurial or public principles and practices may easily establish themselves if the original SSE is not sufficiently sound on its foundations and its objectives. In this case we see a straightforward "economicization" of the SSE which is not necessarily strengthened by these alliances. While this has played an important innovatory role, it gradually leads to less internalization of social questions within economic activities. The TCEC thus leads to a revitalization of economic development, often through the relocalization of activities, stimulus to local savings, and a "greening" of activities, but with no knock-on effects on the population (except in terms of jobs, training, or perhaps economic inclusion) from its mode of involvement, of consumption, etc. Some TCECs however that activating non-market dynamics (social, cultural, festive, etc.) enable the population to take ownership of this innovatory operation which may then become part of deeper transformations in the way regional development takes place.

After some years of experimentation, we are now seeing the liquidation of a number of clusters: the ending of national public funding is the main reason put forward, but this seems to be more of an indicator than a trigger. Initial analysis shows that most often the "fault" within the TCEC results from a lack of coherence between mode of governance and strategic choices. Cluster development may be prioritized over its organization: in these cases, founder members feel excluded from the cluster's dynamics; they see no effects on their own activity, while new activities do not reach break-even point. They may then be led to review their commitment, to the point of withdrawing the resources they have put in, and throw into question the viability of the cluster. At the same time, new actors do not necessarily feel themselves to be involved in the overall dynamic in the same way as the founders were.

Conclusion

The objective assigned to TCECs is the sustainable development of the territory, region or local area, through mutualization and cooperation, considered to be vehicles for innovation.

Itself an organizational innovation, a TCEC enables SSE actors to become de-compartmentalized, forging mutual links and links with economic and social actors both public and private. But the long-term place of the SSE in this process has been questioned: just an initiator or a formative element? The same goes for the effects a TCEC may have on the SSE: a strengthening or a weakening? Innovation also impacts on the way new activities are created, in a collective way which enriches the local economic fabric: is this just about economic and environmental wealth, or beyond that, an improvement in wellbeing and the population's empowerment over their daily life? Innovation, finally, in the exploration of new fields which the SSE alone cannot carry out: does this take the form of a capitalistic contribution to a relational service or *vice versa*, or does it also transform modes of production and use? This innovation is most often based on mutualization as a pooling of various resources: property, logistics, administrative, skills, employment, etc.; this mutualization enables economies of scale and access to additional resources. But the transition to real cooperation is more problematic: pooling resources does not automatically lead to a mutualization of projects; division of labor, and even subcontracting, takes more often the form of partnerships rather than long-term reciprocal commitments. While a common vision unites actors on local and regional issues, it is rare to find a real common strategy which is profitable to all (except in the more reduced framework of a particular industry or sector). This is why TCECs reveal the difficulties inherent in making diverse cultures and objectives converge within a region: while the economic dimension increasingly includes the environmental transition, the economic factor quickly becomes predominant; it has difficulty in finding a place within a social dimension of truly pioneering solidarity, democracy and economic citizenships. The competitive economic pressure on each separate actor often wins out over the cooperative principle, which can only be based on the non-market commitments of members and communities, particularly as cooperative regulation is not (yet?) considered to be effective in itself, and because sustainable development criteria are not included in evaluation models. On its own, the social and solidarity economy does not seem to have sufficient recognition to change representations, and thus visions of regional or territorial development. It is thus called upon to perform some real "advocacy work" to get other actors within the community (craft associations, employers, public institutions, trade unions etc.) to share and champion a new, more socialized mode of development.

References

Bourbousson C., 2016, "La création d'un PTCE comme espace de régulation territoriale sectorielle : le cas des éco matériaux dans les Hautes Alpes", paper for the *XVIes Rencontres du RIUESS, Les « communs » et l'économie sociale et solidaire. Quelles identités et quelles dynamiques communes ?*, May, Montpellier, France.

Bourbousson C., Richez-Battesti N., 2015, "Caractériser les formes organisationnelles des coopérations territoriales : les cas de deux PTCE de la région PACA", paper for the *XVes Rencontres du RIUESS*, Reims, France.

DATAR, 2010, *Territoires 2040, Aménager le changement*, Paris, DATAR.

Fontaine G., 2016, "Analyser les conditions favorables à l'émergence de communs, le cas d'un PTCE d'économie solidaire', paper for the *XIVes Rencontres du RIUESS*, Montpellier.

Le Labo de l'ESS, juin 2017, *Enquête d'analyse 2016 des PTCE : synthèse des principaux résultats*, Paris, Le Labo de l'ESS, <http://www.lelabo-ess.org/IMG/pdf/enquete_annuelle_des_ptce_web_portrait.pdf>, consulted on 2 October 2017.

Fraisse L., 2015, *PTCE*, "Éléments de caractérisation", Travaux du groupe Analyses et Connaissances, Le Labo de l'ESS, <http://www.lelabo-ess.org/IMG/pdf/elements_de_caracterisation_des_ptce_laurent_fraisse_-_avril_2014.pdf>, consulted on 2 October 2017.

France Active/Labo ESS, 2014, "PTCE et dynamiques économiques. Entretiens auprès d'un échantillon de 9 pôles témoins", Travaux du Groupe Analyses et Connaissances, Le Labo de l'ESS, <http://www.lelabo-ess.org/IMG/pdf/etude_ptce_2013_fa_dynamiques_economiques.pdf>, consulted on 2 October 2017.

Gaglio G., J. Lauriol, du Tertre C. (dir.), 2011, *L'économie de la fonctionnalité, une voie pour articuler dynamique économique et développement durable*, Toulouse, Éd. Octarès.

Gardin L., Jany-Catrice F. (dir.), 2016, *L'économie sociale et solidaire en coopérations*, Rennes, PUR.

Gianfaldoni P., 2015, "Le PTCE une forme originale de polarisation en ESS ?", paper for the *XVes Rencontres du RIUESS*, Université de Reims, France, 27-29 May.

Gumuchian H., Pecqueur B., 2007, *La ressource territoriale*, Paris, Economica.

Henry P., 2015, "Pôles territoriaux de coopération économique dans la culture : des regroupements pragmatiques dans des secteurs d'activité de grande incertitude", Paris, Le Labo de l'ESS, <http://www.lelabo-ess.org/IMG/pdf/poles_territoriaux_de_cooperation_economique_culture_des_regroupements_pragmatiques_dasn_des_secteurs_d_activite_de_grande_incertitude_philippe_henry_-_aout_2015_pdf>, consulted on 1 December 2017.

Lévesque B., 2016, "Économie sociale et solidaire et entrepreneur social : vers quels nouveaux écosystèmes ?", *Revue interventions économiques*, 54, <http://interventionseconomiques.revues.org/2802>, consulted on 1 October 2017.

Malo M.C., 2001, "La gestion stratégique de la coopérative et de l'association d'économie sociale, *RECMA – Revue internationale de l'économie sociale*, 282: 84-94.

Matray M., Poisat J., 2013, "Les PTCE, une dynamique citoyenne et institutionnelle d'innovation sociale", paper for the *XVIes Rencontres du RIUESS*, Montpellier, France.

Perret C., Gagnon C., 2015, "La créativité : une ressource pour les territoires fragilisés. Le cas du PTCE Sud Archer à Romans sur Isère", *note de recherche, IREGE*, Université de Savoie, <https://halshs.archives-ouvertes.fr/halshs-01241693>, consulted on 1 October 2017.

Perroux F., 1964, *L'Économie du XXe siècle*, Paris, PUF.

Podlewski T., 2014, "Intelligence collective, dynamiques culturelles et cadre institutionnel : comme se construit un PTCE", paper for the *XV*[es] *Rencontres du RIUESS*, Lille, France.

RECMA – Revue internationale de l'économie sociale, 2017, 343 (Pôle territorial de coopération économique, L. Fraisse, P. Gianfaldoni [dir.]), janvier.

RTES/Atelier Coopératif, 2014, "Les rôles des collectivités territoriales dans les dynamiques PTCE", *Repères*, février, actualisé juin 2016, <http://rtes.fr/IMG/pdf/Etude_PTCE_Actualisee_2016_VFinaleA4_Logos-compressed.pdf>, consulted on 1 October 2017.

Chapter 12

Territorial Legitimacy of Large Social Economy Enterprises

Analysis of a Speech by the President of a Cooperative Group

Alexandrine Lapoutte

Université Lumière Lyon 2

Martine Vézina & Marie-Claire Malo

HEC Montréal

Introduction[1]

This study begins with the 2014 Declaration of the participants of the International summit of cooperatives. In this text, the "local strength" and "overall power" of cooperatives are emphasized. They reaffirm the "strength of the cooperative model" and call for the "growth and sustainability of cooperative businesses," as we need more influential cooperatives that "innovate, grow stronger, and increase their numbers to better meet the needs of individuals and society." The Declaration concludes by stating that, "as builders of local economies and drivers of a more stable, inclusive and human global economy, they are making an indisputable contribution to lasting prosperity." Such a declaration implies that territorial rooting and overall development constitute two facets of a single reality for social economy enterprises, and particularly for cooperatives. The necessity for growth is no longer only linked to

1 The authors wish to thank HEC Montreal for its financial support in the realization of this study.

constraints induced by the globalization of the economy but constitutes the very heart of the cooperative to spread this human entrepreneurial model. These two territorialities are not exclusive to SE enterprises, however. In fact, all enterprises look to benefit from economies of scale and proximity. Strategic clusters are a convincing illustration. What distinguishes SE enterprises in this regard is that their relation to the territory is one of their strong, even distinctive, elements (Demoustier, Richez-Battesti, 2010). As a result, it is necessary for them to legitimize the initiatives likely to appear suspect regarding the actual aspirations of strategic change projects of scale and the coherence with the social and territorial project they carry. Because the progression of SE enterprises outside the territories that spurred them may present risks in terms of maintaining their identity, such initiatives must be legitimized. This legitimization process appears as inevitable when applied to large SE enterprises, whose economic reality is that of enterprises that, like other enterprises, are eager to broaden their territories of activity under competitive imperatives accentuated by the globalization process of their activities.

In this study, we seek to understand how a large SE enterprise legitimizes its relation to its local and broader territories to increase its social acceptance. To accomplish this, we have been through the text-analysis of a speech by the president of a large mutual group in the French cooperative banking sector from an event celebrating the 100th anniversary of its founding. A speech is a relevant material to reveal a legitimization strategy (Phillips *et al.*, 2004). We consider this speech as a singular case and try to understand it as such. Although a single case, to a certain extent, it may have some generalization potential, as large SE enterprises face similar challenges as they grow and globalize. In the following sections, we will present a review of the works examining large SE enterprises regarding their relation to their territories. The analytical framework of the study, supported by Suchman's (1995) legitimacy forms typology, the methodology, and the analysis of the results will follow. We will conclude by discussing the study's main results.

1. Territory and the large SE enterprises

Most territorial analyses devote little attention to SE actors. On the other hand, those who are interested in social economy tend to suggest that its relations to territory are natural. The fact that SE enterprises stem from collective action, usually within a context of geographical proximity, tends to reinforce this opinion (Demoustier, Richez-Battesti, 2010), which does not always stand the test of time, however.

While large SE enterprises are different from large globalized enterprises, they share certain similarities. As Demoustier and Malo (2012) and others remind us, large SE enterprises are enterprises, but not ordinary enterprises. SE identity construction took place through a succession of combinations of two elements: trade and territory in a proto-industrial context; activity and status with the construction of major industry based on the division of labor; politics and the public in the shadow of public policies; and enterprise and market in a neoliberal context (p. 21). Over the course of this progression, the relation of SE enterprises to their competitive sectors came to dominate their relation to their territories. At the same time, to avoid being trivialized, SE enterprises are urged to revive the territorial and sector-based project of social and solidarity economy. They are called upon to see that the strategic context is defined not only as a sector where competitive forces are at work but also as a territory characterized by movements of cooperation, intercooperation, and solidarity (p. 34). From this perspective, the territory would not have only economic value. The territorial rooting would be part of SE enterprises' identity.

Like other enterprises, however, SE enterprises in general and large SE enterprises in particular can develop and grow like globalized enterprises. The structuring of many large SE enterprises into business units comprising subsidiaries (Côté, 2001) illustrates this. However, there is a real risk of seeing the territorial rooting of large SE enterprises break down due to its being within a capitalist sector-based regime, while the dominant system of rules can overtake the sub-system of SE rules. In this context, the values characterizing SE enterprises may be affected; as a result, the interest of members and of the community may suffer. The growth strategy of SE enterprises may change the territoriality, connectivity, employability, and accessibility (Malo *et al.*, 2001). Mauget (2008) emphasizes that structuring into units comprising subsidiaries causes three side-effects: the organization becomes more distant and complex, and its logics become more nebulous. For Deroy and Thénot (2015), in a dynamic of isomorphism, the market logic dominates the cooperative logic of large SE enterprises, to the detriment of their territorial rooting.

Malo and Vézina (2004) look at the development strategy of social economy enterprises through the lens of tension between the local and broader territories, recognizing the crucial role of the scale, even of the territory, in the governance and management methods of social economy enterprises. To the local and community territory of their origin is juxtaposed a supra-local territory while the model is reproduced in a dynamic of dissemination, resource mutualization, and emergence of a new sector. The entry of capitalist entrepreneurs into those market segments likely to be profitable lead social economy enterprises to choose between three positions over the local-global continuum: a focused or segment model, a globalized and standardized one, such as that of capitalist entrepreneurs or a balanced hybrid, namely a mix of the two previous approaches. While drawn to the standardized model of globalized enterprises, inspired large SE enterprises (Vézina, Malo, 2014) navigate between local and broader contexts. The first is one of proximity and collaboration between actors sharing common logics and hybrid resources. A source of more specific resources, the broader context is also an adverse environment. Inspired organizations also know how to construct intermediary contexts and internal and external networks. It is through their active relations at these three levels/types of environments that inspired organizations ultimately develop their capacity for co-construction with multiple supra-local partners enabling them to progress further toward their regulating, even transformative, ambition (Vézina, Malo, 2014).

Assens (2013) shows that bipolar cooperatives successfully combine the effects associated with economies of territorial proximity and economies of scale through the internationalization of their markets and activities. The strategy of cooperatives developing in a globalized context are constructed according to an ago-antagonist dynamic between the market (supra-local) and the territory (local), which may end in strategic levers in an opposition as well as in a synergy dynamic. From a similar perspective, Chauvin *et al.* (2011) show how cooperative banks choose to reinforce their local rooting through the creation of an innovative distribution network of geographical proximity, to better integrate within the European market dynamic.

These studies echo the concept of glocalization in the field of strategic management. For Saives *et al.* (2011), while "globalist" organizations become rooted in environments that "participate in the process of planetary and dynamic optimization of the organizational arrangements of multinationals' value chains" (Saives *et al.,* 2011: 71), national development models are part of a glocalization strategy. It is therefore by relying on local products and deeply rooted organizations that these firms globalize their activities and markets. One characteristic of these firms is that they combine a local anchorage through local participation with a globalized position for their activities (Saives *et al.,* 2011: 72). In fact, in that study large agricultural cooperatives have been associated to a "glocalist" profile, while capitalist agro-food multinationals would follow a "globalist" approach.

The question of large SE enterprises' relation to their territories is therefore central. While indirectly addressed in research, it gains recognition when growth raises doubt as to their identity as social economy enterprises. In this context, contrary to large globalized enterprises, large SE enterprises are called upon to legitimize initiatives likely to modify, even attenuate, relations to their original territories. One could even posit that the Declaration of the participants of the 2014 Summit of Cooperatives constitutes a legitimization of the identity of cooperatives, even when globalized. In the following section, we present a territorial legitimacy analytical framework.

2. Legitimacy as analytical framework

It is generally admitted that studies on legitimacy fall under one of two main approaches. The neo-institutional perspective focuses on institutional pressures, sources of isomorphism, which organizations face (Di Maggio, Powell, 1983). This pressure is exercised under three forms: mimetism, profession, and regulation. Enterprises would then conform to the norms, rules, and values of their environments.

The resource-based view presents legitimacy as a full resource. According to Pfeffer and Salancik (1978), organizations interact with their social environments to acquire the resources they need to ensure their survival. Therefore, legitimacy ensures organizations society's approval and enables them to obtain the resources they need to survive (Zimmerman, Zeitz, 2002), such as capital, technology, managers, skills, clients, networks, etc.

Enterprises are not passive, however. They actively manage their legitimacy (Oliver, 1991; Suchman, 1995) according to effective, or, more often, symbolic methods, notably speeches (Phillips *et al.,* 2004).

The social pressures tend to garner ambivalent responses from enterprises, tempted to distinguish their formal structures from their daily activities (Weick, 1976).

Today, Suchman's (1995) definition is a reference as a synthesis of neo-institutional and instrumental approaches. According to him, "legitimacy is a generalized perception or assumption that the actions of an entity are desirable, proper, or appropriate within some socially constructed system of norms, values, beliefs, and definitions" (1995: 574).

It is now widely admitted that legitimacy takes one of three forms: pragmatic, moral, or cognitive. Pragmatic legitimacy corresponds to what is useful and of interest. It may be founded on exchange, influence (e.g., the integration of stakeholders into political decision-making processes), or the tendency to grant legitimacy to organizations that take others' interests into account.

Moral legitimacy corresponds to the norms and values shared in an organization. It is based on the evaluation of their character as socially good or better. Suchman distinguishes four sources of moral legitimacy: consequential – how organizations are judged by society based on what they accomplish; procedural – whether they make use of socially accepted techniques and procedures; structural – when their structural characteristics position them within a morally acceptable category; and personal – when they are based on leaders' charisma.

Cognitive legitimacy corresponds to the underlying mental representations or to how organizations make themselves understood in their environments. The first source of cognitive legitimacy is called comprehensibility. In a chaotic cognitive social environment, individuals must arrange their experiences into coherent accounts. Legitimacy comes from available models providing plausible explanations for the existence of organizations. The second source is taken-for-grantedness. "According to this view, institutions not only render disorder manageable, they actually transform it into a set of intersubjective 'givens' that submerge the possibility of dissent" (p. 583). Nevertheless, this strength is counterbalanced by pluralist political cultures. Finally, according to Suchman, organizations engage in strategies aiming to gain, maintain, or repair their legitimacy.

Legitimacy seems to be a pertinent lens through which to study the SE enterprise, as it underlies a collective project. Two normative contexts characterize the SE enterprise, namely the market logic and the legitimacy unique to the institutional field of SE, such as in fair trade (Huybrechts, Nicholls, 2013). In fact, cooperatives and other SE enterprises justify themselves in relation to the norms, values, and beliefs of SE, and that of the capitalist economy – the dominant system. Their system of rules is not the dominant system as it constitutes a sub-system of this later (Vienney, 1994). However, their field spurs a utopic project (Desroche, 1976) whose aim is to contribute to the emergence a social and solidarity economy that would transform market rules into social market rules (Demoustier, 2001). SE enterprises, as inspired organizations, are able to invent and create their context by drawing on a social transformation perspective (Vézina, Rousselière, Malo, 2014).

With two levels of territories, large SE enterprises must, on a global scale, embrace a less well-known model that creates its own context and ensures its legitimacy in a world that is not one of social and solidarity economy. In contrast, at the local level, the goal would be to maintain a legitimacy acquired through recognized territorial rooting. In a study of important stakeholders, Lapoutte and Cadiou (2014) show that the contribution of SE enterprises to their territories is not generally recognized. It would thus seem all the more pertinent to examine the justifications related to the territorialization of large SE enterprises.

To maintain the legitimacy of their relation to their territories, large SE enterprises could tend to draw on the three forms of legitimacy (see Table 1). The cognitive legitimacy is associated with the underlying models and with the interaction between the enterprise and the broader society. It is at this level that the question of the differentiation or trivialization of cooperative enterprises is essentially arising. The SE enterprise is accepted because its relation to its territory is understood, in accordance with available models, and is even self-evident. On the moral level, the SE enterprise justifies its action by referring to shared norms, which may be values of the capitalist economy or of social and solidarity economy. It is accepted following a positive normative evaluation, because it does what is right for its community. On the pragmatic level, the SE enterprise justifies its action in a calculating manner according to what is useful. It is accepted because it is useful to its community (employment, economic development, etc.).

Table 1: Large SE Enterprise Territorial Legitimacy Analytical Framework

Type of territorial legitimacy	*Rests on*	*Indicators*
PRAGMATIC How is the large SE enterprise's relation to its territory useful?	The enterprise's usefulness for stakeholders on the territory	The consideration of interests in terms of exchange, influence, or predisposition
MORAL How is the large SE enterprise's relation to its territory consistent with shared norms?	The values linking the enterprise to its territory	Impacts, procedures, structures, and leadership
COGNITIVE How does the large SE enterprise understand its relation to its territory?	The representations of the relation between the enterprise and its territory	Models making the relation to the territory plausible The givens of the relation to the territory

Source: the authors

Our analytical framework aims at integrating the three types of legitimacy to the double relation the large social economy enterprise maintains with its territory, local and global.

3. Methodology: analyses of a president's speech

According to the neo-institutional perspective, firms tend to show their congruence with the environment (legitimacy in this case) through actual or symbolic actions. Communication and, more specifically, speeches (Phillips *et al.*, 2004) appear to be a common means of legitimizing enterprises. While a multitude of discourses may be held regarding an organization (notably by employees and unions), we are interested here in the speech of a president, reflecting the legitimacy professed by the organization.

Jean-Pierre Denis is president of Crédit Mutuel Arkéa (CMA) and is also president of Crédit Mutuel de Bretagne (CMB). Historically, the relation to the territory is strong, as the group is rooted into the local economy and recruits locally (Moulévrier, Suaud, 2014). The Crédit Mutuel Arkéa Group comprises Crédit Mutuel Bretagne, Crédit Mutuel du Sud-Ouest, Crédit Mutuel Massif Central, in addition to 20 subsidiaries. With 3.62 million members and a balance sheet boasting

€110 billion in 2015, Crédit Mutuel Arkéa is a major player in bank insurance. It is deeply rooted in France (present in 19 of 22 French regions), Belgium, and Luxembourg and provides banking services across Europe through its subsidiaries. As a cooperative mutualist group, Arkéa constitutes one of the organizational mutations in SE that questions SE's relation to territory (Richez-Battesti, Malo, 2012). The Group's strong presence in the economic and competitive spheres makes it sensitive to the trend toward trivialization, institutional isomorphism, and legitimacy concerns.

The speech analyzed in this study contains statements Jean-Pierre Denis made during a roundtable with two other presidents of mutualist groups. None of these large SE enterprises would exist today if it were not for the creation of the Office central des œuvres mutuelles agricoles du Finistère, in Landerneau, in 1911, within the context of the assertion of Britanny's identity (Ford, 1993). It was for the occasion of the "1911-2011, 100 years of mutualism at Landerneau" event (<www.landerneau-mutualisme.fr>) that the three presidents were invited to take part in a roundtable in 2011. An anniversary is a key moment for enterprises to justify and actualize their identity. The statements were made before a large audience of local stakeholders of these large SE enterprises: members, directors, executives, and employees (around 800 participants).

Jean-Pierre Denis has been president of the Crédit Mutuel Arkéa Group and Crédit Mutuel de Bretagne since 2008. This senior public servant was also a senior executive in large private enterprises, before joining the banking sector (box 1).

Box 1. Short Biography of Jean-Pierre Denis

1988:	Following studies at HEC and at the ENA, he became *Inspecteur des Finances*
1992:	Deputy chief of staff to Jacques Chirac at Paris City Hall
1995:	Deputy secretary general of the Élysée
1998:	External growth operations advisor at the Compagnie générale des eaux (which became Vivendi)
1999:	CEO and president of Dalkia (Vivendi and Veolia Environnement groups)
2003:	Elected president of the directoire de la Banque de développement des petites et moyennes entreprises (BDPME). He was also president and CEO of the Crédit d'équipement des petites et moyennes entreprises (CEPME) and president and CEO of the Agence nationale de valorisation de la recherche (Anvar)
2005:	President and CEO of Oséo, public body responsible for SMBs financing

The theme of the roundtable was "Identity and perspectives". The three key speakers were called upon to speak one at a time on seven questions/themes (see box 2). The audio transcription of the roundtable resulted in 9,163 words, 42% of which were from the president of the CMA.

Box 2. The 7 Questions Asked During the Roundtable

1. Can you draw us a picture of Crédit Mutuel Arkéa and Crédit Mutuel de Bretagne?
2. How did it free itself from the Office Central? And how did it morph into CMA today?
3. What is the legacy of those years?
4. How are the governance and decisions organized?
5. How important is territorial rooting for Crédit Mutuel Arkéa?
6. With regard to the crisis, do you think your enterprise is still better equipped, and will this crisis impact the Group's results?
7. Let's end on the prospects for development. How do you see the coming years?

In the following section, we analyze the president's speech through the lens of various forms of legitimacy that he draws on when addressing the organization's relation to its territory.

4. CMA territorial relation legitimization forms

In this section we analyze the president speech according to our analytical framework of territorial legitimacy.

4.1. Pragmatic legitimacy: A contribution to the local territory's activity and a supra-local zone of activity

Pragmatic legitimacy relates to the satisfaction of interests, to usefulness, and to calculations. At the local level, the enterprise presents itself as a contributor to the territory's activity, as a major direct financer of Brittany's economy ("a direct financial institution important to Britain's economy"), for several reasons: financial services available for several actors (taxpayers, enterprises, associations, local groups), many skilled jobs, access to services through territorial networking, and investments in real estate with decision centres confirmed near Brest (box 3).

Box 3. Pragmatic Legitimacy

Local

And I insist, many skills, a great deal of know-how, a strong capacity to innovate, through jobs, highly skilled jobs. What I think characterises our Group the most today is its high expectations, its skill, its professionalism. Today, we count on Brest to play a central role, where we design and manufacture the products we distribute, 2,400 collaborators, we recruit several hundred a year, mainly in Brittany.

I invite you to subscribe to our new B shares … these social shares, which increase the Group's capital, allow us to invest in the Breton economy … on the contrary, it is a rational way of seeing our region's development.

But regardless of my point of view, the responsibility of elected officials is not limited to setting general objectives. It is really to get involved in the core of the enterprise's activity, to set the course. It is my essential responsibility as president of the Group to create the conditions for elected officials to be able to influence the enterprise's decisions transparently.

Supra-Local

… is obviously present in Brittany; 6,000 of our collaborators carry out their activities in Brittany, but we also have a certain number of subsidiaries that are active in most of France's regions; I believe we are active in 20 out of 22 metropolitan areas.

You know that we have the chance to have in the Group an online bank called Fortunéo, whose head office is in the Brest agglomeration and which is a major player today in online banking in France and Belgium.

…being in a position to expand

We identify two types of pragmatic legitimacy: exchange and influence. The territory provides resources (skills and savings), while the enterprise contributes to the territory's development (exchange legitimacy). The enterprise reaffirms the integration of members in instances of governance (influence legitimacy).

The supra-local level is barely addressed; the territory here is national, even international. The president presents it mainly as an area of activity and conquest, by evoking, on more than one occasion, the competition context.

4.2. Moral legitimacy: A shared project for the success of the Breton territory, a supra-local territory run through territorialized governance

The moral legitimacy rests on a normative evaluation of the enterprise's relation to its territory. Here, the shared norms are linked, through history, to the values (cooperation and solidarity) inherited from the central office. Today, they are expressed mainly through a "local development" and "territorial solidarity" project, the enterprise being a "long-term partner of the Breton economy." Cooperative governance links the enterprise to its territory through the presence of elected directors in local credit unions (box 4).

Box 4. Moral Legitimacy

Local

The first [strong element the legacy rests on] I was going to mention is the spirit of cooperation.

So, in terms of the local credit unions, yes as well, obviously, and I would like to mention our 3,000 elected directors in local credit unions who closely follow the development of each credit union's activity … They certainly bring all their know-how and knowledge of the field, and their sense of proximity is also exceptional.

We also try through our mutual assistance funds to support our members who are in difficulty because life's accidents, personal accidents, put them in the red, as we say. We also try through the local credit unions, which visit the sensitive areas monthly, to bring personalized solutions to those most in need. We also try to bring this extra support provided by today's bank.

Today, through Synergie Finance, which offer capital development within the Group through a nice structure we just put in place, Arkéa Partenaire, which holds €400 billion, which isn't insignificant, we are trying to give Breton enterprises the means to realize their projects. It is a form of territorial solidarity that we want to express. We want to do it intelligently, by supporting Bretons who have good ideas but sometimes do not have the resources to convince bankers. We are not looking to mix types here. What is important to us is to be an enterprise that supports the people and invests sustainably, not to make an exorbitant profit but to accompany Breton enterprises over the long term. Therefore, we want to be a long-term partner of the Breton economy.

Supra-Local

From there, I would like to say that we at CMA are shielded from catastrophes when they arise. The only … if I take Greece as an example, today, everyone is talking about it. For the CMA Group, Greece represents nine and a half million euros. Let's not forget that the enterprise generates about 300 million surpluses per year. Even if Greece completely defaulted and were in a situation where it could no longer honour its debts, this wouldn't affect the Group's accounts very much

Sure, we have to make a surplus in this world, but our goal is to build long-term solutions, to provide services to our clients and members, services that meet their needs. This is what spirit of cooperation means; it is not to turn a profit for the performance it generates.

At the core of the system, elected officials have this essential responsibility. This is for the CMB and CMA federations. We are equipped with federal commissions; I won't go into detail tonight, but they are specialized committees exclusively made up of elected officials who closely follow the enterprise's development. But regardless of my point of view, the responsibility of elected officials is not limited to setting general objectives. It is really to get involved in the core of the enterprise's activity, to set the course.

As can be stressed from the president's speech, moral legitimacy is appreciated mainly through the consequences of the enterprise's actions – local development and actions of solidarity – but also through procedures and structures related to cooperative governance.

The speech is silent on the consequences of the enterprise's actions on the supra-local territory. The president emphasizes that the development of international activities does not pose a risk for the local territory. Thus, the development seems reasoned and prudent, as it does not threaten the cooperative Group or the durability of the local project. Growth serves members over the long term.

The Group corresponds mainly to the supra-local (broader) territory, but its governance remains localized. It is a "group," Crédit Mutuel Arkéa, made up of three regional federations. This group unites territorialized organizations and is not run quite like the others. Its administrators are attached to human values and strive to satisfy their clients and members over the long term. Through federal commissions made up of elected officials, the latter, as well as professionals, run it jointly and express the concerns of the local and supra-local territories, thereby expanding the cooperative territory beyond the local level.

4.3 Cognitive legitimacy: Born here, with a view to grow

Brittany remains the territory of origin and of reference. This rooting influences strategic decisions. Thus, the relation to the territory implicitly refers to the rooting of the enterprise in its territory and to a co-construction of the enterprise and of its territory (box 5).

Box 5. Cognitive Legitimacy

Local

… in Landerneau, where we were born.

Finally, I would like to add a visceral attachment to the territory. We made the choice long ago, whose permanence we continue to confirm through recruitments and investments, and by setting up and developing in North-Finistère, to expand in Brittany, obviously; that is our market of reference.

It is true that, since the important decisions engaging the Group are made here, in North-Finistère, we don't see things quite in the same way.

Supra-Local

CMB is the backbone of the Group, and CMB is not a fully mature enterprise; it is a young enterprise. It took on its modern shape in 1979, and it has enormous potential in front of it, this nice enterprise. And with Jean-Pierre Le Tennier, its CEO, we try to work on giving it more pep and an appetite for conquest. So, notice to clients who aren't entirely convinced, but I don't think there are many who doubt our will to develop.

At the same time, of course, I think this is part of the model, of the pioneering spirit that drove the creators of the Office Central a hundred year ago, of knowing to open up and be in a position to expand.

The enterprise's relation to its territory refers to the biological and natural model of birth. On the cognitive level, the speech integrates growth into the cooperative model: development and growth are consistent with the pioneer model. The metaphors of biological birth and of the life cycle are always drawn on to explain that the enterprise is still young; therefore, development appears to be taken for granted.

Our results are synthesized in Table 2.

Table 2: CMA Territorial Legitimacy Analysis

Territory Form of Legitimacy	*Local*	*Supra-Local*
Pragmatic	Contribution to the territory's activity and participation in the decision-making	Market opportunities
Moral	A shared project for the success of the Breton territory	Cooperative territorial governance on various scales Long term growth to serve members
Cognitive	Born here Development base Cooperative and territorial bank model	Growing is natural Pioneer model for expansion Cooperative entrepreneurial model

Source: the authors

5. Discussion and conclusion

We conducted this study in order to understand how a large SE enterprise legitimizes its relation to its local and supra-local territories. The process by which a large SE enterprise legitimizes its territorial identity appears necessary, even though the latter constitutes a specificity as well as a potential impediment to the enterprise's expansion, and even to its identity as a large enterprise. To take into account how a senior administrator at the helm of a large SE enterprise legitimizes its relationship with its local and supra-local territories, we have drawn on the three forms of legitimacy developed by Suchman (1995): pragmatic, moral, and cognitive.

The analysis we conducted of the speech given by the president of this large mutualist group in the French cooperative banking sector at a public event reveals a strong will to account for the relationships that the large SE enterprise maintains with its territory of origin. In fact, while the themes of the panel in which the leader participated did not pertain to this subject specifically, we found multiple references to the territory in his intervention as a whole. It seems that, even though its future depends on sector-based development leaning heavily toward globalization, the territory remains a strong identity reference (Demoustier, Richez-Battesti, 2010) for this large SE enterprise.

How does the large SE enterprise justify this double territoriality? According to the speech, territorial rooting can satisfy members as much as international development, as long as they participate in the common project underlying the mutualism model. The speech focuses on pragmatic legitimacy, moral legitimacy, and cognitive legitimacy. These three forms are expressed differently with regard to the local and supra-local territories. At the local level, the president asserts his enterprise's identity as one of a territorial cooperative bank. The local territory is legitimized, based on the very origins of the organization (cognitive legitimacy), whose common project for the territory's success (moral legitimacy) depends on its maintaining its decision-making centres locally and taking decisions in members' best interest. It contributes to the territory's social economic development (pragmatic legitimacy) while sharing the norms of the enterprises of its sector. The local territory has an economic value providing resources (places for setting up and for recruiting salaried collaborators). It is also an expression of a social project that is historically constructed and reaffirmed through current strategic decisions.

The references to the supra-local territory were inspired by a discourse borrowed from the entrepreneurial logic. Thus, growth appears to be natural, even integral to the cooperative's enterprise DNA (cognitive legitimacy). While the president mentions a context of crisis and of competition, the supra-local territory is seen more as a source of market opportunities, opportunities to exploit the business assets (technology and distribution networks) and skills (professionalism and sales capability) (pragmatic legitimacy), as long as the development is long term and aims to better serve members. Multi-level cooperative governance (moral legitimacy) ensures balance between the local territorial project and the supra-local entrepreneurial one. Governance is therefore at the core of the local and supra-local territory legitimization process (moral in this case) of the large SE enterprise. In addition, the speech emphasizes the important role of monitoring, even when international activities are concerned, played by elected officials in specialized federal governance structures.

At the cognitive level, therefore, the speech actualizes the mutualism model by revealing growth as natural. While growth and development are not debatable, the way to justify them seems original. Where one may have express classic arguments related mainly to economic contingencies (international context, competition, regulatory imperatives, etc.), growth seems to be more of an element of the cooperative project of a mutualism model seeking to construct its international context by expanding the cooperative institutional field. Thus, the large SE enterprise resists isomorphism to move forward in a proactive and voluntaristic manner inspired by its mutualist identity (Vézina, Malo, 2014), in the very spirit of the Declaration of the Summit of Cooperatives, that was referred to earlier. However, there doesn't seem to be any economic and social development project *for* the supra-local territory. The latter is mentioned only as a market. In this way of preserving the local territory while expanding internationally, there seems to be an instrumentalization of one territory (supranational) by another (local). Considering that a compromise is necessary, one must admit that it reveals the limits within the spirit of cooperation.

The supra-local level speech is not so much articulated, as it refers to relatively few specific information (number of countries, types of services, modes of development, etc.). The supra-local remains nebulous. Given that the speech was delivered before a local audience, this could be due to the president's desire to adopt a perspective that is appropriate to the audience as much as omitting those more controversial dimensions related to the cooperative group's identity such as references to some territorialized strategic constructions (Saives *et al.*, 2011: 70) characteristic of glocalization strategies. This would have showed more specifically how the organization combines the local territory (specific resources, local innovation skills, organizational culture, and participation of citizens to territorial activities) with the expansion of its activities on a broader scale. Is this speech but a first step in the longer process of reducing the cognitive distance to internationalization?

This present work has some limitations. The conclusions must be understood within the specific scope of this study, which does not aim to analyze the organization's practices but rather a speech by the organization's president. In addition, this speech was given before a local audience. It may be that this speech reflects the necessity to legitimize how the organization sees its relation to its local territory and how the supra-local territory compares to the local territory as another scale of the mutualism model. While this is a single case study, its findings may be generalized, given the issues and challenges large SE enterprises face in their relation to their territory. A comparative study of speeches by administrators of large SE enterprises and of speeches delivered to other types of audiences would shed more light on the subject.

This study's scope of analysis provides a strong point of view from which to theorize the relation of large SE enterprises to their territories, which seems neither overly rooted in the local territory (idealist conception) nor under-rooted in the supra-local territory (capitalist conception) but always related to identity. Thus, this study completes the analyses of the relation of SE enterprises developing on a local scale of action to their territories. Local SE enterprises undergoing a change of scale will find grist for reflection on the social construction of their relation to their territories in a dynamic of isomorphism or in one where the cooperative model is propelled.

References

Assens C., 2013, "Entre territoire et marché. La stratégie bipolaire des coopératives agricoles", *Revue française de gestion*, 230: 35-55.

Chauvin B., Mendez A., Richez-Battesti N., 2011, "De la Nef (Nouvelle économie fraternelle) à la BEE (Banque éthique européenne). De l'émergence du banquier itinérant ?", *La Revue des sciences de gestion (La RSG) : Direction et gestion des entreprises*, 3-4 (249-250): 87-95.

Côté D. (dir.), 2001, *Les holdings coopératifs*, Bruxelles, CIRIEC international/ DeBoeck Université.

Demoustier D., 2001, *L'économie sociale et solidaire : s'associer pour entreprendre autrement*, Syros, la Découverte.

Demoustier D., Malo M.-C., 2012, "L'économie sociale et solidaire, une économie relationnelle ? Questions d'identité et de stratégie !", *in* E. Bayle, J.-C. Dupuis (dir.), *Management des entreprises de l'économie sociale et solidaire, identités plurielles et spécificités*, Bruxelles, De Boeck, p. 15-40.

Demoustier D., Richez-Battesti N., 2010, "Les organisations de l'économie sociale et solidaire : gouvernance, régulation et territoire", *Géographie, économie, société*, 1 (12): 5-14.

Deroy X., Thénot M., 2015, "L'évolution des logiques coopérative et de marché dans les coopératives agricoles françaises" *Revue française de gestion*, 250: 31-47.

Desroche H., 1976, *Le projet coopératif : son utopie et sa pratique, ses appareils et ses réseaux, ses espérances et ses déconvenues*, Paris, Les Éditions Ouvrières.

Di Maggio P.J., Powell W.W., 1983, "The iron cage revisited: institutional isomorphism and collective rationality in organizational fields", *American Sociological Review*, 48 (2): 147-60.

Ford C., 1993, *Creating the Nation in Provincial France. Religion and Political Identity in Brittany*, Princeton NJ, Princeton University Press.

Huybrechts B., Nicholls A., 2013, "The Role of Legitimacy in Social Enterprise-Corporate Collaboration", *Social Enterprise Journal*, 9 (2): 130-46.

Lapoutte A., Cadiou C., 2014, "Gouvernance et entreprise mutualiste : la légitimité en question", *Recherches en Sciences de Gestion-Management Sciences-Ciencias de Gestión*, 101: 175-94.

Malo M.-C., 2001, "La gestion stratégique de la coopérative et de l'association d'économie sociale", *RECMA – Revue internationale de l'économie sociale*, 281-282: 84-95.

Malo M.-C., Lévesque B., Chouinard O., Desjardins P.-M., Forgues É., 2001, "Coopératives financières, cohésion sociale et nouveau territoire local à l'ère de la mondialisation", UQAM, *Cahier du CRISES*, No. ET0108.

Malo M.-C., Vézina M., 2004, "Governance and Management of Collective User-Based Enterprises: Value-Creation Strategies and Organizational Configurations", *Annals of Public and Cooperative Economics/Annals of Public and Cooperative Economics*, 75 (1): 113-37.

Malo M.-C., Vézina M., Audebrand L., 2012, "Deciphering Tensions in the Development of Co-operatives: Insights from the Montréal School on Co-operative management", *Ekonomiaz*, 79: 265-95.

Mauget R., 2008, "De la coopérative au groupe coopératif agroalimentaire : évolution ou dénaturation ?", *in* Munoz *et al.* (dir.), *La gouvernance des entreprises coopératives*, Rennes, PUR, p. 57-73.

Moulévrier P., Suaud C., 2014, "Les usages institués et stratégiques du passé d'une organisation bancaire. Le Crédit Mutuel", *Sociologies pratiques*, 2 (29): 73-82.

Oliver C., 1991, "Strategic responses to institutional processes", *Academy of Management Review*, 16 (1): 145-79.

Pfeffer J., Salancik G.R., 1978, *The External Control of Organizations: A Resource Dependence Perspective*, Stanford Ca, Stanford University Press.

Phillips N., Lawrence T.B., Hardy C., 2004, "Discourse and Institutions", *Academy of Management Review*, 29 (4): 635-52.

Richez-Battesti N., Malo M.-C., 2012, "ESS et mutations organisationnelles", *RECMA – Revue internationale de l'économie sociale*, 325: 36-47.

Saives A.-L., Desmarteau R.H., Kerzazi L., 2011, "Modèles d'affaires, proximités et territorialisation des entreprises. Les cas de l'agroalimentaire au Québec", *Revue française de gestion*, 4 (213): 57-75.

Sommet international des coopératives, 2014, *Déclaration*, <https://www.sommetinter.coop/sites/default/files/library/sic2014_declaration_fr.pdf>, consulted on 21 July 2017.

Suchman M.-C., 1995, "Managing Legitimacy: Strategic and Institutional Approaches", *Academy of Management Review*, 20 (3): 571-610.

Vézina M., Malo M.-C., 2014, "Inspiration et invention", *in* Tannery F. *et al.* (dir.), *Encyclopédie de la stratégie*, Paris, Vuibert, p. 739-46.

Vézina M., Rousselière D., Malo M.-C., 2014, "Conjuguer innovation et adaptation : la stratégie de développement par hybridation de la coopérative agricole généraliste", *in*, Sommet international des coopératives (dir.), *Le pouvoir d'innover des coopératives*, <http://www.sommetinter.coop/files/live/sites/somint/files/pdf/Articles%20scientifiques/2014_45_Vezina.pdf>, consulted on 21 July 2017.

Vienney C., 1994, *L'économie sociale*, Paris, la Découverte.

Weick K.E., 1976, "Educational Organizations as Loosely Coupled Systems", *Administrative Science Quarterly*, 21 (1): 1-19.

Zimmerman M.A., Zeitz, G.J., 2002, "Beyond survival: Achieving new venture growth by building legitimacy", *Academy of Management Review*, 27 (3): 414-31.

General Conclusion

Territorial Regimes and Changes in Sociopolitical and Socioeconomic Regulations

Xabier Itçaina

Centre Émile Durkheim, CNRS, Sciences Po Bordeaux, University of Bordeaux

Apart from the arguments to be expected on the specific articulation between work and capital within their business model, supporters of the Social and solidarity economy (SSE) frequently emphasize the territorial anchoring or anchoring of their ventures in order to distinguish themselves from conventional capitalist firms. If we take this argument seriously, then this territorial anchoring should be seen as having at least two potential consequences. On the one hand, territorial anchoring offers specific resources to social economy ventures: better connections to the needs of the territory, together with fluid relations with local policy-makers and businesses thanks to historically-constructed mutual trust and social capital. On the other hand, territorial anchoring means that social economy ventures are particularly sensitive and permeable to local factors, be they of an economic, cultural, social, political or institutional nature, that may have less virtuous effects on their development. These factors might be local political patronage, social and ethnic divisions, local economic crises, or structural weaknesses (areas which are isolated, agrarian, mono-industrial, etc.) To put this another way, territorial anchoring is not virtuous *per se*. Rather, its effectiveness depends on a positive combination of economic, social, spatial and political factors.

The articulation between the SSE and territory is not self-evident (Pecqueur, Itçaina, 2012). For the contributions in this volume, the challenge was one of disentangling these interrelations by avoiding two pitfalls. The first, the angelic or idealist perspective, sees the SSE as the answer to all neoliberalism-related ills. The demystifying perspective, by contrast, emphasizes the relentless routinization[1] and institutional isomorphism of SSE enterprises, which eventually end up resorting to market-oriented and/or public economy-oriented models. Local case studies can extricate us from this dilemma. Close observation of complex local configurations where public, private, associative and cooperative actors and issues are deeply entangled enables us to achieve a distanced and non-ideological understanding of the territorial dynamics of the SSE.

The inherent risk of local studies, obviously, is one of juxtaposing merely local monographs, without any increase in generalization. We prefer to think that a comparative reading of all chapters in this volume offers a way to overcome this obstacle. Based on the empirical contributions made, this Conclusion seeks to sketch out a potential research program around the territorial dynamics of SSE, at the intersection of political sociology, economic sociology and spatial and regional economics. We shall proceed in five stages. We first review the general theoretical stance shared by all the contributors to this book, itself an emanation of the CIRIEC International SSE and Territory Working Group (1). We then focus on four themes introduced by contributions to this volume, which offer just as many research avenues: the interplay between the territorial scales of the SSE (2); the territorial structuring of the SSE as a response to changes in public (3) and market (4) regulations; and finally, the relationship between SSE dynamics and territorial cultures and identities (5).

1. Towards a constructivist approach to territorial regulations

At the very minimum, and as highlighted in the Introduction to this book, all chapters share an approach to the territory understood as an institutionalized geographical space, in the sense of a stabilized set of rules, norms and expectations (Smith, 2011: 469; Ruggie, 1993). This approach firmly rejects any essentialization of territorial belongings and, *a fortiori*, rejects any naturalization of the way local enterprises, of whatever sort, are rooted or anchored. In this respect, Andy Smith proposes a useful

[1] See, for instance, Errasti *et al.* (2016) on the "co-opitalist" evolution of Mondragón, or Hély and Moulévrier (2013) on the nature of work in French associations.

distinction between "rooted", "anchored" and "autonomous" firms. The rooted firm would present the following features:

> not only does the company source a significant part of its raw materials or components locally, but it also generates its finance *via* local banks, other credit organizations, and public policies. Moreover, a certain amount of its products are sold locally, but it also generates its finance *via* local banks, other credit organizations, and public policies [...] More importantly still, rooted companies are far more dependent upon the skills and availability of a localized labor force than their autonomous and anchored counterparts. In short, these firms are virtually un transferable to other localities because at least three, and often four, of the basic planks of their business logics are deeply inscribed in the social fabric of their current location. (Smith, 2016: 154).

These distinctions between the levels of territorial implantation of firms, that could be applied to SSE companies, echoes another of our general stances, again already stated in the introduction, and that defines territory as:

> a coming-together of actors, in a specific spatial context, which aims to define and then try to solve, in a constrained environment, a shared social or productive problem. Territory building consists in the first place of defining the boundaries of a problem, starting with its territorial limits, and envisioning resolution scenarios. This coming-together will vary according to the productive activities to be undertaken as well as public policy (Pecqueur, Itçaina 2012: 48, our translation).

This approach echoes the perceptions of territory conveyed by the cognitive approaches to local development, which rightly point out that territory building always is always associated with the construction of physical boundaries. In this perspective, territory "is perceived as a space of economic coordination, of knowledge and solidarity, based on proximity, a space of identity, a place outside which a certain mistrust prevails, a space of differentiation and discrimination between insiders and outsider" (Kahn, 2010: 629, our translation).

The relations between an anchored economy and an a-spatial economy is also at the heart of proximity economics. For Pecqueur, a territory is above all "a central space for coordination between actors looking to solve newly-encountered problems of production. When this is the case, we see a combination of the anchored and the nomadic activities of firms" (Pecqueur, 2006: 29).

In other words, our case studies help to enrich a broader and interdisciplinary perspective in terms of SSE *territorial regimes*, in a dialogue between the political sociology of territorial mobilizations, the economic sociology of the SSE, and local development studies. We aim to replicate with the SSE a research perspective which was initially designed to analyze more broadly the non-economic or indirectly economic factors of local development (Palard *et al.*, 2007). These factors concern: (a) the social and historical construction of trust between territorial actors; (b) the way the economic and political regulations of a territory, including territorial governance and following the definition offered by Demoustier and Richez-Battesti (2010),[2] relate to one another; (c) the way economic actors contribute to the definition of public problems within a territory (Lascoumes, Le Galès, 2007; Gusfield, 1980), making these problems public or confining them more narrowly (Gilbert, Henry, 2012). Applied to the SSE, this perspective embraces different SSE dimensions: the SSE as a territorial heritage, the entanglement of the SSE in territorial governance and territorial regulation, and the political work undertaken by actors in respect of the SSE. This last point is crucial and, by focusing on collective action, prevents any culturalist and deterministic considerations from emphasizing the intrinsic properties of some territories considered to be naturally suitable for local development through the SSE. In this sense, the concept of political work (Jullien, Smith, 2014; Smith, 2016), does justice to the agency of the actors concerned by referring to a three-dimensional form of collective action: problematization (the making of collective and/or public problems); instrumentation (the construction and use of policy instruments); and legitimization. If, following Smith (2016), we agree that the economy's political dimension can be seen when actors mobilize or seek to silence values in order to modify or maintain economic institutions, then the SSE is eminently political, given the continuous activation of values presented by actors as specific to themselves.[3] Any reference to territory

[2] For Demoustier and Richez-Battesti (2010: 8) *territorial regulation* refers to "how activities, jobs, incomes, capital flows, which ensure the regularity of the productive system, interact and are coordinated". In contrast, *territorial governance* refers to the "institutional design of decision making about territorial development through public debates, public action, and, more specifically, policy-making" (our translation).

[3] Of course, the SSE does not have a monopoly over the value-laden economy. Studies on industrial sectors (Jullien, Smith, 2014; Smith, 2016) have provided evidence that even the most capitalist sectors mobilize values – freedom, security, equality, tradition, according to Smith (2016) – and combine these in various ways in their

then becomes an argument within a markedly value-based discourse. The territorial anchoring of the SSE is presented by its promoters as a political lever, and the local scale becomes the most suitable one for collective action to realize the founding values of the SSE: social justice, equity, democratic governance of companies, and full participation of the SSE in territorial development.

More specifically, political sociologists have proposed a theoretical framework labelled as "territorial institutionalism" in order to address the relationships between policy-making and sector-based territorial economies. Although initially designed to study industry, this framework might advantageously be tested on relations between the SSE and territories. Carter and Smith (2008), on the empirical basis of the fishing and wine sectors, define territorial institutionalism as referring to three uses of territory in relation to the political assignation of authority:

- Justifying the frontiers of public policy: the way policy instruments institutionalize sector-specific definitions of territory. For instance, the institutionalization of an SSE department in a French Regional Council or in a Spanish Autonomous Community will impact on the territorial structuring of SSE actors, in terms of representativeness and political work.
- Defining the eligibility of actors within institutional orders: how do actors (within each industry, in the Carter and Smith model) have access to decision-making arenas thanks to the legitimacy they derive from representing a given component of a sector (producers, manufacturers, public authorities, etc.)? However, and even for multinational companies, this legitimacy is never a purely sector-based one. Instead, it depends on the legitimacy of their socio-economic and political integration within specific territories. Legitimacy also hinges upon "how actors 'dramatize' their own representativeness by evoking territory in their public discourse" (2008: 270). Again, and our contributors testify to this, emphasis is given to the positioning and legitimacy struggles undertaken by promoters of SSE within the bureaucratic, economical and scientific fields.
- Territory as a resource for either politicizing or depoliticizing regulatory contradictions and ambiguities: territory may frequently be used to depoliticize tensions and contradictions

political work. Values such as the general interest, public service, and equity, are also very much present in the public economy.

internal to institutional orders (as configurations of actors and instruments). The territorial reference thus becomes a way to reframe arguments in terms of the general interest. Conversely, reference to the territory may be used to politicize an issue. For instance, within the SSE this is the case for short food circuits or for local currencies presented as socioeconomic alternatives with an openly political dimension.

Despite their generality, these preceding remarks mirror an epistemological starting position shared by the contributors to this volume. A comparative reading of the case studies serves to enrich this posture and help isolate some elements that might contribute towards constructing a more advanced framework analyzing the relationships between the SSE and a given territory. Four avenues for research can thus be identified from this reading.

2. The interplay between the territorial scales of the SSE: multi-situated actors

An initial point here concerns the scales of analysis. Working on spatially-localized case studies does not mean that territorial analysis must be limited to the observation of micro-configurations, with no possibility of generalization. A closer look shows that any interplay between actors is always multi-scalar (micro-, meso- or macro-), and that territorial dynamics are structured around a continuous back-and-forth movement between different scales of collective action and policy making. For instance, the development of a local farmers' market at Cesena, in Emilia-Romagna (Chapter 5), only makes sense as a local response to the emergence of global public problems. For consumers, these would include food safety, the quest for quality and ecological concerns, and for producers, the problem of marketization and the dilemmas posed by the globalization of agricultural markets. Equally, when in the village of Chãos, in the center of Portugal (Chapter 8) a social stock exchange makes possible a Centre for biodiversity and reinterpretation of bees promoted by a cooperative, the micro-local response addresses problems which are much more global: the decline of rural territories, the decline of traditional forms of production, or the inadequacy of conventional financial tools. In other words, recentring on the local and the logics of proximity is quite the opposite of any confinement.

Observation of the political and/or the institutional work (Lawrence, Suddaby, 2006) of SSE actors highlights their capacity to perform at distinct scales of collective and public action. This approach is well illustrated by the capacity of local actors in Romania (Chapter 5) and in the Basque Country (Chapter 3); in the former case they were able to capture European policy instruments and consolidate the re-institutionalization of the SSE in a post-communist context, and in the latter case, to consolidate cross-border relations. Interplay can here be observed at various levels simultaneously: micro- (local), meso- (province, region, state, EU) and macro- (as responses to global challenges).

3. The territorial structuring of the SSE as a response to changes in public regulation

The different territorial configurations of the SSE constitute institutional responses, in the sociological sense, to the public problems territories have to cope with: water supply in Venezuela (Chapter 6), demographic changes and an ageing population in the Spanish Basque Country (Chapter 9), public health, with the case of visually impaired people in the south of Brazil Chapter 10), and the emergence of new forms of job insecurity in Portugal in the aftermath of the 2008 economic crisis (Chapter 8).

Collective action undertaken by SSE actors cannot be understood without taking account of changes in the market environment and in public policy. In this respect, the deliberately broad geographical frame of this book (Western and East-Central Europe, North and South America) necessarily throws up sharp contrasts. In a first configuration, the development of the SSE itself may emanate from state or supra-state institutions. Chapter 6 shows how the Venezuelan state promoted cooperativism during the Bolivarian revolution following the coming to power of Hugo Chávez in 1998. This political change led to an exponential but short-lived increase in the number of cooperatives. The same case studies raise the nagging question of the boundaries of the SSE when water technical boards are categorized as SSE institutions, despite being largely driven by public authorities. In post-communist Romania, as previously noted, the impetus for the development of the SSE and social enterprise, in its variety of meanings (Defourny, Nyssens, 2017) owes a great deal to European policy incentives. Conversely, in other cases, the local development of the SSE mainly represents a response to the weakening of public policies and to the retrenchment of the welfare state. In Porto, the economic crisis is reactivating older forms of the social economy such as the Porto Stone Masons' Cooperative and its intra-mutual solidarity mechanisms (Chapter 8). In Gipuzkoa (in the Spanish Basque Country), debate on the possible delivery of social welfare services on a cooperative basis has taken place in a context marked by the limits of provincial policies which, despite wide-ranging autonomy as regards welfare policy, are faced with the problem of an ageing population (Chapter 9). Through a Delphi survey conducted among welfare policy makers, this chapter evidences contrasting views of the SSE and a perception of cooperativization as an indication of the public authorities' disengagement from the welfare sector.

Territorial restructuring is, for the SSE, one of the responses to these changes in policy-making. In this regard also, responses vary widely throughout the case studies. Three principal scenarios can be identified. The first consists of *local SSE actors combining in territorial hubs or clusters*. The IEP sites in Flanders (Chapter 7) are good examples of this logic, constituting spatially concentrated hubs or locations in cities that accommodate public, profit and non-profit organizations that jointly strive for a (more) solid economic participation of socially deprived citizens, both as a consumer and as a provider of labor.

In France, the PTCEs (Pôles territoriaux de coopération économique, Territorial Clusters of Economic Cooperation), set up in 2013 and then included in the 2014 SSE Law, innovate by establishing territorial clusters of SSE actors in partnership with policymakers and with market-oriented private actors (Chapter 11). PTCEs, be they territorial or sector-based, add the SSE dimension to the territorial clustering of economic development, under its different forms (competitive clusters, industrial districts, local productive systems) (Gianfaldoni, 2017). A second response consists of *structuring SSEs in accordance with network- and sector-based principles*. The process of institutionalization of solidarity-based and responsible finance in Quebec illustrates this strategy (Chapter 1). Drawing on sociological institutionalism, the authors conceive territory first of all as an institutional field of activity, organized on a simultaneously territorial and networked basis. A third organizational response by SSE actors consists of inventing a sort of mobile or nomadic territoriality, as illustrated by the original figure of the itinerant NEF (Nouvelle économie fraternelle, New Fraternal Economy) banker in France (Chapter 2). In this precise case, a bank with a rather centralized structure and a limited marketing network, aims to cover the territory better. Through the experience of the itinerant banker, the NEF constructs its own uses of the territory. Fieldwork conducted in the Provence-Alpes-Côte d'Azur region provides evidence of the positive impact of the itinerant banking system, with an increase in the number of loans especially in rural and deprived areas of the Alpes-de-Haute-Provence and the Hautes Alpes departments. Inevitably, this original relationship to the territory fuels internal tensions within the bank between marketing skills and organizational skills.

4. Reference to the territory as a response to changes in market regulation

The territorial reference may also constitute a resource for SSE actors when responding to market constraints. References to territory in this case become a means of differentiating the SSE within a competitive environment, as well as a discursive instrument of legitimization at the local scale. This dual use of territory is particularly prevalent among major SSE operators seeking re-legitimization. Chapter 12 well illustrates this positioning in its analysis of the role played by territory in the discourse of the President of the Crédit Mutuel de Bretagne. The authors distinguish three types of territorial legitimacy among those activated by this major SSE operator. *Pragmatic territorial legitimacy*, in the first place, refers to the utility of the relationship to the territory for the company. *Moral legitimacy*, for its part, stresses the coherence of the link between the SSE enterprise and its territory provided by its norms and values. Finally, *cognitive legitimacy* refers to the way a major social economy company understands its relationship with the territory.

Using this framework, the authors emphasize how the leader of this mutual bank stresses the bank's support for Breton companies, while remaining silent on the effects of its transnational development while a social economy enterprise. Interplay between scales is minimized: the supra-local is presented as a market and as a series of opportunities, and not as a threat to the institutional identity of the enterprise. By way of contrast, local anchoring is legitimized through an evocation of the organization's origins (cognitive legitimacy). The bank's common project for the territory's success (moral legitimacy) depends on its maintaining decision-making centres locally, and on taking decisions in the best interest of its members. It contributes to the territory's social economic development (pragmatic legitimacy) while sharing the norms of the enterprises within its sector (Chapter 12).

This analysis might usefully illustrate Smith's theoretical proposal (Smith, 2016) that the success of the activation of the "local" reference by economic actors depends, above all, on how representations of the territory are conjured up in order to change or reproduce institutions that are relevant to an economic activity. More precisely, "what needs to be ascertained is the extent to which a locality has an impact upon the value-fueled problematizations around which institutions are challenged or defended, the policy instruments they maintain or modify, and the modes of legitimation used to do either" (Smith, 2016: 160).

On this point, Smith's political economy approach echoes what the economy of proximity should say about the role of the territorial reference in shaping the differential advantages of productive processes. Pecqueur (2006) shows that, unlike the neoclassical argument on comparative advantage, reference to the territory enables companies to evade their production problems by differentiating their product in order to make it totally specific and thus escape competition. A good illustration is provided by the footwear producers of the Cholet area (*Ibid.*). Producers, in this case, first looked to move upmarket in order to drive up prices. In a second phase, they tried to control fashions upstream in order to have a product completely different from standard imported footwear (Pecqueur, 2006: 26). This case study, on the theoretical level, illustrates well the complementarity of the proximity economy approach and the political sociology of territorial policy-making. Indeed, the constitution of the entrepreneurial fabric in the North-East of Vendée is also highly dependent on the socio-political and cultural socialization structures which are specific to this territory (Berthet, Palard, 1997). This interdisciplinary dialogue, although relatively advanced for the conventional market economy, has still to be developed for the SSE.

One might find comparable uses of the territorial reference by other major SSE operators immersed in commercial logic and market practices. The reference to territory, however, has difficulty in resisting market pressures and economic contingencies. In Mondragón, Errasti *et al.* (2016) and Ortega and Uriarte (2015) show that, during the major crisis that affected the Fagor Electrodomésticos industrial cooperative in the years 2005-2013, the activation of cooperative solidarity mechanisms peculiar to Mondragón could not make up for strategic choices resulting from the hasty internationalization of one of its industrial components. In other terms, territorial solidarity, when moving from talk to action, cannot always correct market contingencies. We shall not pursue this topic, but this case study might fuel the ongoing debate between economists and socio-economists on the comparative advantages and disadvantages of the cooperative as an institutional form for a firm (Richez-Battesti, Defourny, 2017).

In other words, and if we refer to the regulationist approach, the contributions to this volume tend to reintroduce the territorial factor to analysis of restructurings of the SSE as responses to a global transformation of the largely superseded State-market frame of reference. In this respect, the territorial approach permits the reintroduction of a meso-scale of observation of SSE actors responding to macro-economic and societal changes (see General Introduction). We thus need to question the role of the territorial SSE, as a collection of economic institutions, in going beyond traditional compromises on wage relations, as well as the relationship with consumption and with the environment. This would feed into the research perspective on territorial development proposed by Lévesque (2014: 263) by associating the proximity economy, institutionalist analysis, and the sociology of social movements.

5. SSE, cultures and territorial identities

Finally, the contributions show that territorial identities and cultures can offer a solid basis for collective action around the SSE. Without reopening a longstanding debate (see, among others, Thériault, 1998; Kahn, 2010), we should nevertheless emphasize the distinction between two approaches, the first relating the SSE to territorial *culture*, while the second relates the SSE to territorial *identity*.

On the one hand, it is necessary to take into consideration the role played by cultural variables in building a "readiness to cooperate" that can lead to specific mobilizations around local development through the SSE. The notion of "culture of development" as proposed by Kahn (2010: 639) could be extended to the SSE. This notion refers to: "the development orientations related to the objective economic situation of the region, to its history, its economic trajectory, its population, its social capital, etc. For a given territory, a 'culture of development' refers to a state of regional organization and of institutions globally oriented towards an economic objective" (our translation).

From this perspective, territorial resources are not limited to the usual production factors and include cultural dimensions (such as the natural and cultural collective heritage, traditions, and language) that take part in the development effort. The chapter on the Romanian case (Chapter 5), starting from a social capital perspective, offers a case study located in the rural area of Horezu and marks out promising avenues of research into the potential interaction between customary institutions for managing the "commons" (in this case grazing lands and forest) and SSE initiatives.

Barely sketched out in this book, these anthropological perspectives would merit closer examination in the case of rural and/or isolated areas with a view to understanding the extent to which some production factors usually seen as inherited factors of stagnation can, instead, be transformed into territorial resources for development. This conversion involves the actors in political work consisting of re-interpreting the representation of customary institutions (work management schemes, management of common public goods, reciprocity relations between neighbors, collective rights, etc.). These institutions are no longer seen as concerning societies exclusively oriented towards the reproduction of a closed institutional order, but as repositories of values and instruments that can be transposed in the contemporary term SSE. Actors select from the values associated with customary schemes and practices by drawing an implicit distinction between those mechanisms which are consistent with current conditions of socio-economic exchanges and those which are not. In her ongoing dissertation research on the Inuit cooperatives, Anne-Marie Merrien[4] points out that while cooperatives provide a new institutional framework for traditional Inuit values such as solidarity and sharing, they nevertheless represent cultural disruption in various respects, if not a transition towards a monetary economy which had been largely ignored until then. Selling food, for instance, and not giving it away or swapping it is, in many respects, a radical change which the cooperative may assist and make socially acceptable.

---

4 Merrien A.-M. (s.d.), Le modèle coopératif comme moyen de reconnaissance identitaire. Le cas des coopératives au Nunavik (provisional title), Université de Montréal, Faculté des Arts et des sciences, Doctorat en Sciences humaines appliquées (in progress). See also Southcott (2015).

In the province of Soule, in the Basque Pyrenees, anthropologists (Fernández de Larrinoa, 2009) have observed a continuity between the customary institutions of shepherds for the collective management of summer pastures and the production of milk and cheese (*olha*), and a new cooperative (Azkorria, founded in 2006) which was designed to facilitate cheese production and, above all, marketing. At the same time, the cooperative represents a dual economic and political break. Firstly, the cooperative is reinforcing a long-term transition towards the market economy, but this is by constructing a certain amount of territorial specificity (quality-labelled cheeses) in order to create a market niche less open to deregulated competition. Secondly, and more politically, the cooperative sees itself as taking part in an alternative system of peasant farming, and as being part of a New Economic Social Movement (Gendron, 2001) with a widespread socio-territorial area of operation. Political criticism is aimed both at the institutions regulating local farming and the major agro-food companies – including cooperatives – engaged in expansion and opening subsidiaries, thus challenging their territorial anchoring.

In both these respects, the Soule cooperative is a form of modernization of longstanding collective action schemes. The cooperative, as an institution, to a certain extent reproduces longstanding customary principles of turn-taking and reciprocity which used to be peculiar to shepherding communities (Ott, 1993). At the same time, cooperation allows us to think in terms of collective action at multiple scales. Cooperation relates to the collective action of small farmers, well-structured politically and in trade union terms. This is based both on reproducing the traditional model of the small family farm (*etxea*: the household in Basque), and its adaptation, especially by helping those setting up a farm outside the family circle or by developing rural tourism or short food circuits (Welch-Devine, Murray, 2011; Itçaina, Gomez, 2015). It is not our intention here to make daring comparisons between Inuit cooperative members, Horezu farmers or Pyrenean shepherds. Nevertheless, the territorial activation of one and the same institution, the cooperative, enables us to shed light on ambivalent mechanisms of interactions between culture and economic institutions. These mechanisms remain largely underexplored in the case of isolated rural territories.

This use of culture as a territorial resource needs to be distinguished, in our view, from the uses of *identity*. Reflecting on the new forms of political and economic regionalism in eight European regions, Keating,

Loughlin and Deschouwer (2003) point to the risk of confusion between culture and identity. To escape from it, these authors propose a ternary approach to culture. Conceived of restrictively, culture is the field targeted by cultural policies. Culture may then designate the values and practices of a society which help to structure behaviors and expectations. Culture can also equate to identity. This notion may itself, when it is applied to regional identity, appear in the form of three constitutive elements. The cognitive dimension of identity refers to the level of knowledge of the region possessed by its inhabitants. The affective dimension designates the level of attachment to the region, or the extent to which this dimension provides a frame of reference for a shared identity and for solidarity, which may find itself competing with other identities. Finally, in its instrumental dimension, regional identity may be used as a basis for campaigning and for collective action. These three dimensions may constitute historical stages in the construction of regionalist militancy, but not all regional experiences necessarily lead to the activation of identity.

However, studies of territorial economic development and of the SSE are far from unanimous in attributing crucial importance to explanations from territorial cultures or identity preferences. In his research on the restructuring of small- and medium-sized enterprises (SMEs) in Saint-Étienne, Le Galès (2006) shows that the hypothesis of "economic exchanges under identity preference constraints" noticed by Jean Saglio (1991), is not necessarily valid, and that we should instead look closely at the way that competing local goods and services are constructed in order to understand local dynamics. Nevertheless, the activation of territorial identity by policy makers and/or economic social movements might in certain circumstances help to explain certain territorial dynamics, including those related to the SSE.

In this respect, Chapter 12 shows how a major mutualist bank in Brittany refers to a collective memory of mutualism in Landerneau (where in 1911 the Central Office for Farmers' Friendly Societies in Finistère – Office central des œuvres mutuelles agricoles du Finistère – was created). As said earlier, territorial identity becomes a means, for a mutual bank, of reasserting its organizational identity. Chapter 3 also illustrates the way that territorial actors, this time in the Basque Country, use the SSE to give an economic content to an assertion of identity (or to translate identity in terms of economic development). This political work is based on a discourse emphasizing a community of values between the SSE and regionalist approaches to endogenous, solidary-based and ecological economic development. The cross-border uses of the SSE was initiated by Basque social movements, along lines distinct from those adopted by the public authorities. In a second phase however, Basque supporters of the SSE took advantage of the new policy instruments for cross-border cooperation that had been set up by public authorities, starting with European instruments. Thus, to use the language of territorial institutionalism, there has been an interplay of actors engaged both in politicization (the SSE as a way to consolidate a cross-border Basque cultural and political community) and in depoliticization (European instruments of cross-border cooperation between SSE actors as a solution to functional and practical issues).

Conclusion

Clearly, an edited volume will never have the same coherence as a monograph or a specific case study. However, the chapters of this book all contribute towards a balanced approach to the territorial regimes of the SSE which interweave socio-economic approaches to local and community development, analysis of SSE governance, socio-political approaches to the construction of territorial public problems, social mobilizations and territorial policymaking. This enquiry asks only to be gone into in greater depth.

Acknowledgement: the author thanks Mike Fay for his help in translating this chapter.

References

Berthet T., J. Palard, 1997, “Culture politique réfractaire et décollage économique. L’exemple de la Vendée du nord-est”, *Revue française de science politique*, 47 (1): 29-48.

Carter C., Smith A., 2008, “Revitalizing public policy approaches to the EU: ‘territorial institutionalism’, fisheries and wine”, *Journal of European Public Policy*, 15 (2): 263-81.

Defourny J., Nyssens M. (dir.), 2017, *Économie sociale et solidaire. Socioéconomie du 3e secteur*, Louvain-la-Neuve, De Boeck, p. 73-116.

Demoustier D., Richez-Battesti N., 2010, “Les organisations de l’économie sociale et solidaire : gouvernance, régulation et territoire”, *Géographie, économie, société*, 12 (1): 5-14.

Errasti A., Bretos I., Etxezarreta E., 2016, “What do Mondragon coopitalist multinationals look like? The rise and fall of Fagor Electrodomésticos and its European subsidiaries”, *Annals of Public and Cooperative Economics*, 87 (3): 433-56.

Fernández de Larrinoa K., 2009, “Pastoreo en Sola. De la trashumancia a los pastos de altitud y a las queserías en el fondo del valle”, *Ager. Revista de desploblación y de desarrollo rural. Journal of depopulation and rural development studies*, 8: 25-43.

Gendron C., 2001, “Émergence de nouveaux mouvements sociaux économiques”, *Revue Pour*, 172: 175-81.

Gianfaldoni P., 2017, “Le PTCE comme forme spécifique de polarisation : quels principes novateurs de structuration et de gouvernance ?”, *RECMA – Revue internationale de l’économie sociale*, 343: 40-56.

Gilbert C., Henry E., 2012, “La définition des problèmes publics: entre publicité et discrétion”, *Revue française de sociologie*, 531: 39-55.

Gusfield J., 1980, *The Culture of Public Problems: Drinking-Driving and the Symbolic Order*, Chicago, The University of Chicago Press.

Hély M., Moulévrier P., 2013, *L’économie sociale et solidaire : de l’utopie aux pratiques*, Paris, La Dispute.

Itçaina X., Gomez A., 2015, “Territorial identity and grassroot economic activism: the politicization of farmers’ mobilizations in the French Basque Country”, *Partecipazione e Conflitto*, 8 (2): 478-503.

Jullien B., Smith A., 2014, “Introduction. Studying the EU’s government of industries”, *in* Jullien B., Smith A., *The EU’s Government of Industries: Markets, Institutions and Politics*, London/New York, Routledge, p. 1-31.

Kahn R., 2010, “La dimension culturelle du développement territorial”, *Revue d’économie régionale et urbaine*, 4: 625-50.

Keating M., Loughlin J., Deschouwer K., 2003, *Culture, Institutions and Economic Development: A Study of Eight European Regions*, Cheltenham (UK)/Northampton (USA), Edward Elgar.

Lascoumes P., Le Galès P., 2007, *Sociologie de l’action publique*, Paris, A. Colin.

Lawrence T.B., Suddaby R., 2006, "Institutions and institutional work", *in* S.R. Clegg, C. Hardy, T.B. Lawrence, W.R. Nord (eds.), *Handbook of Organizational Studies*, 2nd ed., London, Sage, p. 215-54.

Le Galès P., 2006, "La restructuration des PMI à St Étienne après la crise : traces du passé et limites de l'intégration horizontale", *Sociologie du travail*, 1 (48): 17-36.

Lévesque B., 2014, "La contribution de la 'nouvelle sociologie économique' à l'analyse des territoires sous l'angle de l'économie plurielle", *in* B. Lévesque, J.-M. Fontant, J.-L. Klein (dir.), *L'innovation sociale : les marches d'une construction théorique et pratique*, Québec, Presses de l'Université du Québec, p. 245-64.

Ortega Sunsundegui I., Uriarte Zabala L., 2015, *Retos y dilemas del cooperativismo de Mondragón tras la crisis de Fagor electrodomésticos*, Cuardernos de Lanki (10).

Ott S., 1993, *The Circle of Mountains: A Basque Shepherding Community*, Reno, University of Nevada Press.

Palard J., Itçaina X., Ségas S. (dir.), 2007, *Régimes territoriaux et développement économique*, Rennes, PUR.

Pecqueur B., 2006, "Le tournant territorial de l'économie globale", *Espaces et sociétés*, 1 (124-125): 17-32.

Pecqueur B., Itçaina X., 2012, "Économie sociale et solidaire et territoire : un couple allant de soi ?", *RECMA – Revue internationale de l'économie sociale*, 325: 48-64.

Richez-Battesti N., Defourny J., 2017, "Les coopératives", *in* J. Defourny, M. Nyssens (dir.), *Économie sociale et solidaire. Socioéconomie du 3e secteur*, Louvain-la-Neuve, De Boeck, p. 73-116.

Ruggie J.G., 1993, "Territoriality and beyond: problematizing modernity in international relations", *International Organization*, 47 (1): 139-74.

Saglio J., 1991, "Échange social et identité collective dans les systèmes industriels", *Sociologie du travail*, 33 (4): 529-44.

Smith A., 2011,"Territoires", *in* R. Pasquier, S. Guigner, A. Cole (dir.), *Dictionnaire des politiques territoriales*, Paris, Presses de Sciences po, p. 469-74.

Smith A., 2016, *The Politics of Economic Activity*, Oxford, Oxford University Press.

Southcott C. (ed.), 2015, *Northern Communities Working Together: The Social Economy of Canada's North*, Toronto, Toronto Press, Scholarly Publishing Division.

Thériault Y., 1998, "L'identité culturelle et le développement coopératif : réflexions à partir des expériences acadiennes et québécoises", *in* D. Malabou (dir.), *L'expérience coopérative : expériences et recherches francophones*, Limoges, Presses de l'Université de Limoges.

Welch-Devine M., Murray S., 2011, "'We're European farmers now': transitions and transformations in Basque agricultural practices", *Anthropological Journal of European Cultures*, 20 (1): 69-88.

List of Contributors

Fernando Gregorio Aponte Godoy is a lawyer (University of Zulia), specialized in Labor Law and social security (Rafael Urdaneta University). He holds a *Magister Scientiae* in Regional Development (University of Los Andes). He is a social researcher and a legal advisor of CAYAPA *Revista Venezolana de Economía Social*. He is a member of the Board of Directors of CIRIEC Venezuela.

Leonardo R. Argüello L.: economist and magister in Regional development from the University of Los Andes, Venezuela; specialist in municipal public management by the Santa María University; Program in Governance and Management of Public Policies by the Andean Development Corporation and Universities George Washington of USA and Catholic Andrés Bello; Program for the Supervision of Public Management by the Spanish Agency for International Cooperation and the Court of Accounts of Spain; diploma in Cooperativism. Professor and collaborating researcher at the University of Los Andes. Board of Directors of CIRIEC Venezuela.

Cristina Barna is a social economy expert at Solidarity laboratory since 2014, and also an associate professor, currently collaborating with different Romanian universities. She holds a doctorate in Economics from Bucharest University of Economic studies, Romania. Cristina was a member of the GECES, European Commission Group of Experts on Social Entrepreneurship (2012-2014) and also a member of GECES sub-group on social impact measurement (2013-2014) as academic & think-thank. She is a member of International Scientific Commission – Social Economy of CIRIEC International. She co-authored scientific papers, research reports and books on various subjects from social economy field. In the recent years she published: *Romanian credit unions – self-organizing for financial education and inclusion (2017)* – paper nominated as one of the three finalists of the European Microfinance Network (EMN) Research Award 2017, *European toolkit for starting up* *cooperatives and social enterprises in rural areas* (2017), *Understanding agricultural cooperatives: A start up guide* (2017), *Financial inclusion through social economy* (2015), *Atlas of Social Economy: Romania 2014, Handbook of social enterprise's manager* (2012).

Susana Jacinta Queirós Bernardino is an adjunct professor of Management at the Polytechnic of Porto – Institute of accounting and administration (ISCAP), Portugal, and a researcher at CEOS.PP – Centre for organizational and social studies of P.Porto. She completed her under-graduation degree in Management at the Faculty of Economics of the University of Porto. She got her PhD in Management in 2014 from the Portucalense University. Her research interests focus on social entrepreneurship, entrepreneurship and social and solidarity economy.

Andrea Bassi (PhD in Sociology and Social policy) is an associate professor of Sociology at the Department of Political and Social Sciences – Bologna University. He teaches: "Quantitative Methods for Social Research" and "Social Justice and Equity Studies" at the School of Political Science and "General Sociology" and "Sociology of Nonprofit Organizations" at the School of Economics and Management. His research interests include: studies on nonprofit organizations in the field of social and health services, particularly concerning the relationships between public administration and nonprofit deliverers; systems of measurement of organizational performance and social impact of nonprofit organizations. He has 20 years of experience as a Manager of nonprofit institutions in Italy, associations, social cooperatives, voluntary organizations and foundations, both at the local and national level. He has been Director of the research unit of FIVOL – Italian Foundation for Volunteers (1995-1996) in Rome; Director of IREF – Institute of Research in Education and Training (1997-1999) in Rome; Director of Flaminia Foundation (2000-2006) in Ravenna. He is member of ISTR – International Society for Third Sector Research and EMES – European Network on Social Economy. He has been Director of the Summer School ESSE – European Summer School on Social Economy – Bologna University. He is Director of the High Education Course in "Humanitarian and Health-Social Management", Bologna University. He is a member of the National Observatory on Associations, Ministry of Labor and Social Policy.

Marie J. Bouchard is full professor at the Université du Québec à Montréal, Canada. Regular member of the Centre de recherches sur les innovations sociales (CRISES), she currently leads the research area on Collective enterprises. She is a member of the scientific council of Territoires innovants en économie sociale et solidaire (TIESS). She was co-lead of the Community Housing Research Partnership of the Community-University Research Alliance on the Social Economy (CURA-SE) (2000-2010). She held the Canada Research Chair on the Social Economy (2003-2013). In 2015, she was appointed president of the CIRIEC International Scientific Commission on the "Social and Cooperative Economy."

Michelle Bylemans is a researcher at the University of Antwerp (i.e. the Faculty of Design Sciences), within the disciplines of (interior) architecture, urban design and special planning. In her research, she uses the method of Research by Design on both new built projects and redevelopment projects with a socio-economic focus. In particular, she focusses on the impact of visualization techniques (e.g. plans, sections, reference-images, 3D-images, 3D-models, etc.) that are used while presenting these projects.

Béatrice Chauvin, with a large experience of executive in cooperative banks in France, received her PhD from Aix Marseillle University in Management. Her research was about the transformation of the NEF. She is now head of a food cooperative in the south of France.

Simon De Nys-Ketels is a PhD candidate at the Department of Architecture and Urban Planning of Ghent University, where he graduated in 2012. He continued his studies, obtaining an additional Master degree in economic sciences, majoring in globalization at Ghent University in 2014. He started working as a research fellow at the Antwerp University, exploring the relationship between social economy, architecture and urban planning. Since 2015, he is pursuing a PhD at Ghent University, in which he focuses on the architecture and urban planning of (post-)colonial medical infrastructure in the Democratic Republic of Congo.

Danièle Demoustier is an honorary economist at Sciences Po Grenoble, France, where she was director of the postgraduate studies module

(DESS) *Développement et expertise de l'économie sociale* (Development and training in social economy). She contributed to numerous training seminars for social economy enterprises and organizations and is engaged in their general assemblies on a regular basis. She has authored numerous publications on the social and solidarity economy. In 2003, she published her book *L'économie sociale et solidaire : s'associer pour entreprendre autrement* (la Découverte). In 2015 and 2017, she collaborated with Nadine Richez-Battesti and Jean-François Draperi on the publication of the *Atlas national de l'économie sociale et solidaire*. Together with Rafael Chaves, she also co-edited the book *The Emergence of the Social Economy in Public Policy / L'émergence de l'économie sociale dans les politiques publiques*, published in 2013 by Peter Lang in the Social economy & public economy series.

Benito Díaz is a sociologist from University of Zulia, School of sociology, Venezuela. He obtained his degrees in English Language from the University of London, King's College; MSc in Health Planning and Financing from London University, London School of Economics and Political Sciences and London School of Hygiene and Tropical Medicine, United Kingdom. He obtained his PhD from the University of Liverpool, School of tropical medicine, United Kingdom. He is a professor and a recognized researcher at the Universidad de Los Andes. He is the editor of *CAYAPA Revista Venezolana de Economía Social* <www.saber.ula.ve/cayapa>, and the founder and a member of the Board of Directors of CIRIEC-Venezuela.

Anjel Errasti Amozarrain is a senior lecturer in Strategic Management and Business Economics at the Faculty of Economics and Business of the University of the Basque Country (UPV/EHU) in Donostia-San Sebastian, where he is also a researcher at the GEZKI Institute of Cooperative Law and Social Economy. His research interests focus on cooperatives and social economy, public policies, employment, Mondragón cooperatives, multinational corporations and globalization.

Marc Errotabehere is a PhD student in Management Sciences at the University of Pau et des Pays de l'Adour (Centre de recherches et d'études en gestion). His dissertation is entitled: "Studying a process of innovation through the dynamic capacities theory: the case of a regional retail bank (Crédit Agricole d'Aquitaine)". His research interests focus on strategic management and innovation in the banking sector. In 2017, he presented a paper on "Towards a new form of counselling in business starting: the case of a School attached to a mutualist bank" (*Les pratiques et les défis de l'accompagnement entrepreneurial : Cas des start-up, des jeunes entreprises et des PME*, International conference Cadi Ayyad University, Marrakech, 2-3 March 2017).

Enekoitz Etxezarreta Etxarri is a lecturer at the University of the Basque Country (UPV-EHU) and secretary of GEZKI Research institute on Cooperative Law and Social Economy. He graduated on Economics and Social and Cultural Anthropology and completed his postgraduate studies on Development Economics at the UPV/EHU. In 2012, he obtained his PhD on the participation of the social economy in the area of social services. His main research areas are social and solidarity economy, social innovation and social entrepreneurship.

Sara Fabbri holds a Master in Social Economy from the University of Bologna, Forlì Campus.

Mario Fagiolo: Economist from the University "La Sapienza" in Rome, Italy; Magister in Administrative Sciences, Management mention, by the Universidad de Oriente; PhD student in Development Studies at the Central University of Venezuela (CENDES-UCV). Diploma in Cooperativism. International collaborator in development programs promoted by the Lay Movement for Latin America. He is a professor and recognized researcher at the Universidad de Oriente, Venezuela. Activist of the Venezuelan Cooperative Movement. Founder and Board of Directors of CIRIEC-Venezuela. Founder of the *Observatorio Sucrense de Economía Social* (OSES).

José de Freitas Santos is a full professor of International Business at the Polytechnic of Porto – Institute of Accounting and Administration (ISCAP), and researcher at CEOS.PP – Centre for Organizational and Social Studies of P.Porto. He obtained his PhD in 1997 from Minho University. His research interests include tourism, regional development, social entrepreneurship, internationalization and digital marketing. Besides presentations on these topics at various conferences in Portugal and abroad, his articles have been published in several domestic and international journals.

Júlia Graeff is a researcher in social innovation at the Center of Socioeconomic and Administration Sciences (ESAG) of the State University of Santa Catarina, Brazil. She holds a doctorate in administration from the Federal University of Paraná, Brazil. She has experience in consulting in strategic management, process analysis, human resources and socio-environmental responsibility projects. She is a researcher at the Observatory of Social Innovation in Florianópolis and the Laboratory of Education for Sustainability and Social Innovation, Florianópolis, Brazil.

Angel Higuerey Gómez is a full professor and a recognized researcher at the Universidad de Los Andes, where he is the current Director of the Instituto Experimental de Investigaciones Humanística, Económica y Social (IEXIHES). He holds a PhD in Economics from the University of Las Palmas de Gran Canarias, Spain, a Master and Specialist in Tax Law from the Santa María University and; a Degree in Administration, from the *Universidad de Oriente*, Venezuela. He is a member of the Board of Directors of CIRIEC Venezuela.

Xabier Itçaina is a CNRS senior researcher in political sociology at Sciences Po Bordeaux (France), and director of the Centre Émile Durkheim (UMR5116 CNRS, Sciences Po Bordeaux, University of Bordeaux). He is a former Marie Curie Fellow at the European University in Florence (2012-2013). His current research is concerned with three areas: (a) Catholicism and politics in Southern Europe; (b) the territorial dynamics of social economy in Southern Europe; (c) political anthropology of identity politics in the Basque Country. Among his recent publications are: with D. Demoustier (2018), *Faire territoire par la coopération : l'expérience du PTCE Sud Aquitaine* (La Librairie des Territoires, forthcoming); with I. Favretto (eds.) (2017), *Protest, Popular Culture and Tradition in Modern and Contemporary Western Europe* (Palgrave); with A. Roger and A. Smith (2016), *Varietals of Capitalism: A Political Economy of the Changing Wine Industry* (Cornell University Press); with A. Giorgi (eds.) (2015-2016), "Religion and local politics in Southern Europe", 3 section issues of *Religion, State and Society*, 43 (2), 2015; 44 (1), 2016; 44 (3), 2016.

Alexandrine Lapoutte is an assistant professor in management at Université Lumière Lyon 2, France. She belongs to the steering committee of the postgraduate studies module (Master 2) "Social and Solidarity Economy". As a regular member of the research center COACTIS (EA-4161), she leads researches on social economy stakeholder governance. She is a member of national (RIUESS) and international (CIRIEC) research associations focused on social economy.

Eusebio Lasa Altuna is graduated in Economics and Business administration and he completed a Master degree in Social and Solidarity Economy. He is a lecturer at the University of the Basque Country (UPV/EHU, Applied Economy I department) and a member of GEZKI Research institute on Cooperative Law and Social Economy. His main research area, with several publications and lectures, is on cooperativization and public administration. He also works on local socio-economic models.

Marie-Claire Malo is honorary professor at HEC Montréal (Department of management) and associated member of *Centre de recherche sur les innovations sociales* (CRISES) whose coordination is at the UQAM. She co-authored the book *La gestion stratégique, une approche fondamentale* and she trained several cohorts of students to the analysis of strategic coherence, in Québec and in France. She has published extensively in various languages on topics related to the social and solidarity-based economy. She contributed to the mandates of various organizations: Centre de gestion des coopératives, Centre d'étude en responsabilité sociale et écocitoyenneté (CÉRSÉ), CIRIEC-Canada and its journal, CIRIEC international and its journal, *Coopérative de développement régional* (CDR) in Montréal, Coop-HEC, Corporation de développement économique communautaire (CDÉC) in Côte-des-Neiges and Notre-Dame-de-Grâce, Émile-Girardin Foundation, Institut de recherche en économie contemporaine (IRÉC), Territoires innovants en économie sociale et solidaire (TIÉSS).

Deolinda Meira (Portugal) is an adjunct professor of Commercial Law at the Polytechnic of Porto – Institute of Accounting and Administration (ISCAP), and researcher at CEOS.PP – Centre for Organizational and Social Studies of P.Porto. She holds a doctorate in Cooperative Law from the University of Vigo. Her current work focuses on the legal framework of cooperative and social economy, which has been the subject of several scientific communications, monographs, book chapters, and articles. She is a co-editor of the Journal CES (*Cooperativism and Social Economy*) published by the University of Vigo, Spain. She also engages in consulting activities and participates in projects about the legal framework of cooperatives and other entities of social economy. She was a member of the Committee for the Revision of the Portuguese Cooperative Code (revision introduced by Law No. 119/2015, of 31 August), created within the CNES (National Council for the Social Economy).

Juan Carlos Pérez de Mendiguren is a lecturer at the University of the Basque Country (UPV-EHU). He graduated on Economics and Business Administration and completed his postgraduate studies with an MA on Development Economics at the University of East-Anglia (UK). In 2014 he obtained his PhD on Economics, conducting research on concept of Solidarity Economy and on the Network of Solidarity Economy Firms of the Basque Country. Juan Carlos is also a member of HEGOA (Institute of Development and International Cooperation of the UPV-EHU), for which he carries out teaching and research duties. His current research interests focus on the Social and Solidarity Economy, Social Enterprise, and Development. He has lived in different countries and has extensive fieldwork experience in South America and Southern Africa, particularly in South Africa where he lived and work as researcher on rural development for nearly four years.

Nadine Richez-Battesti is economist at Aix-Marseille University, France. She is co-head of the postgraduate studies module (Master2) "ESS: Organization and projects", and a regular member of the Institute of Labor Economy and Sociology (LEST-CNRS) where she currently leads research on social and solidarity economy and on social innovation. She is member of several research associations in France and in the international level (ADDES, AES, CIRIEC, EMES) and she contributes to numerous training seminars for social enterprises. In 2012, 2014 and 2017, she collaborated with Danièle Demoustier and Jean-François Draperi to the *Atlas national de l'économie sociale et solidaire*. She has been involved in the last years in European contracts about Third Sector and about Mapping Social enterprise for France. She has published extensively about SSE in various academic journals.

Maurício Serva is professor at Universidade federal de Santa Catarina (UFSC), Brazil. He holds a doctorate in administration from the Fundação Getúlio Vargas, Brazil. Since 2007 he is director of the Núcleo de Pesquisa em Organizações, Racionalidade e Desenvolvimento (ORD) at UFSC, where he currently leads a research area on organizational studies. From 2002 to 2012, he was president of CIRIEC-Brazil.

Nathalie Vallet is an academic expert in the disciplines of strategic decision-making and organizational theory within public and social profit organizations. Over the last 20 years she has initiated several research projects in which complex policy challenges are related to solutions combining the disciplines of public management, architecture, interior architecture and urban development. As such, she has for instance conducted research into the future strategic roles of public libraries, labor courts, local governments, penitentiary organizations, local police and social economy organizations. Since 2012, she is engaged in the faculty of design sciences of the University of Antwerp (Belgium) where she also fulfills the role of vice-dean since 2017.

Ancuţa Vameşu is a member of CIRIEC and president of *Laboratorul de Solidaritate*, a non-profit independent research organization conducting experimental projects of social enterprise development, financial inclusion and participatory local economic development, advising the credit union movement, and other social economy organizations in Romania. Her research activities concentrate on the non-profit sector and social economy organizations in Romania. In the 1990s she coordinated Romania's participation in the Johns Hopkins University international comparative research project of the non-profit sector. She has designed and coordinated research projects on various segments of social economy in Romania, on national accounts of social enterprises in Romania in cooperation with the National Institute of Statistics and the Ministry of Labor using CIRIEC Manual of satellite accounts, and initiated the *Atlas of Social Economy in Romania*. She has co-authored several papers on social economy and social enterprises in Romania most notably: *Romanian credit unions – self-organizing for financial education and inclusion (2017)* – paper nominated as one of the three finalists of the European Microfinance Network (EMN) Research Award 2017, *Financial Inclusion through Social Economy (2015)*, *The NGO Sector in Romania-trends, profile and challenges 2010.*

Martine Vézina is an associate professor in the management department at HEC Montreal. She teaches management in the areas of strategy, social economy, social innovation and change management. For the last twenty-five years she has been interested in better understanding social economy organizations from the perspective of their management specificities at different stages of their development from a resources-based perspective. She enquires about the mechanisms of social innovation by large institutionalized social economy organizations. Martine Vézina is a member of CRISES (Centre de recherche sur les innovations sociales et la transformation sociale), CIRIEC-Canada and TIESS (Territoires innovants en économie sociale et solidaire). She is also involved in the laboratory for collaborative economy of the EDDEC institute (Environnement, développement durable et économie circulaire) at University of Montréal. She is member of the advisory board of the Centre for Co-operative Studies (University of Saskatchewan). She is also involved in boards of social economy organizations in the different fields.

Tassadit Zerdani holds a PhD. in Administration. She is a lecturer at the Department of Organization and Human Resources of École des Sciences de Gestion (ESG), Université du Québec à Montréal (UQAM), Canada, and a professional researcher attached to the Centre de recherche sur les innovations sociales (CRISES) and Territoires innovants en économie sociale et solidaire (TIESS).

Social Economy & Public Economy

The series "Social Economy & Public Economy" gathers books proposing international analytical comparisons of organizations and economic activities oriented towards the service of the general and collective interest: social services, public services, regulation, public enterprises, economic action of territorial entities (regions, local authorities), cooperatives, mutuals, non-profit organizations, etc. In a context of "large transformation", the scientific activity in this field has significantly developed, and the series aims at being a new dissemination and valorization means of this activity using a pluri-disciplinary approach (economics, social sciences, law, political sciences, etc.).

The series is placed under the editorial responsibility of CIRIEC. As an international organization with a scientific aim, CIRIEC undertakes and disseminates research on the public, social and cooperative economy. One of its main activities is the coordination of a large international network of researchers active in these fields. Members and non-members of this network are allowed to publish books in the series.

Series titles

Vol. 1 – CIRIEC (sous la dir. de Bernard Enjolras), *Gouvernance et intérêt général dans les services sociaux et de santé*, 2008, 265 p.

Vol. 2 – CIRIEC (Marie J. Bouchard), *The Worth of the Social Economy. An International Perspective*, 2009, 268 p.

Vol. 3 – CIRIEC (Philippe Bance & Luc Bernier), *Contemporary Crisis and Renewal of Public Action. Towards the Emergence of a New Form of Regulation? / Crise contemporaine et renouveau de l'action publique. Vers l'émergence d'un nouveau mode de régulation?*, 2011, 333 p.

Vol. 4 – CIRIEC (Rafael Chaves & Danièle Demoustier), *The Emergence of the Social Economy in Public Policy. An International Analysis/ L'émergence de l'Économie sociale dans les politiques publiques. Une analyse internationale*, 2013, 367 p.

Vol. 5 – CIRIEC (Luc Bernier), *Public Enterprises Today: Missions, Performance and Governance. Learning from Fifteen Cases / Les entreprises publiques aujourd'hui : missions, performance, gouvernance. Leçons de quinze études de cas*, 2015, 367 p.

Vol. 6 – CIRIEC (Marie J. Bouchard & Damien Rousselière), *The Weight of the Social Economy. An International Perspective*, 2015, 334 p.

Vol. 7 – CIRIEC (Xabier Itçaina & Nadine Richez-Battesti), *Social and Solidarity-based Economy and Territory. From Embeddedness to Co-construction*, 2018, 374 p.

www.peterlang.com